LEARNING
AND
BEHAVIOR

THE MACMILLAN COMPANY
NEW YORK · CHICAGO
DALLAS · ATLANTA · SAN FRANCISCO
LONDON · MANILA

IN CANADA
BRETT-MACMILLAN LTD.
GALT, ONTARIO

LEARNING
AND
BEHAVIOR

REED LAWSON, Ph.D.
Department of Psychology
The Ohio State University

NEW YORK – THE MACMILLAN COMPANY

First Printing

Library of Congress catalog card number: 60-5156

The Macmillan Company, New York
Brett-Macmillan Ltd., Galt, Ontario

Printed in the United States of America

*
*
* **TO MY MOTHER AND FATHER**

✳ ACKNOWLEDGMENTS

✳

✳

I am deeply indebted to the following individuals who contributed materially to the development of this book: Professors
Harold Babb, Hobart College, and Melvin H. Marx, University of
Missouri, for their critical readings of early drafts, and Miss Miriam
Odell, The Ohio State University, for her diligent aid in preparing
the reference list and the illustrations. I am also sincerely grateful
to the American Psychological Association, The Journal Press, and
the University of Nebraska Press for permission to reproduce and/or
adapt materials on which they hold the copyrights.

Reed Lawson

* TABLE OF CONTENTS

LEARNING
AND
BEHAVIOR

SECTION I

*

*

* *SIMPLE*

* *HABIT*

* *FORMATION*

CHAPTER I

✳
. ✳

✳ THE SUBJECT MATTER AND
LANGUAGE OF "LEARNING"

"LEARNING" AS A GENERAL FRAMEWORK
FOR PSYCHOLOGICAL THOUGHT

The concepts and the principles revealed by the study of learning form the basis of a large part of psychology as it is taught in the United States. The role of learning has been emphasized frequently in perception, in problem-solving, in personality development, in child behavior, and in the formation of individual differences. Much of current applied psychology is concerned with problems that are basically problems of learning—how to train, educate, or re-educate people; how to change their political views; how to change their buying habits. All such modifications or alterations of behavior can be discussed in terms of learning; their accomplishment can be thought of as the occurrence of new learning, and the ease with which any of these changes is effected can be shown to be at least partially determined by the rigidity that previous learning had given to the older patterns of behavior.

This strong emphasis on learning in the United States is a rather unique cultural phenomenon. In no other country, with the exception of the Soviet Union, does learning consume so much of the attention of academic psychologists. Increasing interest in learning can be noted in Japan and in England, but this may be a result of the impact of American psychology on academic circles in those countries (e.g., many contemporary Japanese psychologists received their advanced training in the United States).

No one would deny that the behavior of organisms is often changed or influenced by a process that can be called "learning." But it is quite another matter to assert or to imply that this process is a fundamental determinant of action. Psychologists in Western Europe, for example, consider perceptual, motivational, or biological influences upon behavior to be of more paramount importance. Gestalt psychology—which originated in central Europe—is a viewpoint that does not regard learning as a "basic" influence. Past experience (learning) is seen, rather, as affecting one's perception of a given situation; it is the perception, however, that ultimately governs one's overt activity, and perception is not entirely dependent upon learning for its substance and form.

Whether one considers learning, perception, motivation, genes, the stars and planets, or anything else to be the most pervasive influence on an organism's behavior is largely a matter of choice. Any investigator's particular choice is not a chance event, to be sure, but it is not entirely determined by the "scientific facts." Indeed, some philosophers of science assert that it is not possible to test with the methods of science whether the laws of learning, for example, are the basic laws of psychology.

Now, this is a book about learning. I would not have attempted this project if I were not fairly conversant with the topic. This familiarity, in turn, is the result of my interest in learning. So the reader can reasonably anticipate that I will often talk enthusiastically about learning. Such enthusiasm can be infectious, and I hope this will be its main effect here. But enthusiasm can also breed myopia, tunnel-vision, or other forms of partial blindness. I hope that I will be indulged if I show occasional moments of blurred vision (I also hope they are only occasional). Even if one does not become a "convert" to behaviorism, or decide to devote his life to research on learning, this book may still activate a few cortical areas in a pleasant, if only momentary, fashion. In brief, this book talks about behavior almost exclusively from the standpoint of learning. This is a legitimate and interesting way of looking at behavior, but it is not the only way of looking at behavior.

In our own culture, however, there is a firm belief that learning—the capacity to adjust oneself to an environment that is constantly presenting new problems, new barriers to the individual organism—is one of the most important consequences of the interaction of an organism with its environment. From such a belief stems the further notion that the more we know about the exact ways in which environment influences behavior, the better will we be able to alter the environment so that we, or our heirs, can attain our goals in life more easily.

The view that a person's behavior at a given time is greatly affected by his previous experiences throughout life, gives to the topic of learning the breadth and scope that it now has in American psychology. In about 1900 some American psychologists, who came to be known as functionalists, began emphasizing this ability to adapt to the immediate demands of an ever-changing environment as one of the chief survival mechanisms used by the individuals of many species, especially the higher primates. Man himself affords the most dramatic example of the utility of this ability.

The American public's interest in science is basically utilitarian. The men whose names come to mind most readily when you think of "American scientists" are Eli Whitney, Samuel Morse, A. G. Bell, Thomas Edison, Robert Fulton, and so on. Actually, none of these men are famous because of their contributions to "science"; they are remembered because they invented things that made life easier in some way or other, but invention is only a relative-by-marriage of science.

I have no intention of disparaging the highly creative and extremely beneficial work that is invention. But invention and science are not actually the same activities. They overlap little or not at all in their ultimate aims.

Scientists want to understand what is going on about them in the universe and it matters little to them that some of this knowledge is of little or no practical value. As yet, for example, the discovery of the planet Neptune has not radically changed the lives of anyone; yet the fact that its presence had been deduced prior to the development of a telescope powerful enough to discover it simply by random exploration is a source of vicarious pride and satisfaction to many people.

The scientist's basic belief is in an orderly universe, and his main goal as a scientist is to perceive and describe some of this orderliness. Certainly the scientist who enjoys the profits of technological advancement cannot take a "holier-than-thou" attitude toward those who make more tangible contributions to the world. Any attempt by scientists to do so is snobbery and, furthermore, it is foolish, since it is biting the hand that feeds them. Gratitude for the benefits of technology, however, need not take the form of adopting technology's goals as one's own. Science, no more than art or religion, needs to justify itself solely because its products are "useful," in the more limited meaning of that term.

Many of the people who study learning share this view of the role of science. It is important for the student to realize from the outset that some of the problems with which psychologists in the field of learning are concerned do not derive their interest or importance from the practical consequences that would stem from the solutions of these problems. Learning, to some of us in the field, is primarily an opening to the study of the general problems of how organisms behave the way they do.

In conclusion to this discussion, we hasten to add that one should not get the impression that scientists of any sort go out of their way to avoid working on problems of value to society in general. The point is simply that such a goal is not the main determinant of scientific interest.

Let us turn now from the matter of *why* we study learning and give some consideration to *what* it is that we study.

WHAT IS LEARNING?

No simple, capsule definition of learning that could be written in plain English will include all of the characteristics that psychologists attribute to the term. There are two major reasons for this inability to be succinct.

1. The Diversity of "Learning Situations"

Since the concept of learning is widely used in American psychology, it obviously is being applied to a multitude of concrete situations. The variety of learning situations is so great that it is hard for a psychologist to be accurate and yet use familiar terms in describing the points of similarity between such situations. When we consider, in the ensuing chapters, all of the experimental situations in which learning can be studied, it will become clear that there are two ways in which learning experiments can differ from each other in their specific details.

First, there are a large number of procedures by which learning can be produced. Consider, as an example from outside the laboratory, the number of different kinds of study methods that are used by college students. Some of these are more effective than others, perhaps, but the fact remains that there are several alternative ways of attaining the college degree and/or a college education. Students learn, for instance, what courses to take and what courses to avoid (wherever they have a choice in the matter) in order to achieve most efficiently whatever it was they sought when they entered college in the first place; on the other hand, some students let other considerations determine their choice of courses, but develop techniques for getting as much or as little knowledge out of such courses as they want to get, while at the same time maintaining an acceptable grade average. Both of these modes of adjustment are the result of learning, but they involve—as we shall see—somewhat different training procedures (the fact that said training is largely informal does not alter the fact that adjustment to a college curriculum involves training, or learning).

A second source of diversity in learning experiments is the number of behavioral changes that are regarded as indications that learning has taken place. A rat running through a maze by the shortest path to the goal, a pigeon tapping a plastic plate with its beak whenever a light is turned on, a monkey consistently choosing one of two differently marked boxes every time they are offered to him, and the child who stops calling the postman "Daddy"—all these are kinds of behavioral changes that are considered to reflect the occurrence of learning.

2. Learning Is Not a Thing

The most important reason why it is hard to define learning is that learning is *not* a concrete, observable event. The basic notion of the school of psychological thought called behaviorism is that the raw data of psychological research *must be* the observable actions of an organism (which are called *responses*) that occur in the presence of observable environmental changes (which are called *stimuli*).

Many years ago, E. C. Tolman (269) made prominent the idea that behavior is influenced by many variables; learning, Tolman said, is the name given to only a small number of the demonstrable relationships between environmental events (stimuli) and behavioral changes (responses).

The full implications of this position have not always been realized, and the recent history of learning research has seen many instances of attempts to demonstrate experimentally that some given variable did or did not affect learning. We don't prove the existence of learning; we define it. The fact is, we can rather arbitrarily select the environment-behavior relationships—or, as we shall call them, *stimulus-response relationships*—which will and will not be included in our definition of learning. Scientific observation can only show what variables affect the relationships in which we have already declared an interest; thus, we can never *prove* by the methods of science that something does or does not affect learning, in an absolute sense, but only within the confines of our definition of learning.

Thus, radically different definitions of learning are possible, and the differences in opposing definitions cannot be resolved by an appeal to facts. Because learning is a matter of definition, a variety of *theories* of learning are possible. Learning theories make either implicit or explicit *assumptions* about the fundamental nature of the hypothetical learning process. These theories are extremely interesting, and the controversies between different theorists have resulted in the addition of much fascinating and important experimental work to the field. While we shall give much attention to the experimental work so spawned, we shall give little attention to the general theories of learning themselves. There are two reasons for this decision, one practical and one largely a matter of opinion.

The practical reason is simple enough—there is not sufficient time or space to cover both the facts and the theories of learning within the confines of a single course. It is my opinion that, when a choice must be made between the two, the choice must be to emphasize the facts, to the exclusion of the theories. This choice is in no sense anti-theoretical, but as theories derive from and relate to the facts, the reason for first understanding the latter should be obvious.

Now, it is impossible to eschew completely the mention of theory, no matter at what level of analysis one seeks to present the field of learning. There are three cases in which I have gone into theoretical problems at some length in this text:

(1) First of all, some theoretical problems have seemed of such importance to learning psychologists that attempts to resolve these problems determined the nature of much experimental work. In some cases, it is not possible—even with the advantage of historical perspective—to present the data of such experiments without describing the theoretical problem from which they arose. To do so, would make the experiments incomprehensible. The outstanding instance of this in this text are those experiments dealing with the theoretical problem of the essential nature of a reinforcing event, to which the whole of Chapter 4 is devoted.

(2) Sometimes a theoretical notion may serve as an effective teaching device, even if the notion itself is quite controversial. For example, although many psychologists (including myself) are quite skeptical about the theoretical value of the concept of inhibition, I have not hesitated to refer to it repeatedly in this text, because it does serve as a simple way of linking a lot of apparently disparate data together. This latter task is obviously one of the important functions of a textbook, and any way that serves this end—without, of course, misleading the students—seems legitimate.

(3) Finally, although this is always a risky assertion at the present stage of development in psychology, there may be some theories that are essentially correct. I have presumed to judge the interference theory of forgetting (Chapter 12) as such a theory. This, however, is my closest brush (I hope) with presenting still controversial material as if there were no controversy. Rather than go into all of the complexities of most of the current controversies about interpreting facts, however, I have tried to stay with the factual material available alone.

So we shall study the facts, i.e., the conclusions drawn from scientific observations made by psychologists who said they were studying learning. To be comprehensible, however, such a large body of information as exists in the field of learning needs some organizing framework. If the framework is not to be the theories of learning, what will it be? I have decided to use a "model" of learning.

As I use the term, a model is an abstract *description* of the *observable* aspects of organism-environment relationships. A model has some features in common with a theory, but there is one important difference. The purpose of the model I shall use in this text is to provide a basis for comparing and contrasting the various experimental and everyday events that are the concern of learning psychologists. It is not intended, in itself, to be an explanation of behavior. The correctness of the model, therefore, is not of primary importance; learning situations that do not fit the model, for instance, can perhaps be most easily understood and remembered in terms of why they do not fit. My use of a model takes advantage of only one of several ends that this device can serve; a general discussion of the uses of models, however, is irrelevant to the matters at hand. An understanding of the ways in which models can be used should become clearer as the approach utilized in this text is developed.

DESCRIBING LEARNING IN STIMULUS-RESPONSE TERMS

Let us begin the construction of this learning model by stating in more explicit words what I meant when I said that learning is the name given to some of the demonstrable relationships between environmental events and behavior changes. In particular, learning involves the transition from a time at which a given environment-behavior relationship is unpredictable to a time at which this relationship is stable and predictable. In every instance in which learning is said to occur, therefore, *at least two* observations must be made in order to verify this assertion: We must be able to show (1) that originally a particular organism, or species, does not regularly and reliably make some specific, identifiable action under a given set of conditions, and (2) that after certain events have taken place there comes to be a predictable relationship between the given environmental conditions and said act.

Now, the entire subject matter of psychology consists of the description of the interactions of organisms with their environments. "Behavior" and "environmental conditions" are all-inclusive terms; if we wish to break these concepts down for the purpose of analysis, we must use smaller, more specific units of analysis. The units upon which behaviorists rely are the stimulus and the response. In general, "stimulus" is used to refer to more or less discrete aspects of a particular environmental situation; similarly, "response" refers to specific features of an organism's total behavior.

There are so many different languages in which learning research has been reported by the experimenters themselves that the writer of a text on learning has but two alternatives: (1) to shift back and forth among the various orientations and their different languages, thus effectively bewildering all but the most diligent students; or (2) to select arbitrarily a vocabulary that can best handle the greatest number of specific learning situations. I have chosen the latter course, even though the vocabulary I have chosen may be taken by some readers as an indication of bias on my part. My usage of stimulus-response terminology is intended for one purpose only—to emphasize that the *facts* of a science *must* refer to observable events, no matter what sorts of concepts a theory may employ. Even "stimulus" and "response," however, are emotionally laden terms in contemporary psychology; in a further effort to reduce the implication of a preference for one theory over another in this field, I have

chosen to use (whenever stylistic considerations do not counter-
mand it) the symbols S for stimulus and R for response. The reader
is to understand that this symbolism is not intended as any meta-
physical description of "the way that life is," and so on; S and R
are meant only to be reminders of the *empirical* basis on which any
science must be founded.

The Concept of the Stimulus

Let us consider here not how various psychologists have defined
the term in the abstract, but how the term "stimulus" has been used
in actual practice.

Usually, the term refers to some sort of relatively rapid energy
change in the physical environment of the subject whose behavior is
under observation. In psychology, we never describe completely
all the energy changes occurring in a given situation. Our descriptions always represent a selection from all the possible changes that
could be noted and described in a given situation. Just what aspect
of this total is designated as the stimulus is left somewhat to the dis-
cretion of the experimenter.

In some cases "stimulus" is used to refer to a multitude or con-
glomeration of *actual* and *inferred* changes, and in other cases, it
refers to an observable set of *actual* changes alone. Thus the stimulus
for a movie star waving to his fans as he enters Grauman's may
include a complex array of visual and auditory stimuli arising from
the presence of the enthusiastic throng, but we would be hard put
to correlate the star's actions point for point with specific changes
in this array of stimuli from moment to moment. On the other hand,
consider a fire drill in a public school building. The stimulus for
beginning orderly withdrawal from the building may be spoken of
as the sounding of the fire-bell. Other forms of energy changes are
present and perhaps necessary, but the one that is obviously correlated with this type of behavior is the sound of the bell.

In both of these cases, a thorough description of all the energy
changes occurring is not attempted. What the two examples have
in common, however, is that the stimuli are described so that two

observers could agree that at least these changes were present. Sometimes, to emphasize the multiplicity of environmental events that are relevant in some situations, the term "stimulus-complex" may be used. The student should keep in mind that the symbol S alone may also refer to a complex environment; the exact meaning of S can only be stated for a specific situation.

If all this sounds as if the term "stimulus" is frequently employed in a loose and uncritical manner, this is precisely what it is intended to convey. However, it is to the credit of contemporary psychologists that more and more attention is being devoted to the specification of just what kinds of changes deserve the label "stimulus," and what kinds do not. That the situation is not hopeless is attested by the fact that results from various experiments show considerable agreement even when they employ quite different means of specifying the stimuli involved.

The Concept of Response

Behaviorists frequently define a response as the action of a muscle or a gland, but in only a very limited number of studies does the response observed and measured actually correspond to this definition. In most experiments a somewhat grosser segment of action is studied. "Response" may, in fact, refer to anything that an organism does; the main requirement is that different observers must be able to agree as to when an organism is and is not doing a certain thing.

Perhaps the most common description of response encountered in studies of learning is that formulated in "accomplishment" language. We most often specify, not what muscle or set of muscles contracted, relaxed, and so forth in a given situation, but rather what was accomplished by the organism's actions in relation to certain environmental objects. The statement that "the rat traversed the runway" does not say anything about muscles, except by implication; it states, instead, what was accomplished by muscular action—i.e., a change in location of the animal with respect to the end-points of the runway.

The fact that the same term is used to refer to a wide variety of actions does not result in difficulty within a single experiment, provided adequate description is supplied about the actual form of the behavior investigated. It remains to be seen, however, whether truly general laws can be formulated in terms of S and R relationships when the key terms reflect such a lack of rigor.

Stimulus-Response Variability

In opening this discussion about "what is learning," I mentioned that learning implied a change in an S-R relationship. The observable change in an S-R relationship that is characteristic of nearly all learning situations is a reduction in the variability of the responses that occur in the presence of a particular stimulus. "S-R variability" may mean several things. It may mean (1) that several different responses are made in an unsystematic fashion while an S is present; (2) that on successive presentations of S, different responses occur in a sequence that cannot accurately be anticipated; or (3) that on successive occasions of S the time when a specific R will start or be completed is quite unpredictable. These meanings are not mutually exclusive, of course, and which one will be emphasized in a given learning situation depends largely upon the types of observations that are being made in that situation. "Reduction in variability" simply means that the randomness of the events described above diminishes.

To put this more specifically, it is conventional to say that learning has occurred whenever it can be shown (1) that at one time a given organism's behavior was essentially random, or generally unrelated to some feature of the environment, and (2) that eventually this organism's reactions to this aspect of its environment became rather predictable. By way of simplification, we can call this process the elimination of random activity, or of irrelevant responses.

More familiar terms that are applied to the behavioral changes in learning situations are phrases such as "improvement in performance," or "strengthening of a stimulus-response relationship."

These are useful terms, and they will occur many times in this text, but at this point I wish to emphasize the *observable* events to which statements refer. I am asserting that the basic observable characteristic is a reduction in S-R variability. Now, variability is most accurately and objectively described by numbers. The next logical topics, therefore, are the ways in which S-R relationships can be described numerically.

QUANTITATIVE DESCRIPTIONS OF RESPONDING USED IN THE STUDY OF LEARNING

Although the elimination of irrelevant behavior may be a characteristic of all learning situations, there are many ways of recording this transition in an objective manner. At their present stage of scientific maturity, learning psychologists have no sound basis for asserting that any of these ways is a better measure of learning than any other. There are five such measures, and these can be grouped into three general categories:

Category I: Temporal Measures of S-R Occurrences

1. Response Latency

As an example of this measure, consider a two-year-old boy named Roger Muttle, whom we find in the kitchen while his mother is baking a pie. As we look in on him, Roger is toddling rapidly toward the oven with his arms extended; it seems quite certain that he will put his hands against the hot stove. Realizing this, Mrs. Muttle says, "No, no, Roger, the stove is hot!" Since this combination of sounds will not elicit an automatic response by any two-year-old male, Mrs. Muttle's warning must depend for its effectiveness upon prior learning by Roger that will prevent him from making physical contact with the hot stove.

If Roger has learned to respect this particular set of sounds when made by Mother, it is quite probable that the response he used to make upon touching a hot object—i.e., some response that gets him away from the object—will be made to his mother's warning. In the following chapter we will discuss the technical aspects of this sort of learning situation, but for the moment the important point to recognize is that whether Roger gets burned or not depends upon how quickly he responds (by stopping his approach to the stove) after his mother has issued her warning.

If Roger begins to halt or to withdraw from the stove area after Mother's warning, we would usually consider this a case of learned behavior (since this vocalization by Mother does not automatically produce such a response in all two-year-old human beings). Learning, then, is sometimes inferred from the fact that a response is initiated quite quickly after the relevant S is presented; learning tends to shorten the *response latency*.

Response latency is the time between the onset of the critical S—such as Mother's warning—and the time when an organism initiates the R that is to be (or has been) learned. As learning progresses, response latency decreases; that is, R occurs sooner and sooner after the onset (beginning) of S. There are limits, of course, to the shortness of response latencies; at least one limiting factor is the speed with which a nerve impulse can travel to and activate a muscle.

2. Speed of Responding

Not only does R occur sooner and sooner after S is presented, but, as learning progresses, R is completed faster and faster. Technically, speed of response is defined as the time between the beginning of R and its termination; it is often called "response time," in fact. This measure is most applicable to R's that are actually composed of a series of actions—such as a rat running to food, or a person parking a car.

Category II: Frequency of Appropriate R Occurrences

3. Percentage of R_L[1]

This involves, in the case of the individual learner, the pooling of a block of consecutive presentations of S—say, five, ten, or

---

[1] R_L is a shorthand way of denoting in the abstract the "response to be learned," or the "correct" response. In this way it is distinguished, symbolically, from other responses that may occur in the same setting.

twenty—and computing the percentage of times that R subsequently occurred without any additional manipulation of the learner (as by prompting him). As learning progresses, this percentage will rise; if enough practice is given it will eventually reach 100 per cent in most simple learning situations.

4. Rate of Responding

This is measured in much the same way as percentage of response occurrences except that time in the presence of S, instead of number of S presentations, is the unit of evaluation. In studies in which rate of responding is measured, more than one occurrence of the appropriate R is possible per presentation of S, and S may be continually present for several minutes. As learning takes place, rate of responding characteristically reaches a stable level and pattern (or periodicity) of occurrence.

5. Percentage and Rate Compared

Measures of percentage and of rate are both ratios, the numerators of which are the number of appropriate R's ("appropriate" in the sense that this is the R which is supposed to be learned in a particular situation). The measures differ in their denominators. For percentage, the denominator is a number of discrete S presentations; for rate, it is a period of time during which S is continually present. While these measures are analogous, they are employed in experimental situations that differ in the method of S presentation or variation.

One may wonder about the comparability of experiments in which each S is followed by only one R and those in which many R's may occur each time. Both of these cases resemble many real-life situations. In the laboratory and in everyday life which of these events will occur is determined by whether the first R is followed by the removal of S or by the removal of the means to make R right away again. If a man rises when a woman enters a room, he clearly can't continue to keep getting up; he *can*, however, keep on playing a pinball machine as long as he has coins. It is generally assumed by psychologists that similar laws hold for both of these types of learning situations; at least they are not

seen as sources of *contradictory* principles of learning and behavior.

Category III: Frequency of Inappropriate R Occurrences

6. Frequency, or Percentage of Errors

In order to tally errors it must be possible for the learner to make
more than one kind of R when S is presented, and not all of these
kinds of R's can be "correct." Just how to tell the learner which of
the R's is correct constitutes the bulk of this text, so we shall not
pursue this point now. An error is the occurrence of any R except
the correct one when S is present.

In many situations a person *can* make an R whether or not the
usually appropriate S is present. Sitting alone in a room does
not prevent you, for example, from saying, "Hello" aloud. Another
example of this type of error would be the case of an automobile
driver with normal vision stopping when a traffic light turned
green. Where such an event is possible in learning experiments
it is the practice to count as errors those occurrences of an R for
which the proper S is not present.

The percentage of errors, of course, may be simply the opposite [2]
of the percentage of correct responses. Both measures are obtained
in the same way. They are not mirror images only in situations in
which the presentation of S may be followed by "no R" (i.e., when
presentation of S does not alter the subject's already ongoing activity) or in which the normally correct R can be made in the
absence of S.

Objective Criteria of Learning

I have said that a reduction in random activity is probably the
essential criterion for asserting that learning has occurred in any
specific instance. If this is acceptable, how do the objective measures
of responding just considered relate to this "definition" of learning?
To answer this, let us turn to a fictitious but realistic example:

[2] Literally, 100 per cent—R_L per cent.

After having been out of the house for the first time, your puppy, Grundoon, comes to the screen door and makes these responses: (1) wags his tail, (2) whines, yaps, or barks, and (3) scratches the door. He is let into the house. For whatever reason, you decide that Grundoon's scratching on the door is "the signal that he wants in." Now, by the processes to be examined in succeeding chapters, Grundoon eventually uses only the scratching on the door to get in. The tail-wagging and noise-making drop out. Each of the behavioral measures described above reflects in some manner this fundamental characteristic of learning situations: the reduction of irrelevant behavior.

(1) Over a series of recurrences of this situation, the alacrity with which Grundoon *initiates* the scratching response after he comes to the door would ordinarily be found to increase. This is a crude analog of the laboratory measure, *response latency*. As more and more irrelevant R's drop out, it stands to reason that the appropriate one will come to be made sooner and sooner.

(2) The door-scratching R is not the best means of illustrating *speed of responding*, but it should be clear that as random behavior drops out, the R_L will be made more efficiently, thus more rapidly. The time required to make any given stroke at the door will decrease over a series of occurrences; this is essentially what is meant when it is said that speed of responding increases as learning takes place.

(3–4) As already mentioned, percentage and rate of responding are, in the last analysis, two ways of measuring essentially the same aspect of behavioral change. Our hypothetical pet is in a situation in which *rate* is the appropriate measure; his particular R_L can be repeated frequently in succession. Here also it should be easy to see that with the elimination of inappropriate behavior, R_L will occur more and more frequently. Even in the brief time that Grundoon may have to scratch at the door, the number of such responses will usually increase over a series of these occasions. Psychologists label this measure of change in R *rate of responding*.

(5) Two types of behavior in this situation might be classified as errors. First, barking and tail-wagging could be considered to be errors, since they have nothing to do with gaining entry into the house. A second class of errors would be attempts by the puppy to scratch at other doors through which he would not be permitted to enter (such as neighbors' doors or other doors besides the back door of his own home). In either case, Grundoon would be making irrelevant or inappropriate R's, so of course we would expect *error reduction* to accompany learning.

Excepting occasional ingenious techniques that have not yet become widely used, this exhausts the list of response changes from which learning is inferred directly. There remain a variety of indirect ways of determining what has been learned at some earlier time. These are measures of retention, of transfer of training, and of the persistence of R after it is no longer useful. They are indirect measures because they do not give a picture of learning in progress, but they can be used to demonstrate how well some S-R relationship has previously been established. Consideration of these will be deferred until later sections, since their understanding requires more background in the basic principles of simple habit formation, which principles can be explained in terms of the measures of response change just described.

In the preceding discussion of measures of R-change, I emphasized the technical differences between them. This was primarily for clarification. Learning psychologists are undecided as to the degree to which there are all methods of measuring the same thing. They are at least uncertain about the precise relationships to each other of these ways of observing a change in R, although we did note one feature common to them all. This is an important matter, because if learning is in any sense an actual event, or a specific process, then there must be some way of transforming any particular measure of learning into the units of any other such measure. Such transformations would probably not be simple, but they would have to be possible. Until the transformations are discovered, we must regard learning as the generic term for a number of specific R-changes under specific conditions.

REINFORCEMENT: A FUNDAMENTAL CONCEPT

So far I have said that learning, broken down into its observable components, consists of more than one occurrence of an S-R sequence, with a concomitant change in R. In terms of our model, and in terms of traditional psychological and popular thought, *at least* these events must be observed before we can designate a situation as one in which learning has occurred. But there is one feature that is typical of many, if not all learning situations, and that is the condition that leads to the association of one R instead of another with a given S. The name given to this feature is *reinforcement*. For the present, we wish only to discuss the usefulness of a reinforcement concept. Chapters 4 and 5 will be concerned with a more detailed examination of the empirical status of the concept.

Behavior, by the broad definition that psychologists use, goes on continuously. An organism that is not behaving is literally a dead organism. Even casual observation will verify that, in the presence of a new, or unfamiliar S, an organism will probably make a wide variety of R's. Referring again to the case of the puppy at the door, his original behavior when outside the door would be schematized, in terms of the model, as the occurrence of several R's: barking, or R_b, scratching, or R_{sc}, tail-wagging, or R_w, and so on. All these occur in the presence of the door-stimuli—S_{dr}.

Now, learning is inferred from the fact that after successive presentations of S, one of the R's—in the example, R_{sc}—begins to show one of the systematic changes just considered. If originally the occurrence of R_{sc} in the presence of S_{dr} was unpredictable, what could change this relationship between them? Why does it ever become the case that R_b and R_w become less frequent consequences of S_{dr}, while the relationship of S_{dr} and R_{sc} becomes increasingly predictable?

Logic, as well as everyday experience, suggests that perhaps a relationship develops between S and R because *something else* happens whenever one R occurs in the presence of S that does not happen when other R's occur. Since we assume that observable events in psychology belong either to the S class or to the R class, this "something else" *must* be another S, for if it were only another R we would be right back where we started—i.e., still one more R occurring at random in the presence of S. This additional event is called a *reinforcer,* and to differentiate this stimulus change from those involved in the S-R relationship itself, is designated by the symbol "X."

This is a difficult notion to grasp, so it may help to review the foregoing. Learning is defined in terms of an observable change in an S-R relationship that occurs over a series of repetitions of this S-R sequence. In many laboratory and real-life situations, however, whatever R occurs when a given S is presented is, in the beginning, randomly determined. Why should these sequences ever become non-random? A reasonable guess is that the occurrence of some S-R sequence is followed by some sort of change that is unlike the changes that follow other, similar sequences. (All occurrences of an R are followed by some sorts of changes, of course; at the very least, by proprioceptive feedback—which is the technical name for the stimulation whereby we can tell without looking that our arm, for example, is above our head.) These presumed changes are called *reinforcers* because that is what Pavlov, the scientist who put learning on the map, called them—although psychologists today do not heartily agree with Pavlov's ideas about the nature of reinforcers. The occurrence of a reinforcer will be spoken of as a "reinforcement," "a reinforcing event," or referred to by such statements as, "S-R was reinforced by . . ."

A Laboratory Demonstration of Reinforcement

To illustrate the reinforcement concept, let us consider in some detail an intriguing experiment reported in 1942 by Prof. John P. Seward (236). He placed thirty-two rats, one at a time, into a rather small box containing only a small, metal rod (conventionally called a "bar" by most psychologists) that was actually one end of a lever. The rats were each given one of these three treatments:

REWARD Group

For this group the apparatus was fixed so that a depression of the bar caused a bit of food to fall into a pan near the bar. These rats, as well as those in the other two groups, had been deprived of food for several hours prior to the experimental session every day. After a rat ate this food, it was removed from the box.

REMOVAL Group

Subjects in this group simply were removed from the box by hand just after they pressed the bar. Although also hungry, they got no food while in the box, nor soon afterwards.

Controls

For members of the control group nothing in particular happened immediately after they had pressed on the bar. They were removed at the end of five minutes, unless they had pressed the bar during the preceding ten seconds. Thus, neither food nor removal followed the bar-pressing response in a systematic fashion.

Seward found that ten of twelve subjects in the REWARD Group showed a progressive decrease in bar-press latencies over the training days. Six of the twelve REMOVAL Group subjects showed clear improvement, too. Latency in this case would be measured from the time the rat was placed in the box, facing the bar, until it pressed the bar. Control subjects' latencies were highly variable throughout. However, when the training period ended, all rats were placed on the control group routine—i.e., nothing happened when any rat pressed the bar now. The rats in the REWARD and REMOVAL Groups both persisted in pressing the bar more frequently than did the control rats. This is one of the indirect ways of measuring what, or how much, has been learned under some earlier training procedure. We can conclude that most of the subjects of both the REWARD and REMOVAL Groups had, as we ordinarily say, "learned to press the bar." The controls had apparently not done so.

For the rats in the REWARD and REMOVAL Groups there had been a definite change in the environment soon after they made a particular response. They showed the kind of response change that we expect to occur when learning is taking place. The control rats had no distinctive event occur after a bar-press; there was no evidence that they ever made this R other than randomly. The difference between the two experimental groups and the control group was, as we shall put it throughout the book, that the experimental rats were reinforced when they pressed the bar, while the control rats were not.

THE LEARNING MODEL SUMMARIZED

The only purpose of the learning model that will be used throughout this text is to provide an abstract description of those events that are common to the greatest number of the experimental studies of learning. Although such modest devices as this have sometimes been mistakenly identified as learning theories, nothing of the sort is intended here. Solely that we may relate, compare, and contrast the great variety of specific learning situations to be considered, I am suggesting the model as a sort of analytic "common denominator."

The events that usually can be observed in what are conventionally called learning situations, then, can be summarized thus:

(1) There is a describable physical change or changes (variously called "a stimulus," "stimuli," or "a stimulus-complex") that occurs in the environment of an organism. This is S.

(2) The organism does something (he acts, moves, talks, thinks— in general, he "responds" in some way) in the presence of such stimuli. This is R.

(3) Following this response, an additional physical change occurs in the environment. This may be the addition of a new element to the environment (e.g., the food for REWARD Group rats above) or the elimination of some features of the previous S. (E.g., for REMOVAL Group rats the box and the bar were, in effect, removed after they pressed the bar. The fact that the rat, not the box itself, changes position in space after a bar-press is irrelevant.) This is X.

So we arrive at a "stimulus-response-reinforcement" model of the situation that typifies the conditions under which it is most frequently said that learning occurs. I cannot stress too often that this model is not a description of any laws of learning; its only evangelistic note is an appeal to the observables of psychological research. The only useful way to introduce the field of learning is in terms of the observable events that, in the long run, have always shaped thinking about learning—no matter how speculative the ensuing thinking.

Habit and Habit Strength

So far, we have intentionally clung to a cumbersome terminology in order to establish firmly the empirical referents—the general descriptions of the experimental data—upon which the study of learning is founded. Assuming that these are becoming clear, we shall now attempt to simplify our working language.

Specifically, we can proceed more rapidly if we have a shorthand way of stating that a specific S-R relationship is being, or has been, learned. Nearly all learning psychologists have a brief way of conveying this idea, but there has been no general agreement on a single term. The most common terms have been "S-R bond," "habit," "expectancy," "memory," "engram," and various phrases involving the word "conditioning."

Now, we could spend a great deal of time debating the merits of these different terms, or we could invent a new one. Words are only tools for us to use as suits us best. Without further haggling, therefore, I shall follow the custom popularized by the late, very influential Clark L. Hull (124), and speak of learning as "habit formation," "habit acquisition," or "habit development." "Habit" refers to a functional relationship between an S and an R; the other parts of the terms—"formation" and the like—refer to the assumption that this relationship is established by events that occur over a period of time.

One word of caution must be added. Habit, as used here, means much *more* than it does in the popular vernacular. The man in the street thinks of habits as unconscious, involuntary, perhaps even uncontrollable kinds of stereotyped behavior. The formal procedures of reasoning, for example, are not usually thought of as habits.

We shall give a more extensive meaning to habit, using it to refer to any kind of learned behavior. By this definition, then, the procedures employed in logical reasoning are habitual, just as brushing the teeth or eating with a knife and fork are habitual.

One other term will help us also. This is "habit strength." It refers to how firmly a particular S-R relationship has been established.

As a simple example of the use of this concept, compare a child in the fourth grade with one in the second. Both "know the alphabet" —i.e., they can name all twenty-six letters in proper order. So, in a sense, they both have the same set of habits. Ordinarily, though, the fourth-grader will recite more rapidly and/or more efficiently than the second-grade child. The fourth-grader would also probably have a slightly harder time learning an entirely different alphabet of approximately the same length and with some coincidental similarities in the visual or auditory characteristics of its letters. Thus, although from one standpoint they have the same habits, there is still a behavioral difference; one child knows the alphabet "better," as it is usually put, than the other. Our way of describing such differences, when necessary, will be to say that the *strengths* of the habits involved are different for the two children.

Just a Little More Dogma

So far in this introductory chapter I have discussed one set of assumptions, prejudices, and so on after another. I have pleaded the causes of empiricism, behaviorism, and "pure science." There are not many more controversial issues upon which I can express a dogmatic opinion. The chief ones remaining are: Why study very simple learning situations? And why use rats? The answers to these questions are closely related.

It is the belief of many learning psychologists that the behavior of an organism progresses from a stage at which the learning of simple S-R units is difficult, or tedious, to a point where the learning of complex patterns of S and R events—sometimes of great length—

is simple. Most believe, further, that what kinds of complex behavior we *are* able to learn are determined by the kinds of simple
behavior that we *did* learn in the past. This might be described
as an assumption that learning is a continuous process, wherein all
previous habits are potential influences upon any new learning.

This "continuous process" view has many ramifications. The one
that is pertinent here is that, since simple habit formation is not
regarded as distinct from its more complex derivatives, a thorough,
systematic account of behavior needs as a foundation the understanding of how the very earliest or simplest kinds of learning take
place.

A human infant affords much anecdotal evidence that learning
occurs in the beginning only after tedious practice. The systematic,
controlled observation of learning in babies is rarely possible, however, and even if such research were more common it would not be
sufficient. The infants of any species show behavioral changes that
are as attributable to growth as to practice—at least, the effects of
these factors cannot be satisfactorily separated.

Enter the Rodent

In lieu of studying our own progeny we substitute a subject with
more desirable characteristics—desirable, that is, from the research
standpoint. The substitute is a laboratory animal that has been
required to reach physical maturity in a rather uneventful environment. This gives us a subject that is not likely to undergo radical
structural changes for a while, yet is still rather uneducated—or, as
we say, "naive."

The most popular animal for this sort of use has been the albino
rat or the hooded rat. He is relatively inexpensive to house and
feed. He reproduces rather easily, abundantly, and quickly. He
also reaches physical maturity quite rapidly. All in all, the cost of
raising rats to be used in only one experiment and then discarded
is not prohibitive; in short, much of the rat's popularity is based
on economics. Although there is little doubt that the rat has been
overused, and sometimes inappropriately used as an experimental
subject (21, 105), this is not sufficient reason for *rejecting* informa-

tion derived from the study of this animal's behavior. The major
need is for supplementary information from other organisms, and
in recent years this need has begun to be met. For such experiments
as require only that its subjects be naive members of a species whose
natural peculiarities and abilities are fairly well understood, the
laboratory-raised rat will do as well as any. We shall try to restrict
our consideration of "rat research" to studies that had at least this
much rationale for using the beast.

THINGS TO COME

The ensuing chapters of this text organize the field of learning
into three major sections, with a couple of digressions into related
subjects. The major sections attempt to show the transition from
simple to complex learning. In Chapters 2 and 3 the two main
kinds of simple habit formation situations are described in detail.
"Simple habits" are habits that involve only one stimulus and one
response. "Complex habits," or "complex learning situations," are
those involving the concurrent formation of a number of S-R
relationships. One of the main purposes of this text is to describe
how simple learning situations aid us in the understanding of complex learning. Chapters 6, 7, and 8 describe learning situations that,
from the *procedural* standpoint, are rather straightforward extensions of the practices used to establish simple habits. The habits
that *result* from these procedures, however, more closely resemble
the behavior that characterizes complex learning. These learning
situations, called in this text "simple habit interactions," thus represent a transition between the simplest and the most complex kinds
of learning situations. In the final two chapters of the text (11 and
12) complex learning situations themselves are examined.

The first digression is introduced following the study of simple
habit situations. In Chapters 4 and 5 the present knowledge about
the supremely important concept of reinforcement is examined in
detail. This discussion appears in that place because an under-

standing of simple learning situations is sufficient for an understanding of most of the research bearing on the topic of reinforcement. This material will also increase our knowledge of the most effective simple learning procedures. The next digression occurs in Chapters 9 and 10 and concerns the general adequacy of the approach to learning presented here. First we pause to consider some of the more well-known deviations from our model of learning situations. Next, the concept of motivation is taken up. These topics are deferred until after the study of simple habit interactions because most of the pertinent research involves the use of procedures that are introduced in those chapters.

In brief, the whole book is devoted to a description of the kinds of situations in which learning can be observed to take place. A conscious attempt has been made to show how all these situations may be related to one another, and how the understanding of simpler situations enhances our ability to understand (and thus manipulate) more complex situations. Finally, some evaluations of the logical and empirical status of certain concepts in this field are made. I have tried to keep these to a minimum, but in some places they are unavoidable.

SUMMARY

Americans, psychologists or not, are interested in the reasons why an individual responds in the manner that he does, and in the means by which this behavior may be changed. One approach to the solution of such problems lies in understanding how individuals learn. Although the study of learning has many obvious implications for applied psychology, this is not its sole justification. The behaviorist, at least, regards it as the possible stepping-stone to a general understanding of the behavior of organisms.

There is no concise definition of learning that could describe all of the situations to which the term can be applied. The reason for this is that learning is not a "thing." Learning is not studied directly;

it is defined in terms of a portion of the many functional relationships that can be noted between certain environmental events, called stimuli, and behavioral events, called responses.

Owing to the inability to provide an adequate definition of learning that would suit all points of view, I have afforded instead a model of learning, against which the myriad facts of learning can be compared and contrasted. The model states that learning is a change in responding that occurs as a result of at least one and usually more occurrences of the sequence:

$$\text{stimulus—response—reinforcement.}$$

This is not a theoretical assumption, but simply a point of departure for the study of learning data. We shall find many experimental examples in which one or more of the elements in the learning model are not readily apparent.

SUPPLEMENTARY NOTES

Certain aspects of the discussion of the quantitative measures of learning need further elaboration in order to clarify some fine technical points.

Equating Errors with Irrelevant R's

For simplicity, the description of errors given above emphasized their similarity to irrelevant responses in general. In the sense that any R not systematically related to the occurrence of reinforcement is irrelevant, errors are a subtype of that class, but they are unique in two ways:

(1) Errors are always, by definition, incompatible with the occurrence of the correct response, whereas many sorts of irrelevant responses, as in the example of the dog, may accompany the occurrence of the correct R. By the same token, erroneous R's may be free of any such additional irrelevant characteristics; in other words, an error may be made with the same speed and efficiency as seen in the case of a correct, well-learned R.

(2) Perhaps the most distinctive feature of errors is that they are

observed, measured, and recorded with the same degree of accuracy as is the occurrence of the R_L in the same situation. This is not true of most irrelevant R's; as we have seen, their occurrence is inferred indirectly from the measures discussed. The reasons for this are both practical and lethargic, with an occasional lack of insight involved, too.

Progress in the field of learning has sometimes been impeded by psychologists' lack of systematic information about the factors affecting the occurrence of irrelevant R's. This lack is now recognized and rectified in large part by European students of animal behavior.

Pooling Latency and Speed of R Measures

Quite often experiments combine these measures, i.e., report the time elapsing between the presentation of S and the completion of R. When this is done, either the name "latency" or "response time" may be applied to the measure by a given experimenter. This is not so confusing as you might think, since the part of a report describing an experiment's method will usually reveal exactly what was measured. This book will always use "latency" and "response time, or speed" in their exact and separate meanings.

For many purposes this composite time measure is adequate, but not always. Zeaman (298) has performed an experiment in which response latencies and response times did show different relationships to his independent variable, although the relationships were not incompatible. Specifically, Zeaman trained some rats to run down a runway to get a large piece of cheese, and some others to run to a small piece. The amount of reward for running, then, was the independent variable. Rats who got a large reward ran somewhat faster than rats who received a small morsel, but the differences were not very marked. A much more striking difference was found in the response latencies, with the large-reward animals having the shorter ones. Here, then, is a case in which a composite time would have probably revealed the same general principle about the effect of amount of reward, but some more detailed information would have been lost with such a measure.

The Difference between Rate and Speed of Responding

Students sometimes find this distinction difficult because both kinds of observations involve time measurements. It was also noted that speed of responding usually is used when the defined R is actually composed of a series of R's. In some cases, the speed of R and the rate of R might actually reduce to the same set of observations. Typically, however, the rate of R is applied only in the case in which the same R is made over and over in the presence of the same S. The speed of R, on the other hand, refers to situations in which the members of the series (if the experimental R actually is a series) are not exactly the same and which, furthermore, usually lead to a slight change in S. The rat running along a runway, for example, is moving first one leg, then another; each leg movement tends to change S slightly, since it brings the animal into a different portion of the runway.

The Probability and Magnitude of R as Learning Measures

More advanced students may have noted these omissions already. The omissions were intentional, for several reasons.

"Probability of responding" may have great potential as a theoretical means of giving many behavioral measures a common denominator, but as a direct measure itself it is equivalent to the operations identified above as measures of the frequency of appropriate R occurrences. At least this is the case at present; advances in our ability to chart simultaneously the changes in R_L and in several irrelevant R's, for example, might give a new, empirical meaning to the probability of R.

Magnitude (or amplitude) of response is a quite useful and objective measure of behavior in many laboratory and natural situations. But changes along this dimension are not consistently related to the presence or absence of irrelevant R's—including errors. Similarly, a stable, predictable S-R relationship may involve either a vigorous R, or one using only a fraction of the effort that *could* be expended in its accomplishment. In short, neither the most characteristic change during, nor the most general outcome of, learning situations has a systematic relationship to the variable magnitude of response; its utility is not as a basic measure of learning. Of course, every measure of responding can be made to show changes other than those that are characteristic of simple learning situations. Most important from the standpoint of the approach to learning taken in this text, however, is the fact that there is not yet clear evidence that changes in amplitude of response are systematically related to the elimination of irrelevant responses, unless we confound the measurement of magnitude of R with temporal measures of responding.

CHAPTER 2

✳

✳

✳ THE S-R OF S-R-X:
PAVLOVIAN CONDITIONING

The German psychologist Ebbinghaus was the first to subject learning to scientific investigation, but the Russian physiologist Pavlov must get the credit for being the first to emphasize the extent to which the behavior of higher animals was influenced by learning. The study of learning begins with the study of Pavlov's work (204, 205) because his work did, and still does, represent one of the most thorough, careful analyses of learning phenomena that is known to the field. He was the first to identify and describe a great proportion of the behavioral events that are now familiar to learning psychologists.

Pavlov's influence on the *vocabulary* of learning would alone be sufficient justification for granting him a prominent position in a Hall of Fame for psychologists. Actually, his contribution was much more profound than this. His work provided psychologists with the methods—and, indeed, much of the data—for understanding what is called the S-R part of the learning model used here. In fact, although the belief is not so prevalent as in the past, some psychologists still hold the view that Pavlovian conditioning is itself *the* model of learning, that it reveals the empirical essentials of the learning process.

34

The Case of the Impatient Dogs

Pavlov stumbled upon the phenomenon he came to call conditioning in the course of some experiments he was performing to determine the role of salivation in digestion. For this research he had prepared some dogs so that their salivary flow went not into their mouths, but into little glass containers attached to the dogs' heads. One of his techniques was to put a small amount of meat into the dog's mouth and to note, among other things, the consequent flow of saliva. This experiment had not gone on very long when Pavlov noted that the dogs did not always wait for the meat before they began to salivate. It looked as if the secretion (a response, in our terms) could be started simply by the *sight* of the meat.

Pavlov had the quality that characterizes great scientists—curiosity. So he took time away from his research on digestion (for which he would one day earn a Nobel prize) in order to check this new phenomenon more systematically. He replaced the sight of food with the ticking of a metronome, since this sound could be more easily and completely controlled.

The results were as the physiologist had expected: a dog would come to salivate when the metronome sounded, even though no meat powder was given immediately. All that was necessary to make this happen was to repeat several times the sequence,

Metronome ticking . . . Meat powder in mouth . . . Salivation.

Now, some people are willing to go so far as to attribute sufficient "intelligence" or "ability to reason" to a dog so that it might not puzzle them that the dog could "see a connection between" the sight and taste of meat. Only the most avid dog enthusiast, however, could fail to be impressed by the fact that a stimulus (ticking metronome) which had a purely coincidental relationship to the receipt of food could come to arouse essentially the same response (salivation) as did the food itself. We should also note that salivation is not a "voluntary" response; there can be no explanation of this S-R relationship in such terms as "the dog salivates when the metronome ticks because he thinks this will get him some food." We reject such explanations in general, of course, because they beg the question, but this mode of thought is especially inapplicable here, since the dog cannot "control" his salivary flow.

Pavlov realized that this experiment proved far more than that dogs are especially astute observers of their surroundings, and he quickly shifted his attention, as a physiologist, from the stomach to the brain. He devoted the remaining forty years of his life to the study of conditioning, the pre-eminence of which in learning is acknowledged by the fact that his procedure is now generally called "classical conditioning." For *this* work, which revolutionized psychology in two large countries and has been one of the important influences on psychology everywhere, he did not receive a Nobel prize; so much for the world's view of psychology as a natural science.

THE ESSENTIAL FEATURES OF CONDITIONING

Pavlov went on to show that the procedure by which he had got the salivary response to occur when a metronome ticked could also be used to teach many other new S-R relationships to dogs. Equally important, Pavlov and subsequent workers showed that his technique could be used with a wide variety of species. By 1931, Razran (216) was able to report that sixteen different species had been successfully conditioned; the phylogenetic range was covered almost competely in this list, from protozoa to man. The standard features of this seemingly universal method of training are the following:

1. A Neutral Stimulus Is Presented

Ideally, a neutral stimulus—symbolized by S_n—elicits no R at all. More realistically, though, R's that could be described as "orienting toward S" or "attending to S" can often be noted. A dog, for example, will prick up its ears at the sound of a metronome, just as a person will turn his eyes toward an object that moves in the periphery of his visual field. Such R's as these are not usually important in conditioning, since they can be controlled, utilized, or eliminated. S_n is usually neutral, however, in the sense that it does not evoke any response that is like the one to which it will become associated via conditioning.

2. An Unconditioned Stimulus Quickly Follows S_n

Of fundamental importance for Pavlovian conditioning is the pairing of the neutral stimulus with a stimulus that is already known to produce a specifiable response. This latter stimulus is called an *unconditioned stimulus*—represented by UCS—because its relation to the response it evokes is not dependent on any training factors. Meat powder in the mouth, for example, is the UCS for salivation; a dog does not have to be taught this relationship. The response produced by a UCS is called, similarly, an *unconditioned response*—UCR. A UCS-UCR relationship is relatively invariant and can usually be altered only by fatigue or certain drugs. Even then the alteration is only temporary. S_n-UCR is the Primary Relationship.

These first two steps in the conditioning sequence are actually three: S_n followed by UCS which, in turn, is followed by UCR.

Because of the invariable relationship between UCS and UCR, is it reasonable to speak of Pavlovian conditioning as being a case of associating an S and an R, although the experimenter literally controls the pairing of two S's only. The UCS, however, is only an effective means to the desired end—its occurrence guarantees the occurrence of the R.

3. The CS-CR Sequence Develops

Conditioning is said to have occurred when, after several repetitions of the sequence S_n-UCS-UCR, it becomes possible to produce a response similar to the UCR simply by presenting S_n alone. When this happens, it is customary to speak of the formerly neutral stimulus as a *conditioned stimulus,* symbolized as CS, and to call the new response now associated with this stimulus a *conditioned response*—CR.

Learning, therefore, is inferred in the Pavlovian situation because there has been a change in the relationship between an S and an

R. Without the S_n-UCS pairings the would be little or no expectation of this S and R combination occurring.

Specifically, the response changes that occur during a series of conditioning trials are either (a) decreases in the latency of some aspect of the UCR or (b) increases in the number of times that a part of the UCR will occur without the aid of the UCS. In other words, a conditioned response is one that finally comes to occur *before* the UCS is presented, or even when the UCS is not presented at all.

Comparison of UCR and CR

In brief, the process of conditioning is a shift from the sequence, S_n-UCS-UCR, to the sequence, CS-CR. The difference between S_n and CS is purely terminological; physically, they are one and the same. This is not true of the difference between UCR and CR.

The CR resembles the UCR, but occurs without the onset of the UCS. Furthermore, the CR typically differs in observable details from the UCR:

(1) One class of differences is quantitative: conditioned salivation is not usually so copious as unconditioned salivation.

(2) Some CR's differ from the initial UCR in the degree of complexity or amount of muscular involvement. Consider a case such as that in which the UCS is an electric shock to a dog's paw. The UCR in most such cases is a diffuse sort of behavior—straining at the harness used to keep the dog relatively immobile, barking, tail and ear movements, all of these and more may occur originally in addition to the act most directly related to the UCS: withdrawal of the leg from the electric grid. When conditioning has been established, however, most of what we would usually call "excited" behavior has dropped out. The CR, unlike the UCR, is a calm, smooth, leg-withdrawal response. This change in R during learning is an instance of what I have already described as the elimination of irrelevant responses.

(3) CR's may sometimes differ from UCR's in that, while the UCR is a direct response to the UCS—by definition, of course—the

resulting CR may sometimes have the appearance of the behavior we would ordinarily call "getting ready for the UCS to occur." An example of this behavior has been described by Mowrer (195):

If a rat is placed on a grill that can momentarily be energized with electricity and if on each occasion that the resulting shock is presented a tone of moderate intensity is sounded for one second in advance, . . . after as few as two or three paired presentations of the conditioned and unconditioned stimuli, one can [with some subjects] observe reactions, such as flattening of the ears and disturbed breathing, that clearly indicate that the tone has become a signal of impending shock (195, p. 28).

This kind of CR is often spoken of as a "preparatory response." In some respects it represents a transition between "true" Pavlovian conditioning and some of the other kinds of learning to be considered in the next chapter. The animals who developed the reactions described above did *not* acquire a response to the tone that resembled the UCR to shock (i.e., leaping off the grill momentarily).

Where is the X in Pavlovian Conditioning?

It has not taken very long for my warning about the looseness of the fit of the model to make itself manifest. So far in this chapter I have said much about the CS-UCS relationship, or the S-R relationship of the model, but where is the reinforcer in Pavlovian conditioning?

Pavlov called the occurrence of the UCS a reinforcement. Now, once a CR has begun to occur slightly before its UCS is presented, then it *would* be possible to equate UCS and X. In such a case, the UCS would literally be occurring in the position in time that we have allocated to reinforcers (i.e., *after* the response). But in the beginning of conditioning the UCS most certainly does not *follow* the R-to-be-learned. Therefore, the *onset* of the UCS can not be a reinforcer in terms of our model. We shall see that reinforcement is most important in the early stages of habit formation, and that is just the time when UCS-onset precedes R_L.

Actually, any statements about the possible reinforcers in Pavlovian conditioning would be only guesses. The terminal events of Pavlovian conditioning just have not received the same attention as have the earlier phases of the S-R-X sequence in this situation. That is why the schematic representations of conditioning shown in Figure 1 have so few indications of the terminal events (for example, when the CS is stopped relative to UCS termination). After the characteristics of reinforcers have been examined in more detail, I shall suggest some possible X events in Pavlovian conditioning situations.

TEMPORAL FACTORS IN PAVLOVIAN CONDITIONING

The CS-UCS relationship is not only the distinguishing feature of Pavlovian conditioning, but the exact nature of this relationship determines the strengths of the habits formed by this technique. It is no wonder, then, that four subtypes of Pavlovian conditioning are differentiated by the ways in which the CS and UCS are paired with each other. These differences, summarized in Figure 1, are:

Simultaneous Conditioning

With this procedure, CS and UCS are presented simultaneously; the times of their onsets coincide.

Delayed Conditioning

In this case the CS comes on before the UCS is presented. Usually the CS remains present until after the UCS has been presented; if it is terminated simultaneously with UCS onset, this is still classified as delayed conditioning.

Trace Conditioning

This differs from delayed conditioning in that *both* the onset and the termination of the CS occur before the onset of thes UCS. The term "trace" comes from the reasonable assumption that no R can be associated with an S that is not present at the time this R is made. Since, in this kind of conditioning, the external CS has ceased by the time the UCR occurs, Pavlov assumed that there was some neural trace of the CS still present at the time of the UCR's occurrence. Be sure to recognize that at present this is only an assumption, no matter how reasonable it may seem. The reasonableness is buttressed by the fact that conditioning can actually be obtained by this method.

FIGURE 1

Types of Pavlovian Conditioning Based on the CS-UCS Interval

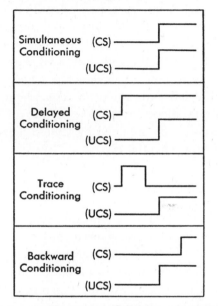

Inflections stand for stimulus onsets, deflection represents stimulus termination. To clarify the differences in these types, all UCS's are represented as occurring at the same point in time in each instance (the base line represents the passage of time; usually only a few seconds, at the most, are involved in any of these sequences). Termination of S is shown only where it is part of the specifications for a type of conditioning. The student should understand that UCR presumably occurs soon after UCS onset. ·

Backward Conditioning

Here the onset of UCS—and thus the UCR itself—*precedes* the presentation of the CS. This certainly *could be* a possible category of the class of CS-UCS intervals. Whether backward conditioning can actually be obtained, however, has often been doubted by psychologists. Pavlov first denied the actual possibility of this kind of conditioning, although he listed it as a class-member of the interval categorization. Later he said it could be done, but the resulting CR was weak. Prof. Gregory Razran, upon whom American psychologists are dependent for much of their information about recent developments in Russian experimental psychology, reports that backward conditioning of a stable sort has been repeatedly obtained in Russia (217).

In the United States, however, psychologists have not been successful in effecting by the backward conditioning procedure any of those changes that are accepted as indices of learning—e.g., increased percentage of CR's with increased pairings of UCS and CS. At best, this issue remains in doubt pending a thorough comparison of the Russian and American research in this area. (For a discussion of one alleged exception to the rule that backward conditioning has not been obtained by United States psychologists, see the *Notes* for this chapter.)

The Optimal Conditions for Pavlovian Conditioning

The foregoing classification of possible types of Pavlovian conditioning situations was a capsule survey of Pavlov's own taxonomy. It has been found that the study of these classes—both the real and the imagined—is helpful to the student's understanding of the Pavlovian method in general. All the types named above do not, however, represent equally important events.

We have already seen that backward conditioning is a curiosity, but hardly an effective way of obtaining any learning. Similarly, the data in Figure 2 will now dispose of simultaneous conditioning as a phenomenon of more than theoretical interest. This figure describes the results of a carefully conducted and carefully analyzed study of CS-UCS time relationships in the critical range of such intervals.

Figure 2 is a collection of "learning curves." They show the composite improvement (from the experimenters' standpoint) in CR performance obtained in six different groups of subjects—each represented by a different line, or "curve," in this figure—each of which was trained with a different CS-UCS interval.

The response conditioned in this experiment was that of withdrawing the forefinger from an electric grid. The UCS, of course, was a shock; the CS was a tone. The subjects received one hundred trials altogether. On eighty of these the UCS followed the

FIGURE 2

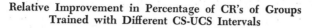

Relative Improvement in Percentage of CR's of Groups
Trained with Different CS-UCS Intervals

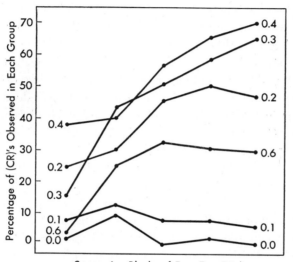

The CS-UCS interval used for each group is indicated by the numbers at the beginning and the end of the graph showing that group's performance at successive stages of training.

These results suggest that little conditioning occurs with CS-UCS intervals less than 0.2 secs., and that the most favorable interval is near 0.4 secs., a finding that has been verified many times. These curves were derived from data reported by Fitzwater and Thrush (79), in the *Journal of Experimental Psychology*, vol. 51, p. 60. Used by permission of the American Psychological Association.

CS by one of the fractions of a second indicated before and after each curve. On the other twenty trials the UCS was not given. These test trials occurred once in every block of five trials. Each curve represents the composite behavior of ten college students. Each point on a curve is the ratio of the total number of observed

CR's occurring in any group over the forty (i.e., 4×10) possible such occurrences during four consecutive test trials. The figure indicates that with simultaneous conditions, namely, 0.00 sec. difference between the onset of the CS and the onset of the UCS, or nearly simultaneous conditions (0.10 sec. difference in the two events), nothing resembling learning can be discerned. It seems that a very short delay is the most effective CS-UCS interval.

What about trace conditioning, as opposed to delay? After all, trace conditioning is actually a special form of delayed conditioning, differing only in that with trace conditioning the CS is over before the UCS begins. Although many more combinations of events need to be studied carefully, the available data indicate two principles: (1) within the optimal range for conditioning (i.e., about 0.45 sec. between CS and UCS onsets) no one has yet demonstrated a difference in the effectiveness of trace and delayed conditioning techniques; (2) with longer intervals, but still short enough for conditioning to occur at all, delayed conditioning does seem to be somewhat superior to trace conditioning (19, 147, 220). In other words, if the CS-UCS interval becomes long (i.e., exceeds 1.0 sec.), then it does make a difference whether the CS is still present when the UCS finally occurs; for shorter intervals, however, the difference in time between the *onsets* of the two stimuli seems to be the critical factor. This, of course, is consistent with the "neural trace" hypothesis; such traces would be expected to grow weaker with time, leading to poorer conditioning as the time between *CS termination* and *UCS onset* increases.

Time Between Conditioning Trials

Not only is the timing of the CS-UCS interval important in determining the stability of a Pavlovian habit, but so is also the timing of the presentation of successive CS-UCS pairings. This variable's effect is somewhat simpler than that of the CS-UCS interval. A definitive study by Spence and Norris (257) showed that as the time between successive CS-UCS pairings is increased, the conditioned response becomes more stable more quickly. The data in support of this statement are shown in Figure 3. In this experiment, a CS-UCS interval of 0.60 sec. was used, the CS was an increase in the brightness of a patch of light, the UCS was a puff of air directed at the eye (which causes an unconditioned blink reaction); Spence and Norris considered any blink of the eyelid to be a CR if it occurred from 0.25 sec. to 0.60 sec. after the CS was presented. As Figure 3 shows, training with a longer inter-

FIGURE 3

Rate and Stability of Conditioning as a Function of Time Between Conditioning Trials

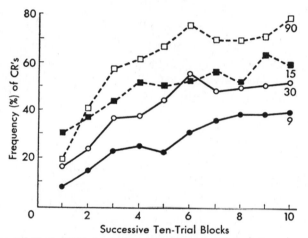

From Spence and Norris (257), in the *Journal of Experimental Psychology,* vol. 40, p. 718. Used by permission of the American Psychological Association.

This figure shows the acquisition of a conditioned eyeblink in four groups of college students who were each given 100 CS-UCS pairings with a different amount of time between successive trials. The average intertrial interval used is shown (in sec.) at the end of the graph for each group.

trial interval results in the more rapid development of CR's and also a more predictable CS-CR relationship; the apparent reversal of this relationship for the 15- and 30-second interval groups is actually not a reliable difference—in other words, these particular intervals had essentially the same effect.

Until we get into relatively complex learning situations, we shall find that this same relationship between the spacing of practice and the speed of habit acquisition holds fairly well for non-Pavlovian situations as well. This is one of the remarkable features of Pavlov's type of learning situation: most of the relationships discovered with this technique have quite striking analogs in other sorts of learning situations as well.

TWO OTHER TYPES OF PAVLOVIAN CONDITIONING

To complete the taxonomy of this technique, two more phenomena remain to be discussed, viz.:

Higher-Order Conditioning

The characteristic shared by all UCS's is that they each can elicit a fairly specific R of some sort. The stimuli almost always used for this purpose by Pavlov were, indeed, members of un-learned—i.e., unconditioned—S-R units. But their "unconditioned-ness" is, theoretically, only an incidental (although desirable) characteristic of UCS's. Viewing them most abstractly, UCS's are a very convenient way of getting some R's to occur. Other kinds of S can also provide the same service. For example, a well-established CS could achieve a similar end to that accomplished by employing a UCS. This was first shown by one of Pavlov's students, Frolov, who paired a new S_n with an already established CS. The results resembled those obtained with S_n-UCS pairings of a conventional sort: S_n ultimately came to evoke a CR similar to, but not identical with the CR elicited by the first CS. Pavlov named this process "higher-order" conditioning.

Higher-order conditioning, then, differs from other types of conditioning in only one main respect: Instead of a true UCS, higher-order conditioning uses an already established CS to elicit an R in the presence of a new S_n. Hypothetically, the chain of higher-order CR's originating from one UCS should have no limits; once a CS has been established, it should be possible to use it as a quasi-UCS for the development of a further S-R relationship, similarly with this new CS, and so on, as long as each preceding CS is occasionally paired with its original UCS, or UCS-substitute, to keep up its own strength.

Actually, few American psychologists are sure that they have ever seen the development of higher-order conditioning in the laboratory. This is not an attempt to revive any of the semantic issues discussed in Chapter 1. Higher-order conditioning has rarely been demonstrated in an American psychological laboratory, although Eccher and Culler (67) have done so. The higher-order CR's that have typically been reported in the United States (e.g., 77) were very unstable and some extraordinary reinforcement procedures had to be used in order to maintain them.

Russian psychologists, on the other hand, are reported to have observed impressively high orders of conditioning. So few United States psychologists can read the Russian language that we must be content with meager, abstracted reports about developments in scientific Russian psychology. Were sufficient details known, the differences in the results with higher-order conditioning procedures found in the two countries might become readily understandable.

In some of the other learning situations that we will soon consider, phenomena *analogous* to higher-order conditioning can be seen. Upon closer examination they usually turn out to be complicated by the presence of other conditions that are not specified by the Pavlovian definition of this procedure; these extraneous conditions, furthermore, often make it possible to relate the alleged higher-order conditioning to more readily observed types of learning situations. Examples of this will be seen in Chapter 3 (p. 96). Perhaps the whole difficulty here is verbal, i.e., a matter of what features of a complicated procedure one wishes to emphasize. After all, even simple instances of Pavlovian conditioning are not always completely distinguishable from the procedures to be discussed in ensuing chapters under other names. Until higher-order conditioning receives more empirical verification, however, it would be best for the student to be skeptical of the extensiveness of this process.

Temporal Conditioning

If meat powder is put into a dog's mouth regularly, say every half an hour, the dog will eventually begin to salivate just before the end of each half-hour "waiting period." In this experimental demonstration, care is taken to prevent the regular occurrence of any externally produced S other than the UCS. In unique characteristic of temporal conditioning is that a CR—in this example, salivation just prior to presentation of the food—develops even though there is no observable CS. Time is not an observable CS.

To my knowledge, few psychologists oppose the assumption that there are certain internal stimuli that operate in much the same way as do the more manipulable types of S's, and that these might serve as the CS complex for a temporal CR. If this assumption is granted, then the most relevant research on temporal conditioning would be investigations aimed at understanding the nature of such internal stimuli. This sort of research, however, is somewhat outside the main interests of most learning psychologists, with the result that there has been little study of temporal conditioning. This may someday be found to have been unfortunate; for example, imagine our collective chagrin in the field of learning if a phenomenon that we have more or less ignored for thirty years should ultimately be shown to reveal many important relationships. It is *always dangerous* to assume that we understand a phenomenon when we have, in fact, not studied it thoroughly. Scientists continue to do this because there are many instances in science where such calculated risks (as to what to pursue and what to ignore) have, indeed, paid off.

STIMULUS FACTORS AFFECTING BEHAVIOR

In America, Pavlovian conditioning has been used primarily as a means of studying the S events in the S-R-X sequence. In Pavlovian conditioning studies, the experimenter has a degree of control over the S and the R not usually found in the kinds of learning situations to be discussed in the next chapters. The result, as we have said, is that much of what we know about the effects of specific stimulus conditions on behavior comes from research by the Pavlovian method.

S Variability from Trial to Trial

Rarely in the laboratory, and almost never in ordinary learning situations, is the learner confronted by *exactly the same* combination of stimuli on each learning trial. Simply by shifting his bodily position, for instance, an organism will be getting somewhat different visual, auditory, and proprioceptive stimuli than previously. Since such shifts are common, the truth of the opening sentence is obvious. It is believed that the effect of this is to make the actual (i.e., usually observed) progress of learning less regular than textbook or theoretical descriptions imply. The individual learner's response latency, for example, does not literally decrease on every trial; errors do not steadily become fewer; response rate may fluctuate widely during the early stages of learning; and so on. Such deviations from the idealized learning "process"—wherein every reinforcement of an S-R sequence produces an improvement in the next performance of R—are typically attributed to "experimental error." Presumably, experimental error is correctable by the refinement of one's experimental techniques. Is this true of learning?

Yes, it is, and Virginia Voeks (280), one of the many women who have made important contributions to experimental psychology, has shown that the more closely we approach the *exact duplication of* S on each trial, the closer will we approach the theoretical course of learning. Voeks placed college students in a situation in which a mild buzzing sound was followed by a puff of air directed toward the eyeball. Such a puff of air will cause a person to blink—it is a UCS. After sufficient pairings of buzz (S_n) and puff (UCS), people learn to close their eyelid (CR) when the buzz (CS) sounds, so that the air puff strikes the lid harmlessly. Following the considerations above, Voeks sought to control more of the actual sources of stimulation than merely the onset and duration of the buzz and the air puff. Here are excerpts from her own description of how she established control over most facets of the total S.[1]

[1] For reading ease I have rearranged the order of the material in this quotation somewhat, and have omitted the conventional denotation for deletions;

To reduce the apprehension with which many subjects start their first experimental session, the experimenter chatted with the subject, answered his questions, and appeared, at least, to allay his fears about possible shocks, snakes, and other noxious stimuli. The experiment began only when the subject appeared comfortable and confident he could do what was expected of him. To mitigate increasing "nervousness" about the need for finishing the session, the subject [had been] asked to allow an hour before he signed up; on arrival, he was told that although it might seem longer, we would stop after no more than 45 mins. No subject was run during his examination week nor immediately before any class test.

Throughout each trial, the subject depressed a telegraph key with each hand. The keys were depressed "as soon as possible" after a signal "with a firm smooth motion," held down "with a constant pressure" until a buzz terminated, and (were) then released. Depression of both keys activated the buzz; contact was broken if either key was released slightly, thus affording a check on the relative constancy of pressure. A stiff spring was used in the keys, so the response involved muscles of the arms and shoulders as well as of the hands.

At the start of each trial, the subject breathed in rhythm to the experimenter's saying, "Ready, inhale, exhale, inhale, hold." The words were spoken slowly; on the last "inhale," the subject inhaled "as deeply as possible," and in response to "hold," held his breath and depressed the keys.

Besides stablizing the key-response, this routine should have increased the similarity of the on-trial stimuli arising from the diaphragm, intercostals, and other muscles of the chest, shoulders, and upper arms.

A soundproof room was used; all necessary movements by the experimenter were highly routinized; except for these, she was nearly soundless; the subject's head was surrounded by a box, sharply limiting his visual field; he was requested not to talk during the experiment (unless fatigued or something seemed to be going wrong) (280, p. 139).

These conditions are hardly typical of everyday learning situations, and yet even with all these precautions Voeks could not

---

these alterations, which do not distort the meaning at all, have been approved by the publisher of the article (The American Psychological Association). Furthermore, I have avoided the typical space-saving device used by psychological journals, that of denoting the experimenter as E, the subject as S. This book will use a plethora of symbols anyway, and especially many involving the letter S.

From the *Journal of Experimental Psychology,* vol. 47, p. 139. Used by permission of the American Psychological Association.

be sure that S was exactly the same on every trial for a given subject. She came closer to this goal, however, than almost any other experimenter.

Under such conditions, learning came close to its textbook depiction. In most cases, once a subject began to make eyeblink responses to the buzz alone he never again failed to make this learned response. In addition, the average magnitude of responses to the buzz alone was nearly always greater in succeeding blocks of trials until the maximum (full closure during the CS-UCS interval) was attained. In other words, when S is almost exactly the same on each trial, learning actually does progress in so orderly a manner that we can predict with a high degree of accuracy what a subject's response will be like on a given trial, if we know what his behavior on preceding trials has been.

Habits that develop under more typical conditions of S variability may show a more erratic sort of acquisition, but they do have one mark of superiority—they are more resistant to change once they are established. An experiment by Mackintosh (177), which was the opposite of Voeks' study in that it permitted S conditions to vary far *more* than is customary in laboratory studies of learning, has demonstrated this.

In the final analysis, variability of S from trial to trial gives to learning an erratic course, but also gives the resultant habits their ultimate flexibility of application. Most learned R's, that is, can be evoked by a somewhat wide range of S conditions; in other words, several S-R relationships are usually established in a given learning situation, instead of just one. This has definite advantages in survival value over the habit that involves one, and only one, particular stimulus pattern. There is, however, a process other than controlled or uncontrolled variation in an S complex from learning trial to learning trial that makes many cases of simple habit formation cases of *multiple* habit formation, even involving S's that are *not* presented during training. This process is called *stimulus generalization,* and it, too, was first observed (and named) by Pavlov.

Stimulus Generalization

As we know, if a 1000-cycle tone (the frequency of a tone, analogous to what we ordinarily think of as its "pitch," is measured in "cycles per second") is repeatedly paired with a UCS such as food, a dog will come to salivate when this tone is presented alone. What will happen now if the dog hears an 800-cycle tone for the first time, instead of the usual 1000-cycle tone? There is a great deal of evidence to indicate that the dog will make a weak version of the CR to this new tone; this in spite of the fact that the 800-cycle tone has never been associated with the UCS. This is called *stimulus generalization*.

Students often wonder why this phenomenon is not called "response generalization" instead. "To generalize" is often used as an active verb in our speech, and, in that sense of the word, the stimuli themselves certainly do no generalizing. There is no good reason why this phenomenon is called stimulus generalization, but it is too late to change the term now. Actually, it will do as well as any other label.

Stimulus generalization, then, is the term denoting the fact that once a learned relationship between an S and an R has been established, other S's similar to the training S will also become capable of arousing this R, even though they have never been related directly to the R. So, in the process of establishing a functional connection between S_1 and R_1, we automatically produce other connections between stimuli similar to S_1 and the response, R_1. This phenomenon is evident in the youngster who is just learning to talk. If the family dog is called "Sturdley," the child will in time come to designate the animal by this same verbal label. Once the child has learned to call *his* dog "Sturdley," he is more than apt to go around calling all the dogs in the neighborhood "Sturdley" as well. He may persist in this for quite some time though the neighborhood dogs may vary a lot in size, color, shape, and so on, not only from one another, but from the real Sturdley as well.

Clearly, this phenomenon has some significance for individual adaptation. For example, if a young child who is burned by the hot stove could not generalize this experience to other stoves of somewhat different physical features (or even the same stove viewed from a different angle), adaptation through learning would be most inefficient; he would have to be burned by each new stove he encountered before learning to be wary of it.

The phenomenon of stimulus generalization was first noted in the Pavlovian learning situation and this method was long a favorite means of studying generalization. An experiment by Hovland (117) is a classic study of the Pavlovian type concerning the strength of generalized habits. Hovland first selected four tones of different pitches, each of which was judged by many people to be equally different in pitch from the next lower-pitched tone (i.e., tone 1 differed in pitch from tone 2 by the same subjective degree as pitch 2 differed from pitch 3). Then he conditioned the GSR's of half of his subjects to the lowest pitch on his scale, while the others were conditioned to the highest tone; the UCS was an electric shock. Later, each of the other three tones was sounded for each subject, the object being to determine the magnitude of response occurring to these "unfamiliar" tones (they actually *were* somewhat unfamiliar, even to experienced young adults, because they were "pure" tones). By properly counterbalancing the presentation order of the test (generalization) tones for different subjects, it was possible to pool the results from all subjects and obtain the curve shown in Figure 4. Generalized habit strength is clearly a function of the degree of similarity between the original and the test stimuli.

Although first observed, and perhaps most easily demonstrated in the Pavlovian conditioning set-up, stimulus generalization is not limited to this particular situation. The phenomenon is believed to be fundamental to the process of transfer of training (Chapter 7) and to much complex learning. Learning psychologists agree that stimulus generalization does occur, and that the strength of a learned R is a decreasing function of the difference between the original training S and any other similar S. Beyond these generalities, however, disagreement predominates. In particular, there are great differences of opinion about the shape of the generalization curve.

In 1943, Hull (124) offered a formula for the generalization phenomenon that was based upon Hovland's data. Many learning psychologists have since observed generalization gradients (as the relationships between S similarity and R strength are often called) that do not match Hull's hypothesized gradient. It seems that there

FIGURE 4

Hovland's Generalization Curve for the Conditioned GSR

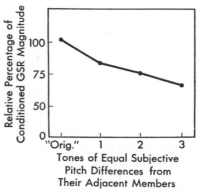

From Hovland (117), in the *Journal of General Psychology*, vol. 17, p. 136. Used by permission of the Journal Press.

Here the mean amplitude of the GSR established during conditioning (to the original tone) is taken as representing 100 per cent, and the remaining points on the curve show the relative reduction of the GSR amplitude to tones with known degrees of subjective difference in pitch from the original tone.

may be more than one generalization gradient, depending upon the methods of establishing them. This possibility will be considered again later, after we have studied more of the learning phenomena themselves.

For the moment, recognize that (1) stimulus generalization does occur, and that (2) it is directly related to the degree of difference between the training and the generalized S's. More exact specification of the latter relationships could be of great value both for behavior theory and for the application of learning principles to concrete situations. As yet, however, the knowledge of the precise form(s) of the generalization gradient is inadequate.

The Effect of CS Intensity

The intensity of a stimulus is a rather limited dimension of S. It is fairly well correlated with certain physical events—e.g., decibels of sound, brightness of light, and the like. Obviously, it is not among the most striking or important stimulus dimensions for those who are interested in personality or the social facets of human behavior. Nevertheless, stimulus intensity does play a role in the performance of learned behavior, and there is even a chance that the relationship of R strength to CS intensity may be the basis of other behavioral laws of a broader scope.

In current American psychological thought, CS intensity is held to affect the observed strength of the CR, but not to affect the rate of acquisition of the CS-CR relationship. In other words, the more intense the CS the more vigorous the CR, but the number of CS-UCS pairings necessary to develop a stable CR remains the same (19, 146). Just as with stimulus generalization, the role of stimulus intensity in behavior has been demonstrated in many non-Pavlovian situations.

ELIMINATING CONDITIONED RESPONSES: EXTINCTION

Since a CR is established by repeated pairings of the CS and the UCS, it would be reasonable to expect that repeated presentation of the CS *without* following it with the UCS might lead to elimination of the CR. This is exactly what happens; repeated unreinforced presentations of the CS lead to changes in the CR that are the opposite of those described as indices of learning in the first chapter.

The procedure of presenting the CS repeatedly without following it by the UCS was named "experimental extinction" by Pavlov. In current usage this has been shortened simply to *extinction*. Later in this text there is an entire chapter on this procedure, so we will not examine it in great detail now. But there are a few terms and phenomena in this area about which it will be helpful to know a little since they are relevant in other contexts as well; it is to these that we now turn for a moment.

Inhibition

Extinction is a procedure; it can be most generally described as the repeated evocation of a learned response without reinforcing it. Extinction itself is not a behavioral phenomenon, nor is it an "explanation" of any behavioral phenomenon. To account for the observable fact that continued nonreinforcement of a response leads to the weakening and ultimate cessation of this response, we must appeal to other principles or hypotheses.

Pavlov "accounted for" the behavior observed during extinction by positing a neural process that he called "inhibition." The unreinforced occurrence of a CR, he said, causes inhibition to accumulate; when inhibition is sufficiently great, the CR will cease.

Inhibition is a purely hypothetical event, as far as anyone now knows. It is roughly analogous to "fatigue," but the important difference in the two concepts is that there is a known physiological process underlying fatigue, while no such physiological event can now be indicated in the case of inhibition.

Spontaneous Recovery

Suppose that extinction has proceeded to the point that a CR is completely "suppressed"; repeated presentation of the CS has failed to produce any more CR's. What if we now wait a few hours, then reintroduce the subject to the experimental situation and again present the CS? As it turns out, the subject will usually respond again to the CS. For the first few presentations of the CS it will look as if the subject had had no previous extinction sessions.

Pavlov, apparently at a momentary loss for hypothetical processes, called this phenomenon "spontaneous recovery." We now know that this relationship between the effects of extinction and the effects of rest is no more "spontaneous" than is the fact that you are now reading this material; it is a highly predictable facet of learned behavior. Nevertheless, the term has taken hold, and we continue to use it.

The most conventional interpretations of spontaneous recovery relate it to the concept of inhibition. As viewed by Pavlov and later by Hull (124), inhibition was assumed to be a labile process, accumulating with unreinforced occurrences of the CR and dissipating with rest, i.e., no presentation of the CS or anything similar for some period of time. As inhibition diminishes, the CR regains some of its strength, thus manifesting "recovery."

Related evidence for some extinction-produced process that waxes and wanes with time comes from comparisons of "massed" and "spaced" extinction trials. Massed extinction trials are those that occur in as rapid succession as the experimental situation will permit; if one extinction trial follows another within 1.0 minute or less, the extinction series is usually called massed. Spaced extinction trials, obviously, are those that occur infrequently enough for the subject to get some rest between trials. The sky is the limit as to how far apart spaced trials can be, but the intervals most often employed in experimental work range from fifteen minutes to twenty-four hours. In almost every instance where spaced and massed extinction conditions have been compared, a greater decrement in CR strength has been shown, for any constant number of extinction trials, under the massed condition than under spaced extinction. This would follow from the assumption that inhibition is something that builds up during nonreinforced occasions of the CR and diminishes when the subject is allowed to rest.

Conditioned Inhibition

If inhibition can be "washed away" by rest, however, how could extinction ever result in the rather permanent cessation of responding that is known to occur with repeated or prolonged extinction series? How could a CR ever be eliminated if there were enough rest permitted between extinction trials? In the long run, we know, the effect of nonreinforcement supersedes the effect of rest, but how can an inhibition notion account for this? Certainly another concept is needed to complete the Pavlovian-Hullian picture of extinction. Again the great Russian psychologist came up with an answer that is still quite popular.

Since Pavlov regarded inhibition as a real event, he conjectured that it shared some of the characteristics of observable responses, and could be conditioned just as could any R. Extinction could thus be viewed as a new conditioning situation in which inhibition is a sort of UCR that is produced by repeated nonreinforced occurrences of a CR. Since the old UCS—used to establish the earlier CR—is no longer present, but the old CS *is*, a new relationship begins to be formed: that between the CS and "inhibition." Thus, after sufficient pairings, a new phenomenon develops. This is called *conditioned inhibition*, i.e., a learned inhibition of the earlier CR.

As with other conditioned responses, conditioned inhibition is impervious to the "ravages of time" per se. It does not, that is, weaken with rest between S-R repetitions. As the number of unreinforced occurrences of the CR increases, so does the strength of the "inhibitory CR," as it is called; this happens whether extinction trials are widely spaced or compactly massed. Eventually, so this viewpoint goes, the strength of the inhibitory CR will exceed that of the original CR—the one undergoing extinction—and when this happens, the original CR will itself cease to be evoked by the CS under any circumstances.

In terms of the "reality" of the concepts of inhibition and conditioned inhibition, the foregoing account is, of course, highly speculative. But conditioned inhibition is a neat way of handling the following sorts of facts:

(1) It is true that if extinction series are repeated again and again with a constant rest interval between, spontaneous recovery will be noted; the amount of recovery, however, shows a progressive decline over the initial trials of a number of such series, and it becomes easier and easier in each successive extinction period to eliminate the original CR. This would suggest that not all of the inhibition accumulated during the previous extinction session has dissipated, even with long rest intervals.

(2) If conditioned inhibition is the same as any other conditioned response, then we should be able to evoke it—outside of the extinction situation in which it is *assumed* to operate—by presenting the appropriate CS. Some fairly old experiments supported this deduction; these experiments used the following procedure:

First, the sequence CS_1-CR_1 underwent extinction (thus presumably, making CS_1 an inhibitory stimulus). Then another habit, CS_2-CR_2, with few or no features common to the first conditioning sequence, was developed. Finally, under conditions usually conducive to the performance of the latter habit, CS_1 and CS_2 were presented together. It was found that this combination would not produce CR_2.[2] So it seems that inhibition, whatever it is, can be conditioned; it seems, further, that conditioned inhibition can be manipulated in the same way as can any other CR.

(3) Pressing even further the similarity between conditioned inhibition and observable CR's, it might be asked whether inhibition will show the stimulus generalization effect. Hovland (118) investigated this, too. He repeated the general form of the experiment discussed in connection with Figure 4 (p. 54), but with important changes. For one thing, he developed an equally strong, identical CR to all four of the pure tones (the same tones as used in the earlier study) with each subject. Then half of the subjects were given extinction trials with the lowest tone only, while the other half had repeated nonreinforcement associated with the highest tone only. This procedure, of course, resulted in a rapid decline in the magnitude of the GSR to the particular tone used. Finally, all subjects were tested on the remaining three tones; this was the crucial part of the experiment— the question was, what would be the effect of extinction at one point on this range of stimuli on the CR's associated with the three similar S's? The results are shown in Figure 5.

The Comparative Generalization of Excitation and Inhibition

A comparison of Figures 4 and 5 reveals that inhibition does not generalize to the same extent that "positive," or observable, conditioning (sometimes called "excitation," to contrast it with inhibition) does. After the establishment of a CR to the original

[2] As a control measure, some subjects for whom CS_1 was still an S_n—i.e., it had been neither a conditioned stimulus nor a conditioned inhibitor—were tested on the same combination-CS of CS_1 and CS_2; in this case, CR_2 occurred.

tone of Figure 4, there is a relatively strong tendency to make this same response to tone 3, for instance. On the other hand, extinction with the original tone does not produce nearly so great a generalized decrement in the CR to tone 3 (see Figure 5).

FIGURE 5

An Empirical Relationship that Can Be Interpreted as
The Effect of Generalized Conditioned Inhibition

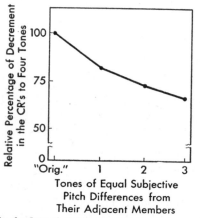

Tones of Equal Subjective
Pitch Differences from
Their Adjacent Members

From Hovland (118), in the *Journal of Experimental Psychology*, vol. 21, p. 59. Used by permission of the American Psychological Association.

In this curve, it is assumed that the effect of extinction in regard to the original tone has been to produce a decrement in the associated CR strength of 100 per cent. The validity of this assumption does not matter; the important effect displayed here is the degree to which the CR's to similar tones are also weakened. Such weakening is attributed, in Pavlovian language, to the generalization of conditioned inhibition.

The difference in the generalization gradients of excitatory and inhibitory tendencies is factual and verifiable, no matter what may be your opinion of hypothetical concepts such as inhibition. We shall find that concepts of the kind just considered can be helpful in organizing and analyzing many learning situations. Conflict situations, in particular, have turned out to be amazingly tractable by analysis in fairly traditional Pavlovian terms (188). But there are objections to this positing of abstract unobservables. The inhibition approach emphasizes the failure of something to occur; it is always difficult to prove that one has observed "nothing happening." *Something* is always happening in a psychological experiment. To some psychologists it is disturbing to have to appeal to hypothetical events until all observable alternatives have been exhausted. The following approach to extinction is sometimes offered as a more positive, empirically oriented substitute for inhibition theory.

Counter-conditioning

A CR can also be eliminated by substituting another CR for it. This procedure is called *counter-conditioning*, and involves the following steps:

(1) The relationship, CS_1-CR_1, is established; this means that UCS_1 need not be presented in order to get a response to CS_1.

(2) Now, to eliminate CR_1, we not only withhold UCS_1 (extinction), but also present a new unconditional stimulus UCS_2 whenever CS_1 is presented. UCS_2 elicits a response that is different from CR_1.

(3) This pairing of CS_1 and UCS_2 will conflict with the previously established CS_1-CR_1 habit. Ultimately, the organism learns a new habit consisting of CS_1 and CR_2.

The details in any specific situation, of course, are far more complicated, but these major features of counter-conditioning have their parallels in many techniques of habit-alteration—including those not concerned with habits established by Pavlov's method. In fact, the counter-conditioning framework is applicable to the Pavlov-Hull account of extinction described above. They differ in that in the inhibition theory of extinction, the last-formed habit (conditioned inhibition) is defined only negatively, in terms of the absence of CR_1; similarly, UCR_2—inhibition, in their terms—is not observed or controlled as in the usual Pavlovian situation. Much of Chapter 8 will be devoted to a further discussion of this controversy.

THE SIGNIFICANCE OF PAVLOVIAN CONDITIONING

Pavlov's extensive research program affected psychology (learning in particular, of course) in two major ways:

(1) By the time his work became known in the United States,

Pavlov had already carefully collected and organized a large body of data. He and his students were the first to describe and name phenomena and procedures such as conditioning itself, stimulus generalization, extinction, and spontaneous recovery that are still regarded by most learning researchers as being among the basic descriptive units of behavior science, appropriate even in non-Pavlovian situations.

(2) Pavlov's work was first delved into and appreciated in the United States by the behaviorists, who recognized it as an ideal representation of the very kind of psychological research that, up to the time this work became known, they had been championing in the abstract. The "discovery" of conditioning by Watson (282) and his co-workers enabled behaviorists to make positive suggestions about psychological research.

Originally, behaviorism was largely a negative viewpoint; it was a rebellion against the introspectionist methods of Wundt and, in this country, of Titchener. A school of thought that emphasizes only what should not be done *may* succeed in altering the viewpoints against which it is opposed, but will not itself survive long without a more positive program.

We will never know whether behaviorists would have developed their own methods of psychological research. Just when they needed such a program they discovered one that seemed custom-made. Pavlov's method was objective, well-controlled, precise, and versatile; behaviorism embraced it enthusiastically.

Conditioning in Nature

The preceding discussion emphasized the virtues of Pavlovian conditioning as a research method. What about conditioning as a portrayal of everyday learning events?

Opinion on this matter is still divided, but the trend is increasingly away from attempts at a literal depiction of natural learning situations in terms of the basic Pavlovian conditioning sequence. At present, it is felt by most psychologists that the learning situations to be considered in subsequent chapters of this text more closely resemble the natural circumstances in which learning can occur. On the other hand, it can not be emphasized too often that the vocabularly developed by Pavlov is, in large part, used to describe natural learning situations succinctly. If Pavlovian conditioning is an artificial type of learning, then its artificiality has been of the same useful type as have many other laboratory phenomena in the natural sciences.

The psychologists who most literally believe that Pavlovian conditioning often occurs outside of the laboratory are those who hold viewpoints similar to that of O. H. Mowrer (197). Mowrer's position, putting it most simply, is that there are two types of learning situations and these result in distinct classes of habits. The commonly observable types of learning are called "problem-solving" by Mowrer. By these methods the organism learns responses that are pertinent to its motives or needs. The second class of learning situations is that in which, according to Mowrer, the events of Pavlovian conditioning occur. This learning results in the acquisition of new drives, or, more accurately, in the conditioning of biological drives to more and more stimuli in the environment. Acquired drives are considered to develop by the continguous occurrence of a CS, a UCS, and a UCR which is, in this case, a response resulting from activity of the autonomic nervous system. Without accepting all of Mowrer's implications, quite a few psychologists agree with the general notion that learned drives (particularly, fear) may be established by Pavlovian methods: a CS is associated with a UCS for which the UCR is something that we call "drive increase." We shall return to this point when we consider avoidance conditioning.

SUMMARY

Pavlovian conditioning is a highly refined method of observing learning in the laboratory. Its essential steps are the pairing of a neutral stimulus, indicated by S_n, with an unconditioned stimulus, indicated by UCS. The latter is called "unconditioned" because it will nearly always evoke a specifiable response, a UCR. After sufficient S_n-UCS pairings, S_n will come to evoke some portion or facet of the response formerly made to the UCS alone. When this occurs, we speak of a *conditioned stimulus*—CS—eliciting a *conditioned response*—CR.

Pavlovian conditioning data do not *directly* reveal much about the ways in which ordinary people learn ordinary things. The method is a highly abstract technique for examining some phases of the "learning process." At least four major contributions to American psychology can be credited to Pavlov, his students, and his method of studying learning:

(1) Pavlovian conditioning was the ace in the hole for the school of thought called "behaviorism." We can never know now whether it was truly essential or not, but Pavlov's work provided the most convincing argument for the behaviorist position that Watson, in the early days of the movement, had been able to find. The great Russian physiologist proved the feasibility of a truly objective approach to psychological research, which was the cause Watson championed.

(2) At a more empirical level of evaluation, Pavlovian conditioning has, as mentioned above, supplied much of the information about the S-R relationships in the learning situation, and about their effects on the ultimate behavior pattern produced. The conventional, or most technically correct, methods of establishing a true CR do not reveal much about the X part of our S-R-X model of learning. Pavlovian researchers have been especially concerned with the stimulus events that influence the establishment of a conditioned habit. As we have repeatedly emphasized, this is not a criticism of our model nor (most certainly) of Pavlov's method. Some laboratory procedures are best for certain purposes, but complete duds for other, related aims. Thus it is with Pavlovian conditioning.

(3) Although, in general, the Pavlovian method of developing habits is regarded as highly artificial, it is also believed by many psychologists to be the means by which nonbiological drives are developed in humans.

(4) Pavlov first observed and sketched the broad hypothetical outlines of the phenomenon called "extinction," which has since become a highly important technique for the study of various learning problems.

While one need not regard as gospel every definition or hypothesis put forth by Pavlov, the student of behavior will make a serious mistake if he ignores the Pavlovian method and the phenomena revealed by it. To appreciate the utility of much of the data discovered by the Pavlovian method, we need to consider much more learning research. His was not only the first approach, but it remains one of the most comprehensive and systematic attacks upon a large area of behavior. While we are about to leave Pavlovian conditioning as a focal topic, we shall never get far away from the concepts and hypotheses that have been treated in this chapter.

SUPPLEMENTARY NOTES

Methodological Points

The Concept of a Learning Trial

This is a very arbitrary unit. Roughly, it corresponds to an opportunity to respond. In Pavlovian conditioning, a trial would begin with the occurrence of an S_n or CS and end with the occurrence of a UCR or CR. During extinction, however, the UCR would never occur, and the CR is expected to cease eventually; in such cases we must resort to an arbitrary time limit for defining a trial. This time limit is not hard to decide upon in the Pavlovian situation— the CS-UCS interval used during training provides a meaningful reference point.

The necessity of defining the beginning and end of a trial in a consistent, objective manner is apparent in the study of such problems as the effect of spacing of trials upon the rate of extinction. Clearly, the interval between trials cannot be controlled if there is. no systematic basis for deciding when a trial has begun or ended.

On the Neutrality of S_n

Ideally, as mentioned when the topic was introduced in the text, the neutral stimulus used in a conditioning study should not elicit any response resembling the UCR or the CR-to-be-established.

Sometimes, however, it may be true that the neutral stimulus actually does arouse a weak version of the response to be conditioned to it, even before conditioning has taken place. The most noteworthy example of this in the human subject is when the response in question is the GSR. The GSR (which stands for "galvanic skin response") is measured by passing an extremely weak electric current (imperceptible to the subject) through the skin of one palm; the GSR is a drop in the skin resistance that will occur momentarily when some S, such as an electric shock to the other hand, is presented. Almost any stimulus, however, will cause a few GSR's to occur. Since, except for this one consideration, the GSR is a fairly easy medium for studying Pavlovian conditioning in humans, the common practice is to adapt the GSR to whatever stimulus is to become the S_n. Adaptation is accomplished by repeatedly presenting the S—such as a light or a tone—until the GSR ceases to occur upon its presentation alone. In other words, through the process of adaptation we can actually transform a stimulus into a neutral stimulus, by our definition of "neutral," even though it was not such to begin with. Of course, this procedure is only for experimental purposes; in a practical use of Pavlovian conditioning it might actually be very helpful if you could find an S that has already evoked a weak form of the R you planned to use—the development of a strong R to this S should be just that much easier.

Backward Conditioning Research in the United States

The history of the backward conditioning controversy in America really began with the appearance, in 1930 and in 1932, of two carefully performed and carefully reported experiments by Helen M. Wolfle (290, 291). Contrary to Pavlov's assertions, she reported that backward conditioning could indeed occur. In both studies, some subjects made a few CR's when a CS, which had always *followed* the UCS on training trials, was presented alone. Her procedure was essentially the same as that of Fitzwater and Thrush, described on page 43 except, of course, for the fact that the UCS came before the CS.

During the next few years, many attempts were made to obtain backward conditioning with other species or other (CR)'s, but never with the success that Wolfle had described. Not until 1947, in fact, were findings similar to hers again obtained. Spooner and Kellogg (259) used the method that is always most likely to result in the verification of previous research findings—they repeated the essential features of Wolfle's own procedure, something that seems not to have appeared necessary to other scientists during the intervening fifteen years.

Although Spooner and Kellogg found exactly what Wolfle had, they regarded their data somewhat more skeptically. They also noted a further characteristic of the backward conditioning data that had, up to then, gone unnoticed. Finger-withdrawal responses did occasionally occur when the CS was presented alone after several UCS-CS pairings, but this fact was the only support for the assertion that backward *conditioning* had been obtained.

First of all, it was a rare subject who showed any improvement in the percentage of CR's occurring during the test sessions, although the number of UCS-CS pairings was increasing from test trial to test trial. Second, *progressive decline* in the percentage of CR's over succeeding test trials was typical of more subjects than was improvement in CR performance. Third, the number of subjects who never gave any CR's formed an impressively large minority. All these characteristics can actually be seen in Wolfle's own published data summaries. Spooner and Kellogg also reported that latency of CR did not decrease as more and more conditioning trials were given.

In other words, none of the changes generally agreed upon by psychologists to be characteristics of learning have been observed in the case of backward "conditioning." The progressive changes that most often occur in this situation are just the opposite of those from which learning is inferred. The fact that some few CR's do occur is noteworthy; to assume that this of necessity implies the occurrence of learning, in the Pavlovian sense, is very shortsighted.

Sometimes people ask, doesn't the *decline* in CR's with more backward conditioning trials suggest that the subjects are learning *not* to respond? This question misses the point of what is involved in conditioning. If one were sitting at a desk with one hand resting flat, palm down, and he heard a light tapping sound (Wolfle's CS), would he raise the forefinger of this hand (the CR of her experiment)? Not many people would. If one has not learned an R to an S, it should hardly be necessary to employ backward conditioning, or any other kind of conditioning, to teach the person not to make this R when the S occurs.

There are two reasons why we have devoted so much space to a phenomenon that, as we see, should not have been categorized with other kinds of Pavlovian conditioning to begin with. First, some fairly recent secondary sources still mention, albeit briefly, that backward conditioning is a way of forming a habit by Pavlov's technique. The fact that they dismiss the method as inferior does not alter the theoretical implications that would follow if it were true that habits of *any* quality could sometimes be established by this procedure. For example (and this is the second reason I have spent so much time on this matter), the general discussion of learning and reinforcement in the first chapter would have been quite different if it could be shown that repetitions of the sequence, R_1-S_1, could eventually lead to the sequence S_1-R_1.

*

*

CHAPTER 3

* # THE R-X OF S-R-X:
OPERANT LEARNING

The type of learning that is most characteristic of everyday situations has been called "problem-solving," "trial-and-error learning," "instrumental conditioning," or "operant learning." As with all terms, each of these is equally useful, providing only that we know to what it refers. In this book a preference will be shown for the term, "operant learning"; this label was suggested by B. F. Skinner (247) who has done much to further our systematic knowledge about this important area.

As an example of the general features of operant learning, let us first consider an experiment performed by Azrin and Lindsley (13). The general purpose of this study was to show how one could get pairs of children to work together (cooperate) using standard operant learning techniques:

During any experimental session, two grade-school children of the same age and sex were brought into a room containing little else except a table and two chairs. At each end of the table, near the chairs, were three holes, with the holes at each end aligned symmetrically with respect to one another. On each side of the table there was also a stick (called a stylus) with a metal tip; these were attached to the table by electric cords, and fitted the holes in the table.

The children were told that the table and its equipment were the parts of a game that they could play or not, as they choose, while they were in the room. Each child was then told to place one of the sticks in each of the three holes at his end of the table. Finally, the experimenter showed the children some jelly beans and said merely, "While you are in the room some of these will drop into this cup." The cup referred to was attached to one side of a transparent screen that separated the two sides of the table; the screen prevented one child from operating both styli at once.

When both styli were placed in corresponding holes at the two ends of the table within a fraction of a second of each other, an electrical circuit closed activating a machine that released one jelly bean into the cup beside the screen. The experimental question was, could pairs of children learn to cooperate in their stylus manipulations, given no more instruction (or even encouragement to play with the table at all) then here described?

As it turned out, learning was shown by ten pairs of children; the learning measure here was rate of "cooperative" responses. Since only one jelly bean was delivered on each occurrence of the correct combination of responses, the children ordinarily worked out an agreement for sharing the rewards (e.g., by taking turns at getting the candy). In those cases where one child insisted on taking all the candy, the rate quickly dropped to zero.

THE MAJOR CHARACTERISTICS OF OPERANT LEARNING

The fact that the subjects worked in pairs, and that the response measured was actually the combined actions of the two subjects, in no way detracts from the experiment's exemplification of the basic ingredients of operant learning. While the Azrin-Lindsley study is a rather novel application of the operant learning procedure, it is only one of innumerable instances in which this method has been successfully demonstrated with adults, children, chimpanzees, down the scale to the rat and beyond. In every case both the procedure and the outcomes are highly similar.

The essential features of operant learning are these:

S Characteristics of Operant Learning

It is not always necessary to have an S and an R as explicitly and clearly defined in operant learning as they typically are in Pavlovian conditioning situations. In many cases, as in the study just described, various S's could be used by different subjects in the same learning situation.

Although simple operant habits can be formed in situations where S_L can be only vaguely identified, this is not necessarily so. Once an operant habit has been established, especially in the laboratory, it is often possible to vary independently different aspects of the learning environment, and note the effects of the absence of (or changes in) certain elements of the total S situation on the performance of the habit. In this way it may be possible to identify more exactly the stimuli involved in the habit. Such an analysis is, at least hypothetically, possible in most operant learning situations.

It is not always the case that S is not known or controlled in operant learning. The major exceptions are the *discriminated operant* habits. Such a habit is established when an R is reinforced if it occurs in the presence of certain S's, but not reinforced if the same R occurs when these S's are not present in the subject's environment. This procedure, called "discrimination learning," is discussed extensively in Chapter 6; it is mentioned here only to point out that there *are* operant learning situations in which S is specifiable, controlled, and an important aspect of these situations. Actually, such situations are in the majority in nature. Only when simple habits are being considered alone do cases of very vague specification of the crucial stimuli predominate. This, in fact, is one of the features differentiating simple habit formation from more complex learning situations.

R Characteristics of Operant Learning

Unlike the Pavlovian method, the operant learning procedure does not use direct control over the occurrence of R as a means of originally associating S and R. In operant learning, it is "up to the subject," so to speak, whether he will ever make the desired R—i.e., the one to be reinforced—under the appropriate stimulus conditions.

In the Azrin-Lindsley experiment, for instance, the instructions put the children under no pressure to insert the styli in the holes at any time after the experimenter showed them how to do it. Furthermore, there were, at most, only subtle implications of a relationship between the styli and the jelly beans; there was certainly no hint that both children had to make a similar R almost simultaneously in order to obtain a jelly bean. In other words, operant learning depends for its initiation upon the chance, or random occurrence of the correct response.

I have already pointed out that there is no universal agreement about the meaning of a "response," as a general term, other than that independent observers must be able to agree as to whether a given segment of behavior has or has not occurred at a specific point in time and space. In most Pavlovian situations the CR and UCR *could* be described in anatomical terms, although this is not always done. In operant situations the common mode of describing an R is in terms of its accomplishment.

Most responses effect some change in the organism's environment, even if only temporarily. We often describe behavior in terms of "the rat pushing the lever," "the pigeon pecking the disk," "the child pointing at the correct object," or "the student giving the right answer." All these descriptions are couched in terms of what the organism's actions accomplished, rather than in terms of the physical movements of the organism itself. There is nothing unrealistic about this practice; to paraphrase an old saying, nature does not seem to care how you play the game—at least within limits—but whether you win or not.

To put it another way, there *are* many ways to skin a cat, and if skinning a cat is what is important (either in nature or in society) then *any* behavior that achieves this will be reinforced. Since it is a change in the environment that actually provides the reinforcement in many operant situations, it should be clear why a specific, potentially physiological definition of R_L is unnecessary in many cases of operant learning.

Operant learning situations, therefore, can vary from ones in which the R_L is fairly specifically defined to those in which any one of a variety of R's—in the physical sense—may be reinforced. By the definition of simple habits being used in this text, the latter situation—R_L vaguely defined—is typical. Complex habit formation begins with cases in which a variety of actions by the organism *could* accomplish the same thing, but only one or a few of these are permitted to be effective. More about this in a while.

Methods of Increasing the Frequency of R_L Occurrences

Actually, neither teachers nor experimenters need (or usually do) literally trust to luck during the early stages of an operant learning situation. There are several specific techniques for reducing the randomness of behavior in a given situation, and we shall see many of these throughout the text (in the illustrative examples and experiments especially). There are, however, two general methods for restricting the variability in responding that could possibly occur in a situation in which the subject has no special habits to employ (this is called a "new learning" situation). These techniques are important because R obviously *must* occur before it can be reinforced; *variable* behavior precludes, by definition, the frequent occurrence of any specific R, and some possible R's might never occur. The techniques for diminishing behavioral variability, then, are ways of increasing the chances that the R to be reinforced will occur fairly often, relative to the occurrence of irrelevant or erroneous R's.

1. Reducing the Possibilities for Irrelevant Responses

The Skinner box, briefly described in connection with the Seward study in Chapter 1, illustrates this technique very well. This "box" is just that—an empty cubicle, barren of anything except a "bar" or lever, and, in most cases, a receptacle in which food or water is deposited upon the occurrence of the proper R. In the Skinner Box, the R that is reinforced is the movement of the intruded bar.

Now, there is just not very much that a rat can do in such an environment, so, as long as the rat is active, the chances are very good that it will often move the lever accidentally. The more often "bar-presses" (as this sort of R is called) occur by chance, the more frequently they can be reinforced. After a few reinforcements, of course, the occurrence of R_L begins to become less than accidental.

2. Increasing the Possibility That Any R's Will Occur

One effect of the procedures described as "increasing the subject's motivation (or drive)" is to raise the overall level of the subject's activity or responsiveness to the environment. Just as it is important to prevent the subject from making *too many different R's* in a new operant learning situation, it is also important to insure that the subject will not make *too few R's of any kind.* For trial-and-error learning to occur, the subject must try things, so we cannot permit him to grow bored and/or fall asleep.

It should be apparent that the most effective general method of insuring the occurrence of R_L in an operant learning situation is a combination of both techniques just described: keep the subject active (by motivating him), but make sure that he does not do too much else besides perform R_L. Either technique by itself will usually aid in the progress of operant learning; together they are almost always effective.

X Characteristics of Operant Learning

In many cases of operant learning the S is not even identified by the experimenter, much less controlled; the R_L's occurrence is also independent of the experimenter's actions, except indirectly. So far, this situation does not sound like a particularly scientific tool for the investigation of learning, or anything else. The value of operant learning as a research method, however, becomes clear when we turn to the X part of our model; operant learning is our best means of observing the role of reinforcement in learning. The reinforcing agent is clearly identifiable in operant learning situations; this characteristic best differentiates operant learning from other types of learning situations.

Not only is the reinforcer clearly identifiable but its presentation is completely under the experimenter's control, so that the presentation of the reinforcing stimulus has a specific relationship to the occurrence of R. In experimental cases of operant learning this relationship is often determined by the nature of the apparatus that is involved in the performance of R_L. In the Skinner box, if food is used as the reinforcer, it can be arranged that a movement of the lever *automatically* releases a food pellet into the box. In the maze or runway, if the animal goes in the proper direction it will automatically end up in the presence of the reinforcer (such as food). In the study of cooperation, described earlier, the nearly simultaneous closing of the proper circuits released a jelly bean into the cup via a chute that led from a dispenser in the adjoining room (so that the whole supply of jelly beans would not be in sight of the subjects; this same arrangement is used, of course, with the Skinner box).

In operant learning situations in which the subject does not manipulate something that could automatically provide X, the experimenter or teacher must be prepared to present it himself when the correct R occurs. Sometimes this presents practical problems, of course, and such problems account for many of the real life instances in which learning does not proceed in the manner that the teacher anticipates or intends. This is why a greater variety of experimental situations will not be encountered in the following discussion of operant learning and reinforcement (although the variety actually is rather large); if you are interested in studying some aspect of the R-X relationship, it would not be good sense to employ a learning situation in which this relationship can not be controlled easily. There is, however, a great deal of evidence to show that in a concrete, practical situation the principles of operant learning can be applied once the teacher has had the ingenuity to provide for control over the R-X relationship.

The final point to be made about reinforcers in operant learning situations is that they are usually rewards. The nature of rewards is discussed in detail in the two succeeding chapters; for the moment, it will suffice to describe a reward as any object or event for which an organism is known to show definite preference, under a given set of conditions. Food is a reward to a hungry organism, to mention just one obvious example. Both in the laboratory study and in the everyday application of learning principles, rewards are usually the most efficiently controlled and the most effectively employed type of reinforcing conditions. But this does not mean that rewards are the only possible sorts of reinforcers; that they are not is suggested, for instance, by the REMOVAL group animals of Seward's experiment (see Chapter 1, pp. 22–23.)

Operant Learning Characteristics Summarized

(1) In operant learning, the S is complex, not easy to specify in detail in all cases, and does not have a controlled onset or termination. This is not always true of operant learning, but is quite frequently so.

(2) The R_L's occurrence is not determined by the experimenter, i.e., there is no UCS. Steps *can* often be taken to make the R_L's occurrence highly likely, but the experimenter does not determine precisely when it will and when it will not occur.

(2a) The learner is usually motivated in successful, efficient operant learning situations, since this is a way to make the occurrence of the R_L more likely. As with reward, the concept of motivation is sufficiently complex to merit a chapter of its own. Until the material of Chapter 10 is taken up, however, let us understand motivation to mean any procedure that is designed to keep the organism active—either in a general or in a specific way.

(3) The reinforcer is clearly identifiable.

(4) The presentation of the reinforcer has a specific, controlled relationship to the occurrence of the R. This is always true in laboratory instances of operant learning, and is also the case when operant learning methods are being used effectively in practical situations.

(5) Reinforcement is usually some form of reward; again this is a *typical* characteristic of operant learning, but it is not without exceptions. (When reinforcement is a reward, the symbol X_{rew} will be used in this text.)

TYPES OF OPERANT LEARNING SITUATIONS

There are several different procedures that share the foregoing characteristics, and these can be spoken of as types of operant learning, although it is not intended by these distinctions to imply that different learning principles apply to each. Some of these classes of operant learning may, indeed, seem to involve differences in the kind of learning that is effected, but the distinctions to be made here are based on procedural differences alone.

Three major kinds of procedural differences provide the bases for the distinctions between the types of operant learning situations that can be noted. Probably most important are the kinds of *motivating* and *reinforcing procedures* that can be used; there are also differences in the relevant *response characteristics*. A taxonomy of operant learning should consider at least these three dimensions. These are shown in Table I.

TABLE I

The Dimensions Along Which Operant Learning Situations Can Vary, with the Subcategories of These Dimensions

DIMENSION R: The Rs Critical to the Occurrence of Reinforcement	DIMENSION Mot: The Motive Conditions Holding at the Time of Learning	DIMENSION X: The Reinforcement Conditions Used to Effect Learning
1. Only one R	1. Independent of any given learning situation	1. Pertinent to the motivating conditions
2. Many Rs of the same kind	2. Inextricably related to the given learning situation (motivation relevant)	2. Not pertinent to the motivating conditions (a) "Unlearned" (b) "Acquired"
3. Many different R's		

Dimension R of Operant Learning

This dimension of operant learning concerns the number and the similarity of the responses that must occur before reinforcement will be presented. We can divide operant learning situations into three types on this dimension: (1) The cases in which the occurrence of only one R is critical for the presentation of X; (2) the cases in which more than one R of the same kind must occur before X is forthcoming; and (3) the cases in which multiple (i.e., two or more) R's, each different, are required before reinforcement occurs. The difference between case (1) and case (2) is chiefly quantitative—the relative number of R's, considered to be the same, that are necessary before X occurs—but the difference between case (2) and case (3) is qualitative as well.

Case 1: One R Determines X

Here X follows the occurrence of a fairly specific R, and it is not important what other R's may precede or follow the critical response (viz., R_L). The distinction between these cases and those requiring the occurrence of several R's in succession prior to reinforcement must be arbitrary. As Skinner has shown, even the seemingly simple bar-pressing situation (in which a rat presses a lever and every instance of this is followed by a food reward, or reinforcer) can actually be described as a series of S-R relationships (i.e., an instance of case 3 in Table I).

The Azrin-Lindsley study provides an example of such a situation. In that experiment the crucial response for any given subject was the placement of his stylus into the hole directly opposite the one into which his partner had placed, or was about to place, his own stylus. Obviously, verbal communication between subjects would facilitate this cooperation, but this communication was only indirectly related to reinforcement. Reinforcement was not contingent upon any particular form of communication, nor was it given if such communication was not followed by the appropriate R on the part of either subject. Only the response that resulted in the proper (as defined by the experimenters) placement of the stylus was reinforced. The fact that learning occurred under such arbitrary conditions, and, in fact, occurred very quickly, justifies the experimental use of the "one-R" analysis, even though it can usually be shown that instances of case 1 are actually an experimental fiction in operant learning.

Probably there are some studies that were treated as being of the case 1 type—i.e., one-R—that could be more easily understood had they been studied in terms of case 3 on Dimension R, but there are many experimental and real-life examples of situations in which learning can be obtained when the environment of the subject is so constructed that one and only one occurrence of an R determines whether reinforcement will then occur.

The fact that further subdivision of such situations may be possible is not crucial. Scientists seek verifiable relationships, and it is unquestionable that such relationships can be obtained in situations where the occurrence of only one R determines the occurrence of X. All simple operant learning situations—both in the laboratory and in the workaday world—are of this sort.

Case 2: Repetitions of the Same R before Reinforcement

This is a simple extension of case 1. A given R must, or at least can, be made repeatedly (how often is up to the teacher) before X occurs. The same reservations apply equally to cases 1 and 2; it is always possible that some further and different R's actually occur between the last R in the crucial series and the ultimate attainment of the reinforcer, especially if X is a reward. This class of operant learning situations (multiple R's of the same kind) is especially useful in the study of reinforcement schedules (Chapter 5). It suffices to say here that it is possible to obtain verifiable relationships between the number of R's required per X and both the rate of acquisition and the predictability of R's during habit maintenance.

Case 3: Several Different R's per X

This is perhaps the most commonplace sort of operant learning. Here the subject makes a series of R's before any reinforcement is presented. As mentioned above, the two previous classes of this dimension are largely oversimplifications of the present case, especially if we adhere rather closely to a muscle-group definition of R. A rat running down a runway (with food obtained after every run) makes, as we have said, numerous different R's, if muscle movements are considered. Essentially the same R-X relationships can frequently be noted whether we define R in a broad way ("running down a runway"), or in a very discrete manner ("the left forepaw moved x mm. in y msecs."). Therefore, the possibility that most cast 1 examples of Dimension R would reduce to case 3 types, if enough instances were observed carefully, does not seem critical in the long run. But we never should overlook the possibility that a specific one-R situation may be incomprehensible unless further analyzed as an instance of case 3 here.

In summary, Dimension R turns out to be very flexible, which is in keeping with the fact that in operant learning R is typically neither controlled nor observed with the meticulous care that it receives in Pavlovian conditioning. The way in which a scientist categorizes (and thus observes) any given operant situation on this dimension is largely determined by his interests and prejudices. It is often sufficient to have a fairly casual definition of events that you must observe carefully. We must never forget, however, that we may not be sufficiently analytic in a given instance of operant learning.

Dimension Mot of Operant Learning

A general description of this dimension can be given quickly. If we hold in abeyance the problems concerned with the definition of motivation or drive, the subcategories of this dimension are rather easily differentiable.

There are cases in which the procedures that increase motivation are *independent* of the procedures that constitute the learning situation at a given instant. For example, if we have deprived an animal of food for a number of hours, the animal is just as hungry whether we put him into an operant learning situation or not. This is an example of case 1 of Dimension Mot in Table I.

On the other hand, some means of motivating the subject *must* be employed in the context in which we expect learning to occur. Mrs. Muttle, when attempting to teach young Roger to exercise caution about the stove, relies on the fact that her cry, "No, no, Roger, musn't touch!" will be closely followed by withdrawal behavior by Roger if he does indeed go ahead and touch the stove. The whole development of pain-avoiding behavior by Roger will be discussed in a later section, but the point here is that Mrs. Muttle ultimately depends upon the stove's heat to produce random behavior, some of which she intends to reinforce when it occurs. The fact that the stove may be hot at times when Roger is not around is trivial; in terms of what his mother hopes he will learn, the motivator is relevant. This is an instance of case 2 on Dimension Mot.

Dimension X of Operant Learning

As with motivation, we shall temporarily take an easy-going approach to the problem of defining reinforcement. This problem is carefully examined in the next chapters. Granting this temporary *laissez-faire*, we may differentiate reinforcers of all kinds into two types: (1) those that are *pertinent* to whatever motivation conditions have been used to facilitate the occurrence of R_L, and (2) those that are not pertinent. Within the latter class (reinforcers not pertinent to the motivational conditions), there is a further subdivision—(2a) reinforcers whose effectiveness is apparently not dependent on special prior training of any sort (called "unlearned") and (2b) those that *are* dependent on prior training (called "acquired" reinforcers). All these distinctions will be examined further in this chapter.

In the foregoing breakdown of reinforcement situations in operant learning, reinforcers are delineated in terms of their relationship to motivation. This indicates another role that motivation can play: not only can motivation be used to insure the occurrence of R_L, but it can also be used to insure the effectiveness of a reinforcer. In other words, the procedures that we call "motivating the subject" may have either or both of two effects: (1) Motivation may increase a subject's general responsiveness to any kind of stimulation, or

(2) motivation may increase a subject's responsiveness to *certain* S's, thus making it more likely that such S's can serve as reinforcers.

The Dimensions of Operant Learning: Summary

The simplest way to summarize the previous two sections would be to say that Dimension Mot and Dimension X interact as differentiators of operant learning types. Motivation may be produced by procedures that are independent of any given learning situation, or these procedures may be among the essential features of a given learning situation. In either case, the means of reinforcing R_L may be pertinent to the motivating conditions, or the reinforcement may be unrelated to them. If unrelated, it is useful to inquire whether X is an acquired or innately reinforcing agent. Any of these six basic types of operant learning situations, furthermore, may involve any of the three categories of Dimension R, with only a few possible exceptions. There are, then, altogether eighteen possible combinations of the various subcategories of these three dimensions. Of these, sixteen can now be shown to have identifiable representatives in the experimental work involving operant learning.

The whole purpose of this delineation is to emphasize the wide variety of operant learning procedures that are known. It would be expecting a great deal to ask anyone to commit these sixteen to eighteen subtypes to memory. The somewhat detailed analysis of the six types of operant learning (in terms of motivational and reinforcement conditions) that involve only case 1 of Dimension R will suffice to illustrate the important differences along the motivation and reinforcement dimensions of analysis. It should be understood that, with exceptions to be noted, a similar analysis could be applied to cases 2 and 3 of this dimension.

SIX REPRESENTATIVE CASES OF OPERANT LEARNING

The following experimental descriptions are but a glimpse of the means with which behavior scientists have examined operant learning. Innumerable examples could have been cited for most of the following cases, and the cases not taken up in the succeeding paragraphs have received almost as much study as those that I do take the time and space to discuss in detail. Throughout this text examples of these other operant types will be used to illustrate other behavioral phenomena. Bear in mind, therefore, that the following examples all involve case 1 of Dimension R—i.e., only one R is crucial to the occurrence of reinforcement, and every time that this R occurs it is to be reinforced.

1. One R/Motivation Independent/Reinforcement Pertinent

We need only refer to the Seward experiment (236) described in Chapter 1 to exemplify this most simple of operant learning situations. REWARD group animals were deprived of food for several hours prior to placement in the Skinner box. When a subject pressed the bar—R—a food pellet was delivered, and the subject ate it. The rat's hunger was not dependent upon being placed in the Skinner box (thus, motivation was independent); one and only one response (bar depression) determined the occurrence of reinforcement, and the reinforcing agent was relevant (*pertinent*) to the subject's motivation (food for a hungry rat). As you remember, learning was most easily obtained under such conditions in Seward's study.

2. One R/Motivation Independent/Reinforcement Not Pertinent, Unlearned

When the subject's motivation is not directly determined by the particular learning situation in which he finds himself, then reinforcement may either be pertinent or not, considered in relation to the motivation of the subject.

Seward's experiment illustrates both of these relations. Both his REWARD group and his REMOVAL group were hungry when placed in the learning situation (the Skinner box). Only the RE-WARD group received food, however; the REMOVAL group did not. Both learned the bar-pressing response. So we say that the reinforcement for the REWARD group was *pertinent*, since it could be assumed to have changed the motivational conditions of the subject (i.e., to have reduced the subject's hunger). The reinforcer (removal from box) for the REMOVAL group presumably left these subjects' hunger unchanged, so this X was *not pertinent* to the motivation conditions; that it was not pertinent, however, did not make it ineffective.

3. One R/Motivation Independent/Reinforcement Not Pertinent, Acquired

The reinforcer in Seward's REMOVAL group was not only not pertinent to the motivating conditions, but it was unlearned, i.e., it was not dependent upon prior experience with removal for its effectiveness as a reinforcer. There is another class of reinforcers, however, that is just the opposite: *secondary reinforcers,* as they are called, are stimuli having no intrinsic ability to attract the subject's attention (except fleetingly). They are analogous to S_n's in Pavlovian conditioning.

As an example of an acquired, irrelevant reinforcer consider a portion of an experiment I once conducted (158, Exp. II). First, rats were trained to run down a straight runway; sometimes they ran into a white endbox, sometimes the endbox was black. Whenever the white endbox was in place, the subject was fed (the rats were always hungry at the time of training); the black box contained no food. After several trials with each endbox in place, the situation was changed. Now a simple, one-choice maze was introduced. This maze, called a U-maze, was shaped like a two-tined fork (see Figure 6).

In such a maze, the subject cannot see either endbox at the choice-point. If, under such conditions, a rat develops a preference for one side of the maze over the other (i.e., he consistently goes right or left, instead of going to either side randomly), we might assume that learning has occurred. Now, it is known that rats will show left or right "turning preferences" even when the consequences of going to either side are the same. These turning preferences are controlled by giving several trials without any endboxes in place (the rat is removed as soon as he makes his choice, whatever it is).

After the "naturally preferred side" was determined, the white endbox (in which food had previously been given for running in the straight runway) was placed at the end of the path leading from the *nonpreferred* side of the maze choice-point. At the end of the maze leading from the preferred side was an unknown endbox having

FIGURE 6

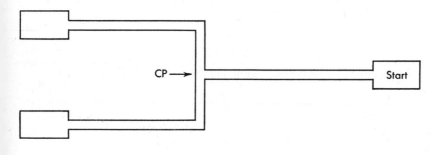

A U-maze

black and white vertical stripes. In other words, a box previously associated with food was placed at the end of the path along which the rat was least likely to travel frequently, and a strange box was placed at the end of the path most often chosen by the rat.

Thirty-eight of forty rats thus treated reversed their "natural" preferences and, over a series of these maze trials, made a majority of their turns at the choice-point (CP) into the path leading to the box previously associated with food. This box did *not* contain food at the time of these maze trials, although the subjects were still hungry.

Thus, this is an operant case involving one R (the turn at the CP), an independent source of motivation (hunger), and a reinforcer not directly related to the motivational conditions (since the box no longer contained any food). The overwhelming proportion of preference reversals indicates that these conditions were sufficient for learning to occur.

4. One R/Motivation Relevant/X Pertinent

Consider a rat who finds himself in a box that has an electrical grid for a floor, which is divided in half by a small partition. Electricity can be passed through the floor on either side of the partition independently; in other words, the grid on one side of the partition could be "hot" while the floor on the other side was "cold." A schematic side view of such an apparatus is shown in Figure 7.

FIGURE 7

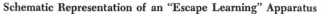

Schematic Representation of an "Escape Learning" Apparatus

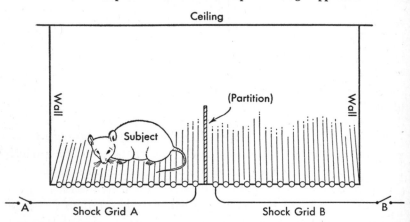

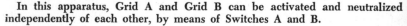

In this apparatus, Grid A and Grid B can be activated and neutralized independently of each other, by means of Switches A and B.

Notice that the dividing partition is considerably lower than the ceiling and walls. The reason for this is that we wish to teach the rat to jump over this partition; "jumping the hurdle" is the R_L in this situation. Given the conditions depicted in Figure 7, a rat can easily be taught, usually within a few minutes, to make this R.

The steps on any of the first few training trials are these:

(1) Switch A is closed, making grid A "hot."

(2) The subject becomes active, but in a diffuse, undirected way.

When shocked, rats will usually move around on the grid vigorously, attempting to jump out of the box, to scale the walls, to hang on to the ceiling, and so on.

(3) As in any good operant learning situation, this apparatus is so arranged that the R that is very likely to occur is that which results in getting the subject over the partition onto grid B.

(4) Since grid B is not charged, scaling the partition results in the termination of the electric shock.

(5) We now allow the subject to regain his composure on grid B, then we open switch A (stopping the shock on that side) and close switch B (starting the shock there). Essentially the same pattern of random activity will begin again and will only cease when the R is made that gets the subject across the partition onto grid A (which is now cold).

Ultimately, the rat will quickly respond to the onset of shock on either grid with an efficient jumping response that successfully terminates the electric shock.

The use of electric shock (always below the voltage and amperage levels that would lead to bodily harm of the subject) is a favorite method of psychologists for studying the effects of *noxious stimulation*. A noxious stimulus—symbolized as S_{nox}—is a convenient way of motivating the subject by means that are, in terms of Table I, inextricably related to the given learning situation. For brevity's sake, we refer to these situations as cases in which motivation is relevant.

Escape Learning

The foregoing example of the *One R/Motivation Relevant/X Pertinent* case has a special name among learning psychologists. It is called *escape learning*. While it is not the only kind of operant learning that fits the operant classification under discussion, escape learning is probably the clearest illustration of this type. Although, according to the scheme developed here, escape learning is only a special case of one type of operant learning, the extensiveness of its occurrence in everyday learning has led to a great interest in its dynamics. So I am going to digress from the development of

Table I somewhat, and discuss the features of escape learning at length for a while.

Escape learning is unique because of the role of S_{nox} in this situation; altogether, S_{nox} serves three functions in the escape learning case:

(1) The onset of S_{nox} motivates the subject: the subject's general activity is increased by the presence of S_{nox}.

(2) Since it is present at the time when R_L occurs, S_{nox} is an important part of the S of the S-R-X model of escape learning. In fact, S_{nox} will usually be *crucial* to the occurrence of the escape response.

(3) The termination of S_{nox} serves as the reinforcer of R_L. In general, a pertinent reinforcer is always an event that constitutes a reversal of whatever procedures had earlier been instituted as a means of motivating the subject. In this case, the reinforcing event is the successful termination of the electric shock (which is, as you have seen, an automatic result of the occurrence of R_L—the usual case in operant learning).

There is a superficial resemblance to Pavlovian conditioning in some aspects of escape learning, since R_L could be said to be a UCR to S_{nox}. While this is true, the R_L in escape learning is but one of a number of different UCR's that may originally be elicited by S_{nox}—several other R's were, in fact, described above in connection with the first occurrence of the shock. In Pavlovian conditioning such a diversity of UCR's is rarely possible. Furthermore, in Pavlovian conditioning it may or may not be the case that the occurrence of R_L terminates the UCS—certainly this is not exactly what happens in conditioned salivation, for instance. In escape learning, R_L *always* should terminate S_{nox}, if escape learning is actually to develop.

Another difference between Pavlovian conditioning and escape learning is that in escape learning there is no CS in the Pavlovian sense; S_{nox} is not only the UCS for a variety of R's, but when escape learning has taken place, the onset of S_{nox} has become the CS. In no conventional type of Pavlovian conditioning does the UCS become the CS.

A pretty subtle differentiation is being drawn between operant and Pavlovian procedures in the case of escape learning. All attempts to classify natural events, however, must involve some fairly arbitrary distinctions. In the case of escape learning, present evidence and current viewpoints in learning do not require that all cases of Pavlovian conditioning and operant learning be mutually exclusive. This is because the differences in these two situations are primarily methodological. Experimentally, they are believed by most psychologists to reveal different aspects of a common sequence of events (e.g., S-R-X, as we have chosen to describe it). We place escape learning in the operant group because (1) it is possible to specify the R-X relationship and (2) there is no CS of the usual sort.

Avoidance Learning

There is another large group of learning situations that fits the *One R/Motivation Relevant/X Pertinent* type. This is the group generally classified as instances of *avoidance learning*. In avoidance learning, the subject, instead of making an R that terminates S_{nox}, makes an R that *prevents the occurrence* of S_{nox}. In simple avoidance learning cases, the avoidance R may be exactly the same as the escape R, differing only in that it occurs *before* S_{nox} instead of afterwards. Not only is this kind of situation presumably a frequent occurrence in everyday life, but it is also a very common experimental method of studying some of the more complex relationships that sometimes operate in even relatively simple (i.e., one-response) learning situations.

Avoidance learning is only possible if there is some way for the subject to "know" that S_{nox} is about to occur; in other words, there must be a warning signal. If, in the situation shown in Figure 7 and discussed in connection with escape learning, we had added some stimulus (such as buzzing sound) that always came on just before S_{nox} began, then eventually the subject would be observed to jump over the hurdle as soon as the buzzer began to sound. All simple avoidance learning by relatively unsophisticated organisms evolves from escape learning situations. Initially, that is, the subject learns an R that will terminate noxious stimulation. If some additional S is invariably paired with S_{nox}, this S will eventually be sufficient for the arousal of the former escape R, or an R very similar to it. Psychologists who have experimented with aversive stimuli have often noted the fact that merely introducing the subject to the situation in which S_{nox}'s occur may become a sufficient warning signal. After a while, for example, a rat will struggle when you try to put him back in an apparatus where he has previously been shocked.

In terms of the learning model, escape and avoidance learning differ in the S and the X components. In escape learning, S is always the onset of S_{nox} and X is the termination of S_{nox}; in avoidance learning, S can be any kind of stimulus that has been frequently associated with the subsequent onset of S_{nox}, and X *appears to be* the absence of S_{nox} (or the failure of S_{nox} to occur). While this is a fair description of the X in avoidance learning, in terms of observables over a period of time, it presents problems for an understanding of the reinforcing agent in this kind of learning situation.

The only organism that can be aware of the fact that something has *not* happened is man. Man can talk. He can not only talk, he can abstract. Spoken words, printed words, even "thoughts," no matter how poorly these communication media are understood by psychologists, are at least physical events; they are changes or variations in stimulation. This enables us to transcend the confines of immediate events, and the most unique consequence of this ability is that events that have never taken place *can*—by virtue of being talked about—affect behavior in essentially the same way as do events that "really do" happen.

Thus, it is not surprising to find that human beings are capable of avoidance learning, for humans are able to conceptualize the fact of S_{nox} *not* occurring. But rats can be trained to make avoidance R's too. Only the most blatant anthropomorphism (which is the device of describing animal behavior in terms of human characteristics—e.g., labeling the grasshopper "lazy") could allow us to think of the rat as being able to "realize" that something has not happened. To put this still another way, consider again the apparatus of Figure 7, as a case wherein the avoidance R is to leave the area in which the shock is about to be turned on. Objectively, this amounts to jumping from one cold grid to another (now cold) grid. Except for geographical location, what has changed? And if nothing has, why jump?

Can we assume that the rat is capable of telling himself that the grid from which he has just departed was about to become the conductor of an electrical charge? No, we hesitate to attribute such a skill to the rat, for there are many other learning situations in which a similar ability would also be useful for the rat, but it fails to assert itself.

Need we, then, assume that it is actually possible for no change in the environment to reinforce behavior? No, scientists shy away from this alternative, too. The failure of something to happen is not a useful concept in science. Science depends upon observation and we cannot observe nothing.

So, in avoidance learning, we are confronted with the puzzle that non-verbal organisms can be influenced by developments that apparently can only be regarded as actual events by organisms capable of both speech and abstraction. Obviously, we err in some way. Either nonverbal organisms *can* be influenced by the failure of something to happen, or it is possible for a null event to be indicated by other than verbal means. Conceivably, such an Aristotelian (dichotomous) analysis of the logical possibilities is itself the source of error, but as yet scientific thinking remains committed to such reasoning. Of the alternatives, the one most compatible with conventional scientific thought is that in avoidance learning there is a positive event, an actual change in the environment that substitutes for (or represents) the failure of S_{nox} to occur. The most generally accepted account of avoidance learning is that which has been propounded by psychologists such as O. H. Mowrer (196) and N. E. Miller (189), both of whom were influenced in their thinking by Clark L. Hull (124).

Fear Conditioning

The basic axiom in the Mowrer or Miller account of avoidance learning is that the pairing of S_n with S_{nox} transforms S_n into a "fear-producing" stimulus. S_n, that is, becomes more than a cue for the observable avoidance R; it becomes a noxious stimulus in its own right. Its presence alone becomes sufficient to make the subject afraid. Avoidance learning, by this view, is seen to be a special case of escape learning wherein the subject seeks to escape from the formerly neutral stimulus (which has acquired noxious properties via its association with the original S_{nox}).

Such a conceptualization places the phenomenon in the realm of behavior that is related to what *does* happen on any given trial (termination of the warning signal), rather than to what *does not*. If a theory were all that is necessary to achieve a reunion of facts and scientific prejudices, however, then we would be able to spin a better yarn about the degree of our understanding of learning and behavior than we are able to do. Unfortunately, the rules for "making science" are more demanding than this. Axioms or assumptions themselves need not be (technically, they cannot be) amenable to direct, empirical test, but they should generate deductions (usually called *theorems*) that can be verified empirically. The Mowrer-Miller fear-conditioning concept fares rather well when evaluated by that standard. If avoidance conditioning is hypothesized to be escape learning wherein the S_{nox} is the former S_n, then there are at least three testable deductions that could be made:

(1) According to the fear-conditioning view, it should be possible, after sufficient pairings of S_n, to teach subjects to escape from the former S_n even if they had no specific escape training in relation to the original S_{nox}.

Kalish (136) has reported such a finding. First, the subjects (rats are nearly always used in such work) are confined in a small area, the floor of which is a shock grid. The apparatus is such that, aside from the momentary relief afforded by jumping off the floor, no R is systematically associated with shock termination; on the other hand, some S_n invariably comes on just before shock onset. So S_n *is* paired with S_{nox}, but not with any effective escape R.

Then the rats are taught to jump a hurdle in order to terminate the combination of a buzzing sound and a light—the previous S_n

that had been paired with shock in the earlier training situation (which was only a slightly different environment from that used for the test trials). In other words, Kalish's method demonstrated the development of an escape R to an acquired S_{nox} in spite of the fact that the subjects had had no escape training in connection with S_{nox} itself.

(2) If the pairing of S_n with S_{nox} permits the development of S_n into a noxious, or fear-producing, stimulus, even when no overt R is systematically reinforced in the presence of the S_n-S_{nox} compound, then this should be demonstrable outside of *any* escape learning situation.

This hypothesis has been confirmed by Amsel and Cole (6) and others. The first part of such a demonstration is just the same sort of pairing of S_n and S_{nox} as employed by Kalish (above). For S_n, Amsel and Cole used a flickering light.

Following this phase of the study, the subjects were deprived of water for a number of hours, then placed in a box containing a graduated waterbottle. Tests had been made to determine how much any given rat would drink in a half-hour when as thirsty as in the test period. During the test drinking period, the flickering light was presented intermittently. Amsel and Cole reported that this greatly reduced the drinking behavior. They also had some control rats with the same thirst and drinking experience, but no pairings of the flickering light and shock. When the light was presented during the test drinking period, control rats also showed some decrement in amount of water consumed, but not nearly so much of a drop as noted in the experimental animals.

Here, no R was associated with S_n during the initial phase of the experiment, nor was the effectiveness of S_n as a conditioned fear stimulus tested in any sort of escape or avoidance situation. Even in a fundamentally "pleasant" situation (where the animal's thirst was being quenched), the acquired S_{nox} was able to arouse behavior that was incompatible with drinking water.

Notice that it is a reasonable, though unimportant assumption that the acquired S_{nox} set off fear reactions in the rats. To call this pairing of S_n and S_{nox} a means of conditioning fear is simply a convenient way of summarizing the procedure. Whether the rat "really does" become afraid of S_n is irrelevant; as Amsel and Cole have shown, it makes a difference to have a flashing light repeatedly paired with the onset of electric shock. One of the ways in which it makes the difference is that the subsequent presentation of the flashing light in another situation (in which the subject's normal behavior is fairly predictable) will disrupt the subject's ordinary activity in this situation.

(3) Finally, it would be expected that even if S_n were paired with S_{nox} under circumstances that permitted the subject to learn to escape the noxious stimulus, it still should be possible, later on, to associate *another* escape response with the former S_n alone.

This last "theorem" is supported by one of Miller's own experiments (189), using an apparatus similar to that shown in Figure 7 (page 86). In Miller's study the walls of the two compartments were black and white, respectively, and the partition contained a doorway. Instead of jumping over the partition, a rat could run through it.

Miller always shocked his rats in the white-walled compartment; the door separating the two compartments was always open, and entry into the black-walled area stopped the shock. Thus, the rats originally learned how to escape the shock in the white "room." Since Miller always allowed a little time to elapse between the placing of a rat in the white chamber and the onset of shock, it was possible for the rat to *avoid* shock by running through the door as soon as he was put into the white section.

When a rat reached this level of accomplishment, Miller changed the rules. The door separating the compartments was now closed, *but* a lever was placed in the wall next to the door. Whenever the lever was depressed the door opened, permitting access into the black room. During this phase of the experiment, shock was no longer given in the white chamber, no matter how long an animal tarried in it.

Most rats can learn to press the lever under the conditions just described. Lever-pressing was never associated with escape from electric shock, but that R *was* learned by trial-and-error when its only consequence was the opportunity to leave the white box. This strongly argues that the white compartment itself had become a fear-producing situation.

In summary, then, the Mowrer-Miller view of avoidance learning is that it consists of two discrete stages:

(1) Some neutral stimulus is repeatedly paired with a noxious stimulus, with the result that S_n itself acquires noxious characteristics.

(2) The subject learns a response that leads to the termination of the acquired S_{nox}; such responses need not be related to escape R's already associated with the original S_{nox}, although indeed they frequently are.

Is Avoidance Learning a Special Case of Pavlovian Conditioning?

When one asks if avoidance learning is essentially a form of Pavlovian conditioning, two questions are really being raised. One refers to the superficial resemblance of many features of these two learning situations; to this facet of the question the same answers can be given as were given in the case of escape learning. As the experiments by Amsel and Cole, Kalish, and Miller each showed, avoidance learning has some decidedly non-Pavlovian characteristics in respect to the exact procedures used in the two cases.

Unlike escape learning, however, we cannot dismiss the relevance of Pavlovian procedures so easily in attempting to understand the *etiology* of avoidance R's. Many psychologists, indeed, have strong suspicions that Pavlovian conditioning is *part* of the procedure from which avoidance R's develop. Specifically, the first stage in avoidance learning—the pairing of S_n and S_{nox}—is widely regarded as being a crude version of Pavlovian training methods. Few of the observations that are considered crucial in Pavlovian research, however, are made during avoidance learning studies. As a result, we do not really know what the possible role of various UCR's might have been in Kalish's preliminary training, for example. Miller never reported the UCR's produced by shock in his apparatus, and so on. An instance of the difference in perspective that can occur when UCR's *are* directly studied in an avoidance situation is Kimble's work (149) described in the Supplementary Notes to this chapter (p. 117).

If we permit ourselves to ignore such frailties in the research on avoidance learning, then this phenomenon seems to be adequately accounted for by some form of the Mowrer-Miller fear-conditioning hypothesis. Whether one regards the first stage in the avoidance learning development as an example of Pavlovian learning is, in view of the lack of data, a matter of opinion rather than fact. It is a matter of fact, though, that most contemporary learning psychologists typically apply Pavlovian terminology to the avoidance learning situation; the acquired-fear stimulus is called the CS and the S_{nox} is labeled the UCS.

Avoidance Learning in Adult Humans

In the preceding chapter I mentioned that we would encounter several phenomena analogous to the procedure that Pavlov called "higher-order conditioning." One example of this can be seen in the behavior of adult humans, who are, by and large, sophisticated verbal subjects. With such subjects it is frequently sufficient to instruct them, prior to a learning task, that some stimulus condition is "wrong," or somehow "undesirable." Brody (34), for example, gave subjects the task of keeping a pointer on a black spot that moved irregularly over an illuminated screen; sometimes the light on the screen went off, and when this happened it was impossible to follow the spot, thus lowering the subject's score. The subjects learned that by adjusting a knob on the apparatus they could get the light back on (escape learning). Then a tone began to sound for 1.8 seconds before the light on the screen went out; if the subjects made the knob adjustment within the 1.8-second period they could prevent the light's going out. Brody found that the knob-adjustment—R—came to be associated with the tone in essentially the manner that was predicted from the knowledge of the course of development of avoidance R's in animals.

After this excursion into the ramifications of a single class of operant learning situations, let us return to some other general types of operant learning.

5. One R/Motivation Relevant/X Not Pertinent, "Acquired"

This instance of operant learning is one of the more typical kinds of operant learning situations that confront human beings. Except for the fact that humans are usually called upon to learn more than a single R, the experimental and anecdotal examples of this class of operant learning are legion. If we dissect any rote or serial learning problem into its components, however, we may justifiably (albeit arbitrarily) speak of the One-R case in many human learning situations. It doesn't matter that few human learning situations actually involve only a single R_L. As we have seen, many of the distinctions between cases 1 and 3 of Dimension R are highly arbitrary. The present analysis of operant learning, as with our abstract learning model, is presented so as to describe the fundamental variables underlying operant learning, *not* to describe our perception of the real world.

Some features of an experiment by Hubbard (122) demonstrate the case of *One R/Motivation Relevant/X Not Pertinent, "Acquired."* His subjects (college students) sat in front of a table and blackboard; on the table were some telegraph keys, on the blackboard were two lights and a tiny window that exposed a revolving series of one-digit numbers. Hubbard gave his subjects the following instructions:

This is a learning problem. At regular intervals this green light will come on, and then this shutter will open, exposing a number. When you see the number, press one of the keys. If you press the right one this red light will flash. If you press the wrong one, nothing will happen. You won't have to press very hard. Use only your first finger, and when the shutter is closed, keep your finger off the keys. Since I can't answer questions, let's go through the instructions again. (122, p. 236)

The instructions were read again, without the last sentence. After the experimenter had ascertained that a subject was comfortably positioned before the apparatus, he said ". . . I'll be listening for some things, so I won't be able to talk with you, and please don't talk to me." (122, p. 236) Then the experimenter put on a set of headphones in order to discourage the subject from talking to him;

this is a conventional control in human learning experiments—the reduction of extraneous conversation to a minimum is a way of reducing a major source of individual differences between subjects. As the experimenter himself sat down, his final statement was, "Remember, the red light tells you when you're right. Ready? Here we go."

Under these conditions, fifty-four out of no more than fifty-seven college students were able to learn to associate the correct key-responses with the various numbers displayed in the small window. The exact meaning of "were able to learn" is that none of the fifty-four successful subjects required more than sixty trials altogether to learn the possible S-R connections, so that they could make correct R's—no matter what the S—on nine consecutive trials.

In terms of our classificatory scheme, the reinforcer here was not pertinent, because the subjects were not literally motivated to work for red light occurrences, per se. Red light occurrences did reinforce the R_L's, because the subjects learned (from the experimenter's instructions) that if they "did the right things" (the relevant motivation) this light would flash on. Motivation is relevant here because it is hard to imagine that many people would automatically try to match switches and numbers; the verbal statements of the experimenter that the subject should "do the right things" is clearly important, and clearly part of the learning situation. The fact that the subjects' responsiveness to such strictures is due to a long past history of learning does not alter the other fact that the subjects do go through the kinds of motions that are conducive to learning in the particular experimental situation because Hubbard asked them to do so. Thus, motivation is inextricably related to the learning situation as such.

6. One R/Motivation Relevant/X Not Pertinent, "Unlearned"

Experimental examples of this final (in terms of reinforcement and motivation variables) operant class are very rare, chiefly because learning psychologists, until recent times, were distracted by theoretical problems that drew attention away from learning situations in which reinforcement was not some sort of reward. For all of Hull's positive contributions to the understanding of behavior (or to the methods for achieving such understanding) he and his advocates did psychology the disservice of severely restricting interest in non-reward reinforcers. For that reason experimental examples of non-pertinent reinforcers are hard to find. I have been able to find only one fairly adequate experimental illustration of the present category, and I completely failed at finding the parallel examples for the cases called multiple R's of the same kind, and multiple, different R's. This is why I spoke of only sixteen operant learning types, instead of eighteen (which is the number of possible combinations).

The treatment given to the previously described group in Hubbard's experiment (above) during a second phase of his experiment provides us with one of the few examples of this class that is to be found in the experimental literature. After a subject in this group had made thirty consecutive responses (with the red light as the cue for a correct response), the conditions were changed. The green (signal) light and the numbers continued to appear as before, but the red light no longer came on when a correct R was made. Instead, a tone sounded after every correct R; the definition of a correct R remained the same as during initial training, too. This tone had not been mentioned to, nor experienced by, any subject in this group prior to the time of this shift in the reinforcement conditions. Thus, it was certainly not pertinent to a subject's motivation in this situation. Nor did it have any acquired reinforcing value, since the instructions had not indicated that it was a signal for correct, as the red light was. But was it a reinforcer?

At first, after the tone had replaced the light, the average number of correct key depressions dropped far below the original level of performance, although the tone followed just the same S-R sequences as had formerly been reinforced by the red light. After twenty trials with only tone reinforcement, however, about eighteen out of twenty-seven subjects were again making the reinforced R. Over a series of forty such trials, these subjects made an average of 26.04 correct responses, compared to only an average of 15.00

for subjects originally trained with both tone and light for correct R's and then—during the same forty trials—given *neither* stimulus after any R. This difference was statistically reliable, when evaluated by a statistical test that ignores individual variability from trial to trial.

This experiment is not literally an example of learning, at least not of original acquisition of R_L. As already mentioned, *Motivation Relevant/X Not Pertinent, "Unlearned"* cases of operant learning have received less than their share of scrutiny so far. Hubbard's study, however, was not far off the point; a general principle illustrated by this experiment is that learning (more accurately, *habit maintenance* in this case) occurs even when reinforcement has little or no relationship to motivation. Nevertheless, the use of a pertinent X is usually more effective for practical purposes.

OPERANT ANALOGS OF VARIABLES AND PHENOMENA OBSERVED IN PAVLOVIAN CONDITIONING

The chief utilitarian argument for the study of Pavlovian conditioning is that it provides a convenient means for the precise study of certain behavioral phenomena that also occur in more natural kinds of learning situations. Let us now briefly examine the evidence for this assertion by considering some operant learning demonstrations of phenomena first discovered and named by Pavlov and his students.

Stimulus Generalization

A simple, effective demonstration of stimulus generalization in an operant situation has been offered by Grice and Saltz (95). They trained rats to approach either a white disk 20 sq. cm. in area, or one 79 sq. cm. in area, nose under a flap in the center of the disk, and get a food pellet from a cup behind the disk. After the animals had learned to make this response efficiently, the two groups were subdivided into several smaller groups each of which was given a series of nonreinforced trials with a different-sized disk in place in front of the food cup. The animals trained initially with the 79 sq.

cm. disk were given extinction with disks of either 79, 63, 50, 32, or 20 sq. cm. in area; those who originally learned to respond to the 20 sq. cm. disk were tested with disks of either 20, 32, 50, or 79 sq. cm. in area. In this experiment, the amount of generalization is evaluated by the relative resistances to extinction of the subjects in the various test groups; the results obtained by Grice and Saltz

FIGURE 8

An Example of Stimulus Generalization in an Operant Situation

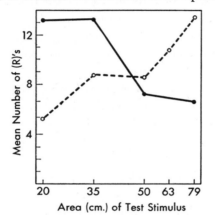

Area (cm.) of Test Stimulus

From Grice and Saltz (95), in the *Journal of Experimental Psychology*, vol. 40, p. 705. Used by permission of the American Psychological Association.

The curve consisting of four filled circles shows the resistances to extinction of groups of rats first trained to approach a disk of 20 sq. cm. in area, then shows one of the circles indicated on the base line but not reinforced for occurrences of R_L. The graph with five open circles shows the same data for groups of animals first trained on the disk of 79 sq. cm. The use of resistance to extinction is the most common means of quantifying stimulus generalization in operant learning situations.

are shown in Figure 8. The results are exactly what one would expect from our knowledge of stimulus generalization: as the test S is made more and more unlike (i.e., either larger or smaller than S_L—the stimulus in the presence of which R_L was reinforced during training), it becomes more and more easy to "eliminate" R_L by no longer reinforcing its occurrence.

Stimulus generalization, then, is the name given to the fact that if an organism learns to make a given response in one specific situation, this also decreases the variability of his behavior in other, similar situations. In nature, it is often true that similar situations can be adjusted to by similar behavior, so this phenomenon has obvious survival value. If a bear, more or less by accident, once discovers honey in a tree that has bees buzzing around it, then it probably will be fruitful for him in the future to investigate other trees that also have bees flying around them, even though the tree, the actual sound of the bees, the surroundings, and so forth, may vary quite a bit from one instance to another. Generalization prevents the discrepancies from dissuading the bear's investigation. Like most surivival mechanisms, of course, it is not flawless—generalization may cause an organism to persist in a maladaptive response as well as in an adaptive one.

When we seek to teach an organism by operant techniques it is often convenient to capitalize on this generalization phenomenon. For example, much of the information about certain features of operant learning situations comes from experiments using pigeons in which the basic S-R relationship involved is always pecking at a disk (this is directly analogous to the bar-pressing procedure, adapted to one of the neater characteristics of the pigeon). In many of these experiments it is not particularly useful to have to go through the process of establishing a strong pecking response in the experimental apparatus (although the means for doing this are, of course, quite well understood). A means of speeding this process up is to place in the pigeon's home cage a panel that consists of many paper disks pasted over holes in a board. The disks are the same size as the disk in the experimental apparatus. Behind each paper disk is some grain which the pigeon gets whenever he pecks at one of them, causing it to tear. At first the paper covering is very thin, so that almost any accidental contact by the beak will break it, revealing the grain. On successive days the paper is made stronger and stronger—thus making the disks more and more like the plastic disk that the pigeon will have to peck in the apparatus (food is presented in a trough just below the disk in the apparatus). Thus, via stimulus generalization a pigeon treated in this manner in his home cage will come to the apparatus with a strong tendency to peck at circular forms on walls; so, fairly complicated S-R-X conditions can be started much more quickly with such subjects than with pigeons who must first be repeatedly reinforced for the elementary pecking response (the simple habit upon which all more complex problems are to be based). Analogous devices are often used to speed up learning in children and even adults (such as the use of examples that refer to already familiar events).

The Relative Generalization of Approach and Avoidance Habits

Habits that are established by the use of rewards as reinforcers are sometimes spoken of as "approach" habits, after the terminology inaugurated by Kurt Lewin (168) as a means of analyzing conflict situations. Avoidance habits have already been discussed in this chapter (p. 89). Naturally, we would expect stimulus generalization to apply to both kinds of habits, and so it does. But there is one very remarkable and very important difference in the operation of this phenomenon in the two cases: *Approach habits generalize over a greater range of stimuli than do avoidance habits.*

Among the clearer laboratory demonstrations of this is one reported by Miller and Kraeling (190): [1]

First an approach habit was established by training hungry rats to run down a wide white alley to secure food. The food was concealed by a hinged shield which could easily be pushed out of the way. Then an avoidance habit, inhibiting the approach, was established by putting increasingly strong shocks on the food shield until the animals failed to touch it. Finally, the generalization of this approach-avoidance conflict was tested by comparing the response in the original stimulus situation with that in two new situations differing by varying amounts from the original one. This was accomplished by dividing the [subjects] into three groups which were tested respectively (a) in the wide white alley (*same*), (b) in a narrower gray alley (*intermediate*), and (c) in a very narrow black alley (*different*).

As control for any effects of the alleys per se, half of the [rats] received their original training in the narrow black alley so that it was the *same* and the wide white alley was *different*. . . . Control [subjects]

[1] From the *Journal of Experimental Psychology*, vol. 43, p. 218. Used by permission of the American Psychological Association.

were kept on the same feeding cycle as the experimental ones, but instead of being trained to approach and avoid in the alley, they received pellets of food in restraining cages. Then they were tested in the same way as the experimental [animals]. (190, p. 218)

The results were reported in terms of the percentage of subjects in each group who reached the goal area within 60 seconds on at least one of the four test trials. These percentages were as follows:

> Tested in *same* alley: 23 per cent
> Tested in *intermediate* alley: 37 per cent
> Tested in *different* alley: 70 per cent
> All controls combined: 15 per cent

The conclusion that approach habits generalize more than avoidance habits is based on the following reasoning. For 77 per cent of the subjects tested in the same alley where they had been trained, the avoidance response was clearly the stronger tendency. If generalization occurs equally for approach and approach responses, we would expect approximately the same proportion of subjects (about 3:1) to show a predominant avoidance tendency. This is certainly not what occurred; 70 per cent of the subjects made approach responses during test trials on a quite different apparatus. Nor is this because this situation is so different that the animals are just responding randomly; if this were true, the control subjects should have shown a lot of approach responses, too, since they *are* responding randomly, having had no training. Thus we conclude that the generalization of an approach response extends over a wider range of stimuli than does that of an avoidance response originally associated with the same S_L.

The discovery of this important principle has enabled psychologists to make quite precise analyses of conflict situations. It has already been noted that a similar difference appears to hold for the generalization of the effects of repeated nonreinforcement compared to the effects of repeated reinforcement; some evidence for this latter statement comes from the Hovland experiments discussed in Chapter 2 (pp. 53 and 59). The only factor limiting the precision of the predictions that can be made from these principles is that, so far, we have not discovered a universal rule or set of rules for describing in absolute terms the amount of generalization to be expected following a given training situation. The search for these continues. At present all that has clearly been established for stimulus generalization is that the strength of R_L in the presence of a stimulus that is similar to, but not identical with S_L,[2] is mainly influenced by two variables: (1) the similarity of the stimuli concerned, and (2) the strength of the original habit (with the exception noted for extinction and avoidance). In an extension of Grice and Saltz's design, Margolius (178) verified that greater similarity of S_L and S_L' produced greater generalization (which is the fundamental point that has been made all along), and also that the greater the strength of habit, the more generalization; these influences are apparently independent. The student should be warned, however, that even these assertions meet with exceptions when we turn to more complex situations where original training does not consist simply of the repeated reinforcement of one S-R relationship.

Stimulus Intensity and Operant Learning

Another source of distortion can be introduced in generalization effects by varying S_L in the intensity dimension. As we noted in Chapter 2 (p. 55), increasing CS intensity (which, of course, changes the CS from that used to establish the habit) does not necessarily weaken the CR that occurs. Presumably this is because we have the effect of intense stimulation confounding the effect of changing the CS.

The traditional view of the effect of stimulus intensity was stated in terms of the *absolute intensity* of the stimulus. Recent work (31, 134) has provided evidence that it is the *relative intensity* of S_L as compared to the background in which it occurs that is the critical factor. Since the older studies of stimulus intensity typically used

---

[2] To indicate symbolically that some stimulus is similar to a given stimulus, a prime will be added to the symbolic notation already in use to denote the latter. In particular, S_L' will be used frequently to represent stimulus that is similar to some other stimulus that has been used in a learning situation (i.e., that was an S_L).

background stimuli of rather low intensity (darkened, or very quiet rooms), the results obtained appeared to support the absolute interpretation; actually, under such conditions the absolute and relative intensity effects would parallel each other (raising the absolute intensity would increase the contrast). Johnsgard (134), in a very definitive experiment, has shown the standard intensity effect (i.e., increased strength of R_L) when a light of very low absolute intensity, but shown against a background of medium brightness, was used *either* as S_L or as S_L' (the generalized stimulus).

Although the role of stimulus intensity is probably not great in controlling most behavior, the discovery of the way in which this phenomenon is produced does have some implications of potential importance. Particularly, it suggests an area of common ground for psychologists of diverse interests and persuasions; much more evidence will be presented in Chapter 6 that makes it increasingly difficult for "perceptual" psychologists and "learning" psychologists to continue working quite independently of each other, as they have tended to do in the past. In short, the study of the effect of stimulus intensity on learned behavior is one example of a more general rule: as research on specific, rather isolated segments of behavior gets closer and closer to an understanding of the specific topic, the relationship of this behavior to other areas of investigation usually becomes more and more obvious. This is true even when no effort is being directed specifically toward unification.

Extinction Phenomena in Operant Learning

The extinction procedure in operant learning has already been described in this chapter in connection with the Hubbard (122) and Grice and Saltz (95) experiments. It consists simply of withholding the reinforcer when the appropriate R occurs. Since half of Chapter 8 is to be devoted to an examination of the many facets of operant extinction results, we need not go into much detail for the present.

It suffices to say that withholding X in operant situations has essentially the same effect as does withholding UCS in Pavlovian ones: the previously stable S-R relationship becomes less predictable. In Pavlovian situations, it may be literally correct to say that the CR ceases to occur in the presence of the CS as a result of extinction. This is because, prior to conditioning, the probability of the CR being made in the presence of the CS may have been zero. In many operant situations, as we have seen, there may be some relationship of S_L to R_L albeit an erratic one, prior to any reinforcement of the sequence; operant learning, indeed, often depends upon this fact, especially in natural situations. Therefore, the final outcome of operant extinction may not be the complete disappearance of R_L.

Antonitis (9), for example, studied the effect of consistent reinforcement followed by consistent nonreinforcement (symbolized NoX in this text) on the performance of a very simple operant response. He had rats stick their heads through a hole to obtain food pellets. This is a very pure case of simple operant learning because this particular R does occur in rats with a detectable frequency without any specific reinforcement. Antonitis reported that initially this S-R sequence was very variable; that, in accordance with my description of the fundamental consequence of learning, reinforcement reduced the variability in the performance of this sequence, and that extinction (consistent NoX) caused the variability to increase again. The response was never eliminated, however.

A simple way of summarizing the effect of extinction following the relatively consistent reinforcement of a simple habit (either operant or Pavlovian), then, would be to say that extinction will ultimately reinstate the pretraining relationship between the S and the R concerned.

Spontaneous Recovery

Just as the effect of extinction seems to be highly similar in Pavlovian and operant learning situations, so also does the additional phenomenon of spontaneous recovery have quite common characteristics in the two cases. Spontaneous recovery is the term given to the fact that if an organism is removed from the situation for a while following extinction and then returned and again presented with S_L, his performance will initially be better than would be predicted from his performance at the end of the preceding extinction period.

Not only does spontaneous recovery occur in operant situations just as it does in Pavlovian ones, but the variables that affect the degree of recovery seem to be identical in the two situations. Graham and Gagné (90) showed that the amount of recovery of an operant habit is directly related to the length of the period since the termination of extinction; this is exactly the relationship to be observed in Pavlovian studies (e.g., 70). Gagné (82) subsequently presented evidence that recovery occurs very quickly during the early stages of a rest period, but further increases in the length of the rest period produce smaller and smaller gains. This is similar to the phenomenon noted for the spacing of conditioning trials (p. 44), and we shall find as we go through this text that changes in behavior that are related to the passage of time, per se, almost always show this same effect: the changes occur at a negatively accelerated rate as more and more time goes by.

Other factors that influence the amount of spontaneous recovery are the spacing of reinforced occurrences of R_L (i.e., training trials), the spacing of nonreinforced occurrences of R_L (i.e., extinction trials), and the combination of these two factors. These relationships become very complex, however, and are best deferred until Chapter 8 for a more thorough discussion. The number of reinforced occurrences of R_L, prior to extinction, also affects the degree of spontaneous recovery; more reinforcements are associated with greater recovery (115).

Although the discussion of the past few pages does not yet exhaust the similarities between Pavlovian and operant learning situations, it will suffice to show that they are, indeed, quite great. It can thus be seen why, despite the seeming artificiality of his laboratory situation, Pavlov's discoveries did so much to advance our understanding of the psychological event called learning. Since the primary interest of most students of learning is probably in the variables and effects more characteristic of natural learning situations, the major share of our attention in succeeding chapters will be devoted to the experimental situations that appear to have the most direct bearing on those phenomena.

SUMMARY

The major distinguishing feature of operant learning situations is that they most clearly indicate the relationship between the response and reinforcement conditions in learning. Unlike Pavlovian situations, the occurrence of R_L is not precisely controlled; instead, it occurs at random. Reinforcement of these initially random occurrences of R_L in the presence of certain S's leads to the stabilization of an S-R relationship. That, in a nutshell, is the basic operant learning procedure. The procedure for operant learning also deviates from Pavlov's in that the S involved in the habit may be much more vaguely defined (or, to put it another way, may have to be determined by more indirect methods) than in the typical Pavlovian case; it is not invariably true, however, that S is vaguely defined in operant cases. Finally, operant learning (which is also called "instrumental conditioning," or "trial-and-error learning") is believed by most psychologists to resemble much more closely the way in which learning typically proceeds in everyday life.

Since operant learning is the experimental situation most nearly resembling natural learning conditions, we should expect it to have a multitude of specific varieties. Indeed it does. There are four major ways in which such situations can differ independently: (1) the specificity of the S_L can vary, (2) the number and/or kind of R_L's actually involved can vary, (3) the conditions used to guarantee the initial occurrence of R_L can vary, and (4) the relationship of the reinforcing conditions to the conditions of type 3 can also vary. Six experimental examples of operant learning, primarily concerned with the different combinations of factors 3 and 4 that can be obtained, were discussed at length. Of particular interest in a culture, such as ours, that relies heavily upon punishment or the threat of punishment as a means of producing learning, is the subtype of operant learning called *escape learning;* a related subtype, *avoidance learning*, was shown to be a special case of escape learning in which actual physical punishment was replaced by the threat of punishment.

In the final sections of this chapter, we examined the ways in which variables and phenomena first discovered in Pavlovian situations have been found to operate, or manifest themselves, in operant situations. Although the fundamental techniques in these two situations may differ greatly, it was shown that they have many common characteristics as well. While Pavlovian conditioning no longer captures the interest of a great many American psychologists, it should be quite clear how the study of that type of learning situation truly blazed the trail in the development of many important laws of learning.

SUPPLEMENTARY NOTES

Free vs. Controlled Operant Learning Situations

The problem of defining a learning trial (see Notes, Chapter 2) is greater in some cases of operant learning for two reasons: (1) The already mentioned fact that S's presence is not always controlled or manipulated by the experimenter, and (2) in many operant learning situations the means for making R_L are continuously present, at least for a prolonged period of time. Cases where these two conditions prevail are called *free operant* situations; in such situations exactly when the subject will or will not respond is not related to the presence of the opportunity to respond (i.e., the appropriate *manipulandum*), since this is constant.

The Azrin-Lindsley experiment was an example of free operant learning. These are the situations in which it is typically the most difficult to specify the S to which R becomes associated. Free operant learning is also the case in which habit acquisition is measured by changes in *rate* of responding (see Chapter 1).

The alternative to the free operant case consists of those learning situations in which the *opportunities* for making R_L are somewhat more controlled; for lack of a better term, these will be called *con-*

trolled operant conditions. Experimental situations using mazes, or studying the retention of verbal material, and real-life learning such as the answers to specific questions, learning to drive a car and the like are examples of controlled operant learning. In controlled operant learning there are better hints as to what S might be than is sometimes true in free operant cases.

The term "controlled operant" in no way revises the general definition of operant learning. Controlled operant conditions are those in which the *opportunity* to make R_L is controlled; its *occurrence* is still not under direct control (before training, at least); this is still up to the subject.

The controlled operant method has been most used by psychologists interested in clarifying the similarities and differences between operant and Pavlovian situations in general; certainly, the controlled operant procedure is more like Pavlov's than is the free operant case. The basic differences between Pavlovian and operant situations remain the same in either comparison, but at the same time the above distinctions and comparisons should make it apparent that these differences are in some ways subtle ones.

The Relationship of the Single R and Varied R Cases

As pointed out earlier, it is always possible that these two cases of Dimension R may reduce to one, owing to the fact that the Single R case usually is an abstraction involving more than one R in sequence before X is actually obtained. It happens that Seward reported a good example of this, so I quote him directly:

. . . I am convinced that almost all of the animals in both the reward and removal groups learned something over and above bar pressing. The two groups differed primarily not in amount of learning but in what they learned. . . . The typical rewarded rat after the first trial or two promptly nosed the food pan and hole, returning to them again and again. More gradually the bar became an object of attention, but always as an integral part of food-seeking activity. The removed rats were more variable in their behavior. However, eight of the ten on whom observations were recorded came to anticipate removal. They approached the bar, pressed it with a forefoot, quickly swung around, sometimes looking up

toward the experimenter, and waited motionless a second or two. . . .
(236, p. 254)

In other words, it may depend upon the degree to which an experimenter pursues his analysis whether we can classify a particular
operant learning situation as an example of Single R or Varied
R's. For some purposes (primarily, the development of a general
behavior theory) a differentiation between the two cases may be
extremely important; for many practical purposes (cases in which
it is important to attain maximal control over another's behavior),
the realization of the arbitrary distinction being made here may be
helpful. Recall, however, that Azrin and Lindsley were able to
control what was undoubtedly a most complex bit of social behavior
by simply keeping their eyes on a small feature of the whole situation and reinforcing it.

Seward's Test of Guthrie's Theory Refined

This book treats the "stimulus-change" notion of reinforcement
as an empirical fact, rather than as a debatable proposition. While
numerous experiments have produced results compatible with this
concept, most of these data are also consistent with alternative ideas
about the fundamental nature of the X factor. Seward's experiment
(236) provides the nearest thing to a crucial test of the stimulus-
change hypothesis about the nature of reinforcement.

Even Seward's procedure did not entirely preclude alternative
interpretations, because he removed his subjects from the box by
hand; this physical contact *could* have been a reward for any of
several reasons. A simple variation of Seward's procedure, however,
has recently been employed in which the possibility of subtle reward conditions contaminating the REMOVAL group procedure
was even further reduced.

Lawson and Dawson (162) literally removed the S after a
REMOVAL subject made R_L; a Skinner-type, box was placed inside another, larger box, and when REMOVAL subjects pressed the
lever, the experimenter raised the inner box. There were some
other differences in the details of the two experiments, but these

did not appear to matter, because we got results that confirmed Seward's in every essential detail. In other words, the effectiveness of Seward's REMOVAL technique was not simply due to the effects of uncontrolled rewards. The assertion that a reinforcer is not necessarily a reward seems to have a definite empirical basis, even though the *amount* of evidence is still small.

The Azrin-Lindsley Demonstration and S-R Psychology

The example of operant learning with which this chapter opened was not selected at random. Nor was it chosen simply because it is a particularly clear instance of operant learning; it *is* that, but so are many other researches. The Azrin-Lindsley study (13) illustrated a further point that is often overlooked; contemporary experimental psychology is *not* restricted, owing to its use of "stimulus-response" terminology, to the study of muscle-twitches.

The behavior manifested by the children in this study had two important characteristics:

(*1*) *It was complex.* The simultaneous insertion of the styli involved social interaction, verbal behavior, and so on. The situation could reasonably be described as dynamic. None of the foregoing terms, which are very popular with many psychological interest-groups, contribute anything to our understanding of the Azrin-Lindsley situation. Despite the complexity of the response learned here, an understanding of the basic characteristics of *any* operant learning situation was sufficient to enable these two psychologists to establish the desired habit.

(*2*) *It was not defined in terms of muscle-movements.* This supports the most important point I am trying to make here: an analysis of organism-environment relationships in terms of stimuli and responses need not carry with it any excess implications about what the scope of psychology should or can be. The words "stimulus" and "response" are just that—words. If psychology is to become a natural science, we at least need some concept that refers to changes in environmental conditions, and we need some concept that refers to changes in organismic conditions; in Chapter 1 this was the meaning I sought to attribute to these terms. It may now be clearer what was intended in that introduction: operant learning in general shows us that a detailed, physical definition of S will not always be vital to an understanding of learning situations. Similarly, an S-R approach to the action of living organisms does not require that our descriptions of behavior be even remotely anatomical or physiological, except, perhaps, by implication.

By these statements I do not mean to assert that such descriptions (often called molecular analyses of behavior) are useless. To do *that* would be a direct refutation of the point here: A stimulus-response analysis of behavior does not necessarily imply any particular level of analysis, and it is not incompatible with the study of *any* psychological phenomena.

In short, to know that someone has become an S-R psychologist no longer has the prognostic value it once had. The *cult* of capital-B Behaviorism is dead. It has taken a long time, but we have begun to separate the useful from the negative and the dogmatic in the teachings of Watson and his direct descendants. Today, psychologists who bear the label "behaviorist" study social behavior, verbal behavior, all sorts of complex behavior. The trend is toward a *methodological behaviorism.* This kind of behaviorism has stringent rules about *how to study* psychological events, but it says nothing about *what to study.*

CS-UCS Intervals in Avoidance Learning

One apparent exception to the view that avoidance learning is related to Pavlovian conditioning in more than a superficial way is the difference in the optimum CS-UCS intervals in the two situations. We have seen that 0.45 seconds has been well established as the most effective interval in the standard Pavlovian situation. In avoidance learning studies, on the other hand, intervals of this brevity are rarely even used; furthermore, wide discrepancies are to be noted in the best CS-UCS reported by different investigators. Schwartz (235) and Kish (151), for example, conducted avoidance learning experiments that were concerned with the same problem, but the optimum intervals in the two cases were quite different. Schwartz found that for his task the most stable avoidance R developed when he CS preceded the shock by 6.00 seconds, while Kish found a 3.00 second interval to be the best.

Common sense should make it clear why an interval as short as half a second will rarely be effective in avoidance training. The avoidance situation requires, by definition, that the subject learn to make R_L between the time that the CS begins and the time when the UCS is scheduled to occur; if the R_L is made, the UCS does not occur. Obviously, there must be enough time between the onsets of the CS and the UCS for the subject to make R_L. In Pavlovian situations, the criterion of conditioning is simply that the CR will occur *when the CS is presented alone;* there is no requirement that the CR must occur before the UCS. As in the Fitzwater and Thrush experiment (p. 42), the occurrence of conditioning is tested by the occasional withholding of the UCS; the occurrence or nonoccurrence of the CR does not determine when the UCS is to be given. Since just the reverse of this latter condition is true in avoidance learning, the CS-UCS intervals must perforce be longer, to give the subject time to respond before the UCS occurs. Incidentally, it is just because the behavior of the subject determines whether the UCS goes on in avoidance learning that such situations are classed as an operant learning case, despite their many features in common with Pavlovian situations.

The apparent lack of any optimal CS-UCS interval that applies to a wide variety of avoidance situations probably is due to the same factor. Schwartz, for instance, accounted for the difference in his findings and those of Kish as follows:

. . . The discrepancy would appear to be ascribable to the nature of the respective responses required of S. Typical rat behavior in a wheel-turning situation, under massed acquisition, such as Kish employed, consists of "hanging on" the wheel and rarely moving away from it. Also, a high output of "spontaneous" responses characterizes such a procedure. In contrast, in the present shuttlebox, all S's invariably stayed at the extreme ends of the respective compartments and rarely made spontaneous crossings. It appears likely, therefore, that the present results can be accounted for on the assumption that the 3-sec. interval was simply too short for S to perceive the CS change and complete the response in time to avoid the shock. Thus, they were probably shocked while in the act of performing the response. If this occurred with any consistency, such punishment of the avoidance response would be expected to disrupt the avoidance pattern. The observation of abortive avoidance responses in the 3-sec. group lends credence to this hypothesis. On the other hand, the 6-sec. group had sufficient time in which to complete the entire process successfully before the shock came on . . . (235, p. 350)

It seems reasonable the optimum CS-UCS interval in avoidance situations will always be relative to the response required of the organism.

Another View of the Role of Pavlovian Principles in Avoidance Conditioning

When Mowrer and other spokesmen of the fear-conditioning theory considered the role of Pavlovian phenomena in the avoidance learning situation, they usually concluded that S_{nox} was a UCS for visceral responses such as changes in rate of heartbeats, of stomach- and intestinal-muscle contractions, and glandular secretions (e.g., adrenalin). According to this theory, modified forms of these UCR's become associated with S_n in the usual way.

Certainly there is plenty of evidence that smooth-muscle and glandular R's do occur in fear-producing situations. The methods of recording these R's, however, involve attaching instruments to the subject's body, thereby restricting his movements. As a result, psychologists have not yet simultaneously studied the progress of visceral conditioning and the acquisition of escape or avoidance R's. Future developments in experimental apparatus and/or ingenuity, of course, could make this possible; a step in this direction has been taken by Kanfer (138), who was able to record the development of a conditioned acceleration in heartbeats (to a tone paired with electric shock by the delayed conditioning method) while the subjects were engaged in operant activity (talking).

But most S_{nox}'s also produce skeletal UCR's; these we know how to observe. Do they provide any basis for predicting the course of avoidance-R acquisition?

There is much to be discovered yet, but Kimble (149) has shown that knowledge of certain UCS-UCR relationships can considerably enhance our ability to predict the behavior that evolves in one of the standard stituations used by psychologists to study avoidance phenomena. Kimble trained several groups of rats to

FIGURE 9

Average Latencies of R's Made to Avoid Different Intensities of Electric Shock

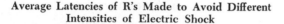

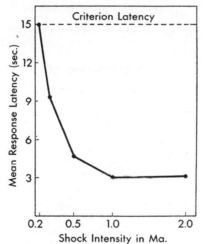

From Kimble (149), in the *Journal of Comparative and Physiological Psychology*, vol. 48, p. 283. Used by permission of the American Psychological Association.

turn a wheel (an R essentially equivalent to the lever-pressing R described earlier) to avoid being shocked. His independent variable was the intensity of S_{nox} used to establish this response, and the dependent variable measure was the average latency of R during the later stages of training. Kimble's results are reproduced in Figure 9.

Certainly these data are consistent with the Mowrer-Miller view of avoidance learning; the stronger the shock, the stronger, presumably, the fear. Increasing fear should lead to learning the avoidance R faster, and performing it more efficiently. This chain of reasoning would force us to predict also that the five groups of Kimble's experiment would differ in resistance to extinction; the greater the fear, the longer should rats persist in making the avoidance R, even though failure to do so would not be punished by re-presentation of S_{nox}. Kimble found no support of this latter hypothesis; the shock intensities during learning did not correlate

FIGURE 10

Relative Incidence of Two UCR's Evoked by Different Shock Intensities

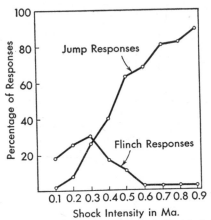

Shock Intensity in Ma.

From Kimble (149), in the *Journal of Comparative and Physiological Psychology*, vol. 48, p. 282. Used by permission of the American Psychological Association.

reliably with the subjects' resistances to extinction (i.e., their tendency to stop making the R_L).

The key to the simplest explanation of these results is given in Figure 10, which shows the relative occurrences of two kinds of UCR's that ten male albino rats made to different intensities of electric current—i.e., the UCS intensity. This graph tells us that a current of 0.4 milliamperes or less most frequently either did not cause the rats to respond in a discriminable way (the sums of the percentages on these abscissae do not equal 100), or elicited a "flinch" response; no matter what fear reactions might be occurring, if any, we would not expect a rat to learn quickly or efficiently to run toward a wheel and set it in motion (the R_L required in the study to which Figure 9 refers) when the occurrence of S_{nox} either does not alter the rat's behavior or, indeed, makes him immobile for a moment. With intensities of 0.5 ma. or greater, as Figure 10 shows, the predominant tendency of the subjects was to jump, or, more generally, to become more active; as in any operant situation, anything that makes a rat more active in a situation in which some kind of activity (wheel-turning, here) can consistently terminate or prevent S_{nox}, increases the chances that the rat will "discover" this activity. Although we might criticize the details of the procedure used to establish the measurements summarized in Figure 10, the predictions to be made on the basis of these data are confirmed in their essentials by the experimental results shown in Figure 9. Furthermore, these data explain why shock intensities did not correlate with resistance to extinction: the overt UCR's to all intensities above 0.5 ma. are essentially the same, and all groups had equal but no better opportunities to learn the appropriate R.

In short, Kimble's study reveals a principle that is being demonstrated more and more often these days: As long as our basic means of determining whether (or how much) learning has occurred reduce to behavioral descriptions, then just as long will our ability to predict the outcome of a given training procedure be directly related to the depth of our knowledge about the subject's behavior *before and during* the training period. While Kimble's work does not rule out the relationships that are propounded by the fear-conditioning account of avoidance behavior, his data do show at least one instance in which so intricate a process as avoidance learning could be better understood as a result of preliminary *behavioral* observations than via hypothetical explanatory mechanisms.

*

*

* # THE BASIC CHARACTERISTICS OF REINFORCERS

If it were necessary to decide which one of the variables studied by learning psychologists is the most important, the answer would surely be reinforcement. By knowing the effects of reinforcement we can best predict and control learned behavior, and only when we can do that can we seriously believe that we *understand* learned behavior. Most of the material yet to be covered (especially in Chapters 5–8) will show the amazingly precise and complex control over behavior that can be exercised by varying reinforcement conditions. In this chapter, let us pause to consider the general nature of the event called reinforcement.

REINFORCERS AS OBSERVABLE EVENTS

Curiously, the determination of the critical aspects of a reinforcer has been treated as a logical problem as often as it has been treated empirically. Arguments about the general nature of reinforcers have enlivened the field of learning for at least thirty years. But the light shed on the issue has not been commensurate with the heat generated by those involved in it.

One source of confusion in discussions of the nature of reinforcement has been a tendency to get this problem tangled up with another, far more basic (and far more difficult), question: Is reinforcement absolutely essential for learning? This latter problem is the sort of theoretical matter that is definitely beyond the scope of this text (except very briefly by way of describing, later on, the background for some studies that are interesting in their own right). It has repeatedly been proved that there is a class of events the relationship of which to some operant S-R sequence can be manipulated in such a way as to affect the stability of the S-R sequence quite precisely. Any such event we call a reinforcer. Whether reinforcement is absolutely essential for any and all learning to occur is quite another question. The present question is: Do the events that act as reinforcers have any other characteristics in common *except* that they can act as reinforcers? In other words, could we predict in advance of actually observing it in a learning situation whether some event would or would not be an effective reinforcer?

Learning is primarily a matter of definition, although our culture restricts the extent to which definitions of learning will vary. All such definitions must specify two things: (1) the nature of the behavioral changes that occur during (or as a result of) learning, and (2) a series of events that must occur (usually more than once) in order to effect these changes. Every series of events must have a distinguishable point of termination. "Distinguishable" implies "observable"; in experimental sciences, furthermore, anything that is observable can, at least potentially, be manipulated and controlled. The terminal event in the sequence that is associated with learning is called a reinforcer by most psychologists.

Thus, the reinforcing (concluding) event in a learning sequence must at least be observable. Insofar as it can also be manipulated, a reinforcer must be a part of the learning organism's environment, or be perfectly correlated with some feature of the environment; by definition, the only way that we can affect an organism is via its environment.

Identifying a Reinforcing Event

Following the reasoning outlined above, the empirical procedure seems clear for determining whether an event is or is not a reinforcer. If an S-R sequence becomes stronger when it is followed by a specific, manipulable event than when it is not, this event can be considered to be a reinforcer. As an example of this, I wish to quote directly from the description of some observations that led to the discovery of a reinforcing event that had never before been suspected of being a reinforcer at the time, not so long ago, when the following experiment was performed by Dr. J. F. Olds: [1]

. . . In the Fall of 1953, we were looking for more information about the reticular activating system. We used electrodes permanently implanted in the brain of a healthy, behaving rat. . . . Quite by accident [in one animal], an electrode was implanted in the region of the anterior commissure.

The result was quite amazing. When the animal was stimulated at a specific place in an open field, he sometimes moved away but he returned and sniffed around that area. More stimulations at that place caused him to spend more of his time there.

Later we found that this same animal could be "pulled" to any spot in the maze by giving a small electrical stimulus *after* each response in the right direction. This was akin to playing the "hot and cold" game with a child. Each correct response brought electrical pulses which seemed to indicate to the animal that it was on the right track. (201, pp. 83–84, italics in original)

Thus, Olds started on his way toward identifying a center of the midbrain, the stimulation of which by a very mild current would serve as a reinforcer. Subsequently, more sophisticated situations were contrived, and many more facets of the effect of this stimulation were examined before a thorough description of its operation as an X could be made. But the rather simple observations just described were actually sufficient to establish the general principle

[1] For the present purpose in quoting this material an understanding of the anatomical terms is not essential. The account of this experiment is taken from Jones (ed.), *Nebraska Symposium of Motivation*, Vol. III, pp. 83–84. Copyright 1955 by the University of Nebraska Press and reprinted by permission of the publisher.

that some sort of brain stimulation was an effective reinforcer. The basis of this assertion was that S-R pairs that were followed by this event (such as going to a specific spot on a table top) occurred more and more frequently. Alternative S-R events (movement in any other direction) were not followed by the same event, and they diminished in strength.

As long as we do not try to answer both of the questions, "What is a reinforcer?" and "Is reinforcement always necessary for learning?" at the same time, then the procedure for defining a reinforcer is simple. This is because we are not prohibited from using the occurrence of learning as a means of finding the answer to the first question, taken by itself. This, in fact, seems to be the way in which most psychologists always do decide whether some event is a reinforcer: if its presentation following a response enables the psychologist to gain some control over that response. Whether this is the only way one can gain control over responding in a learning situation is another proposition entirely; as we shall see in Chapter 9, the negative of this proposition is very difficult to prove by empirical means.

THE LAW OF EFFECT

The Law of Effect was the first behavioral law to be recognized as a behavioral law (as opposed to "laws of consciousness"). It was pronounced by E. L. Thorndike (267) near the turn of the century. By now the readers of this book should have learned the fundamentals of this law without realizing it. Essentially, the Law of Effect asserts that a response is learned, or not learned, depending upon the events (effects) that follow it.

It took fifty years to whittle away at the superstructure of Thorndike's hypothesis, and during the intervening time much unscientific bickering often influenced opinions of this law. One of the important controversies concerning the idea stemmed from the fact that Thorndike contrasted reward with punishment as the basic types of effects. Psychologists have since decided (1) that there are at least three dimensions to effect: positive, negative, and neutral; (2) that positive effects—the ones that strengthen S-R relationships—are not always rewards, as the law was for a long time interpreted to mean; and (3) that neutral effects, rather than negative ones, are the opposite of positive effects, in that they do not produce learning. Negative effects have a role all to themselves, a role that we shall discuss when we consider the concept of punishment (Chapter 8).

As the various examples of operant learning in the preceding chapter showed, it is not difficult to identify a large number of *specific* reinforcing events. The problem that has, off and on, been of great concern to psychologists is the discovery of the features common to all such specific events; in other words, the basic nature of a reinforcing event. All the generalizations that are currently extant fail to fit the known facts in one way or another, but a description of these generalizations will at least enable the student to get a further idea of the variety of events that have been shown to be effective reinforcing conditions.

HYPOTHESES ABOUT THE BASIS OF REINFORCEMENT

As research and discussion concerning the matter continued, there emerged a differentiation between *strong* and *weak* laws of effect. This differentiation has been the basis of most inductive statements about the common denominator of reinforcing events.

(1) The *strong* law of effect is the assertion that reinforcers are always rewards.

(2) The *weak* law admits that other things besides rewards can reinforce. This position is expressed more positively by the statement that reinforcement is any procedure that insures that R_L is the last responce made in the presence of S_L. If R_L is to be the last R made when S_L occurs, the easiest way—perhaps the only logical way—that this can be accomplished is *by changing S_L as soon as R_L is made.*

These two basic positions, which indeed are not mutually exclusive, have been elaborated in a variety of ways by different groups of psychologists. Usually the embellishments of either of these generalizations have taken the form of hypotheses about events within the organism that accompany (i.e., are caused by) the environmental event that terminates the learning sequence.

Rewards as Reinforcers

The psychologists who have espoused some form of the doctrine that rewards are the only X's are legion. Despite the diversity of the ways in which the viewpoint has been expressed, the definitions of reward involved always take one of two general forms:

(1) Definitions are couched in terms of a change in some hypothesized condition of the organism. Such a definition of rewards was most vigorously proposed and most adequately defended by C. L. Hull (124), his colleagues, and their students. Hull's view was that the basic, unlearned conditions that can act as rewards were events that reduced some state of drive. In brief, "drive reduction" was anything that was necessary for the survival of the organism and/or its species. Other events could become rewards by being paired (a la Pavlovian conditioning) with the occurrence of drive reduction, or (as in higher-order conditioning) with learned rewards that had previously been associated with other rewards. The Hullian school further asserted that only rewards could reinforce S-R sequences.[2]

We must admire attempts, such as (and especially) Hull's, to relate the basic laws of psychology to the Darwinist influence that pervades all biological thought, and particularly to the mechanisms of physiology (our closest scientific relative). But other definitions of rewards, or of reinforcers themselves, do not necessarily defeat these admirable aims. Furthermore, there is evidence that is contradictory to all but the most complicated versions of the drive-reduction definition of rewards.

One sort of contradictory evidence comes from a study by Shef-

---

[2] Although Hull himself left the door open for other interpretations of reinforcement, the history of the Hullian school reveals that none of its adherents ever studied non-reward reinforcers, and that many of them have always been quite willing to argue on the positive side of the question as to whether all reinforcers ultimately stemmed from potentially important biological changes in an organism's condition.

field, Wulff, and Backer (238), who raised male rats in isolation from females until sexual maturity. Then they were permitted to explore a runway that led to a sexually receptive female rat. Upon reaching the willing miss, the males were permitted to begin, but not to complete copulation. Frustrating? Not for the males, apparently: on succeeding trials most of them approached the location of the female more and more speedily. Remember, these rats had had no prior opportunity to associate intromission with ejaculation, and it is hard to interpret repeatedly unfulfilled sexual arousal as rewarding in the drive-reduction sense. Nevertheless, the male rats learned.

Even an inexperienced male rat will "pay attention to" a receptive female. This situation, therefore, could be interpreted as an instance in which the runway stimuli associated with going from one end to the other in the apparatus suddenly and radically were altered by coming upon the female. Thus, the female constitutes a marked change in stimuli, and is obviously a reinforcer.

There is, on the other hand, evidence that a beneficial change in an organism's internal environment can, in and of itself, be a reinforcing event. Coppock and Chambers (54) placed rats in an apparatus that prevented any movement except of the head; a hypodermic needle was inserted into a blood vessel in the rat's tail. Thus prepared, the rat was placed in a box in such a position that significant movements of the head to either the left or right would break a photoelectric beam; this activated a counter, enabling the experimenters to determine how many times a given animal would turn his head to each side during a fixed time period. After this had been determined, the apparatus was modified so that now movements to the less preferred side also activated a solenoid, causing a clamp on a rubber tube to be released momentarily. This tube led from a bottle of glucose to the needle in the rat's tail. In short, then, movements of the head to the nonpreferred side now caused a slight rise in the blood-sugar level of the rat, which was hungry (had low blood-sugar) at the time. Control animals received injections of saline solution under the same conditions. The rats receiving the sugar solution showed an increasing tendency to turn their heads toward the side that released the glucose; the control animals did not. This experiment is particularly interesting because it demonstrates the reinforcing effect of an event that is certainly need reducing, and that is also not accompanied by any changes in the external environment (the rats were in a soundproofed box and could not hear the operation of the apparatus; also the releasing of the glucose presumably did not stimulate any of the rat's receptors).

Later, Chambers (49) studied the effects of glucose injections on hungry rabbits. He found that one marked effect was "slight, significant rises" in the animals' temperature, especially in the back and leg, soon after the injections. From this finding, Chambers suggested:

These results may possibly account for some of the rewarding properties of nutritive injections whereby the increment in habit strength may have been obtained in the experiments by Coppock *et al.* The animals may have experienced a general feeling of body warmth, and this may have been rewarding to the food-deprived animals. . . . In addition to, or instead of, mere nutritive need reduction, one may postulate a reduction in temperature stress, or a general feeling of body warmth. (49, p. 567)

So again we find difficulty in attempting to define rewards in terms of survival or need-reducing mechanisms; this is an extremely hard position to relate to empirical observations.

(2) Rewards may also be defined exclusively in terms of observable events, rather than in terms of hypothetical changes within the organism. The most conservative deviation from the drive reduction view of reinforcers is the position that still regards all X's as rewards, but emphasizes the objective method of defining rewards. One of the major nuclei of this approach is the University of Wisconsin Primate Laboratory, directed by Prof. Harry F. Harlow (105).

Defining Rewards Objectively

The criteria for determining whether a given S is a reward can be evaluated in objective test situations, at least hypothetically (i.e., the actual techniques might require more than our skills at a given time could accomplish, but such a determination would not be impossible under better conditions). The criteria that are generally accepted among psychologists as objective evidence that some S is a reward are these:

(1) Rewards are stimuli for which a subject will, under certain circumstances, show a decided preference (relative to other things that are also available).

As an example of this, let us return to the studies by Olds that were introduced above. Having established that electrical stimulation of a mid-brain area was reinforcing, he raised the question of whether it was a reward:

> Still later, the same animal was placed on an elevated T maze. As there was an initial right turn preference, he was forced to the left and stimulated at the end of the left arm. After three such trials, he proceeded to make 10 consecutive runs to the left for electrical stimulation alone, with decreasing running times. Then the stimulus was stopped on the left, and 6 runs were forced to the right with electrical stimulation in the right arm. Up to this point, no food had been used in the maze at all.
>
> Afterwards, the animal was starved for 24 hours. Food was put in both arms of the T maze. The animal was given two forced runs to each arm. He was stimulated in the left arm. After this, he made 10 runs to the left, *stopping at the point of stimulation and never going on* to the food.[3]
>
> We were then convinced that the electrical stimulus *alone* had strongly rewarding effects. . . . (201, p. 84, italics in original)

(2) At least rats, cats, dogs, many primates, and people will usually work hard for rewards. By "working hard" is meant that when conditions are arranged so that it becomes more difficult to perform a response that has previously led to reward, most organisms will not immediately revert to random responding, but will shift instead to the new, more difficult R. This is also true when it becomes necessary to tolerate some degrees of noxious stimulation

---

[3] In all honesty, it must be pointed out that Olds' particular application of this method in this example is by no means perfect. One 24-hour period of food deprivation is generally not sufficient to insure that a laboratory rat will "pay attention to" food even when there are no competing sources of reinforcement in the same environment. This is just another example of the extreme relativity with which any assertion that some S is a reward must be made (see below in text). But while we might quibble with its technical details, the procedure described here *is* a simple, straightforward illustration of the method being discussed. Further, more recent data support the validity of Olds' conclusions.

in order to attain the object or event whose reward value is being tested. These techniques were the basis of a standard apparatus devised to compare the strengths of various rewarding events (133).

(3) Failure to attain rewards, when they had previously been received in the same situation upon the occurrence of the same response as is made at time of test, often results in emotional behavior. If you offer a well-fed, laboratory-adapted chimpanzee a piece of banana, he will make the R's that have usually been followed in the past by the receipt of this delicacy. Should you tease him by keeping the fruit in sight but out of reach, the chimp will eventually act in ways that could be called "frustrated," or "aggressive" (76).

For the really precise determination of the reward value of a particular stimulus the preceding tests may have to be conducted under elaborately controlled conditions. In everyday cases where we wish to control the behavior of some organism, however, such meticulous procedures may be unnecessary; often a fairly casual observation of an organism may suggest effective methods of rewarding it. One of the advantages of rewards as reinforcers is that many of them are effective under a fairly wide range of conditions.

The Relativity of Rewards

With regard to the last statement of the preceding paragraph there is one important reservation to be kept in mind. All *empirical* definitions of reward can be stated only in relative terms. It is actually inaccurate to speak, as I have spoken up to now, of whether a given object or event *is* a reward; this implies that it always is a reward, or never is. The only accurate answer to the question, "Is a given X a reward?" is the apparently ambiguous and unsatisfactory statement, "Sometimes it is, sometimes it isn't."

The most general definition of a reward is that it is something for which an organism shows a preference. "Preference" is inevitably a relative term, since it must always imply some finite set of alternatives. A person may, in all truthfulness, make a statement such as, "I would rather be a great violinist than anything else," but unless the actions that are correlated with this statement alter one's life to the extent that there is finally little choice except between being a great violinist and a mediocre one, the person's behavior may not always reflect this absolute evaluation of his goals when other choices later become possible. Olds' work with the rat, described earlier, illustrates a case in point. Ordinarily, hungry rats prefer food to other things in the environment; even this is only a relative preference, however, as Olds showed: his subjects preferred electrical stimulation to food even when hungry.

Preferences are not only relative to the alternatives available at a given time, they are relative to the past reward experiences of the organism. This will be documented in the next chapter; just to mention an example briefly now, a chimpanzee that is known to accept lettuce as food may become "outraged" if lettuce is offered as a reward for doing something that had previously been paid off with pieces of banana (268).

In addition, preferences are relative to other factors that are influencing the organism at the time he is required to make the choices from which his preference is inferred. Hungry monkeys will ignore the opportunity to engage in activities which at other times are quite attractive to them (105, 107).

Finally, the method of testing for preferences will itself affect the relative rankings of alternatives; this is a now well-known phenomenon in many branches of psychology. To some extent it overlaps the three preceding determinants of the relativity of preferences.

The relativity of rewards is, if anything, even more apparent in human behavior. Most people would agree with the statement that "praise is a highly effective method of rewarding human behavior." But even casual, everyday observations reveal that, as always, whether a given kind of praise will be effective with a specific individual is dependent on many factors. A girl of ten or eleven, for example, may be quite responsive to praise for her athletic ability; three or four years later, if she is still being recognized primarily for her talent at baseball, this may only irritate or embarrass her. A teen-age boy may be quite sensitive about the opinions of him that his peers have, while praise from his teachers and parents may not markedly affect his behavior at all. Examples of the relativity of rewards are practically inexhaustible.

One reason I have emphasized this point so much is that the behavioristic approach to learning is sometimes accused of ignoring individual differences. While it is true that the goal of research is to produce principles of the greatest generality, it should not be inferred from this that the importance of individual and subtle situational differences is being denied. The application of general principles to specific cases always necessitates a knowledge and an appreciation of the equally general principle that "people do differ."

Non-reward Reinforcers

Some psychologists prefer to describe reinforcers in ways that do not demand discussions of such terms as "drive reduction" or "preferences." To differentiate this approach from that just considered, I have chosen to call this the "non-reward" viewpoint. It must be understood that it is very difficult to devise a method of proving empirically that something is *not* rewarding. Insofar as this position serves to emphasize that reinforcing events need not have any relationship to an organism's "needs," "pleasures," and the like, it does add something to the concept of reinforcement that was developed by reward-oriented psychologists. The non-reward positions, too, can be sorted into two subclasses of definitions; like the preceding subdivision they break down into definitions that speak of some hypothetical actions on the part of the organism, and definitions that emphasize a seemingly objective basis for describing reinforcers. Since the conceptual and empirical problems are somewhat different here than in the case of reward definitions, let us take up the subdivision in the reverse order, i.e., from the objective to the hypothetical.

1. The Stimulus-Change Concept

Behind this approach to reinforcers is the assumption that any event that prohibits the occurrence of further, incompatible R's [4]

---

[4] Literally, incompatible R's are those that could not occur simultaneously, e.g., extension and flexion of a limb. It is sometimes handy to use the concept

in the presence of a given S_L, reinforces the association of that S_L with the R immediately preceding this event. This event is most frequently some change in the total S complex. If, immediately after the sequence S_L-R_L has occurred, something happens to S_L to make it somewhat different, obviously any further R's that occur can not be associated with S_L. Guthrie (96) is most closely associated with this description of reinforcers. To him, a reinforcer is any event that causes a given R to be the last R to occur in the presence of the S_L.

Neither the reward nor the stimulus-change viewpoint is entirely adequate. The following experiments point this out; the first seems contrary to reward expectations, the other raises questions about the generality of the stimulus-change concept:

(1) We have already noted Seward's observation (236) that rats simply removed from the apparatus when they pressed a lever gave indications of learning. In the Notes of Chapter 3, the possibility was shown to be very slight that this removal was, in fact, some sort of reward.

(2) An experiment by Zeaman and Radner (299), however, illustrates a puzzling exception to the stimulus-change hypothesis. Their apparatus was a box with a floor fastened only on an axle along its center line. Additional weight on either side of this axle caused the floor to tilt in the direction of the weight. In other words, the floor acted like a simple balance. Zeaman and Radner tried to teach rats to keep going back and forth across the center line under one of two conditions:

LIGHT OFF Group: Rats in this group were placed on one side of the floor while a very bright light illuminated the box. When a rat crossed the center, tilting the floor, the light went off. After a few moments the light went on again; if the rat recrossed the center line the light went off, and so on for several trials.

LIGHT ON Group: For the rats in this group the conditions were just the reverse of those above. They were placed in the box under

---

of "somewhat incompatible," despite this term's lack of exact meaning; in general, it means that the occurrence of a given R will usually preclude the occurrence of some other response in the same setting.

very dim illumination; whenever they crossed the center line, the bright light came on momentarily.

Light on, or light off, both are changes in S, so by the "stimulus-change" hypothesis about reinforcers they would not be expected to differ in effectiveness. They did, however, and quite dramatically. Rats in the LIGHT OFF group made the crossing more and more quickly after the light was turned back on. No similar change in speed of responding was found in the LIGHT ON group; if anything, their tendency to cross when it was rather dark in the box decreased.

Zeaman and Radner showed that not every stimulus change will reinforce. While not devastating to the stimulus-change position, this experiment certainly indicates that the definition of an "effective stimulus change" may be found to have the same sorts of complications as previously noted in the case of rewards.

The failure of "light on" is due to the fact that the albino rat is light aversive. Human beings do not like extremely bright light, but the albino doesn't even have our defenses against such stimulation. Neither its eye nor eyelid have any pigmentation. White rats have a very characteristic reaction to bright light—they will, if possible, get away from it. This experiment suggests that any S that elicits R's that could be described as "attempts to escape, or avoid S" cannot serve as a reinforcement for any preceding R. This does not, however, point to the necessary characteristics of stimulus changes that *will* act as reinforcers.

2. Reinforcement as the S for a New R

Since reinforcing events usually (perhaps always) involve some alteration of the organism's environment, it is conceivable that they may produce some sort of systematic behavior in the organism that is different from the activity that preceded the occurrence of X. Certainly the presentation of a food pellet when a rat presses a lever causes a rat to do something different than he had been doing; specifically, the rat releases the lever and approaches the food receptacle. The behavior in relation to the X itself may be learned (as in the case of responding to the food pellet in the Skinner box), or unlearned (as in the case of the male rat's behavior in the presence of a receptive female; see p. 126). It has been suggested that this may be the crucial feature of those events that are effective reinforcers.

An intriguing experiment in support of this particular position was performed by Coppock (53), using the apparatus previously described (p. 126) in connection with the glucose injection studies. Rats were given 270 pairings of a light and a 5-sec. electric shock; for some rats the light came on 1 sec. before the shock did, for others the shock started 4 secs. before the light, and they terminated together.[5] During the subsequent test periods, the light came on whenever the animal moved its head toward the nonpreferred side and stayed on until the head was moved back to the center or beyond. Quite contrary to what would be expected from a fear-conditioning hypothesis, Coppock found that the animals for whom this light had previously come on just before the shock showed a reliably greater increase (compared to the controls) in frequency of movements to the nonpreferred side, and an increase in the total duration of time spent with the head on the nonpreferred side. Not only did these rats not avoid the light, but the light had the effect usually identified as reinforcing!

Coppock's interpretation of this, putting it very simply, was that the light had been a stimulus for a freezing response; thus, a movement toward the nonpreferred side produced a stimulus that tended to stop further movement. Accordingly, a response (holding head on nonpreferred side) is evoked by a stimulus that occurs whenever a completely compatible response (moving head toward nonpreferred side) is made.[6] This analysis, which is similar to that invoked by Sheffield et al. (238) to account for the reinforcing effect of incomplete copulation, stems from the position that considers the main function of reinforcement to be that of prevent-

---

[5] These specific time relations and the S_n were altered in the second experiment reported in this paper, but the difference between the groups remained essentially the same.

[6] The explanation of greater frequency of R_L is too technical and too complicated to serve any useful purpose in this text, and has therefore been omitted. The interested reader is referred to the original article by Coppock (53).

ing responses antagonistic to R_L from occurring in the presence of S_L.

While the chief exponents of this interpretation of reinforcers have been identified with the non-reward position in general, the view that reinforcers produce specific responses is not actually in opposition to a strict reward position. Especially when using the preference definition of a reward, one implies by the very term "preference" that the organism does something in relation to the reward event. It is not far-fetched to say that something is desirable because of what the organism can do with it, or in its presence.

Reward vs. Non-reward Positions Summarized

The various hypotheses about the essential factor common to all reinforcers range from the view that fundamentally reinforcement is inextricably related to the survival of the organism and its species to the assumption that how reinforcers alter behavior and how organisms survive are problems only coincidentally related to each other. Obviously, this way of formulating the controversy has more than a bit of metaphysics running through it. It has usually been difficult to resolve broad, philosophical disputes by strictly empirical methods.

As for the viewpoints that fall somewhere between these two extremes, the major differences among them may be largely verbal. If we agree to define rewards in terms of some kind of behavior that an organism shows in their presence, then there is little difference between this and the view that reinforcers are effective because they evoke systematic behavior that prevents interference with R_L. It then becomes a matter of to what extent, when we speak of rewards, we are actually implying the existence of unobservable affective states such as that "the organism likes those things," or "wants" them. Definitions of reward that are free from such implications must be practically indistiguishable from all but the most extreme versions of the so-called non-reward hypotheses.

As is typical in the case of such controversies as this, the extreme viewpoints both seem to be inadequate. There are events that reinforce that cannot easily be connected with the organism's needs (defined in terms of survival mechanisms); there are also definite changes in stimulation that do not reinforce the S-R sequences that precede them.

We must therefore conclude that no contemporary description of the general characteristics of *all* X's hits the mark exactly. Further to complicate matters, we shall see in a later chapter that learning has sometimes been obtained in situations in which *no* X event is clearly apparent.

I shall slip out of this muddle (though, perhaps, not too gracefully) by reminding the reader that in Chapter 1, I disavowed the problems of learning theory as being of fundamental importance in this book. At an empirical level, then, the following statements about reinforcement seem proper:

(1) In situations where some sort of R-X sequence *is* identifiable, learning proceeds more quickly and produces a more stable S-R relationship than when an R-X sequence is not clear.

(2) The type of X that is most effective and most practical is an S having the characteristics of a reward—i.e., X_{rew}[7]—keeping in mind that such characteristics are relative and subject to change with changes in various characteristics of the organism or the general situation.

(3) Nevertheless, our ability to comprehend the extensive role of learning as a way of modifying behavior will be severely delimited if we fail to recognize that S's that are not rewards may also reinforce R's. The versatility of non-reward X's may be little compared to that of X_{rew}'s (actually, hardly anything is known about this), but there can still be many occasions when their effect is powerful.

SECONDARY REINFORCEMENT

If an S_n is repeatedly associated with the occurrence of something that is already known to be a reward, S_n itself can come

[7] This symbol will be used in this text when it is important to denote that the reinforcer under discussion was known to be a reward.

to act as an X. A stimulus that has undergone this transformation is called a *secondary reinforcer*. "Secondary" is used here in the sense of "learned" or "acquired"; the term was coined by Hull, but is now used by most psychologists without necessarily implying an acceptance of Hull's position regarding the nature of reinforcement. Perhaps the S_n may even become a reward, too, though the laboratory evidence for this is rather shaky and indirect.

There are no known demonstrations of the development of a secondary reinforcer—symbolized as S^r—through the pairing of an S_n with a non-rewarding reinforcer. We have already seen that the versatility of non-reward reinforcers has not yet been studied to any appreciable extent.

Methods of Forming $(S)^r$'s

There appear to be two major ways of establishing a connection between an S_n and some X_{rew}:

(1) Where S_n is functionally related to X_{rew}, the subject must actually do something when S_n occurs, or do something to cause S_n to occur, before X_{rew} will be presented.

(2) In the other case S_n is simply an event that is coincidental with X_{rew}'s presentation.

A. J. Mitrano (191) did a study many years ago that demonstrated an S_n-X_{rew} relationship of the first kind. Feeble-minded children were shown a machine, much like a cigarette-vending machine, that took poker chips and gave candy bars in return. After the children had learned the connection between poker chips and candy bars (this is the S^r establishment—poker chips were the means of getting candy bars), Mitrano brought another machine into the experimental room. This second device was similar to a slot machine except that it had no intake slot, only an opening from which poker chips exited. The children had only to pump the crank in order to obtain poker chips, which could then be exchanged for chocolate bars by inserting the chips in the other machine.

After this two-part behavior sequence was established, Mitrano went on to compare the relative reinforcement strengths of the chips and candy. For some children the poker-chip machine was disconnected without their knowledge; pulling the lever no longer produced any chips. For the other subjects the poker chips still continued to come out, but the candy machine didn't work—the insertion of a chip in it only resulted in the loss of the chip, no candy.

The results were very illuminating in regard to S^r's. As we might expect, the children who could still get poker chips out of the slot machine continued to work this machine longer than did the children for whom this machine was disconnected. Remember that, functionally, the end result for both groups was the same—no candy. But the continued presentation of poker chips, an S^r, increased resistance to extinction of the lever-pulling R. Ultimately, of course, lever-pulling stopped in both groups. This is in accord with the well-known principle that S^r strength itself is subject to extinction, if not backed up by X_{rew} at least occasionally.

The second method of developing an S^r, illustrated by the experiments of Saltzman (227) and Lawson (158) discussed in Chapter 3, appears to be quite similar to a Pavlovian procedure. Some stimulus quite arbitrarily occurs in close temporal relationship to the occurrence of a reward stimulus. As in Pavlov's technique, what is specifically manipulated is the relationship of two stimuli. Unlike Pavlovian conditioning, however, it is rarely clear that the S^r produces behavior like that made in the presence of X_{rew}; in other words, psychologists can not specify the CR that develops as a result of pairing S_n and X_{rew}. The similarity of the S^r and the X_{rew} on which it was based is, of course, in their effects upon the R's that *precede* their occurrence. At present, we can only speculate as to the actual mechanism by which a neutral stimulus is transformed into a reinforcing event, and we have already had enough speculation in this chapter.

Proving S_n Has Become an S^r

The typical methods of demonstrating that an S_n can become an S^r are: (1) to show that a new R_L, followed by the former S_n alone, will undergo those changes that we usually use to infer the occurrence of learning (Chapter 1), or (2) to show that an R

—formerly followed by X_{rew}—will persist longer when followed by the presumed secondary reinforcer (but no longer by X_{rew}) than when followed neither by the S^r nor by X_{rew}. The first method could be called the *new learning* demonstration of S^r, the second the *resistance-to-extinction* demonstration. In both cases, a valuable control observation, as the Hubbard experiment (pp. 97–100) should have made clear, would be the presentation of the S_n to some subjects in the same learning or extinction situation, but without the prior association of S_n with X_{rew}. This has rarely been done; more frequently, the control employed is *another* stimulus that is physically similar to the original S_n, but not associated with X_{rew}. The subjects receiving this condition have previously had the same S^r establishment procedure as the experimental objects. As yet, the provocative possibility suggested by Hubbard's experiment—that almost any stimulus change, no matter how insignificant, can *maintain* a habit already established by effective reinforcement—remains only a possibility.

S^r's have been exploited more by theorists and textbook writers than they have been studied by scientists. It is easy to note the analogy between such demonstrations as that of Mitrano's and events in everyday life such as the effectiveness of money, verbal praise, hobbies, or games. But we are not at all sure, from the laboratory evidence, that it is anything more than analogy.

PAVLOV REVISITED

As emphasized in Chapter 2, possible reinforcing agents in Pavlovian conditioning situations are matters of conjecture, rather than observation. This is because (1) the S-R relationship has been stressed in Pavlovian studies, and (2) functional definitions of operant and Pavlovian learning, such as those used in this text, make these situations almost exclusive (i.e., if X *is* controlled by the experimenter, the situation would usually be called an operant type, by definition).

The distinctions we have drawn, however, between the two classes of learning situations are not entirely verbal. They are drawn in terms of what is *controlled* by the "teacher" in each case, not in terms of what *could be observed* were the proper techniques employed.

Some psychologists do not regard Pavlovian conditioning and operant learning as cast from the same mold. There is a viewpoint that holds that these types of learning situations actually represent different learning mechanisms. The best pedagogical position would seem to be that as long as experimenters observe one set of events in one situation, and another set in the other, what basis have we for deciding the argument? Personally, however, I cannot deny being impressed by some research by Loucks (173); his findings strongly suggest the possibility that it may be necessary to assume a reinforcing event even in Pavlovian situations where none is readily apparent.

Loucks took advantage of two facts: (1) the brain itself contains no pain receptors, so that once the top of the skull is removed (under anesthesia) the brain can be stimulated electrically while the subject is conscious, without discomfort to the subject, and (2) the location of the beginning of the motor nerves in the cortex (the surface of the brain) in many species is known. Loucks, therefore, exposed the motor area of a dog's brain and located the exact point that, if given a mild electric shock, caused the flexion of one of the dog's legs. Here, presumably, is the ideal UCS. Its occurrence is completely neutral to the subject; literally, the subject is never "aware" of the UCS as such, since it never activates any sensory nerves (when the leg begins moving, of course, proprioception occurs). Loucks proceeded to condition the dog's leg flexion by pairing a bell—an S_n—with stimulation of the motor cortex—the UCS. At least, he tried to condition leg flexion to the bell; after 600 S_n-UCS pairings, however, there was no indication that the bell had, or was about to, become a CS.

Loucks then added the feature of feeding the dog after every unconditioned leg flexion (which, in turn, still followed the sound of the bell). Now learning occurred rapidly. Pavlovian conditioning? Operant learning? S-R-X?

S-R-X, certainly, but Loucks' study does not *prove* that reinforcement is a necessity in *all* Pavlovian set-ups. Most assuredly, an X_{rew} is not a feature of all Pavlovian situations. If—and it is a big if—reinforcement *is* a part of Pavlovian conditioning, then the following aspects of various Pavlovian situations *might* suffice for this role:

(1) The simplest case would be that in which UCS is noxious, and UCR terminates UCS. This should be recognized as escape learning, the relationship of which to Pavlovian conditioning was discussed in Chapter 3.

(2) The UCS may have *aftereffects* that are X_{rew}'s. The powdered meat of many of Pavlov's experiments *could* be an X_{rew}. Putting food in the dog's mouth *can not reinforce* the salivary R that *follows* that event. But after the UCR, the UCS does not just disappear—it is swallowed, and the dog is less hungry than it was before.

(3) Either the experimenter or the subject (the latter by responding) may change the S_n—i.e., CS—immediately upon the occurrence of the R_L. As we have said repeatedly, experimenters rarely do this intentionally in the Pavlovian situation; nevertheless, every CS-UCS relationship involves not only the relative onsets of these S's but also their terminations. While rarely related to UCR occurrence systematically, CS's are, in practice, quite often terminated nearly contiguously with the UCR, or CR, when that develops.

If the preceding suggestions should, indeed, turn out to be close approximations to the observable events that are necessary for the establishment of a CR, it would not seriously alter the current distinction between Pavlovian and operant learning. At present, there is no conclusive evidence that Pavlovian conditioning does not fit the S-R-X model. On the other hand, there is no certain basis for asserting that it does. The Loucks data and the many logical possibilities of reinforcement inherent in most Pavlovian situations incline me, however, toward a belief in the applicability of the model. The main hope is that cool heads—and, best of all, the facts—shall prevail.

SUMMARY

In this chapter were considered those features of reinforcers, and of the R-X relationship in general, that are revealed by the study of the most simple type of operant learning situation.

It was concluded that sufficient data do not exist to decide the ultimate, basic features of all events that can be shown to act as X's. It was emphasized, on the other hand, that the characteristics of reinforcers will be determined empirically, not rationally, in the long run.

＊

＊

CHAPTER 5

＊ **THE EFFECT OF
REINFORCEMENT
VARIATIONS IN
SIMPLE OPERANT LEARNING**

Pavlov proved that the objective study of behavior was possible; he also pointed out the general direction that such a program should follow. For application to everyday situations in which people wish to control the behavior of others, Pavlov's techniques are limited. As far as the study of behavior is concerned, this is no reason to criticize the Academician's work. He could hardly be summarily ignored because he found only the beginning of the trail, and not its end as well.

We know that it is easier to translate the discoveries of the laboratory into applications in nature when the laboratory work concerns operant learning situations. We also know that the most important thing to control in an operant situation is the R-X relationship. The numerous ways in which this part of the learning situation can be varied, and the effects of these variations, are the subject matter of this chapter.

Nearly all the studies to be discussed in this chapter have two characteristics in common. First of all, S_L is always constant throughout any training procedure mentioned. I have intentionally chosen studies meeting that condition for this chapter, deferring the problems of variations in S_L until the next group of chapters.

A second feature of most of the research now to be surveyed is that it concerns variations in X_{rew}'s almost exclusively. This is not by choice, but simply because very little detailed study has yet been made of the operation of non-reward X's.

SCHEDULES OF REINFORCEMENT

A great deal of evidence has been amassed in support of the contention that one of the most important kinds of variation in R-X relationships concerns the consistency with which R_L is followed by X. Any plan that specifies what occurrences of R_L will be occasions for the presentation of X is a *reinforcement schedule*. The simplest schedule of reinforcement is that in which every R_L is followed by reinforcement. This procedure has many labels, of which the most common are "continuous reinforcement," "consistent reinforcement," and "100 per cent reinforcement."

Every other reinforcement schedule must, of course, be some deviation from consistent reinforcement. It must involve something less than the invariant reinforcement of a given S-R relationship whenever it occurs. The most common term for such schedules is "partial reinforcement"—in some ways a misnomer, since it could be misinterpreted as a denial of the all-or-none feature of most reinforcers. "Partial reinforcement," "intermittent reinforcement," and "noncontinuous reinforcement" all mean the same thing: that reinforcement is *not* always given after each occurrence of R_L; of these terms, my preference is equally divided between "noncontinuous" and "intermittent"—so I shall use both of them interchangeably.

In short, if a continuous reinforcement schedule is being used, the learning situation is characterized as

$$S_L\text{-}R_L\text{-}X,$$

i.e., whenever R_L occurs in the presence of S_L, X also occurs. Noncontinuous schedules, in contrast, would be illustrated by

$$S_L\text{-}R_L\text{-}X/NoX,$$

meaning that when R_L is made in the presence of S_L it is sometimes reinforced (X) and sometimes not (NoX).

Deviations from continuous reinforcement occur along two dimensions, and take either of two forms on each dimension:

(1) The first dimension of such schedules concerns the *base* for setting up an intermittent (noncontinuous) schedule. This base may be either the number of R's that must be made between successive reinforcements, or it may be time, wherein reinforcement is available "every so often."

(2) The second dimension is an even more obvious dichotomy; it is the dimension of *regularity*. Either a schedule is regular—i.e., the number of R's or the amount of time between successive reinforcements is always the same—or it is not.

Every reinforcement schedule can be described in terms of its position on both of these dichotomous dimensions, as shown in Table II.

TABLE II

The Basic Types of Noncontinuous Reinforcement Schedules

REGULARITY OF SCHEDULE	BASIS OF SCHEDULE	
	NUMBER OF R's	TIME BETWEEN X's
Regular	Fixed-Ratio	Fixed-Interval
Irregular	Variable-Ratio	Variable-Interval

The effects of noncontinuous reinforcement schedules can be observed under two main types of conditions:

(1) They can be observed after a given schedule has been shifted to one of continuous nonreinforcement (extinction). The relationship of intermittent reinforcement to extinction will be taken up in Chapter 8.

(2) While a particular schedule is in effect: while they are in effect, the various noncontinuous X procedures to be discussed below produce qualitatively and quantitatively different operant behavior patterns. Most of the information about the effects of intermittent X schedules comes from the study of free operant situations (see p. 110). In fact, interval schedules apply only in such situations. In the Skinner box, for example, the subject is free to respond at any time, so time can be used as the basis for determining when reinforcement will be made available; in the straight runway, however, many things besides the subject's own behavior and learning determine *when* he can respond, so a reinforcement schedule based on temporal factors would not be an appropriate or efficient means of arranging R-X contingencies. Ratio schedules, on the other hand, can be employed in either free or controlled operant situations.

Note also that the study of noncontinuous schedules is, in effect, the study of the repeated R case on the R Dimension of operant learning situations (Table I, p. 77). By definition, a noncontinuous ratio schedule requires a subject to repeat R_L one or more times as the condition for receiving X; in actual practice, interval schedules also produce behavior that is most easily described in terms of repetitions of R_L. With these points in mind, let us examine the effects on habit maintenance that result from each of these basic intermittent reinforcement schedules.

Fixed-Ratio Reinforcement

This type of schedule involves the reinforcement of every other R, every fourth R, and so on. Such schedules can be expressed in terms of the ratio of responses to reinforcement occurrences, e.g., 2:1, 4:1, etc. A simple, rough analog of this situation in everyday life would be to pay a worker on a piecework basis, e.g., so much money per bushel of fruit picked.

Free operant responding after prolonged training under a fixed-ratio schedule often looks very much as if the subject has learned to make "bursts" of responses. There are moments of such rapid responding that there is no reason to infer that the subject "expects" a reward for each of these R's; the subject—even if it is the albino rat—does not stop long enough between R's in such bursts to be able to ascertain whether X has been given or not. Denny, Wells, and Maatsch (63) studied the rat's approaches to the food tray while working in a Skinner box under a 5:1 schedule for bar-pressing; as training progressed, there was a very steady decrease in the number of tray approaches per block of five bar-presses. With the higher ratios, at least, nonverbal organisms do show some crude "counting" ability.

In controlled operant situations also, the higher ratios may produce some systematic variations in behavior on rewarded vs. non-rewarded trials. On a fixed 2:1 schedule in the runway, for instance, the rat may, if training continues long enough, show slower running times or latencies on trials following rewarded trials (when they will not be rewarded) than on trials following non-rewarded trials (when they will be rewarded). Because controlled operant studies are rarely as prolonged as free operant ones, however, the evidence for the synchrony of behavior with the reward schedule is not so great in the former. More frequently noted in the controlled operant case is simply a greater variability in the subject's behavior under fixed schedules than under variable ones.

Putting Low Ratios into Effect

Even with a 2:1 fixed-ratio schedule (i.e., when the subject is reinforced every second time he performs R_L), there are as many R_L's that do *not* get reinforced as there are occurrences of R_L that do. Such a condition is not conducive to learning in all subjects when it is applied from the start of training, and the subjects are naive. Skinner (247), however, has reported instances in which a laboratory rat maintained a bar-pressing R on a ratio of 192:1! In fact, we can get almost any vertebrate to develop a consistent pattern of responding under fairly low fixed-ratio schedules. Needless to say, no rat can be trained from scratch on an entirely new sort of response when the reinforcement schedule is 192:1. The "secret" of fixed-ratio training is to ease the subject into lower and lower ratios. With a truly unsophisticated subject, it is best to start with a ratio near 1:1; then, when his rate of responding becomes stable, to shift to a lower ratio, then to one still lower, and so on. The major consideration is never to exceed the subject's limits of persistence in the face of nonreinforcement when decreasing the ratio of R_L's to X's.

In a situation in which the primary objective is the efficient use of reinforcement, the best procedure known at present consists of two stages: (1) Beginning with a ratio close to 1:1, and shifting to a lower ratio whenever the subject's behavior becomes stable; (2) when you get into the range of ratios wherein the behavior is very hard to stabilize, shifting back and forth between ratios just above and just into this range until you produce an acceptably stable level.

This method-of-limits approach is not much used experimentally because researchers are rarely interested in just what reinforcement ratio will be most effective with what subject. More often, in the laboratory, the schedule used has been chosen for its efficiency of application, or because a given ratio is critical to some hypothesis. In either case, the ratio chosen is arbitrarily imposed on all the subjects in the experiment, or in one of its subgroups.

Variable-Ratio Reinforcement

These schedules involve a continual variation in the number of R_L's required for successive reinforcements. Such variations, in experimental work, are determined by random-number systems which may be modified so that the *average* number of responses per reinforcement is comparable to some fixed-ratio schedule. The latter situation enables us to compare the effects of regular reinforcement with those of irregular reinforcement, yet hold the total number of reinforcements (per unit of time) constant.

Oddly enough, variable-ratio schedules produce *less* variable responding than do fixed-ratio schedules. Variable-ratio reinforcement is an effective means of maintaining quite steady behavior. Intuitively (i.e., after the facts are in), this effect should be easy to understand: under a sporadic reinforcement schedule the subject never "knows" when an R_L may "pay off." The most adaptive mode of responding, then, will be that which we call "persistent."

Horseplayers and other gamblers have long provided anecdotal examples of the high degree of behavioral persistence that can be subsidized by extremely low average ratios of reinforcement. In fact, examples of variable-ratio schedules in everyday life are innumerable. Take the child who is in the throes of learning to substitute verbal requests and demands for more tiring (for the child) and less efficient modes of obtaining certain gratifications. In the flush of enthusiasm at this new manifestation of "intelligence," the parents may hasten to the child's every (verbal) beck and call. Inevitably, the charm of this wears off for the parents long before it does for the child; they become lax in obeying baby's commands, and sometimes they are more lax than they are at other times. The effect is to place the child's verbal behavior (e.g., "Mommy, bring me dis!") on a variable-ratio schedule; sometimes one or two repetitions of the request will produce an effect, at other times the child must ask five or more times (not always in the same tone of voice, of course). Armed with a knowledge of the effects of variable-ratio reinforcement, psychologists can predict what most parents have long since grimly accepted: it is very difficult to discourage a child's behavior, when, as is often the case, the behavior has previously been on variable reinforcement.

Fixed-Interval Reinforcement

This schedule (which is also called *periodic* reinforcement) is the case in which, following the occurrence of a given X, no further R's will be reinforced until a given amount of time has passed. Once the time interval has elapsed, the first R_L to be made will be reinforced.

The result of fixed-interval reinforcement is to develop a pattern of responding that suggests a sense of time in the subject. That is, as the end of the established interval draws nearer, the rate of responding increases, so that when the predetermined time is up, reinforcement is almost immediate. This effect, called *scalloping* after the shape of the cumulative response curve it produces, is diagrammed in Figure 11. This effect is reproducible in species whose ability to "tell time," in the sense that humans do, is limited.

The fact that a rat can develop a periodicity in its bar-pressing that closely conforms to the periodicity of the availability of rein-

FIGURE 11

"Scalloping": The Long-Term Effects of Fixed-Interval Reinforcement

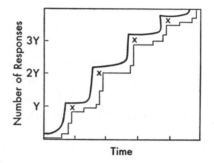

The lower (angular) curve illustrates the general form of the original protocols collected in free operant situations. These are called *cumulative response curves*. A band of paper moves continuously past a recording pen. Every occurrence of R_L moves this pen one notch higher on its holder. Thus, periods of no responding appear as horizontal lines; as the response rate gets faster the curve gets closer to being a vertical line. The hypothetical case shown here is of a well-established behavior pattern under fixed-interval reinforcement. As the time for the next X draws close, R_L's are made with great rapidity; once X occurs, R_L's rate drops nearly to zero. The smoothed version of this curve is shown to indicate why fixed-interval reinforcement is said to produce *scalloping*.

forcement strongly suggests that there are specific S factors to which R_L can, if necessary, become associated even in the simple free operant situation. Little would be gained by speculating here as to the exact nature of such S_L's.

Just as with the previous cases, training by this procedure depends upon a fairly frequent occurrence of R_L during the initial stages of learning. This, again, can be accomplished by starting with an interval that is very brief (close to being equivalent to a 1:1 ratio).

Then the interval is lengthened as rapidly as the subject will tolerate.

The fixed-interval situation bears a superficial resemblance to the "temporal conditioning" phenomenon identified first by Pavlov. The differences in the two cases should now be readily apparent: (1) The R established by fixed-interval reinforcement is *not* always some variation of the R activated by the occurrence of X (e.g., eating is quite distinguishable from bar-pressing) in the operant case, whereas the CR in temporal conditioning has a direct relationship to the UCR used. (2) In periodic operant learning, X will not be presented *until* R_L occurs; in the Pavlovian case, the UCS always occurs at a regular interval, no matter what the subject does. This distinction becomes somewhat less clear, however, in the case of avoidance learning under fixed-interval conditions. In such a situation, *shocks* occur at regular intervals unless the subject makes a specific response. Occurrence of the R_L delays the occurrence of the shock; there is no externally controlled fear stimulus. A stable avoidance response can be developed eventually, although it takes an extremely great amount of training—over 100 hours, during which shocks could occur every 20 secs. unless prevented by R_L, were required in one study using this technique (241).

Clear-cut examples of periodic reinforcement in everyday life are hard to find. A good demonstration of such a schedule requires that no external cues also vary with the availability and unavailability of reward. In the United States, the plethora of clocks, radios, and so on makes such a case very rare. As a mildly good example, however, we might consider the behavior of going to the mailbox to look for mail.

Because the delivery of mail in the United States is an organized business, mail delivery is—with seasonal exceptions—fairly predictable, i.e., regular with respect to time. Suppose that in a given neighborhood, the mail is always delivered close to 11:00 a.m. Now, obviously, a newcomer to the block *could* ascertain this by asking his next-door neighbor, *but this would not be necessary;* functionally, the same relationship between the time of day and the mailman's appearance could be determined by the nonverbal operant learning procedure now under consideration. In fact, it is probably only owing to one's previous experience with many similar trial-and-error situations, accompanied by certain verbal behavior of other people, that a neighbor's statement (e.g., "The mailman usually comes at eleven") could influence one's behavior.

In this very example, however, the newcomer would surely come to associate some external event (e.g., the position of the hands of a clock, or a radio announcement of the time) with the occurrence of R_L-X (going to the mailbox and finding a letter), even if the neighbors were silent. In general, true periodic schedules are not the most efficient kinds of learning situations; as we shall see later, if there is an opportunity to associate any other environmental stimulus with the occurrence of X, organisms will nearly always seize upon these. In the laboratory, however, such stimuli need not exist, and the learned behavior will develop the same way under fixed-interval reinforcement, although more slowly.

Superstitious Behavior

Fixed-interval reinforcement is typically used in connection with a specific R_L, of course, but what if we were to give a subject a reward at regular intervals no matter what he might be doing? Skinner (248) tried this with pigeons, which are ideal operant learners, and the resulting behavior he considered to be an example of "superstitious behavior." That is, the chance reinforcement of some R that the pigeon was very prone to make anyway tended to fixate such responses; reinforcement at entirely arbitrary intervals of time is most likely to follow R's having a high probability of occurrence "naturally." Behavior such as foot-stamping or head-turning quickly became quite repetitious and highly routinized.

The use of the term "superstitious" is intended to convey the fact that the pigeon behaved "as if" a particular R produced X_{rew}, when objectively this was only coincidentally true. It is not hard to go along with Skinner's implication here—much human behavior that does not conform to "objective reality" may develop in essentially the same way. Behavior with an already high frequency of occurrence may, by chance, be followed by some reinforcing event, with the result that such behavior becomes even more frequent. A minor example of this is the comic stereotype of the woman who "repairs" radios and clocks by hitting or dropping them, because this once was followed by reward (the radio started playing again).

Variable-Interval Reinforcement

The final class of noncontinuous reinforcement schedules is sometimes called *aperiodic* reinforcement. It differs only slightly from variable-ratio scheduling, viz., the interval elapsing before another R_L will be followed by reinforcement changes unsystematically after every reinforced occurrence of R_L. From the subject's viewpoint, in fact, variable-interval and variable-ratio schedules may not be differentiable; in either case, the subject can not "figure out" when the next reinforcement will come. As a result, he performs R_L at a steady pace. The chief difference between the two "variable" schedules is that aperiodic reinforcement can only be employed in a free operant situation.

If you have ever seen a newsboy selling papers at a subway entrance during the evening rush hour, you have seen an instance of variable-interval reinforcement. Randomly distributed among the throng heading for the subway are a number of people who want to buy an evening paper to read on the way home. Just when any such person will pass near enough to the newsboy to be able to stop momentarily and make a purchase from him is, from the newsboy's standpoint, entirely unpredictable. The result, as you may know, is an almost incessant cry of, "Get your paper here!" at quite a great rate. Occasionally this behavior is rewarded (by people purchasing papers), but easily 70 per cent of these cries ordinarily are not.

Noncontinuous Reinforcement Schedules Summarized

In general, noncontinuous reinforcement schedules will rarely be easier to use to establish a habit than would a continuous reinforcement procedure. With the proper preliminary training, however, it is possible to bring subjects to the point where even extremely infrequent reinforcement will be sufficient to maintain a consistent level of responding. How often you reinforce will determine the strength of responding. The type of schedule used will determine the pattern of responding you get—an irregular schedule gives the steadiest level of response; a regular schedule produces an irregular response pattern, with continuous reinforcement producing the most erratic performance of all. Furthermore, an irregular schedule in the long run produces an R with greater persistence in the face of continuous nonreinforcement than does any type of regular reinforcement.

In discussing the application of intermittent reinforcement schedules and the difficulties with beginning training under a system that produced X very infrequently, I was implicitly referring to cases in which the "pretraining" likelihood of R_L occurring was low. In such cases, it is true that a certain amount of near-consistent reinforcement must precede an attempt to institute a stringent non-continuous schedule. This preliminary training is simply for the purpose of increasing the momentary level of response strength so that a subject will not cease responding too quickly (i.e., before the next X is due to be given) when a more demanding schedule of reinforcement is imposed.

Actually, there are many other means of supporting or maintaining behavior besides reinforcement. Pavlov showed us one such method, for instance—the UCS. In Chapter 3, I alluded vaguely to a whole host of such devices when Dimension MOT was introduced. As I think of the term, "motivation" refers to any technique for increasing the frequency or efficiency of any R's that do not directly involve training (i.e., pairings of the R with an X). Learning psychologists are just beginning to appreciate the variety of ways in which behavior can be manipulated.

Given an operant response of some strength, however, its manipulation is quite an easy thing via intermittent reinforcement scheduling. The particular frequency and pattern of a schedule used will produce highly predictable results. The evidence for this assertion comes from many experiments and many species. The effects of noncontinuous reinforcement are similar to the results of Pavlovian conditioning in their constancy throughout a wide section of the animal kingdom that has been studied in life science laboratories. This can best be illustrated by a quotation from that great student of operant learning, B. F. Skinner:

. . . Figure [12] shows tracings of three curves which report behavior in response to a multiple fixed-interval, fixed-ratio schedule. The hatches mark reinforcements. Separating them in some cases are short, steep lines showing a high constant rate on a fixed-ratio schedule, and, in others, somewhat longer "scallops" showing a smooth acceleration as the organ-

FIGURE 12

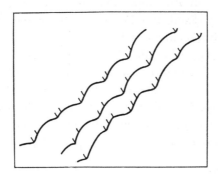

ism shifts from a very low rate just after reinforcement to a higher rate at the end of the fixed interval. The values of the intervals and ratios, the states of deprivation, and the exposures to the schedules were different in the three cases, but except for these details the curves are quite similar. Now, one of them was made by a *pigeon* in some experiments by Ferster and me, one was made by a *rat* in an experiment on anoxia by Lohr, and the third was made by a *monkey* in Karl Pribram's laboratory at the Hartford Institute. Pigeon, rat, monkey, which is which? It doesn't matter. Of course, these three species have behavioral repertoires which are as different as their anatomies. But once you have allowed for differences in the ways in which they make contact with the environment, and in the ways in which they act upon the environment, what remains of their behavior shows astonishingly similar properties. Mice, cats, dogs, and human children could have added other curves to this figure. And when organisms which differ as widely as this nevertheless show similar properties of behavior, differences between members of the same species may be viewed more hopefully. Difficult problems of idiosyncrasy or individuality will always arise as products of biological and cultural processes, but it is the very business of the experimental analysis of behavior to devise techniques which reduce their effects except when they are explicitly under investigation.

We are within reach of a science of the individual. . . . (250, pp. 230–31, italics in original).[1]

FREQUENCY OF REINFORCEMENT

"Frequency" means the number of times that X occurs. If reinforcement facilitates S-R stability, then it would seem to follow that the more often a habit is reinforced, the stronger that habit will be. This is true without important qualification up to a point. Obviously, for any fixed number of R_L occurrences, a continuous schedule of reinforcement will produce a higher frequency of X than will any other schedule. We saw in the preceding section that with prolonged training almost any other schedule is superior to a continuous one. It is this paradox that complicates the discussion of the role of frequency of X in learning. A device that will help partially to resolve this problem is to consider the problems of *habit acquisition* and *habit maintenance* separately.

Habit Acquisition

The acquisition of simple habits is another name for the events that were described and discussed at length in Chapter 1 in the process of developing a definition of learning. When we speak of acquisition, then, we are speaking of that early stage in a habit's history during which a transition is made from a rather unpredictable S-R relationship to a relatively stable relationship.

During acquisition, the role of X's frequency is simple: the more frequently S_L-R_L is reinforced, the less variable the performance of the habit becomes. A simple habit that has been reinforced twenty times is stronger than a simple habit that has only been rein-

---

[1] From the *American Psychologist*, vol. 11, pp. 230–31. Used by permission of the American Psychological Association.

forced ten times. This is true whether we define frequency in absolute or in relative terms.

The Asymptote

The absolute importance of frequency of reinforcement as a determinant of observed response strength seems to decrease as training progresses. In simple learning situations especially, every additional reinforcement produces a less noticeable strengthening of an S-R relationship than did the previous reinforcement. This effect is described in mathematical terminology as a negatively accelerated function (see Figure 13). The result of this relationship

FIGURE 13

Idealized Negatively Accelerated Learning Curves

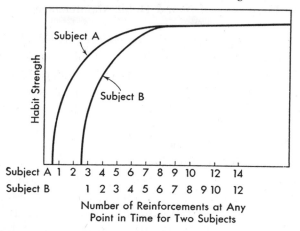

Subject A 1 2 3 4 5 6 7 8 9 10 12 14
Subject B   1 2 3 4 5 6 7 8 9 10 12

Number of Reinforcements at Any
Point in Time for Two Subjects

This indicates how frequency of reinforcement becomes increasingly unimportant as a determinant of differences in behavior, as the number of reinforcements increases. The graph shows habit strength as a negatively accelerated function of frequency of reinforcement, and is an idealized (extremely smoothed out) but not atypical representation of this relationship in simple operant learning situations. Early in training, the differences in numbers of X's at any given time are associated with measurable differences in the performances of the two subjects; later in training, however, only the most refined techniques of measurement might reveal any differences in the behavior of the subjects in the two groups.

is that two R's, both of which have been reinforced a large but quite unequal number of times, may not be measurably different in strength. This is shown schematically in Figure 13.

As the curves show, habit strength in simple learning situations is believed to increase by smaller and smaller amounts with each successive X. Theoretically, every X produces *some* gain in habit strength, no matter how many have been given. Such a curve is called *asymptotic*, and the point in training beyond which it is practically impossible to detect any further change in behavior from trial to trial is called the stage at which the subject has reached the asymptote. Asymptotic performance is quite often used as an indication that learning has occurred.

Frequency of X and Habit Maintenance

Habit maintenance refers to the procedures by which the post-asymptotic performance of a habit is controlled or manipulated. Beyond the asymptote, frequency effects are confounded by scheduling effects. The higher the frequency, the more closely any intermittent schedule approximates continuous reinforcement. But once a habit has been acquired, continuous reinforcement is no longer the most effective procedure for maintaining the habit.

Although it is still true that higher frequencies produce higher rates of responding, we have already seen that continuous X is *not* the limiting condition in this relationship. Any intermittent schedule maintains more stable responding than does continuous X, until the schedules begin to make the occurrence of reinforcement extremely rare relative to the occurrence of R_L. In other words, there is a relationship of frequency to post-asymptotic performance that is very generally like that schematized in Figure 14. That figure must necessarily be extremely vague about the exact relationship, because there are few empirical data bearing on it.

There are two studies that have some bearing on this problem. Brogden (36), working with dogs, and Michels (186), using rhesus monkeys, have reported that the ratios of 1:1, 1:2, 1:3, and 1:4 all produced about the same level of performance, and that all were superior to a 1:5 ratio or lower. This seems to contradict the hypothesis illustrated in Figure 14, but actually it only presents still another facet of the whole problem. Both Brogden and Michels arbitrarily presented the various ratios used to different subjects in different orders (i.e., determined by the conditions of their experimental designs, rather than the performance of their subjects; this

FIGURE 14

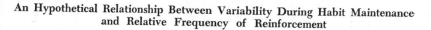

An Hypothetical Relationship Between Variability During Habit Maintenance and Relative Frequency of Reinforcement

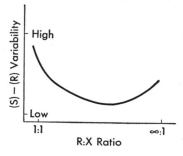

is quite a legitimate procedure which I am not criticizing as such). This is not the standard technique for establishing more and more stringent reinforcement schedules, as described in the preceding section. So these data may indicate that during the period of adjustment to a new schedule, the role of frequency of X is much like what it is during original acquisition (i.e., the higher the frequency the more rapid the rate of acquisition). It is not unreasonable to consider the early phases under a new schedule as being somewhat like original acquisition. This particular interpretation of the Brogden and Michels data is aided by the fact that in both experiments the amount of time a subject spent performing under any given schedule was not great, so pre-asymptotic performance effects could have been a large part of the summarized data they reported.

The relationship of the frequency of X to the various intermittent schedules will differ. The higher the frequency of reinforcement, of course, the less distinguishable will be the types of schedules; presumably, the exact point of equality will vary with the species and the previous learning situations in which an organism has been placed.

In summary, then, we start with the simple law that the greater the frequency of reinforcement, the more efficient is the establishment of an S-R sequence. Once a habit is established, however, the optimum frequency is not 1:1. Exactly what is the optimum frequency is not known, and it probably is complexly determined by many factors; the most obvious of such factors is the particular schedule being used in a given case. Finally, there is a possibility that shifting an organism from one schedule to another is somewhat akin to acquiring a new habit, so that during such transition periods, the role of frequency may be very similar to what it is during original acquisition.

DELAY OF REINFORCEMENT

Our descriptions of X have included the notion that a reinforcer affects the R that *immediately* precedes its occurrence. When the learner makes the response you wish him to learn, you must be very quick to administer the reinforcing agent. If you delay too long, what may happen? Clearly, the learner may make another R unlike R_L; if X is not presented until this has happened, then the chances are that this later response will be the one learned.

In general, any delays in reinforcement are a potential source of trouble, because the organism is *always* doing something unless it is unconscious, and so the presentation of a reinforcer at any time will reinforce *some* response. Reinforcement delayed too long beyond the occurrence of R_L is self-defeating. Not only will R_L not be reinforced, but some other, ensuing bit of behavior will be reinforced instead. This will make it even more difficult to strengthen R_L on subsequent trials.

Delays in reinforcement, then, affect the strength of a given habit indirectly, through the possibility that delayed reinforcement may strengthen an R other than the one that you are attempting to associate with S_L. In the extreme case, in fact, an entirely unexpected habit may develop. All this may seem self-evident on paper; nevertheless, you can find many instances in everyday life where people think they are teaching others to make one R, but are actually reinforcing another one. They are then confused or irritated when their children, pets, employees, or friends do not perform as they had hoped.

The concept of delayed reinforcement depends for its exact specification upon an explicit definition of response. As long as we use varying meanings for R—as discussed in Chapter 1—it is doubtful that any laws relating to inter-response interval and reinforcement can have much generality. Any exact statement of the duration of a delay interval hinges on the point in the occurrence of R at which we begin to time the R-X interval. The major problem, probably, is to decide upon what kinds of activity are irrelevant, i.e., not part of R_L.

A related problem is that of the definition of "immediately." Although we say that there must be some stimulus change immediately after R_L occurs, it is hard to state what "immediately" might mean in actual practice. Especially lacking is the study of delayed reinforcement when X is not a reward. This would be important information, because X_{rew}'s can be presented a measurable time after R_L has occurred, and still, under some circumstances, reinforce R_L. Quite possibly, this would not be true for all kinds of reinforcers. Or would it? We just don't know.

Learning with Delayed Reward

Learning is possible when rewards are delayed, because rewards have a characteristic not now known to be shared by other X's:

when other stimuli—S_n's—are associated with X_{rew}'s, these neutral stimuli acquire the characteristics of reinforcers. These stimuli, as you know, are called *secondary reinforcers* and are symbolized: S^r.

It was Spence (254), one of the best spokesmen of the Hullian position, who related S^r's to learning under delayed reward conditions. Essentially, his notion was that if there were an appreciable delay between R_L and X_{rew}, learning could not occur unless there were some systematic events that consistently filled the time between R_L and X_{rew}.

The events that Spence considered the most likely candidates to fill up a delayed reward interval were secondary reinforcers. Spence conjectured, in particular, that delayed reward learning only occurred when the circumstances of the learning situation made it possible to develop S^r's that would closely follow R_L. This, in effect, indirectly creates a situation in which a reinforcer—although not the one being manipulated by the experimenter or teacher—actually does follow R_L immediately; thus, there is really no longer a delay of all reinforcement. The role of X_{rew} here is to maintain the strength of the acquired reinforcer, and only indirectly to strengthen R_L itself. This interpretation has been supported by an experiment by Grice (93).

A classical study of the effects of different lengths of delayed reward was performed by Perin (206), who set the limit of delay for the rat in a bar-pressing situation at between 14 and 21 secs. Voeks (279), however, pointed out that in describing his procedure Perin had mentioned (in a footnote) that until he had begun the practice of withdrawing the lever following R_L, he had not been able to get learning with *any* delay of reward, no matter how short. Voeks felt that this supported the stimulus-change hypothesis about reinforcers, but we should note that Perin's early failure and his later success in getting some learning with brief delays (10 secs. or less) is also consistent with Spence's hypothesis that there must be some systematic event that follows R_L and precedes the delayed reward.

A final consideration in respect to delayed reward learning is this: the response that is to be associated with a given S_L by a delayed reinforcement procedure must have a fairly high probability of occurrence. Otherwise, it may undergo extinction (owing to nonreinforcement) before the developments described by Spence could begin to have an effect.

Verbalization and Delay of Reward

In human beings, delay of reward is commonplace, yet they learn a great many things. Presumably, Spence's analysis of delayed reward learning applies especially well to these instances in human behavior, because humans *do* have a remarkable capacity to transcend time via their use of symbols, especially self-produced symbols. Verbal cues may help to minimize the effects of delay in two ways:

(1) At the time R_L occurs, an adult human may reinforce himself by saying something to the effect that he has "done the right thing." For example, a person who has just repaired some machinery that can not be tested until sometime later, may say (to himself, or to someone else), "There! That oughta do 'er." Anyone who has watched a small child alone at play can not have failed to observe the amount of such self-reinforcement that is given vocally. Furthermore, if you watch the child when with its parents, the etiology of this mechanism is not hard to discern.

(2) At the time a delayed reward is finally presented, human beings are able to refer this event back to the appropriate R_L. A college student who is making poor grades in a course might try a new, more effective method of studying for it. The delay between using this method and the reward (an exam grade) is nearly always quite appreciable. Nevertheless, the student is capable of relating the two events by the use of language (e.g., "I studied my lecture notes more this time, and got a high B"), thus reinforcing behavior long after it has occurred.

These verbal, atemporal reinforcement techniques can not be relied upon excessively as effective learning devices. In the case of immediate self-reinforcement (example 1 above), there is always the risk that the responses the subject himself rewards are only accidentally related to the true R_L, or not related at all. In the process of "fixing" one part of the machinery, for instance, the mechanic in the illustration above may have moved some other part "out of the way," and, incidentally, into its correct place so that the machinery can work properly. In case 2 above, similar errors can be made, and another source of error may be in defining R_L, long after it has occurred, too ambiguously. It may be that the student above not only studied his lecture notes more than usual, he may have studied all his assignments more than usual. His perception of R_L, thus, is only partially accurate.

Changes in Delay of Reward

There are two basic methods for studying the effects of variations in reinforcement conditions, such as different delays.

(1) Subjects given one treatment are compared with subjects given another treatment. This might be called the *between-subjects* type of comparison. It is a way of evaluating the absolute effects of certain variations in X. It was this type of study on which the conclusions of the last section were based.

(2) The performance of subjects shifted from one treatment to another is examined under both conditions. These are *within-subjects* comparisons; they are the means of studying the differential or relative effects of a given reinforcement condition when it has been preceded by, or is alternated with another condition (all in relation to the same simple habit). These effects are quite important to study, because it frequently turns out that the absolute effect of some specific reinforcement condition is markedly modified by previous or concomitant experience with a somewhat different condition. It is to the relative effects of varying delays within subjects to which we now turn.

Actually, there have been two kinds of within-subjects studies of delayed reward. Somewhat different procedures have been employed for learning situations involving the single-R operant and those involving the many different R's case (see p. 78). Let us consider these separately.

Developing Tolerance for Delayed Reward

If we start a subject in an operant situation with no delay of X_{rew}, then progressively increase the length of the delay, we find that a given long delay does not have the same effect as when it is imposed suddenly. This was shown in an extensive series of studies by Ferster (74) with the pigeon. The pigeon was taught to peck a disk when the box was lighted; by keeping the box dark during the delay period and gradually increasing the delay period, pigeons could be trained to maintain a stable response rate even with delays of 60 secs. When the 60-sec. delay (plus "blackout") had been imposed immediately after no-delay training, all but one pigeon had rapidly ceased responding. Note that this method of developing a tolerance for delayed reward is in good accord with Spence's account of this phenomenon, and is also directly analogous to the techniques described earlier for establishing schedules of reinforcement under which reinforcement is very infrequent. For practical purposes it is quite useful to understand this method of going by very small steps from a time when reinforcement is consistent and immediate to a time when the same behavior can be maintained at a high level even though reinforcement is very infrequent or is delayed until long after the occurrence of the response. The changes in the persistence of behavior and the decreasing reliance on unfailing, immediate rewards for every action seem to be analogous to those behavioral changes that, in everyday life, we call "signs of increasing maturity."

One anomalous effect of shifting reward delay should be mentioned in concluding this section, although it needs more investigation. Harker (102) reported that starting rats, in a bar-pressing situation, on a 10-sec. delay and then reducing this delay to 1 sec. did not result in an improvement in performance. This seems odd at first, but may be due to the fact that any cues immediately following R_L may have become associated with irrelevant, interfering R's during the 10-sec. delay trials; reducing delay would only have the effect of strengthening these even more, thus preventing an improvement in bar-pressing.

Producing Delay by Interrupting an S-R Sequence

The alternative method of studying within-subjects changes in delay of reward involves, as I said, a somewhat different type of procedure. First, the subject is taught a series of responses that transport him from one point in space (the starting area) to another place where X_{rew} is given (the goal area). Delay is then introduced by artificially preventing the immediate occurrence of some part of this sequence of R's, as by physical restraint of the subject.

Holder, Marx, Holder, and Collier (113) showed, for example, that delay introduced in this manner had a *debilitating* effect upon later performance of that part of the R series leading *to* the place of delay, but a *facilitating* effect on the R's *from* the point of delay. That is, rats ran more slowly from the starting point to the delay point, but faster from this point to the goal than when not delayed. At present, the latter effect (facilitation of post-delay responses) is of questionable generality. For example, Amsel and his students have reported verifications of this effect, but Collier and Marx (52) have repeatedly failed to duplicate the results of their work with the Holders (113). The reason for the discrepancies in these researches is not now known.

The effect of delay of reward upon the R's preceding delay, however, is fairly consistent. Just as it is hard to establish an S-R relationship using delayed X_{rew} (see p. 160), so it is difficult to maintain an established habit if delay is introduced after learning has occurred. As with decreased amount of reward, there is usually a period of highly variable responding following the change—emotional behavior is often noted as the subject gets nearer the point in the R sequence at which delay is enforced (39, 40) and also during the delay period itself (84).

QUANTITY OF REWARD

X_{rew}'s, at least, can vary in amount. We can give one rat more food than we give another for performing the same R_L; we can give one person more money than another for the same task. Everyday experiences tell us that these will produce differences in behavior; experimental analysis, however, reveals that the relationship between behavioral differences and differences in X_{rew} amount are rather complex. The full extent of this complexity can not be seen until we have surveyed the more complicated kinds of learning situations that have been studied experimentally. Even the basic operant learning situation, however, reveals that the reward-quantity relationship to behavior is less than a simple one. The amount of X_{rew} does not influence the rate of learning, but is related to the characteristics of the R_L that is established.

Larger amounts of reward produce responses that are faster (56, 289, 298) or of greater magnitude (83) than do smaller amounts.

In none of the above cases, however, were there differences between the reward-amount groups in the number of reinforcements required to develop a relatively stable S-R relationship. Furthermore, Reynolds (223) failed to find differences in resistance to extinction in a simple operant situation, after subjects had been trained with different amounts of food as reinforcement. These facts have sometimes been used to support the argument that reinforcement and reward are not entirely synonymous; that X_{rew}'s have characteristics that do affect behavior, but that are not essential to the fact that they can serve as reinforcers.

Defining "Quantity of Reward"

Perhaps the apparent distinction just stated between reinforcing and nonreinforcing characteristics of X_{rew}'s is a spurious result of a vague definition of "quantity."

Food rewards, for example, have two independent dimensions of amount: (1) the *amount of nutritive material*, i.e., the amount of "biologically useful" material that a given amount of food provides for the organism's body, and (2) the *amount of consummatory activity*, i.e., the amount of manipulation of the reward object necessary to get it into the body.

An experiment by Wolfe and Kaplon (289) illustrates the reason for differentiating between amount of nutrition and amount of consummation. Three groups of baby chickens were taught to run along a straight path for corn. The chicks in one group received one-fourth of a whole kernel of corn per trial; in another group, one whole kernel was given, and in the third group a whole kernel cut into four pieces was given. Chickens get food into their stomachs by seizing a bit in their beaks, then tilting their heads and swallowing, so the first two groups (one-fourth vs. a whole kernel) provide a comparison of the nutritive effects of reward, with consummatory activity constant. As would be expected, the chicks that got a whole kernel eventually ran to the goal faster than did the chicks getting only a quarter of a kernel.

The comparison of the second and third groups is between amounts of consummatory activity per trial, with amount of nutrition constant. The chicks in the third group, who got one kernel in four pieces (requiring four swallows), ran fastest of all. Thus, the nutritive and consummatory dimensions of amount of reward can operate independently to influence behavior; along either dimension, however, the effect on behavior seems to be the same.

The generality of these dimensions is still uncertain, of course; whether all other rewards are similarly multi-dimensional remains for future research to determine. Even for food rewards, in the simple operant situation the amount of nutritive material and the amount of consummatory activity have typically been confounded in most amount-of-reward research. This has probably not made much difference in the conclusions arrived at.

Changes in Amount of Reward

Two investigators have reported what is now accepted as the classic experiment on the effects of shifts in reward amount (56, 289). In both experiments two groups of rats were trained to run in a straight alley, one group receiving a large amount of food, the other only a small amount. Then for half of the animals in each group the amount of reward was changed to the opposite amount. The results were quite striking. On the first few runs after the changes were made, those rats which were shifted from low to high amounts ran *faster* than did those rats which had been getting a large amount right along (recall that in a straight runway situation, rats getting a large reward will run faster than those receiving a small amount). Similarly, the rats which had their reward reduced from the larger amount ran *more slowly* on the first few trials than did those which had been given the small amount from the begin-

FIGURE 15

The Effects of Changing Amount of Reward

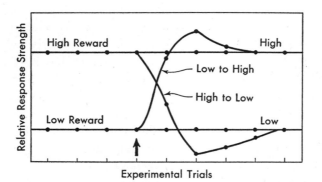

A schematic summary of the Crespi and the Zeaman experiments on the effects of altering the amount of reward for running down a runway for food. Originally, half of the subjects ran to high reward, half to low. Subsequently, half of the high reward subjects were given the low amount, and half of the low reward rats received the higher quantity. The point at which reward amounts were changed is indicated by the arrow. The solid lines beyond this point represent the changes in the behavior of the rats subjected to changes in the quantity of reward. The dotted lines indicate the (unchanging) behavior of the subjects who were continued on the old regimen.

ning. After a while, the performances of the rats in the experimental groups (amount of reward shifted) became indistinguishable from those of their comparable control groups (the groups getting the amounts to which the experimental animals had been shifted). These effects are summarized in Figure 15.

QUALITY OF REWARD

Although learning psychologists occasionally report studies in which they assert that they are varying "quality of reward," it is hard to give an inclusive definition of this term. The basic reason for this inadequacy is that the phrase, quality of reward, is redundant.

We saw in the last chapter that the definition of reward itself is relative, dependent on several factors. Now, the basic method used to determine quality of reward for any group of objects or events is to present a subject with a variety of such stimuli and observe (1) which is chosen by the subject most often, or (2) what proportion of the allotted time the subject spends in commerce with each. This is the very reason why not much research has been directed toward the relation of quality of reward to specific S-R relationships: *the strength of such relationships is exactly the way in which a reward's relative quality is determined in the first place.* Guttman (97), for instance, has shown that the rat's bar-pressing rate is curvilinearly related to the concentration of sucrose used as a reinforcer. As concentration increases, so does response rate— up to a point; for very sweet reinforcers, however, response rate declines. The concentrations that produce such a decline, interestingly, are just those that can be shown by more direct techniques (e.g., cafeteria feeding) to be less preferred by the rat.

One way of resolving this ambiguity would be to define reward in terms of operations other than organisms' preferences, leaving those for the definition of quality alone. Since some psychologists have for years sought without success for an absolute definition of reward, this solution seems more logical than practicable.

An alternative solution that seems to be growing in practice is to amalgamate the concepts of quantity and quality. This represents a marked advance in both sophistication and clarity. Traditionally, "quantity of reward" was reserved, in practice, for variations in some physical, X_{rew} dimension that produced monotonic changes in behavior, while "quality" was applied to objects or events that were not increasingly preferred as certain physical or chemical factors were increased. This is a very arbitrary limitation on the concept of quantity of reward. Quantity should, of course, refer to any physical dimension that can be measured; whether and how variations in these dimensions correlate with behavior variations is an empirical problem. As long as variations in quality, however, *are defined by* the correlation between behavioral variations and a conglomerate of physical and chemical changes, we will not find any relationships between X_{rew} quality and behavior that are not already inherent in our initial definition of X_{rew} quality.

Quantitative and qualitative definitions began to overlap when psychologists sought ways of varying nutritive value while holding consummatory activity constant for organisms with more complex eating mechanisms than the chicken has. Guttman described his work (97), just mentioned, as a study of the effects of a quantitative variation in sucrose concentration. Similarly, R. W. Reynolds (225) studied the effects of variations in the voltage of electrical stimulation of the type discovered by Olds to be rewarding (see p. 128). He not only found great individual differences in rats' responsiveness to various intensities, but he found a generally curvilinear relationship; up to a point, increases in voltage produced increases in response rate, but beyond that rate decreased as the voltage continued to be raised. So we are beginning to find physical dimensions of some reward objects that permit us to quantify them, but the quantification does not relate linearly to behavior; all such discoveries tend to blur the quantity-quality dichotomy of the past.

We understand as yet only a few of the conditions that may influence the relative acceptability of substances or other stimuli; Prof. P. T. Young (e.g., 295, 296) has probably devoted the most attention to this problem, and provided us with much of our present knowledge in this field. All in all, the most profitable and feasible trend in this area would seem to be an increasing amalgamation of the quantity and quality concepts. This will result, surely, in more complexity in the relationship between rewards and behavior, but complexity is not the antithesis of comprehensibility. This trend will also produce more objectivity in our treatments of rewards, and objectivity we *must* have in behavior science.

Single Shifts in Quality of Reward

The work of Guttman (97) and Reynolds (225) involved repeatedly altering the quality of the reward given a particular subject; this was done in accordance with good psychophysical procedure. Another type of within-subjects study of qualitative variation is analogous to that used by Crespi and Zeaman (see p. 169) in the quantity-of-reward context. A particularly clever example of this sort of study has been reported by Goodson, Scarborough, and Lewis (88).

Goodson's experiment consisted in training rats to run to the right-hand side of a T-maze to obtain a mixture of bread and milk. (Bread and milk are foods that are highly preferred by the rat.) On some trials, however, no reward was available in the right-hand endbox. When this happened, the rat was supposed to go from the right-hand goal box to the left-hand one to get bread and milk. Thus, the rats learned two R's during training: (1) the strongest habit (reinforced on six out of every ten trials) was simply to go to the right-hand endbox and eat, but (2) if this box was empty, the rats were to go straight across the cross-piece of the T to the left box and eat there.

The first test trial was the crucial one. It consisted of placing a less-preferred food—a healthy, not unpalatable wet mash of standard laboratory food mixed in tap water—in the *right-hand* endbox. In comparison with a rat's regular laboratory diet, in fact, wet mash is itself a highly preferred food. The question is, how will subjects, which have learned the procedures described above, react to this change—a change of quality of reward? Goodson has consistently found that more than half of the rats in any given demonstration behaved as if *no reward* were present in the right-hand box, i.e., they went immediately to the left-hand box without even tasting the food available in the right-hand box (to which they always ran first, of course). Thus, wet mash in the right-hand goal box was responded to by most rats *as if it were no reward at all*. Demonstrations of this sort are frequently cited as evidence that rats and other nonverbal organisms can form "expectancies" which, in turn, determine their performance.

EFFECTS OF VARIATIONS IN X_{rew} ON Sr STRENGTH

Sr Strength and Reinforcement Schedules

In Chapter 4, I mentioned two major ways of associating S_n's with X_{rew}'s to develop a secondary reinforcer (p. 137), but only discussed one technique in detail. The second method, which involves the coincidental or noninstrumental relating of S_n to X_{rew}, has been analyzed by Saltzman (227).

Saltzman simply trained two groups of rats to run down a straight alley into a white endbox. Animals in one group (Group 100) found food in the box on every run, while animals in Group 50 found food in the box on only half of their runs (2:1 variable ratio). The number of runs was equal, thus the total number of pairings of white box and food was twice as great for Group 100 subjects. The S^r values (or strengths) established by these two procedures were compared by testing the animals in an apparatus and with a procedure that have already been described on pp. 84–85. Using this *new learning* method (as the technique is called), Saltzman found that the white box was an effective S^r for Group 50 subjects, but not for Group 100 subjects. Essentially the same results have been obtained when, after an identical training procedure, the *resistance-to-extinction* demonstration of S^r strength was tried (232).

In a nutshell, Saltzman has shown that S_n-X_{rew} pairings follow the same laws as do R_L-X_{rew} pairings: a noncontinuous schedule of X_{rew} presentations produces a stronger phenomenon (in one case an acquired reinforcer, in the other, a habit) than does continuous reinforcement, *even when the total number of X_{rew} occurrences is much less in the noncontinuous case.*

In the previous chapter I also mentioned that laboratory demonstrations of secondary reinforcers have usually fallen far short of showing the effectiveness that is attributed to analogous events in natural settings. Some studies by Kelleher (141, 142) point this up:

> In Exp. I, two chimpanzees were trained to lever-press on a 5-min. fixed-interval schedule of food reinforcement. They then learned to obtain food by inserting poker chips through a slot. Finally, they operated the lever on a 5-min. fixed-interval schedule of poker chip reinforcement. Poker chips could be exchanged for food at the end of each hour. Both animals initially responded at low rates and eventually ceased responding.
>
> In Exp. II, the animals were reconditioned, and then required to accumulate groups of poker chips before exchange. The size of the required group was gradually increased (2, 3, 4, 6, and 8 poker chips). The rates of responding were directly related to the temporal proximity of exchange for food at the first four groupings. However, responding became irregular when six tokens were required, and extinction occurred when eight tokens were required. (142, p. 575)

It is noteworthy, however, that what success Kelleher did have in controlling behavior by secondary reinforcement came when he used a technique we have already remarked upon twice previously in this chapter: moving by small increments from frequent, consistent presentations of reward to a more and more stringent fixed-ratio schedule of S^r-X_{rew} pairings. The effectiveness of this technique, when applied systematically, can not be overemphasized in this text.

Other Variations in X_{rew} and Sr Strength

Several studies are consistent in reporting that, using the between-subjects method of comparison, the quantity of the reward with which a stimulus is paired does not affect the S^r strength of that stimulus. This is true for the resistance-to-extinction method of testing S^r strength (97, 158), and also the new learning method (116, 158: Exp. II).

It has also been shown that any delay between the occurrence of S_n and of X_{rew} will prevent the development of S_n into a secondary reinforcer (232). Again just as with R-X relationships themselves, the frequency of S_n-X_{rew} pairings is directly related to the S^r strength that is developed (100); the standard reservations about the inter-action of frequency and scheduling of X_{rew} presentations probably apply to this statement, although this has not been studied directly.

SUMMARY

In this chapter five classes of R-X variations were introduced, and their effects on habit acquisition and maintenance examined. The five types of variations were: (1) schedules of reinforcement; (2) frequency of reinforcement; (3) delay of reinforcement; (4) quantity and (4a) quality of reward.

Our knowledge of reinforcement schedules is by far the greatest. We now know that extremely precise control can be exercised over the performance of habits by manipulating the schedule of rein-forcement. A summary principle is this: the more regular the schedule, the more irregular the performance, and vice versa.

All other things equal, the greater the number of times a response has been reinforced, the greater the strength of the habit concerned. However, the interaction of frequency effects with scheduling effects is quite complex and provides many exceptions to the pre-ceding statement. In general, the frequency principle is most ap-plicable to the early stages of habit acquisition; once a habit has been formed, scheduling effects predominate, although frequency will still influence the efficiency of performance.

Evidence is mounting that reinforcement is only effective when it is immediate. If there is any delay between the occurrence of R_L and what is being manipulated as the X in a given learning situation, there will be no habit formation unless some other event comes to mediate the delay between R_L and X. Rewards are par-ticularly likely to be effective when X must be delayed, because S's that occur immediately after R_L may, by association with X_{rew}, come to serve as secondary reinforcers. Human beings have an advantage over other species in delayed reward learning, because our use of language enables us to mitigate the effects of delays relatively easily.

There are still many methodological problems concerning the definitions of quantity and quality of reward, but one general rule does seem to be apparent from the research in this area: variations in the desirability of rewards (however this is ultimately defined) do not affect the rate of habit formation, but do markedly affect the speed or rate with which R_L will be performed.

There are two basic ways of comparing variations in delay, quantity, and quality: (1) different subjects may be given different treatments, or (2) the same subjects may be given different treatments at different times. The second method almost invariably produces differences in performance under the different R-X conditions, especially if the shift is from a good R-X relationship to a poorer one. The first method does not always produce differences in performance, especially in studies of quantity-of-reward effects.

One training procedure of extensive practical value is revealed over and over again when method 2 is used repeatedly. Subjects can be brought to tolerate (i.e., perform effectively despite) extremely long delays in reinforcement, or extremely infrequent occurrences of reinforcement, if they are started with immediate, consistent reinforcement and then gradually eased into more and more stringent conditions. Although no naive organism can learn even the simplest habit if we start training him with a 20:1 reinforcement ratio, or with a 60-sec. delay in X, he can eventually be brought to the point where he will continue to perform under such impoverished conditions.

Finally, it was seen that insofar as they have been studied, variations in S_n-X_{rew} relationships have identical effects on the effectiveness of the S^r developed as do the analogous R-X variations upon response strength.

SUPPLEMENTARY NOTES

Reinforcement Schedules and Human Behavior

As with Pavlovian conditioning, the phenomena that can be reproduced by careful reinforcement scheduling are not limited to a few species or to a few limited features of behavior. Some evidence for this was given in the quote from Skinner (p. 155). More objective evidence is to be had in a series of studies by J. G. Holland (114), who, using adult humans, was able to reproduce all the effects obtained with rats and pigeons. Holland did not even use a particularly powerful reinforcer; the subjects were simply asked to watch a dial and report whenever a pointer moved; the movements themselves were scheduled as the reinforcer. In order to see the dial, a subject had to illuminate it momentarily by pressing a switch; this was the response that was studied.

The effects of reinforcement schedules on human behavior are not, however, limited to very simple, routine tasks. Kanfer (137) has reported a study in which he was able to influence the range of guesses made by subjects in the autokinetic situation by means of reinforcement schedules, and the extent of such influence was directly related to the stringency of the fixed-ratio schedule used.

More Details about Reinforcement Schedules

Although I have repeatedly asserted that psychologists' knowledge of the effects of noncontinuous reinforcement is quite great, space limitations prevent an extensive review of the evidence for this assertion. The skeptical or inquisitive student would do well to check a definitive, technical work entitled *Schedules of Reinforcement,* by Ferster and Skinner (75), for more information on this topic.

Intermittent Reinforcement in Pavlovian Situations

It has often been asserted (e.g., 36, 226) that 100 per cent reinforcement produces more stable responding than does noncontinuous scheduling in a Pavlovian conditioning situation. The implication is that this reflects a basic difference between operant and Pavlovian learning. This does not necessarily follow at all, and such a conclusion reflects two types of misunderstanding about operant learning and reinforcement scheduling that I believe are worth taking the time to clear up.

First of all, it is not necessarily true that operant learning will proceed faster *from the beginning* under intermittent reinforcement

than under continuous. I repeatedly pointed out in this chapter that
we often begin the establishment of an operant habit by reinforcing
every occurrence of R_L. Then, as the habit becomes increasingly
stable, we proceed by small degrees of change at a time to a more
and more rigorous schedule. Thus, habit *acquisition* in both Pavlovian and operant learning develop in the same way, and what is
effective for one is effective for the other. This misunderstanding
comes, I believe, from the fact that studies of Pavlovian conditioning
in the United States rarely go beyond the acquisition stage; the
maintenance of a CR has not been much studied. There is, however, evidence that a CR can be effectively maintained under less
than 100 per cent reinforcement.

In some cases, it is true, an operant habit need not be continuously reinforced, even in the beginning. But when this is true we
invariably find that R_L already—for any of several reasons—occurs
fairly frequently in the presence of S_L even without any reinforcement. If a rat is not extremely frightened or extremely drowsy
when he is put into a runway, there is every reason to expect that
within a reasonably short time he will go from one end of it to the
other. In Pavlovian conditioning this is almost never true. We might
wait hours before a dog would salivate spontaneously while a
metronome was ticking; so, at first, every occurrence of S_n must
be accompanied by the occurrence of the UCS—and presumably X
as well—if a CR is to be established.

In summary, habit acquisition nearly always proceeds most
rapidly the more frequently R_L is reinforced. Only when the chance
occurrence of R_L is fairly high to begin with can we deviate much
from continuous reinforcement; because of the procedural differences in the two situations, R_L may occur rather often by chance in
an operant situation, but rarely (if ever) in Pavlovian cases. This
is the only way in which acquisition in the two situations may differ,
and even this difference is not sufficiently consistent to be treated
as a fundamental one.

SECTION II

*
*
*
*
*

THE INTERACTIONS
OF SIMPLE
HABITS

INTRODUCTION TO SECTION II

Simple Habits

The preceding five chapters were devoted to the principles of learning that derive from and/or apply to the most simple learning situations; simple, that is, from the subject's standpoint, as the procedures for producing these situations may be very complicated and ingenious indeed. The products of such situations I call *simple habits*.

The most general description of a simple learning situation is that it is one in which only one S-R sequence is being affected systematically, and one in which the following conditions apply:

(1) S_L is defined broadly, so that to say that S_L is absent is equivalent to saying that the subject is out of the learning situation, or

(2) S_L is a very specific feature of the environment, but care is taken to prevent the occurrence in the learning situation of stimuli at all similar to S_L.

An example of condition 1 would be the training of a rat to go from one end of a runway to the other; S_L *is* the runway, and, literally, is the learning situation itself as well. Voeks' study, described on p. 49, would be an example of condition 2; most of the events that constituted her CS were completely unlike any stimuli that might have occurred at random in her experimental situation.

Simple Habit Interactions

The study of simple habit situations has revealed principles of wide applicability, but they do not exhaust the list of rules that must currently be known in order to understand and control the behavior of organisms. There are many situations in which more than one habit is involved concurrently. The laboratory study of more complicated learning situations begins with a group of cases in which each of the specific S-R sequences involved is treated

181

much as it would be in a *simple* learning situation. Unlike simple situations, however, the formation of a given habit is affected by the fact that other habits are being, or have previously been, formed under similar conditions.

The phenomena now to be studied, therefore, are called *simple habit interactions*. The basic question with which we will be concerned in the next three chapters is, How does the acquisition of one, essentially simple habit affect the concomitant or subsequent acquisition of another (simple) habit?

SYMBOLS USED IN SECTION II

When we begin to consider the interrelationships among a variety of similar learning situations, standard English becomes quite cumbersome. I have, therefore, sought refuge in the use of symbols. Most of them have already been introduced, but used only sporadically so far. Now that they will be relied upon rather heavily, a brief review will be useful; concrete examples, however, are deferred until they become relevant in the text proper.

1. Stimulus Symbols

S_L: As always, the stimulus or stimulus-complex that is to be, or already has been, involved in some habit.

S_{L_1}, *etc.*: When more than one habit must be discussed in one context, the habits and their components (stimuli, responses, reinforcers) will each and all be differentiated by numerical subscripts. Thus, S_{L_1} is the stimulus component of Habit$_1$.

S'_L: Given that S_L is the stimulus factor in some habit, then S'_L (read, "S prime L") is a stimulus that is in some way similar to S_L. The concept of "similarity" is a tricky one that will be given much attention in Chapter 6; let us just accept the convention, however, of symbolizing any sort of similarity by affixing a prime (') to whatever symbol has already been introduced in a given discussion.

NoS_L: Whereas a prime indicates another event that can be classed as similar to a given event, the prefix *No* will always indicate the *nonoccurrence* of the event indicated. In learning situations this will usually be meaningful only when the indicated event has previously occurred under the conditions being discussed at a given time. NoS_L, then, would be used to indicate that a stimulus is not present at a time when, or place where, it has usually been present.

In short, S'_L and NoS_L represent different degrees of change in S_L. S'_L can be used for any degree of change along a dimension of stimuli similar to S_L. NoS_L is used to indicate the absence of S_L or anything similar to S_L; of course, when anything is absent, something else must be present, but it will be understood that this "something" is not similar to S_L.

2. Response and Reinforcement Symbols

The various means of describing the stimuli involved in learning situations also apply to the identification of the responses in those situations. Exactly the same relationship to R_L, for example, is indicated by the symbol R'_L as the event symbolized by S'_L has to S_L; similarly with NoR_L.

Besides X and NoX, the only symbolism used in connection with reinforcers will be occasional subscripts indicating the nature of the reinforcer more exactly; e.g., X_{rew}.

Habit Somewhat Redefined

To simplify the ensuing exposition, and to highlight the continuity of the various phases of learning. I wish to expand the definition of habit now. Let us consider the results of *any* systematic S-R-X to be a habit; in particular, the consistent recurrence of S-R-NoX will be considered a learning situation if it accompanies or follows the repeated occurrence of some other S-R-X sequence.

The material in this preview should become clearer as the reader progresses into the succeeding chapters. A review of this section is advisable after Chapter 6 has been completed.

CHAPTER 6

✳

✳

✳ SIMPLE HABIT INTERAC-
TIONS: I. DISCRIMINATION
LEARNING

One fundamental result of learning is an increase in the frequency or efficiency with which some R is performed in the presence of some S, but so far we have considered only techniques for enlarging the number of S's that will affect the behavior of organisms.

One of the first subtleties that both nature and psychologists introduce into learning situations is to demand a refinement of the stimulus or response components of a habit; most often, refinement in both are required simultaneously. *Stimulus refinement* means that the environmental conditions under which an R_L will be reinforced are being limited in their permissible variability relative to the conditions under which R_L *could* occur. For example, if we changed the rules so that a rat, who was formerly reinforced whenever he pressed the lever in a Skinner box, was now only reinforced when he pressed the lever while a light was on in the box, we would be "refining" the S_L for the lever-pressing habit. *Response refinement* is any case in which a general definition of R_L (such as many accomplishment definitions) is elaborated by imposing specific anatomical, temporal, mechanical or even purely arbitrary, formal requirements. If we were to decide to reinforce the rat only when he pressed the lever with his left forepaw, we would be "refining" R_L.

After describing the three basic types of discrimination learning situations, we shall consider the relationship of reinforcement variables to discrimination learning. Then we shall consider the stimulus variables involved in such situations, and finally we shall mention two other factors that affect discrimination learning.

THE BASIC TYPES OF DISCRIMINATION LEARNING

To discriminate means "to tell the difference between." Traditionally, psychologists have emphasized the laws governing the differentiation among stimuli as more important in the comprehension of behavior than R differentiation. Probably this has been because objective definitions of stimuli and means of manipulating them were available to psychologists due to the research of other scientists. Actually, the procedures by which an organism is taught to differentiate [1] among R's are so similar to those by which he discriminates S's that neither can be regarded as more basic.

Stimulus Differentiation

For pedagogical purposes, I prefer to treat this topic as if it consisted of two distinct subtypes. In actual practice the two are functionally indistinguishable.

The Discriminative Stimulus: S_L vs. NoS_L

Let us put a rat into a Skinner box in which there is a small light bulb just above the lever. Let us also decide, arbitrarily, that if the rat presses the lever when the light is on, he will be reinforced; when the light is off, no responses will be reinforced. We call the "light on" condition S_L, and indicate the "light off" case by NoS_L.

---

[1] Practice varies among psychologists regarding the use of the terms "discrimination" and "differentiation." Some reserve the former for distinctions among stimuli, and the latter for distinctions among responses; this usage is not always followed, however. As the development of this chapter will indicate, if I were to follow this usage I would need a third term as well to cover certain discrimination learning situations. Accordingly, I will use the terms as synonyms, adding qualifiers (or relying on the context) to indicate whether S and/or R factors are involved.

The most elementary form of stimulus-discrimination learning, then, can be respresented thus:

$$(1) \quad S_L\text{-}R_L\text{-}X$$

vs.

$$(2) \quad NoS_L\text{-}R_L\text{-}NoX$$

These describe the essentials of stimulus discrimination learning: (1) reinforce the desired response when certain stimuli are present; (2) when those stimuli are not present, but R_L can still occur, do not permit R_L to be reinforced. The outcome of this procedure will be a relative increase in the speed or rate of R_L when S_L is present, and a relative decline in R_L's performance when the NoS_L condition is in effect. Note that in both cases a fairly stable S-R relationship results; we can predict when R_L *will* occur, of course, but we can also make predictions about R_L in relation to NoS_L as well. This is why discrimination learning is being presented as a habit interaction situation; two S-R relatonships are being systematically affected concurrently.

S_L in the above situation is often called a *discriminative stimulus* (247), and this term will be used occasionally in this text as a synonym for an S_L that has been employed in a stimulus discrimination situation.

Everyday examples of even this simplest sort of discrimination are easy to find. The telephone bell is one; the mere presence of a telephone is not the critical determinant of whether a person will pick up the receiver or not. In fact, if we exclude for the moment the occurrence of those complex stimuli that are referred to by the phrase, "wanting to call up somebody," then we can safely predict that an adult will not lift a phone's receiver simply because he happens to be close enough to do so. Should the telephone bell begin ringing, however, then a person's behavior becomes highly predictable (especially if the person is alone); in our culture, there are few other stimuli that have such a powerful ability to interrupt almost any other ongoing activity (even sleeping, eating, bathing, and other quite rewarding behaviors). The effectiveness of this stimulus, however, is incidental to the point, which is that the silent telephone is NoS_L, the telephone bell is S_L, and R_L is a series of responses—approaching the phone, lifting the receiver to the ear, and saying something. The reinforcement? Someone's voice coming out of the receiver, obviously; if you doubt this, just observe how quickly R_L ceases to occur if a phone becomes afflicted by one of those mysterious maladies wherein it rings but no connection is made with another phone. Usually only two or three occurrences in rapid succession of hearing the dial tone will suffice to eliminate further responses to the bell for the moment.

Successive Discrimination: S_L vs. S'_L

Now let us replace the rat of the last laboratory example with a pigeon, and modify the apparatus accordingly. Most important, we put two lights above a plastic disk that the pigeon has learned to peck at in order to get food (a simple habit). One light is blue, the other red. Pigeons have good color vision, so we can impose the following rules: (1) When the blue light is on, pecking will be rewarded; (2) when the red light is on, pecking will not be rewarded. This situation can be symbolized thus:

$$S_L\text{-}R_L\text{-}X$$

vs.

$$S'_L\text{-}R_L\text{-}NoX$$

As previously stated, S'_L is a stimulus similar to S_L; in this example, the basis of similarity is a physical one—length of the light waves emitted by the two sources. The outcome will be exactly like that of the previous case. The occurrence of R_L will become stably related to the presence of the blue light, and become predictably reduced when the red light is on.

By carrying the telephone example above one step further, the present case can be incorporated, too. If the phone is on an old-fashioned party line, then all phones on the line ring no matter who is being called, but each phone has a different pattern of long and short sounds. Now the person not only does not respond to the silent phone, he also ignores it when it rings, unless it rings in a particular way.

The distinction between a discriminative stimulus situation and a successive discrimination situation is highly arbritrary. This distinction has been drawn only to illustrate the two forms that simple stimulus discrimination may take. We may ask the subject to differentiate between the presence and absence of some stimulus, or between two somewhat different instances of the same sort of stimulation. In either case, the learning procedures are identical.

Quite often, too, both types of discrimination will be required in the same situation. We can make our pigeon example identical to our party-line telephone anecdote by adding the condition of having both lights off at the same time and not reinforcing any pecks then. So stimulus discrimination situations as a group can be summarized by the following schema:

$$S_L\text{-}R_L\text{-}X$$

vs.

$$S'_L\text{-}R_L\text{-}NoX$$

and/or

$$NoS_L\text{-}R_L\text{-}NoX$$

The essentials of any stimulus differentiation problem are, then, the same: R_L—however defined and identified—is reinforced in the presence of some environmental events, but not others; S_L represents the favorable, or positive environmental condition(s), while S'_L and/or NoS_L indicate unfavorable conditions. Which of the latter symbols is appropriate depends upon the degree of similarity between S_L and any unfavorable (sometimes called negative) conditions. A general description of this dimension itself constitutes quite a conceptual *and* empirical problem that it will be best to sidestep until we have an overview of the whole range of discrimination learning situations.

Response Differentiation

Response differentiation is accomplished by exactly the same method as is used to effect successive stimulus discrimination: reinforce one response to certain stimuli, but do not reinforce other, very similar, responses if they occur in the presence of the same stimuli. In a manner analogous to our stimulus terminology, we speak here of R_L and R'_L. Schematically, response differentiation is represented by the following situations:

$$S_L\text{-}R_L\text{-}X$$

$$S_L\text{-}R'_L\text{-}NoX$$

As long as these differences in responding can be brought under "voluntary control," as it is often called, then the subject can be taught to make such differentiations.

Everyday examples of response differentiation are not hard to find. Anyone who drives a car has learned many differentiations with respect to responses made with the right foot, for instance. There is a certain speed with which one must exert a certain amount of pressure on the brake pedal in order to bring the car to a smooth stop at a prescribed spot. Too much or too little speed and/or pressure will not produce the desired result.

Exactly the same sort of situation can be reproduced in the laboratory with the rat. Usually the lever in the Skinner box is positioned so that it swings through a very small, constant arc when it is pushed by the rat, but Marx, Roberts, and I once built a box with a lever that could swing through an arc of 110° (described in 181a, pp. 99–102). With this apparatus we found that we could readily teach rats to move the lever through as much or as little of this arc as we had arbitrarily decided upon. All that was necessary was to fix the apparatus so that we could immediately and accurately tell just how much the rat moved the lever whenever he pressed it; then we simply released a food pellet whenever the rat moved the bar, say 40°, but not if he moved it more or less than this. Of course, if because of the size of a given rat or other

factors, a movement of just 40° was not a particularly common occurrence, we had to start such training by reinforcing responses
that were *close to,* although not exactly, 40°. This was simply to
insure against the animal giving up too quickly because of nonreinforcement. As training continued, however, more and more of the
animal's responses would be movements of, say, 30° to 50°, and as
this developed we became increasingly strict about the amplitude
we would reinforce.

Many other examples of the same kind of learning could be cited,
but it will suffice to mention just one more which will serve as a
transition to the next topic. I have already referred several times to
experiments with rats in which the T-maze was used; like the
Skinner box, this is a standard learning apparatus that is used to
study many kinds of operant learning (the T-maze, of course, is a
controlled operant learning situation [2]). If we do everything possible
to keep the stimuli both inside and outside of the maze as homogeneous as possible, and then reinforce the rat when it goes to the
right-hand goal box, but not when he goes to the left, this is a
response differentiation situation just like the ones previously described. That is to say, at the choice-point—S_L—one response, i.e.,
R_L (going right), will be reinforced, while R'_L (going left) will not
be. This spatial discrimination, as it is called, is quite easy to learn.

Simultaneous Discrimination Learning

The type of discrimination learning that has been studied most
can be illustrated by the following paradigm. Suppose that we de-
tach the arms of a T-maze, paint one arm white, the other black, and
the stem gray. Now, when the rat comes to the choice-point we can
confront him with this complex stimulus:

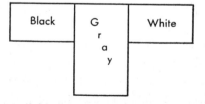

or this one:

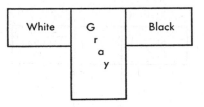

simply by switching the positions of the arms. We arbitrarily impose the rule that whenever the rat traverses the white alley he will be reinforced, but he will not get any reinforcement for running into the black alley. In the jargon of discrimination learning this is called "making white positive and black negative."

Simultaneous discrimination situations have traditionally been thought of as those in which both the correct and incorrect stimuli are present at the same time. Certainly our training since childhood has prepared most adult humans to conceptualize situations such as that above in terms of two alternatives being present at once. There is, however, another way in which many of the simultaneous problems set up in the laboratory *could* be solved, and there is evidence that unsophisticated learners *do* solve them that way sometimes. Let us consider first this case in which the subject need *not* treat the simultaneous problem as one involving both the positive and negative cues on each trial. I call this type *compound discrimination learning* because it involves a straightforward combination of the two kinds of discrimination problems already discussed.

Compound Discrimination Learning

Now, the *simplest* way to describe the black-white problem stated above is to say that "the rat learns always to go to the white side." But while "learning to go to the white" may be the *outcome* of the kind of training here described, it need not be the *original basis* of solution. Proceeding from the analysis of the simple spatial discrimination problem as a case of response differentiation, the most elementary analysis of the above discrimination situation would be to treat it as an instance in which successive discrimination is paired up with response differentiation.

The successive discrimination in a black-white T-maze is between S_L:

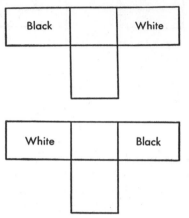

and S'_L:

The response differentiation is R_L—"going to the right"—vs. R'_L —"going to the left." If reinforcement ensues when events S_L and R_L occur together, and similarly when events S'_L and R'_L coincide, the outcome will be a subject *who acts as if* he "knows that white is right."

Since there is still much disagreement about the bases for distinguishing between this and the next subtype of the general class under discussion, it would be futile to present everyday illustrations before discussing the alternative case. So let us proceed to it directly.

"True" Simultaneous Discrimination Learning

The alternative interpretation of simultaneous discrimination situations starts with the assumption that the subject initially attacks a new problem by differentiating among the various features of the given environment; another form of this assumption is that, however a subject perceives the learning situation in the beginning, he *is* differentiating it pretty much the same way as the teacher does by the time he reaches the solution of the problem.

The seemingly critical test of these opposing analyses of simultaneous discrimination learning would be to teach the subject to differentiate S_L and S'_L by the simultaneous procedure, then juxtapose S_L with a variety of other S_L's, and see whether the subject continued to respond consistently to S_L in these new contexts. As a group, the specific, laboratory attempts to meet those conditions have produced ambiguous results. As with most such "either-or" controversies in psychology, the empirical method has been unable to resolve the matter unequivocally in favor of either extreme. On the one hand, we know that verbal subjects do make very subtle distinctions among the features of a given environment. On the other hand, many presumed simultaneous discriminations *could* be solved without the use of an intra-trial differentiation of S_L and S'_L.

Thus, it is not being asserted that organisms can not learn to analyze a complex environment into simpler elements; I hope that this book itself will stand as a refutation of this point. Rather, it is being asserted that discrimination learning is part of the *means* by which such analyses eventually become characteristic of sophisticated learners.

Whether a relatively unsophisticated subject perceives a novel stimulus complex as a whole, or sees it as a conglomerate of distinct elements, probably depends upon a number of factors. The organism's anatomy, particularly the sensitivity of receptors, would affect this; so would the specific composition of the environmental stimuli at the moment in question (some might tend to be more "naturally differentiable" than others). Perceptual tendencies, to use a vague term, are themselves believed to be affected by learning; to put this more objectively, much of the behavior that is presumed to reflect perceptual processes is also known to be markedly influenced by learning experiences. In the next chapter we shall see some very important examples of this. I bring this matter up now in order to emphasize the fact that the discovery of the fundamental basis of discrimination problem solutions is hampered by the circularity of the empirical problem involved. When we use learning to infer the presence or absence of some factor that is presumed both to underlie and to be influenced by learning, how can we answer questions about this factor? It seems necessary to ask, under what conditions does learning proceed by the compound technique, and when does the "true" simultaneous method come into operation?

There is little systematic evidence available on this point, since the problem has rarely been approached in this way.

REINFORCEMENT FACTORS AND
DISCRIMINATION LEARNING

We have already seen that with both stimulus and response conditions constant from trial to trial, there are a number of variations in X that may be introduced. Let us now turn to the intricacies that occur in behavior by varying all three of these dimensions at once. Again, of course, we shall find ourselves talking about X_{rew}'s exclusively, because so far these are the only kinds of reinforcers that have been studied systematically.

Experience with Reward as a Determinant of
Reward-Amount Effects

Visual discrimination learning in the rat, at least, does not seem to be fundamentally related to the amount of reward obtained for correct choices, as long as incorrect choices are followed by no reinforcement at all (159, 221). Even complex response differentiation problems—such as those requiring a sequence of right and left turns prior to reward—also do not appear to be affected by the amount of reward forthcoming (81), although performance in the simple spatial learning situation is so affected (222).[3]

If, however, the *same* subjects are given a number of discrimination problems, for each of which a different amount of reward is used as X, the accuracy of performance on such problems will eventually become directly related to the amount of reward received for correct R's on the different problems. This has been shown for rats (159) and monkeys (185, 234). It is as if an organism must

[3] We must always view negative results (i.e., no relationship between an independent and a dependent variable) with skepticism. Recent research from the laboratories at the University of Wisconsin (233) and the Ohio State University (32, 161) bring the facts of this paragraph into doubt. At this time, however, it is too soon to tell how these findings alter the hypotheses about amount-of-reward effects that are discussed next.

first learn that different amounts of reward are forthcoming in different situations before the response strengths in these situations will differ.

In one of Crespi's experiments on the effects of amount of reward (see p. 168), he noted that rats, *continually* run under small reward conditions for a long time, eventually showed agitated, or emotional behavior just as did those *shifted* from large to small amounts. On the other hand, Zeaman, who repeated the seemingly essential details of Crespi's work, did not report such effects. It may be important that Zeaman used processed cheese as the reward, while Crespi used prepared laboratory-type food. Conceivably, Crespi's low-amount-of-reward rats developed, over a period of time, a rudimentary basis of comparison between the amounts of food available after a run and the amounts available during maintenance feeding in their home cages. Since cheese is rarely included in a laboratory rat's regular diet, Zeaman's rats would not have had the same opportunity for developing a subjective scale of amounts for their particular reward. Speculative as this may be, research does indicate that a subject must have fairly specific experiences with different amounts of reward before he will show differentiable behaviors in most situations using different amounts. Such experiences need not be in an experimental situation. Even experimental subjects must eat, and the eating arrangements may provide the occasion for learning habits (owing to food reinforcement) that could affect some experimental outcomes. Systematic studies of such possibilities have not been reported often enough to provide a basis for a generalization.

Sr Strength and Amount of Reward

When different subjects have an S_n associated with different amounts of X_{rew}, experimenters (116, 158) have repeatedly failed to demonstrate that a secondary reinforcer varies in effectiveness as a function of the magnitude of X_{rew} with which it was originally paired. More recently, however, D'Amato (57) and Powell and Perkins (214) have shown that S^r strength *is* related to amount of X_{rew}, under the following conditions: (1) two neutral stimuli—

S_{n_1} and S_{n_2}—are associated with different amounts of reward, e.g.:

$$S_{n_1}\text{-}X_{rew}(\text{large}) = S^r_{lrg}$$

$$S_{n_2}\text{-}X_{rew}(\text{small}) = S^r_{sml}$$

and (2) at the time of the test for relative S^r strength, both secondary reinforcers are present, and they follow incompatible responses.

As a specific example, D'Amato (57) associated endboxes—S_n's —that differed in color (literally brightness, since one was black, one white) with different amounts of food X_{rew}'s; his subjects were rats. After association with different X_{rew}'s, the boxes' secondary reinforcing strengths were tested by the Saltzman technique (see pp. 84–85). For half of the subjects, he placed S^r_{lrg} at both ends of a T-maze for a subject's first trial; whichever way a rat in this group went, his choice was then followed by entry into S^r_{lrg}. For all remaining trials, S^r_{sml} was placed at the end of the alley that these rats had *not* chosen. For the other half of the subjects, S^r_{sml} was in both places on trial 1, and S^r_{lrg} then placed on the side not chosen. This was an ingenious way of controlling for the fact that rats have turning preferences much like handedness tendencies in people. Altogether, the subjects in D'Amato's study had fourteen trials with S^r_{lrg} at the end of one alley, and S^r_{sml} at the end of the other. Curtains prevented the rats from seeing the endboxes until *after* they had made their choices. The rats as a group showed a significant tendency to turn most often toward the alley leading to the S^r_{lrg} endbox.

In short, the preceding survey boils down to two vague statements: (1) Sometimes the acquisition of habits is affected by the amount of reward forthcoming, but not always; (2) sometimes secondary reinforcers vary in strength according to the amount of primary reward used in their establishment, but not always. The parallels and interrelationships between the findings of these two research topics are especially intriguing to those psychologists who are inclined toward a strict stimulus-response account of the phenomena of learning. One amount of reward can, according to such a view, affect the behavior that precedes it differently than would another amount of reward only if the subject responds differently to the different amounts. What kind of response could this be? Is it a response that itself only develops through learning? If so, what conditions accelerate its acquisition? What conditions facilitate its generalization? For these questions we now can offer only hypotheses, not factual answers.

Similar problems plague the whole area of secondary reinforcers. Pavlovian conditioning, which can be described operationally in terms of pairings of stimuli alone, seems amenable to an S-R description as well. Can the same be said for S^r establishment? Not with any certainty. When the enigmas of amount of reward and S^r development are juxtaposed, more questions are generated while none of the old ones are settled.

The effects of variations in reward-amount are *probably* due to learning, in most cases anyway; all the effects of S^r's, by definition of that term, are due to prior learning. Since it is so frequently useful (and often essential) to describe learning situations in terms of systematic changes in some aspect of behavior that occurs in the presence of S's and is followed by certain consequences, we are reluctant to reject this formulation in the treatment of the present topics. Yet it must be confessed that we can only guess as to the nature of the R's that are immediately involved in either the reward-differentiation or S^r-acquisition situations. Conceivably, no *particular* class of R's is related to either case, but even this has not been convincingly demonstrated.

Quality of Reward and Discrimination Learning

We have already seen (pp. 170–71) that the determination of qualitative differences in X_{rew}'s requires some form of discrimination situation. The subject must be able to show a preference for one consequence of responding over another. This is most easily done when different stimuli are associated (temporally or spatially) with the different consequences (and thus with the behavior leading to these). Since a discrimination learning situation is necessary to determine that different consequences of responding do indeed differ in quality (preference), we should naturally expect that discrimination learning should vary quite predictably with variations in the quality of the rewards that follow different S-R sequences. As I pointed out earlier, any experiment that has as its independent variable qualitative differences in X_{rew}'s, which differences have been independently determined by some other technique, is only a study of the validity (or generality) of this previous technique.

All is not trivia in this area, however. Just for the reasons reviewed above, the discrimination learning situation provides a quite sensitive means of evaluating the reinforcement value of events or conditions. By this method psychologists have established that some rather unconventional occurrences can be reinforcing. For instance, Butler (44, 45) and others in the University of Wisconsin Primate Laboratory (104) have demonstrated that the rhesus monkey will learn to solve mechanical puzzles or learn a visual discrimination problem when the only reinforcement for the correct R is the opportunity to manipulate the environment, or to examine it visually. In a follow-up study, Butler (45) examined the relative preference of monkeys for a variety of visual-auditory incentives. He found that monkeys most preferred to watch other monkeys—which is not surprising—but that they could also be enchanted for hours by the sound and movement of an electric train—which *is* rather unexpected. Barnes and Kish (20) have recently used a discrimination procedure to verify the reinforcing characteristics for the rat of small changes in illumination.

Conventionally, studies of quality effects have involved a *within-subjects* sort of design (p. 172). It is possible, of course, to give any subject only one of a group of rewards already known to vary in preferability, and look for differences in the performances of subjects given rewards of different quality. With children, at least, such differences are rather easy to obtain (265); more so, in fact, than would be predicted from our knowledge of the effects of varying amounts of reward in similar learning situations. This is only a further example of the complex relationships that various rewards may have with behavior.

Delay of X and Discrimination Learning

Delay of reinforcement should have the effect of making a discrimination problem more difficult, because the immediate consequences of R_L, R'_L, and NoR_L will be the same. In such a case, discrimination learning should proceed slowly, just as does simple learning with delayed reinforcement. Discrimination learning, by our method of analysis, anyway, basically amounts to the interaction of a number of potential habits; one of these habits—the correct one —is itself a simple habit. The effect of delayed reinforcement on simple habits is known, and this should enable us to predict the effect of delayed X in discrimination learning. Indeed, it does, as Perkins, Banks and Calvin (209) have shown for both successive and simultaneous discriminations; there is little reason to believe that response differentiation would show any different effect.

The study of delayed X in discrimination illuminates both of these phenomena somewhat. We have already noted Grice's study (p. 162) in which he verified Spence's hypothesis about the factor that made possible learning with delayed reward; this definitive study was most efficiently conducted by using a discrimination situation (in which the difficulty of different simple learning situations could most easily be controlled). Essentially the same design was used by Grice and Goldman (94) to verify the Pavlovian assertion that inhibition could generalize just as excitation (or secondary reinforcement) could, and also to suggest that the development of discrimination learning is importantly influenced by the generalization of inhibition. Thus, the combination of delay of X and a simultaneous discrimination learning problem tells us a little more about both of these phenomena and the bases of their effects on behavior.

The Relative Influence of Nonreinforcement vs. Reinforcement

Every discrimination situation involves some occasions on which R_L occurs and is reinforced, and other occasions on which R_L (or R'_L) occurs and is not reinforced. Many times it might be possible to pretrain the subject with respect to one of the stimulus conditions that will later be involved in the discrimation problem. If so, on which stimulus condition would pretraining be most effective; should we expose the subject to

$$S_L\text{-}R_L\text{-}X, \text{ or to}$$

$$S'_L/\text{No}S_L\text{-}R_L\text{-}\text{No}X?$$

This problem is that of comparing the effects of reinforced and non-reinforced pretraining; would we most speed up the actual discrimination learning by first strengthening the right habit, or by weakening the wrong one?

The previous discussions of the generalization of inhibitory and excitatory tendencies should enable you to anticipate what we find here. When we give the subject repeated experiences with

$$S_L\text{-}R_L\text{-}X,$$

we *increase* the tendency for the subject to make R_L in the presence of stimuli similar to S_L; when we repeat the sequence,

$$\text{No}S_L \text{ or } S'_L\text{-}R_L\text{-}\text{No}X,$$

we *decrease* the tendency for R_L to occur when S_L is present. The latter of these effects, however, is not as marked as the former. As a result, by presenting $\text{No}S_L\text{-}R_L\text{-}\text{No}X$ we may be able to establish the relationship,

$$\text{No}S_L\text{-}\text{No}R_L,$$

without also establishing too strongly the undesirable habit,

$$S_L\text{-}\text{No}R_L,$$

which is undesirable because it will impede our ability to carry out the later training procedure of

$$S_L\text{-}R_L\text{-}X.$$

On the other hand, if the pretraining procedure emphasizes positive training, and builds up the habit,

$$S_L\text{-}R_L,$$

it also builds up the soon-to-be-undesirable habit,

$$NoS_L \text{ or } S'_L\text{-}R_L,$$

which is undesirable because it will slow down the effectiveness of the procedure,

$$NoS_L\text{-}R_L\text{-}NoX,$$

when the full discrimination training procedure goes into effect.

That pretraining on the negative condition is more efficacious for the ultimate and rapid success of discrimination training than pretraining on the positive condition has been verified several times (12, 26, 62, 78). If the number of S_L-R_L-X trials is held constant, speed of discrimination learning can be shown to be a function of the number of NoS_L-R_L-NoX occurrences, or the number of S_L-R'_L-NoX occurrences.

Thus, if there is a choice, it seems best to overemphasize the incorrect S-R events in training a subject to master a discrimination problem. Unfortunately, this generalization—if accurate—runs against the grain of some current educational theories; this is because nonreinforcement, as we shall see in Chapter 8, can produce emotional behavior of its own that may also be undesirable. In the long run, these emotional side-effects may interfere with efficient learning just as much or more than if we keep the X/NoX ratio high. Another practical danger in forcing the subject to experience many instances of the negative sequences in a discrimination problem is that we may continue this too long; eventually, nonreinforcement leads to the extinction of R. If extinction occurs to NoS_L and generalizes to S_L, then subsequent discrimination learning will occur slowly, if at all. For if the subject will not make R_L, we can not make it a part of any habit of his.

Schedules of Reinforcement and Discrimination

We have so far considered only discrimination learning cases that offer continuous reinforcement of the correct response. No more than in simple learning situations, however, is continuous reinforcement of a correct response necessary for learning with differential stimulus conditions. Just as in simple learning situations, it takes somewhat longer to establish a discrimination with less than 100 per cent reinforcement of S_L-R_L, but the same basic rule applies: As long as the appropriate stimulus-response relationship is rewarded at all, learning will eventually take place. This has been shown, for instance, by Goss and Rabaioli (89). They reported that it required the following mean numbers of trials to reach a criterion of fifteen out of sixteen correct responses in a complex successive discrimination situation for groups given 100 per cent, 75 per cent, and 50 per cent reinforcement for correct responses, respectively: 22.3, 35.4, and 42.4. At present, no definitive comparison using traditional statistical methods has been made of the degrees of variability during maintenance, or of the relative resistance to extinction of discrimination habits formed under various schedules of reinforcement.

Secondary Reinforcement and Discrimination Learning

Earlier in this chapter I suggested that many psychologists were willing to assume that S^r establishment must, in the final analysis, be an instance of stimulus-response learning, but that this assumption was rooted more in faith than fact. This is not entirely accurate. There is an impressive body of indirect evidence that S^r establishment follows all the important laws governing the acquisition of operant habits. One case in point is the similarity in the procedures necessary to establish a discriminative stimulus and those involved in developing a secondary reinforcer.

By adhering to the S-R-X model in the case of even the simplest operants, I have emphasized the fact that all responding (and thus all learning) occurs in the presence of environmental conditions (stimuli). What these stimuli are, their similarity to other S's, and so forth may or may not be particularly related to the R-X contingencies that obtain in a given situation. While stimuli *may* have some influence on behavior even when the reinforcement contingencies are rather independent of the stimulus conditions, true stimulus control of behavior is only achieved by the techniques of discrimination learning.

Now, secondary reinforcement is clearly a case of the stimulus control of behavior. While it is a sort of control that is only apparent when the stimulus *follows*, rather than precedes, the R being controlled, many psychologists began, in the 1930's, to suspect that this was not an important difference. It was postulated that an originally neutral stimulus derived its reinforcing characteristics by the same procedures that could be used to make that stimulus the occasion for discriminated operant responding.

In a now classic study, Dinsmoor (65) demonstrated the validity of this hypothesis. Dinsmoor did this in a very direct fashion: he first developed an S_L by the successive discrimination method, then he showed that if this stimulus was now arranged so that it *followed* R_L, instead of the other way around, the response was more resistant to extinction than without this consequence. Dinsmoor produced this effect in a free operant (bar-pressing) situation; Webb (283) has verified it in a controlled operant case.

STIMULUS FACTORS AND DISCRIMINATION LEARNING

Similarity

The conditions that make discrimination learning proceed faster or slower are generally considered to be stimulus factors. Traditionally, two views have prevailed: (1) The similarity of the stimuli involved is inversely related to the ease of learning a discrimination, or (2) the relative strengths of the responses to the S's involved may influence the rate of discrimination learning.

A complication arises in that the two views are not completely distinguishable. "Similarity of stimuli" can only be meaningfully defined in terms of behavior. Similar stimuli are those that are associated with similar, or indistiguishable, responses. Therefore, the two approaches above reduce to one: *The more equal is the association of R_L with S_L, S'_L, and/or NoS_L at the start of a discrimination training series, the more difficult will discrimination learning be.*

But the above is really no answer, only the beginning of one. We must now consider the ways in which it is possible to vary the equality of the strengths of the relationships,

$$S_L\text{-}R_L,$$

$$S'_L\text{-}R_L, \text{ and/or}$$

$$NoS_L\text{-}R_L.$$

Basically, there are two processes by which these relationships can be made more similar. First, *physical* similarity among stimuli produces similarity in responses. Second, stimuli quite disparate physically can be made *functionally* equivalent by reinforcing R_L equally, and on the same schedule, in the presence of these S's.

In examining these two processes in further detail we shall not only see some of the problems involved in concrete discrimination learning situations, but also see some of the conceptual, or theoretical, problems involved in relating the data of simple learning to those of more complex situations. This subject also leads directly to the next major type of complex habit interaction.

Physical or "Unlearned" Stimulus Similarity

All other things equal, there is a correlation between the tendency of a response to be made to different stimuli and the physical similarity of such S's. This assumes that there is *some* basis for a tendency to make a response in the first place. The basis is *stimulus generalization,* the phenomenon first identified by Pavlov.

A particularly interesting study of stimulus generalization in an operant situation has been reported by Guttman and Kalish (99). They trained pigeons to respond (by pecking a disk) to a given wave-length (color) of light; different pigeons were trained with different S_L's. NoS_L was not reinforced during their original training. Now, this sort of training of the very easily elicited pecking response produces an extremely persistent level of such responding. As a result, it was possible for Guttman and Kalish to run their birds through a series of extinction series using several wave-lengths other than the ones on which they had been trained. Effects of taking stimuli of different degrees of physical difference from S_L in any particular order of presentation, and similarly obvious variables, were controlled for. The results are summarized in Figure 16. This figure shows the degree of generalization (i.e., the frequency of responding without reinforcement) to stimuli of different degrees of dissimilarity. As the figure shows clearly, there is a correlation between the rate of responding and the physical similarity of training and test stimuli.

FIGURE 16

Stimulus Generalization in Operant Learning: Response Rates to Wave-Lengths of Different Amounts of Variation from That Used as S_L

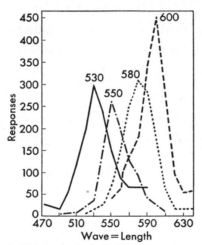

From Guttman and Kalish (99), in the *Journal of Experimental Psychology*, vol. 51, p. 83. Used by permission of the American Psychological Association.

The simplest summary of the stimulus generalization phenomenon is that the establishment of only *one* S-R relationship by simple learning techniques is practically impossible. If an S can be placed on some physical dimension, the establishment of one S-R relationship automatically establishes *other* S-R relationships in which (1) the S's are physically similar to the S_L used during training, and (2) the R's are identical to R_L except in their strengths (i.e., in resistance to extinction, stability, amplitude, and so on).

These effects, of course, are antithetical to those of the discrimination process. Because he found that after conditioning an animal to one CS this subject would make something like the CR to similar stimuli, Pavlov has been interpreted as concluding that *generalization precedes discrimination*. Thus, the Americans influenced by Pavlov have often treated discrimination as the breaking down, or reversal, of the effects of stimulus generalization.

In a crude way it is true that discrimination is the reversal of the generalization phenomenon. The traditional acceptance of this viewpoint, however, has usually carried the further implication that generalization along physical dimensions was the most important, or most basic, form of such generalization.

This can not conceivably be "true," nor can any other broad generalization about the nature of generalization. For one thing, there is no "basic" method for observing generalization occurrences (208).

A generalization test can not occur in a vacuum. As Guttman (98) has pointed out, the classical definitions of generalization could only be tested by hinging everything on one post-training trial. This demands a degree of control of which most contemporary psychological techniques are not capable. Nor is such a test representative of most situations in which the influence of the operation of stimulus generalization may justifiably be inferred. Actually, there are several ways of demonstrating experimentally the effects of generalization. There is the Guttman-Kalish method in which resistance to extinction under various S'_L conditions is the dependent variable. Generalization effects may also be evaluated by observing the acquisition of a habit that involves some S' that is measurably similar to some earlier S_L to which the associated R was somehow different from the current R_L. An example of the effective use of this method is found in a study by Spiker (258).

Spiker presented two stimuli interchangeably; the task of the subjects (preschool children) was to learn which of three switches on an instrument panel should be operated in the presence of each of the stimuli (which were lights of different colors). One switch was never correct, and each of the other two was correct for only one of the lights. This is essentially an instance of Simultaneous Discrimination, Compound Type. Thus, in our terms, the following habit-formation situations were possible in connection with S_L:

$$S_L\text{-}R_L\text{-}X,$$

$$S_L\text{-}R'_L\text{-NoX, and}$$

$$S_L\text{-}R_{neg}\text{-NoX.}$$

For S'_L—the other of the two lights—R'_L would be reinforced, and R_L and R_{neg}—pressing the button that was always incorrect—would not. In the terminology of Chapter 3, the reinforcement here was Acquired, Not Pertinent; correct responses were followed by the presentation of a marble, and each child had been told that if he earned enough marbles in the game, he could exchange them for a toy.

The independent variable in this experiment was the similarity in wave-length of S_L and S'_L. The various pairs of colors used in the different groups are listed in Table III in order of decreasing

TABLE III

Similarity of S_L and S'_L as a Determinant of Relevant and Irrelevant Errors in a Simultaneous Discrimination Situation

Stimuli to which Different R's Were to be Learned		Number of Subjects	Mean Relevant Errors	Mean Irrelevant Errors	Mean Total Errors
S	S'				
Yellow-green	Green	25	21.48	7.44	28.92
Yellow-green	Blue-green	22	17.64	6.95	24.59
Yellow-green	Deep Blue	18	6.44	3.28	9.72
All Subjects Combined		65	16.02	6.12	

Adapted from Spiker (258, p. 394); see text for further explanation. *From the Journal of Experimental Psychology,* vol. 51, p. 394. Used by permission of the American Psychological Association.

similarity between pairs. Table III also shows the numbers of errors associated with each degree of similarity; errors involving the occurrence of the response that would have been reinforced in the presence of the other light (called Relevant Errors) are separated from errors due to the occurrence of R_{neg} (Irrelevant Errors).

In Spiker's words, these data revealed that ". . . with increasing stimulus similarity, there is an increase in the magnitude of the difference between the mean frequencies of the two types of error." (258, p. 394) In other words, as stimulus similarity increased, Relevant Errors increased more rapidly than Irrelevant Errors.

The effect of nonreinforcement generalizes less than the effect of reinforcement of a response. So the tendency to make R_{neg} is changed less by increasing the similarity of the two S_L's than is the tendency to confuse (i.e., generalize) the two R_L's.

Physical Similarity as a Basic Discrimination Variable

Since the physical description of stimuli is the most objective way to describe them, the attempts by psychologists to find relationships between behavior and the physical characteristics of stimuli are quite understandable. Nor have such attempts been unprofitable; some of the most highly refined psychological data are to be found in the area of sensation and perception. And we do find numerous instances in which the behavioral changes that we call "learning" proceed differently, or result in different outcomes, according to the physical features of S's. Despite their separate successes in establishing such correlations, however, a fundamental rapprochement between the fields of learning and sensory psychology has not yet been achieved.

Even when behavioral phenomena that characterize generalization, discrimination learning, and sensory discrimination can all be related to physical similarities or differences in S's, the relationships between these behavioral phenomena themselves appear to be quite unstable. To support this assertion, I need only mention some additional features of the experimental results obtained by Guttman and Kalish and by Spiker; these studies, of course, have just been cited to exemplify the control exerted over learning by physical variations in stimulation.

Guttman and Kalish found essentially the same sort of generalization gradients (as the curves of Figure 16 are often called) for stimuli in the vicinity of a number of different S_L's. It is known, however, that the pigeon *does not discriminate equally well between S's in all the regions of the spectrum studied by Guttman and Kalish* (see 101).

Here is the first anomaly: pigeons generalize to easily discriminated stimuli in almost exactly the same way that they generalize to stimuli that are hard to differentiate. Certainly, these findings do not uphold a theory of discrimination as the breaking down, or the reversal, of generalization.

On the other hand, Spiker pointed out, while describing the pairs of stimuli that he used in his experiment, "The stimuli in each pair [see Table III] are readily discriminated by adults with normal color vision." (258, p. 393) True, Spiker's subjects were not adults, but this can not entirely explain the fact that all his measures of errors showed that greater physical similarity between S_L's was associated with greater difficulty in learning the appropriate R_L's.

This is the second anomaly: even when subjects can readily differentiate between certain S's, the physical similarity of these S's is negatively correlated with the ease of learning a new response differentiation involving these S's.

The reason for this discrepancy is not entirely clear at present. Quite possibly there are some basic differences in the questions that we are asking our subjects when we test their generalization tendencies, as opposed to when we test their discrimination abilities. Certainly the S-R-X contingencies that prevail when we are trying to observe generalization are usually different from those employed when the goal is to get subjects to make discriminations. In general, it seems that aside from the limitations of a subject's receptor systems we can get a subject to discriminate or to generalize to any given extent by varying the S-R-X relationships judiciously. Discrimination and generalization are relative terms, although we typically discuss them in terms that suggest that they are being treated as absolute events. The upshot of these considerations is that we can, to a large extent, make the physical differences between stimuli as important (or unimportant) as we choose. When the physical differences are minimized as the occasions for reinforcement, we may still get evidence of stimulus generalization. In such cases, perhaps generalization is based upon a different process—the one next to be considered.

In ending the discussion of primary stimulus generalization, two matters seem worthy of some concluding remarks. These both concern the role of physical variation in determining the S_L characteristics of behavior.

First of all, in discussing the simultaneous discrimination case, it sufficed for me to consider only S_L and NoS_L as the conditions of stimulation. NoS_L is, of course, always an abstraction; *the absence of anything can only be agreed upon by observers, never demonstrated absolutely,* because whenever some environmental event is absent, *something else must be present.* So, NoS_L always has some features in common with S_L. Many discrimination situations are simply cases in which there are many such features common to the environment defined as S_L and to the environment when S_L is not present.

Obviously, then, the quantitative description of S_L's in many areas would be of benefit. Among the stimulus dimensions that have been suggested as a basis of generalization, perhaps the most promising is that currently being developed by Estes (72). Estes has attempted to formalize and explicate the vague notions about S that I have continually used in this text. Estes' basic hypothesis has been that there is a total situation composed of discernible stimuli, *any number of which* can be described as *a proportion of the total stimuli available* (of the "total situation," that is). There is much more to Estes' theory than this, of course, but the fundamental notion is that the environment at any time is composed of a number of elements any of which may be effective in determining behavior (or associated with behavior) at a given time. If the subject has been trained to respond to any given proportion of such elements, on the average, then stimulus generalization will occur to any other proportion. The divergency of any other proportion from the training proportion has been shown to produce at least as predictable generalization results as can be derived from physically based generalization hypotheses (157).

Mediated Stimulus Generalization

Another type of generalization phenomenon that has been suggested by many psychologists is that due to the *funcational* equivalence of S's rather than to their *physical* similarity. S's are functionally equivalent, by definition, when they elicit a similar response. Mediated generalization is also called learned, or acquired, generalization. There are two steps necessary for its establishment or demonstration.

First, some response, R_a, is associated with two stimuli, S_1 and S_2. The establishment of the S_1-R_a and the S_2-R_a habits should be done quite independently of each other for the purposes of a clear experimental demonstration of this effect.

Second, a new response, R_b, is associated with one of the S's; we shall use S_1 in this example. Again, the S_1-R_b habit is developed in some situation having few or no features in common with the situations in which the habits involving R_a were established.

Now we are ready to test for generalization. Let us present S_2 to the subject in the same general context as that in which the S_1-R_b habit was set up. In the most dramatic case of mediated generalization, the mere presentation of S_2 should be sufficient to evoke R_b. It would be equally valid, however, merely to show that R_b can now become related to S_2 more easily than it could have without the earlier pairing of S_1 and S_2 with R_a.

In other words, the independent pairing of two stimuli with one response, followed by the association of one of these stimuli with still another R, purportedly makes the other S's association with this second R stronger also—even though this S and R have never occurred together (i.e., there was no opportunity for this relationship to be learned in the ordinary ways).

Although this process has been invoked quite often by psychologists in attempts to account for certain complex types of learning, clear-cut experimental demonstrations of mediated generalization are rare. One of the closer approximations to the ideal conditions for demonstrating learned generalization is to be found in an experiment by Bugelski and Scharlock (43). These investigators put their subjects through three learning situations in succession.

In the first learning situation the basic habits acquired were these:

$$(1)\ S_1\text{-}R_1$$
$$(2)\ S_2\text{-}R_2$$
$$(3)\ S_3\text{-}R_3$$

In each case, the S's were printed words, and the correct R's were also indicated by printed words; learning was considered to have occurred when the subject was able to say the appropriate R-words before they were shown to him. All of these words were "nonsense syllables"—i.e., one-syllable words that occur very infrequently, if at all, in the English language; these are often used to study fairly simple learning processes in human beings, because they insure that all subjects will start out with low and nearly equal prior experience with the S's and R's to be involved in the habits the experimenter seeks to establish.

The second learning situation used, as the S's for the new habits, printed representations of the R's learned in the first task. The subjects now had to learn new R's to each of these S_R's, as I shall schematize them:

$$(1)\ S_{R_1}\text{-}R_{1a}$$
$$(2)\ S_{R_2}\text{-}R_{2a}$$
$$(3)\ S_{R_3}\text{-}R_{3a}$$

Finally, the subjects were trained to pair the *responses* of the *second* learning task with the *stimuli* involved in the *first* learning situation, thus:

$$(1)\ S_1\text{-}R_{1a}$$
$$(2)\ S_2\text{-}R_{3a}$$
$$(3)\ S_3\text{-}R_{2a}$$

The first of the three habits in this last situation, S_1-R_{1a}, is a test for mediated stimulus generalization; the other two habits (wherein previously experienced stimuli and responses are mixed up) are control conditions. If learned generalization is operating, the first habit in this third situation should be acquired more easily than the remaining two; this was tentatively verified by the data collected by Bugelski and Scharlock (43), who also reported that their subjects were not aware of any relationship between the different learning situations (which were conducted on different days).

Stimulus generalization due to functional rather than physical similarities, if it *can* be definitely demonstrated, is actually a variation of that group of simple habit interactions that come under the heading of "Transfer of Training." This topic is taken up in the next chapter, in which we will discuss some other techniques for making stimuli more similar or more dissimilar through preliminary training.

Other Factors Influencing Rate of Discrimination Learning

The Effect of the Operant Level of R_L

It should be clear by now that no organism can be taught a habit that involves R's he can not make. Thus, the fundamental problem for the "teacher" in all learning situations, be they experimental or practical, is to determine ways of getting R_L to occur in the presence of the appropriate stimuli. In Pavlovian conditioning, this problem reduces to a search for an appropriate UCS; in operant learning, a variety of techniques exist for increasing the frequency of R_L to a level that will provide sufficient occasions of S_L-R_L-X to permit the establishment of the S_L-R_L habit.

The frequency or efficiency of R_L in a given operant situation prior to the introduction of any reinforcement (i.e., before opportunity for learning) in that particular situation is called the *operant level* of that response. Nearly all studies explicitly concerned with the relationship of the operant level to learning have been conducted in free operant learning situations, so the operant level is conventionally discussed in reference to rate of responding. But there is no reason why the operant level could not refer to *any* of the measures of response strength discussed at the end of Chapter 1. There would seem to be three basic classes of techniques by which the operant level could be manipulated: motivational variations, changes in the number of competing R's that are possible in a given situation, and/or generalization (excitatory).

In discrimination learning, the operant level usually seems to have the same role as does the effect of excitatory stimulus generalization. A high operant level of R_L aids the simple learning process, but impedes discrimination learning. This would be especially true when the differences between S_L and either S'_L or NoS_L constitute a fairly slight change in total stimulation.

Basically, all learning involves reinforcing the sequence S_L-R_L. This may, as we have seen, cause changes in behavior (indistinguishable from those of simple learning) in relation to S's other than S_L. If, for whatever reason, this is not desirable or not practical, then discrimination learning is required in order to refine the S's and/or the R's involved in any particular habit. Obviously, whenever the reinforcement of some S_L-R_L sequence does not produce any increment in a NoS_L-R_L sequence also, then all the material of this chapter becomes irrelevant. Techniques for increasing the operant level of R_L are the bases of one way of increasing the commonalities among these various stimulus situations, because, fundamentally, these techniques are simply other ways of producing greater generalization.

Techniques for increasing the operant level work, at least up to a point, to insure the sufficiently frequent occurrence of S_L-R_L so that any learning could be expected to take place (with the proper reinforcement); beyond some hypothetical optimum operant level, however, further increases should have the same deleterious effects as occur when too much S_L-R_L-X precedes the instigation of discrimination training.

In short, some low operant level is necessary for *any* learning, but attempts to increase the operant level (via motivation, for example) too much will work against the efficient development of discrimination habits. To put this another way, the higher the operant level of

R_L going into a discrimination situation, the more necessary it will be to have a low ratio of S_L-R_L-X occasions compared to the occurrences of NoS_L-R_L-NoX.

The Effects of Time between Discrimination Trials

This topic brings up another facet of the general problem of the effects of distribution of practice. We first mentioned this matter on p. 44; in its most general form, the question is, "Is there an optimal interval between practice trials that will produce the most rapid, or the most stable learning?"

It should be clear that with the variety of learning situations that can be identified, it would be truly remarkable to find that a simple answer to the question of distribution of practice would hold for all of them. In general, the basic issue that has dominated the study of distribution of practice has concerned the role of the hypothetical inhibitory process. This concept was introduced in the chapter on Pavlovian conditioning (p. 56), and in the current chapter we have had occasion to refer to it again. In relation to discrimination learning, of course, the role of inhibition itself is fairly complex, as we have seen.

The majority of evidence indicates that most discrimination learning situations adhere to the general rule that spaced practice (in which the time between trials can be measured in minutes or hours) is superior to massed practice (in which the time between trials is usually described in fractions of a minute). A recent experiment supporting this general proposition is that by Sarason, Sarason, Miller and Mahmoud (231).

Many more experiments have reached the same general conclusion, but beyond this rather unspecific statement little is known.

There are several stumbling blocks to developing a simple, yet specific, statement about an optimal intertrial interval in discrimination learning; of these, the major ones are:

(1) There is first the fact that we know hardly anything about the effects of time on the generalization effects. This is particularly true in reference to operant learning situations. Now, something analogous to the generalization processes we have discussed must

play an important role, at least in the more primitive forms of discrimination. Therefore, it would seem to stand to reason that one of the ways in which an intertrial interval could influence discrimination learning might be via the effects of time on the magnitude of generalization effects. No direct evidence exists relevant to this point.

(1a) In this connection, however, it is conceivable that the three-way interaction of time with inhibitory and excitatory generalization phenomena might be so complex as to produce no useful principles. This amounts, in other words, to saying that there may be no *direct* relationship between intertrial intervals and discrimination learning per se.

(2) We know that discrimination learning is itself not a unitary phenomenon. There are at least three basic procedures included under this classification. In view of this, why should we expect a simple relation between discrimination learning and distribution of practice? Conceivably, different distributional phenomena are optimal for different discrimination situations. Again, there are few systematic data that are relevant to this question.

SUMMARY

The most basic forms of learning can be characterized as procedures by which the extent of environmental control over behavior is *expanded*. More "complex" forms of learning, on the other hand, provide the means by which:

(1) The responses involved in habits become highly specific (i.e., less variable—an obvious extension of the basic learning processes as I have defined them), or

(2) The stimuli involved in any given habit are reduced in number or kind, so that increasingly specific S-complexes become critical in the determination of behavior.

The learning situations that achieve either or both of these aims most directly are called discrimination learning situations.

The basic way to effect any kind of discrimination is to reinforce

only specific R's under very specific S conditions, and withhold reinforcement for any deviations in either R_L or in the conditions under
which R_L occurs. Thus, every discrimination learning situation
involves the concurrent alteration of more than one S-R relationship;
in any given situation, some relationships are strengthened, some
weakened—with the latter being the predominant occurrence. There
are three basic types of discrimination learning: (1) Successive
Discrimination, (2) Response Differentiation, and (3) a combination of these first two, Simultaneous Discrimination.

Concerning the factors that will influence the ease or difficulty of
establishing a discrimination habit, one principle seems to apply to
all: Since discrimination learning involves the strengthening of one
highly specific habit, and the concomitant weakening of very similar
habits, anything that will supplement the procedure of differential
reinforcement will facilitate discrimination; similarly, anything that
tends to make the strengths of these habits more alike will impede
the speed of discrimination learning.

SUPPLEMENTARY NOTES

More on Stimuli and Discrimination Learning

It should be clear now that the ability of most psychologists to
predict the outcomes of discrimination learning situations will not
be appreciably enhanced by a detailed knowledge of the characteristics of the S_L, S'_L, and NoS_L conditions involved. We have not yet
found a simple formula for describing the relative ease or difficulty
of discrimination situations in which the nature of the similarities
and differences in the positive and negative stimuli is very complicated; unfortunately, these similarities and differences are, indeed,
often complicated in natural discrimination situations.

The student should not leave this topic with the impression
that psychologists have been reluctant to tackle the problems posed
by more complex stimulus interrelationships; this is not true. But
it is my impression that the ingeniously complicated discrimination
situations that have so far been set up in different laboratories have

not been the source of well-demonstrated guiding principles. The detailed discussion of the myriad situations being studied for this purpose, therefore, is better left, for the time being, to technical reports, rather than incorporated in a textbook.

Nor does the current lack of a sure set of rules about the role of stimuli in discrimination learning mean that we know nothing about this sort of learning. As a matter of fact, for practical purposes one can set up many successful discrimination situations simply by keeping in mind the general nature of the habit interaction models depicted in this chapter. There is evidence that if the kinds of subjects in which one happens to be interested can make some differential reaction to two given S's, then with enough diligence and the proper application of reinforcement one can accomplish discrimination learning. This advice, of course, does not give much solace to those who seek *efficient* discrimination training methods.

The failure to discover the relevant stimulus variables in discrimination learning via the direct, generalization-oriented approach has caused some psychologists to try turning the problem around. They have employed well-established discrimination learning techniques as a method of determining how subjects do analyze their environments. They seek to answer such questions as, "Are some stimulus differences 'more naturally' responded to than others?" "What kinds of stimulus-reinforcement contingencies are subjects capable of handling?" "Just how complicated can the positive and negative stimulus differences be?" These questions are put in more sophisticated language, to be sure, but basically these seem to be the questions.

This is a reasonable approach to some of the problems of this area, and one that may some day reap great profits. As yet, it is still too new, too unorganized, and too concerned with resolving alleged theoretical controversies whose bearing on the major problem is questionable. As soon as more direction is given to this attempt to discover the stimulus-response relationships that are *brought to* a discrimination situation, and how these aspects of behavior determine the solution of various discrimination situations, progress in this field may occur quite rapidly.

Stimulus Generalization and Discrimination

The general importance for the prediction of stimulus generalization effects of (1) the method by which an S_L is made part of a habit and (2) the method by which the strength of some generalized habit involving an S'_L is evaluated has been stressed by Perkins (208). It is his contention that specific generalization effects can best be predicted from an appreciation of the interaction of these procedural matters with the similarity factor per se. This is a truism, but it still is sometimes overlooked: no phenomenon, such as stimulus generalization, can be described independently of the operations by which the phenomenon is measured. Reinhold and Perkins (218) have shown that this principle accounts in great part for stimulus intensity effects as well. The basic point is this: we do not as yet have, as has often been assumed, a firm empirical basis for deciding whether discrimination learning determines generalization effects, or vice versa; in fact, Perkins' analysis of this area suggests that there is no absolute basis for making such a decision.

Discrimination Theory and Distribution of Practice

It should be pointed out that many psychologists' concern with the effects of intertrial intervals on discrimination stems from an interest in a theoretical problem, more than from a concern with any practical matter. The theoretical issue is whether organisms, particularly nonverbal ones, *compare* the consequences of one discrimination trial with those of another. To put it somewhat facetiously, this issue seems to amount to asking whether most organisms solve discrimination problems by contrasting analytic tables similar to those presented in this chapter.

The issue, of course, can be regarded more seriously than this. It concerns the relationship of perception to learning. There are many psychologists, influenced by the very important contributions of the German Gestalt psychologists, who regard perception as a more fundamental process than learning—i.e., that perceptual factors influence learning. As a reconsideration of Chaper 1 should bring

out, many psychologists can not understand how this sort of controversy can be regarded as an empirical one. We can only tell what
another organism perceives by the way that he responds to various
stimuli; this is exactly the way we infer learning also. Furthermore,
organisms will respond to very few stimuli in *any* systematic fashion
until some learning has taken place. Therefore, it would seem to
be impossible to *compare* the roles of perception and learning in the
determination of behavior. All we can reasonably hope to do is to
develop clear, useful, and (if this appeals to most psychologists)
mutually exclusive *definitions* of learning and perception; definitions
that are, of course, couched in terms of observable relationships
between an organism's behavior and various features of the environment.

There is plenty of room for a meeting of minds between per-
ceptually and learning-oriented psychologists; the latter are quite
content to talk about S's in the abstract, on the assumption that there
are characteristic, unlearned ways in which organisms filter and
organize the total amount of stimulation to which they are subjected at any time. As long as there is an implicit belief that these
two fields of basic psychological research are, in some obscure way,
in competition, obviously there will be little communication and a
lot of redundant research.

Concern about an intertrial comparing mechanism need not, however, get into the above speculations. It *is* reasonable to ask whether
massed practice might not aid some sorts of discrimination learning,
because it provides more opportunities for comparing the events of
one trial with the events of one just preceding. With nonverbal
organisms this hypothetical mechanism would involve such things
as stimulus traces (see p. 40).

Presumably, an empirical or pragmatic interest in a comparing
mechanism could stem from the obvious fact that human beings do
such comparing at least occasionally. Unfortunately, the rather undirected research related to this problem has been complicated by
half-hearted attempts to relate it to the preceding theoretical pseudo-
problems, and also by some fairly uncritical thinking about discrimination learning in general. We can only formulate and conduct

profitable research on complex problems after we have analyzed such problems and related them exhaustively to the simple phenomena about which we *do* have a fair amount of knowledge. It is not true that the study of simple problems will reduce the solution of complex psychological problems to mere child's play. But an understanding of the great deal of knowledge we do have about simple psychological phenomena will at least prevent psychologists from making errors unworthy of any child when they do attempt to study complex problems.

In summary, then, an understanding of the possible bases of the comparing mechanism, or of how far down the phylogenetic scale this phenomenon can be detected, requires a more sophisticated approach to discrimination learning that has been so far in evidence. If these *are* straightforward questions, there should be a straightforward way of answering them.

✳

✳

✳ SIMPLE HABIT
INTERACTIONS:
II. TRANSFER OF TRAINING

Habits do not develop in "psychological vacuums." Responses rarely occur in the presence of totally unfamiliar stimuli, and are not usually reinforced by completely novel events. More characteristically, environment-organism interactions tend to make subsequent contacts between the organism and a somewhat different environment more predictable. Experimental psychologists call this phenomenon *transfer of training*.

Transfer of training refers to the fact that once a given habit is formed (*training*), this development will affect the subsequent acquisition and/or performance of behavior patterns involving similar habits (*transfer of training*).

Anecdotal Examples of Transfer

There are almost limitless examples of this phenomenon to be seen in human behavior, e.g.:

(1) During and immediately after the period centering about 1900, when immigration to the United States was extremely high, many immigrants' children were found to be doing poorly in United States public schools. Obviously, many factors contributed to this condition, but one determinant is of especial interest to students of learning: A large segment of those having difficulty in school were children who came from homes in which, within the family group, the language of their parents' birthplace was still spoken.

Why did such children have more than their share of scholastic trouble? For many children the difficulty was very likely due simply to the fact that they spoke one language *in* school, and another *outside*. Success with our language is a prerequisite for success in our schools—or was at the time which I am now describing. For the offspring of bilingual homes, their previous (preschool) and current experience outside of school had already established, and was maintaining, many habits *incompatible with* success in the school situation. They were receiving, therefore, minimal training at best, and, more frequently, contradictory training on the set of habits that they most needed for scholastic achievement.

(2) For an entirely different effect of transfer of training, consider the typical college mathematics curriculum. Mastery of the calculus and analytic geometry depends upon a prior understanding of algebra and trigonometry. Success with differential equations requires some knowledge of the calculus, and so on. Each more advanced course is most easily mastered by those who have best learned the preceding material. In some other academic fields the progression from the elementary to the advanced courses is not so clear-cut as in mathematics, but the principle is the same: some concepts, facts, theories, and so forth are easier to learn if, as the clichés go, the student "has the background" or the "prerequisites."

The Experimental Model of Transfer

These anecdotal illustrations can be represented, for the purposes of more exact study of transfer of training, by the following basic experimental situation:

	STEP ONE	STEP TWO
TRANSFER Group	Learn Habit A	Learn Habit B
CONTROL Group	Rest, i.e., do nothing related to the activities involved in Habits A or B	Learn Habit B

The important comparison here is between the rates at which the two groups acquire Habit B. Assuming the necessary control measures—such as equating the groups for general skills, for motivation, and the like—any difference in the groups' acquisition or retention of Habit B will mean that there has been some transfer of training from Habit A in the TRANSFER group.

Transfer as Habit Interaction

Since the study of transfer of training is specifically aimed at understanding the influence of one habit on another, it is clear why this area of learning can be considered a case of habit interaction. Now, it is not true that transfer phenomena always involve simple habits, as I have defined them, but there are two reasons for introducing the topic in terms of simple habits: (1) Transfer, like discrimination learning, is regarded as one of the basic processes by which the manifestly complex behavior of humans and their closer relatives develops from simple habit formation. In fact, many learning psychologists feel that the failure to recognize the pervasive role of transfer of training has been the basis of many meaningless controversies—controversies between different learning psychologists, and controversies between learning psychologists and those starting from a different basic orientation. If we make bold assertions such as these, it is incumbent on us to demonstrate our evidence. (2) A consideration no less important in a textbook is that this is a simple way of introducing transfer of training to the student. In order to cover all the matters to be treated under this topic, I shall have to consider some situations that do not involve only simple habits, but these will not complicate things too much.

BASIC CLASSES OF TRANSFER EFFECTS

The Two Dimensions of Transfer

Transfer of training has two dimensions along which it may vary. Now, a habit, in our terminology, is the relationship between a S and an R. Habit A involves the relationship S_A-R_A, and Habit B is S_B-R_B. Theoretically, at least, both the stimulus and response members of various habits can be compared with each other in terms of their degree of similarity. The ways and difficulties of making such comparisons were discussed in the previous chapter.

To illustrate the four general ways in which transfer of training may manifest itself, let us consider five hypothetical individuals, each of whom has just bought the latest model of an automobile equipped with automatic transmission. One of these individuals, Mr. C, has never driven a car nor any other vehicle before; we shall use his changes in performance (as he learns from scratch about driving) as a basal comparison point in reference to which we can describe the behavior of the four other buyers. What we are interested in is the relative ease with which these five people adapt various aspects of their behavior to this new car, i.e., the rates at which they learn to drive it with a minimum of effort or error.

One of our subjects, Mr. H. P., had previously driven an earlier model of the same car he has just bought; it was also equipped with automatic transmission and was approximately the same size and shape. Obviously, Mr. H. P. is not going to have very much difficulty learning to drive his new car. In fact, the minor adjustments in his former driving habits will occur so quickly and with so little interference to efficient driving that he will probably never think of his first few days in the new model as a learning experience. Why? Because the differences in stimuli between his old and his new car are very slight, and largely unrelated to the responses that are most important in driving the new car effectively. The color may be different, the dashboard may be rearranged somewhat, but essentially Mr. H. P. can do the same things with his hands, feet, and eyes that he was accustomed to doing in his old car, and he will be able to drive with at most only a fleeting loss of efficiency. This is a case of *High Positive Transfer:* the stimuli associated with the critical responses involved in driving are very similar in the old and the new cars, and the responses themselves are identical. Relative to Mr. C, or to any of the other people we will consider, Mr. H. P. will adapt himself to his new car most rapidly.

Mr. L. P., our second hypothetical car-owner, has much more to learn, because he has never previously driven a car, although he had become quite skilled on a bicycle. He must, of course, learn to drive, but he will still have a somewhat easier time of it than Mr. C, who had never operated any kind of vehicle before. In learning to ride a bicycle, Mr. L. P. had to learn to make calculations about time and space while traveling at relatively high speeds. Although he still has much to learn about driving, he should acquire effective steering and braking habits faster than Mr. C. This is a case of *Low Positive Transfer:* there are many similarities in the nonvehicular S's that occur in both bike-riding and driving, and the responses to these stimuli are crudely compatible (using the feet to stop, the hands to change direction or keep on course). Relative to Mr. C, Mr. L. P. will adopt effective steering and braking habits more readily.

Mr. C will have an advantage over our next driver, however, in one respect. Mr. H. N. has been accustomed to a car with manual transmission (involving the continual use of the clutch and gear-shift). While it is not too difficult to discard useless habits (unless they were established by avoidance techniques), there will be a period right after he gets the car when Mr. H. N. will find himself pawing the floorboard with his left foot and searching under the steering wheel for the gear-shift just after starting or whenever he wishes to stop or slow down. Mr. C, of course, will never display this pattern of behavior, and is not confronted with the problem of eliminating it. This is a case of *High Negative Transfer:* for Mr. H. N. the similarities between his old and his new cars are almost as great as in the case of Mr. H. P., but some of the responses appropriate to the old machine are inappropriate in the new one. As is typical in the case of negative transfer of training when the earlier training did not involve avoidance techniques, however, the effect is only transitory. Relative to a subject lacking the same background, though, there is an initial impairment in efficiency due to the carrying over of now inappropriate responses.

Our final subject, to round out the picture of transfer effects, has previously done all his driving in England in English automobiles. Mr. L. N. is accustomed to driving on the left side of the road while sitting on the right side of his machine. Compared to our Mr. C, Mr. L. N. is at first going to show a stronger tendency to go to the wrong side of the car when he wants to go for a drive, and he will probably have a stronger tendency to get into the wrong traffic lane than would Mr. C. This is a case of *Low Negative Transfer:* there are sufficient similarities between his new car and his old (and also in the outside stimuli) to induce Mr. L. N. to make formerly acquired responses that are now inappropriate. Unlike Mr. H. N., however, there are also many differences in the old and new S's confronting Mr. L. N., so that his tendency to repeat the earlier habits will not be so strong and they will be replaced more easily. Relative to Mr. C, however, Mr. L. N. will have some relearning to do.

Habit Interactions H+, H−, L+, L−

These four hypothetical instances represent the main points on, and the interactions between, the two dimensions that have classically been identified in transfer phenomena. These dimensions are:

(1) Transfer can vary in the *direction,* or nature, of its effect. The learning of Habit A could *impede* the learning of Habit B, or it could *facilitate* the learning of this habit. Psychologists speak of these two possibilities as, respectively, *negative* transfer—which was described in example 1 above—and *positive* transfer—which was illustrated by example 2.

(2) There will also be differences in the degree, or *amount,* by which a given habit affects later learning. Habit A might be found to have only a mild interfering effect upon the acquisition of Habit B, or it might be a very marked deterrent to the acquisition of this habit.

The preceding discussion should have served to introduce you to the basic transfer-of-training phenomena. These may be summarized in two principles which were first formulated and explicated by Bruce (41) and Wylie (293). Accordingly, the following statements, taken together, constitute what are called the *Bruce-Wylie Laws of Transfer:*

(1) The amount of transfer of training is determined by the degree of similarity of the stimuli involved in the two learning situations.

That is, the more similar are S_A and S_B, the greater will be the effect of having learned Habit A upon the ability to learn Habit B later on.

(2) The direction, or kind of transfer, is determined by the compatibility of the responses involved in the two habits. Some students may prefer to think of this principle as consisting of two parts, viz.:

(2a) When R_A is compatible with R_B, positive transfer occurs; this means that the earlier practice of R_A aids in the later performance of R_B.

(2b) Negative transfer occurs when the evocation of R_A precludes the possibility of the successful, or efficient, performance of R_B; in other words, when R_A and R_B are incompatible.

(It can also be mentioned that a particular habit might have no effect whatsoever on some kinds of later learning. The experimental demonstration of this is not literally possible, since it would require the acceptance of the null hypothesis. For practical purposes, however, "no transfer of training" can usually be defined fairly well. For instance, it is unlikely that learning Latin and learning how to shoot a rifle would affect one another in any important way.)

The interaction of the two dimensions of simple transfer is shown verbally in Table IV. In that table only the learning tasks for the TRANSFER groups (see p. 223) are shown; it should be understood that (using the classic transfer design) the CONTROL groups learn only the habits involved in each task 2 described in the table.

These basic types of transfer situations will be identified as additional cases of simple habit interaction. To emphasize the two-dimensional character of even simple instances of transfer, two identifying symbols will be used for each case. Interactions of Type H are cases in which the interacting habits involve very similar S's (i.e., the first two rows of Table IV). Type L interactions are between habits with low similarity in their S-components (the last two rows of Table IV). When the habits involve compatible R's (rows 1 and 3, Table IV) a $+$ follows the appropriate letter. A minus sign, on the other hand, indicates an interaction between

TABLE IV

Basic Transfer-of-Training Phenomena

Compatibility of Responses	Stimulus Similarity	Symbolic Representation of Preceding Relationships		Type of Transfer
		Habit A	Habit B	
High	High	S-R	S'-R'	High, Positive
Low	High	S-R	S'-NotR	High, Negative
High	Low	S-R	NotS-R'	Low, Positive
Low	Low	S-R	NotS-NotR	Low, Negative

This table summarizes the Bruce-Wylie laws of transfer of training. A prime (') means that the indicated S or R is similar to the corresponding event in Habit A. "NotS" or "NotR" means that there is little similarity or compatibility between the designated events in the two habits.

Reinforcement conditions are not depicted here because these do not enter into the differentiation of the basic types of transfer.

habits that require incompatible R's (rows 2 and 4, Table IV). To summarize, the four basic types of transfer of training shown in Table IV will be called Habit Interactions H+, H−, L+, and L−, respectively.

Figure 17 shows another way of depicting the interaction between S and R variables that is the basis of transfer phenomena. This mode of illustration was worked out by C. E. Osgood (202). It shows in graphic form the same relationships we have been discussing for the past several pages.

THE RELATIVITY OF ALL TRANSFER EFFECTS [1]

In my terminology, the transfer design that characterizes most of the preceding discussion in the simplest way is:

[1] Although the nomenclature, interpretations, and specific line of development in this and the following sections are my responsibility, I did benefit greatly from reading a paper on transfer methodology by Prof. B. B. Murdock (199).

	Task 1	Task 2
TRANSFER Group	Habit A	Habit B
CONTROL Group	Not Habit A	Habit B

But this is unsatisfactory, because "Not Habit A" actually does not state what the subjects of the control group might be bringing to bear upon the learning of Habit B. There are an infinite number of activities that would satisfy the condition, "Not Habit A."

FIGURE 17

Osgood's Transfer Surface

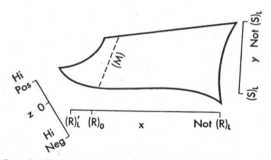

Adapted from Osgood (202), in the *Psychological Review,* vol. 56, p. 140. Used by permission of the American Psychological Association.

Osgood's surface represents the fact that transfer phenomena are dually determined by both S and R variables. If one is not used to 3-dimensional graphs, he can get the essential features of this surface by taking this page and turning up the lower right hand corner while turning down the upper right corner.

The z-plane shows the degree (distance from the zero line) and the kind (upwards or downwards from zero) of transfer from some task 1 to any task 2. The x (response) variable runs from responses highly similar to those of task 1—R'_L—to very incompatible responses—Not R_L. On the y (stimulus) dimension the variation is between stimuli quite like those in the task 1 habit and S's totally unlike the task 1 stimuli—i.e., from S_L to Not S_L. Line M is the point of intersection between the x and z planes; in other words, all the cases that fall on this line would be cases of "no transfer" (0 on the z-axis) because these are situations in which the R's of the two tasks have no common features (the R_0 point on x).

Most learning psychologists have become sufficiently sophisticated that they require control subjects to do *something* for a period equivalent to that occupied in learning task 1 by the experimental subjects. These control task 1 activities fall into two general classes: they may be either (1) some routine or commonplace activity that is not expected to result in any appreciable learning, or (2) some learning activity that has a known transfer effect on Habit B.

No matter which of these task 1 control activities are used, one basic fact is not changed: Transfer effects can be compared only to the behavior on task 2 of control groups treated within the same experimental framework. All transfer effects, therefore, are relative. Things can only be otherwise when we can decide that a specific control group reveals an "asbolute zero" transfer effect. This decision would require that we have a far more valid and general means of scaling S and R similarities than, as mentioned before, now exist.

The Weakness in the Bruce-Wylie Laws

No one could deny that the behavior of an adult organism is some complex function of his past learning plus the current S, R, and X conditions. The understanding of the first-named factor is the province of students of transfer of training. Until recent years, such students worked almost exclusively within the context of the Bruce-Wylie principles.

In the abstract, the Bruce-Wylie laws of transfer cover all the logically possible cases of these sorts of habit interactions. But the predictive ability of these laws, it must be confessed, is poor. This is because learning psychologists have not adopted any definitive means of scaling either stimulus similarity or response compatibility.

This gap in our knowledge has resulted in the evolution of a two-pronged attack in the study of simple transfer situations:

1. "True" Transfer Research

This is research oriented toward understanding the transfer phenomena themselves. In studies of this sort the habits established during task 1 can be analyzed and described in reference to general, abstract S and R classes. Ideally, task 2 can be similarly dissected. Either way, the outcome of such research can be used to evaluate hypotheses that state general transfer principles.

An example of a general transfer hypothesis would be: "When the S's of tasks 1 and 2 affect different sensory modalities, the *degree* of transfer of training will be determined exclusively by the amount of functional, as opposed to physical, similarity between S_1 and S_2." To test such an hypothesis, an experimenter should use tasks in which the stimuli can readily be agreed upon as affecting different sensory modalities. Furthermore, he should have some means of controlling, or measuring, the degree of functional equivalence of S_1 and S_2. Such considerations as these are what I meant when referring to "habits . . . analyzed and described in reference to general, abstract . . . classes."

2. Developing S- and R-Scales

These kinds of transfer studies involve cases in which the S and R components of task 2 are much better understood than are those of task 1. The purpose of such research is, usually, to analyze the components of task 1 indirectly by: (1) noting the direction and degree of transfer from task 1 to task 2, and (2) assuming that the laws of transfer apply.

By observing task 2 performance with and without prior exposure to some task 1, it is sometimes possible to make inferences about either of two relationships: (1) the similarity of the stimuli used in the two tasks, or (2) the compatibility of the responses required in the two tasks. Such inferences are frequently necessary because of our lack of understanding of how to scale all sorts of stimuli and responses along their respective dimensions. When we are uncertain as to the degree of compatibility of two sets of responses, for example, it seems reasonable to use a transfer design, observe the direction of transfer from task 1 to task 2, and then draw our conclusions about R compatibility based on an interpretation of the observed results in terms of the Bruce-Wylie laws. Of course, the satisfactoriness of this mode of attack on the problems of generalization and compatibility is dependent upon the adequacy of the Bruce-Wylie laws and upon the compliance of a given experiment with the requirements of these laws.

An even more exploratory type of research that utilizes the transfer design is that in which we attempt to infer, from performance on task 2, exactly what S-R relationships were formed in task 1. This indirect approach is necessary whenever different kinds of habits could actually produce the same behavioral result in task 1. One of the classic examples of this use of the transfer design is found in research on the problem of transposition.

Transposition

It is assumed that readers of this textbook are able to understand concepts such as "greater than," "not as much as," "almost the same as," and the like. I could, therefore, hardly assert that it is not possible for an organism to learn to respond differentially to S's between which the differences are most easily described by reference to each other. This is called *relational learning*.

Relational learning refers to any situation where it can definitely be shown that a subject has learned to used a relationship (e.g., "when A is bigger than B") as the critical cue in a simultaneous discrimination problem. There is little point in denying that sophisticated human learners, at least, use such cues consciously in many learning situations.

Whether relational learning can occur without the prior learning of the use of verbal responses, however, is a matter of debate. The debate is important, too, because a psychologist's decision on this point markedly affects his analysis of discrimination learning situations. The nature of *that* analysis, in turn, will pretty well determine one's stand on a great many topics in behavior theory.

The method of studying relational learning is called the *transposition* experiment. This is a transfer design, thus its inclusion here. It is a transfer design because no single learning situation can enable us to determine which of the following alternatives is being used by a subject in order to solve a particular discrimination problem:

(1) The relationships between stimulus elements that are present on every trial,

(2) The absolute characteristics of stimulus elements that are present on every trial, or

(3) The differences from trial to trial that are due to different combinations of the stimulus elements on successive trials.

The basic way of deciding between these possibilities was developed by the Gestalt psychologist, Köhler (153). This method involves devising two discrimination problems such that if a given one of the above-named possibilities is used as the method of solving the first problem, the subject's initial attempts to solve the second problem can be predicted from the standard transfer principles.

For years transposition experiments were designed with only the first two of the three alternatives (above) in mind. Of the two, alternative 2 seemed to have the most vitality; Spence (253) presented a brilliant theoretical and empirical defense of this interpretation of the bases of discrimination learning.

In the long run, however, learning research with infra-human species has made it increasingly implausible to assume a basic ability to differentiate the environment at any given moment except insofar as the anatomy of a given organism's receptors might make some fractionation inevitable. For the time being, at least, the third alternative (which I have used as the underlying assumption for the whole of Chapter 6) seems to handle the data most easily.

Complex Transposition Designs

While the transposition design was being used to wrestle with the theoretical problems just described, the versatility of that design was gradually recognized. It became clear that relational learning was not a basic phenomenon, yet was still a fact as far as trained organisms were concerned. If, as it seemed, this was an acquired ability, then the next logical question was, "How is it acquired?" This question seemed most readily answered via a more complicated variation of the transposition design.

A study by Kuenne (156) inaugurated this phase of transposition research. She first required preschool children to chose between these three pieces of cardboard:

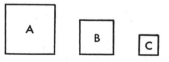

A selection of form B was always rewarded, while choices of A or C never were. This was true no matter what was the arrangement (order) of these forms on any given trial. In other words, it was possible to solve this problem on the basis of "always pointing at the middle-sized one."

After the children had solved this problem, Kuenne gave them this one:

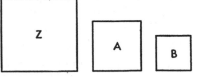

Again the middle-sized one was rewarded. If relational learning is a basic attribute, stimulus-element A should now be chosen by a preponderance of the children. As has already been implied, this result is not obtained unequivocally.

When Kuenne further analyzed her findings, she discovered a relationship between a subject's I.Q. and amount of transposition. In other words, the more likely it was that a child could formulate verbally the hypothesis of "middle-sizedness," the more likely it was that this child would tend initially to select stimulus A on task 2, even though this same stimulus was "wrong" on task 1.

So far, this more complicated sort of transposition study has utilized stimulus dimensions that were probably quite familiar to the subjects already. Also, the other major independent variable has involved differences between subjects over which the experimenters have no control (e.g., differences in "intelligence test" scores). Although a thoroughgoing program of research to work out the details of this particular problem is not beyond the realm of imagination, such a program is not known to be in progress at the present time.

COMPLEX EFFECTS OF PRIOR LEARNING

Although the Bruce-Wylie laws are logical, and verifiable to the extent that our quantification procedures now permit, they do not appear to be exhaustive. That is, there are additional effects of prior learning that do not follow from these laws alone. Some of these effects, indeed, seem to be contradictions of a literal interpretation of the principles so far discussed in this chapter; whether they are truly contradictions or merely complications is still undecided. All the effects of prior learning now to be discussed seem to indicate that something more than specific S-R connections are being formed when an organism is exposed to multiple, successive learning situations. Unfortunately, this vague statement will only be clarified slightly by the succeeding discussion; our understanding of the basic mechanisms involved in these phenomena is not at all good.

Discrimination Reversals

Suppose a subject learns a simultaneous discrimination problem. Then, once he has learned it, the correct and incorrect S-R relationships are switched. This switch is called a *discrimination reversal problem.*

Theoretically, a discrimination reversal should produce maximum negative transfer effects. The S's are, without question, identical, and the correct R's in the two cases are certainly completely incompatible. This is true, at least, for the S's and R's as typically identified by experimenters. In practice, experimenters using this procedure are far from unanimous in demonstrating that discrimination reversals invariably reveal negative transfer. This should be no surprise, because we have already seen that the experimental psychologists' conceptualization of the S and R elements of learning situations is, unfortunately, often inadequate.

The frailties of the high negative transfer paradigm, when applied to the discrimination reversal situation, are most readily brought out in two special instances of this experimental problem:

(1) When the experimentally identified S's are highly complex, or

(2) When the discrimination reversal procedure is repeated again and again, always using the same S-R relationships. This case is most appropriately examined in the next chaper after certain other principles have been introduced.

Concerning the complex S case involving only one discrimination reversal, failures to obtain negative transfer seem to occur most often in experiments in which there is the greatest uncertainty about the general classes to which the S's or the R's of those studies might be assigned. In other words, the first reversal of the correct S and R combinations in a discrimination problem should produce negative transfer. When we do not really understand the habits that are formed (and those that are eliminated) during the original training period, this expectation may not always be confirmed.

If we understood better the S's and R's of complicated discrimination problems in some cases, we might find that the negative transfer hypothesis was not even warranted. Still another factor that may prevent negative transfer in discrimination reversal is the phenomenon of learning how to learn; this will be considered in more detail in just a few pages.

The basic point being made here is that experiments using the discrimination reversal technique are still another source of data that are not easily related to the transfer models of Bruce, Wylie, and Osgood. This particular source of contradictory results, however, is probably not a crucial criticism of these models; the most perplexing outcomes are produced by using problems that are not easily fitted to *any* transfer model. Nevertheless, the need for modes of describing S and R similarities in reference to other than physical dimensions is underscored by the discrimination reversal type of experiment.

Stimulus Predifferentiation

Arnoult (11) has succinctly described the background and basic problem in this area: [2]

At one time it was an accepted dictum in the field of verbal learning that attaching a new response to an old stimulus, according to the A-B . . . A-K paradigm, would lead to negative transfer. About 15 years ago a number of experiments began to be reported in which the same paradigm was used to produce positive transfer. The main characteristic

[2] From the *Psychological Bulletin*, vol. 54, pp. 339, 341 and 349. Used by permission of the American Psychological Association.

of these new studies was the fact that the two sets of responses were sufficiently different that there was essentially no generalization between them: neither incompatibility nor facilitation. It was hypothesized that the pretraining "predifferentiated" the stimuli so that they were more "distinctive," or less "confusing." In recent years a substantial number of experiments have been devoted to this problem of stimulus predifferentiation; many potentially relevant variables have been investigated, some methodological improvements have been suggested and incorporated into later studies, and a number of hypotheses have been offered to account for the positive transfer obtained under these conditions. (11, p. 339)

Arnoult identified four types of predifferentiation designs as shown in Table V, and concluded:

A summary of the results obtained in experiments in which various kinds of predifferentiation training were given indicates that the following generalizations may be made: (a) *Relevant* S-R training (if it can be accepted as falling into the category of stimulus predifferentiation) is the most effective form of verbal pretraining; (b) *Relevant*-S pretraining is, in most cases, more effective than any pretraining method except *Relevant* S-R training; (c) *Irrelevant*-S, or performance set, pretraining is usually poorer than other pretraining methods; and (d) *Directed Attention* pretraining is often as effective as *Relevant*-S pretraining. (11, p. 341)

After attempting to account for these results, Arnoult reached much the same conclusion as have many other psychologists: ". . . more saisfactory hypotheses to account for transfer effects will be developed only when it becomes possible to give a more adequate quantitative description of the stimulus." (11, p. 349)

Learning How to Learn

Let us give a monkey or a small child a two-choice problem to solve: if the subject chooses a certain one of the two objects presented to him, he gets a reward; the choice of the other object results in no reward. At first, the subject may take from seven to ten trials to develop a consistent (correct) choice-response. After about fifty different problems of this kind, however, it takes only one trial for learning to occur. That is, the subject responds randomly (e.g., a given subject may always take the object on the left, or the one that

TABLE V

Examples of Possible S-R Pairs Used During Different Kinds of Predifferentiation Training When the Transfer Task Involves Moving a Control Upward in Response to a Red Light and Downward in Response to a Green Light

KIND OF PRETRAINING	PRETRAINING		TRANSFER TASK	
	Stimulus	Verbal Response	Stimulus	Motor Response
Relevant S-R	Red light	"Up"	Red light	Up
	Green light	"Down"	Green light	Down
Relevant S	Red light	"Cow"	Same as above	
	Green light	"Horse"		
Irrelevant S	Bright light	"Cow"	Same as above	
	Dim light	"Horse"		
Attention	Red light	None	Same as above	
	Green light	None		
No pretraining	None		Same as above	

is most colorful, but essentially he is simply making a blind try) on the first trial, and if this choice is correct, he rarely makes the opposite choice when this problem is again presented; if this first choice is wrong, the subject rarely chooses this object again. This is true even though the two-choice objects for any given problem are unrelated to those used on previous problems. The comparative development of learning sets in monkeys and children is shown in Figure 18.

This kind of behavior indicates that the subject has, as we say, learned how to learn—he has learned a "principle," although, with the monkey, this principle cannot be a verbal one. This kind of learning does not fit our learning model, but it is hard to say in what way it does *not* fit. Viewing it one way, the discrepancy is in terms of S factors—in one sense, the stimuli in any particular problem are not the important determinants of the observed behavior; the subject actually learns not to rely on any object's similarity to one used in a previous problem. Looking at it in a different light, it could be the

FIGURE 18

The Development of Learning Sets in Children and Monkeys

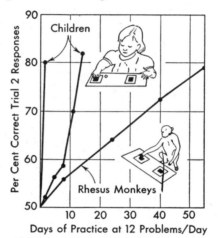

Days of Practice at 12 Problems/Day

From Koch and Meyer (152), in the *Journal of Comparative and Physiological Psychology,* vol. 52, p. 388. Used by permission of the American Psychological Association.

These data show the performances of children, 29 to 66 months old, and monkeys, 18 to 40 months old, on comparable learning set problems. The first curve is the performance of the children who learned fastest, the second for those who took longest to establish a learning set. In the children, rate of learning how to learn was reliably correlated with the Stanford-Binet Mental Age.

R which does not match our model; it is not a specific choice tendency that is being learned over a series of such problems.

What is perhaps most important about this particular phenomenon is that its implications for human learning could be almost unlimited. As Harlow has put it:

The variety of learning situations that play an important role in determining our basic personality characteristics and in changing some of us into thinking animals are repeated many times in similar form. The behavior of the human being is not to be understood in terms of the results of single learning situations but rather in terms of the changes which are affected through multiple, though comparable, learning problems. Our emotional, personal, and intellectual characteristics are not the mere algebraic summation of a near infinity of stimulus-response bonds. The learning of primary importance to the primates, at least, is the formation of learning sets; it is the *learning how to learn efficiently* in the situations the animal frequently encounters. This learning to learn transforms the organism from a creature that adapts to a changing environment by trial and error to one that adapts by seeming hypothesis and insight. (103, p. 51, italics in original)

Learning how to learn has not been observed in lower animals. The cat does not show much of this sort of ability to profit from experience in an abstract way, nor even the marmoset, a very low-order member of the primate family (187, 281). This clearly suggests the role of some kinds of brain mechanisms, but vague neural hypotheses can contribute nothing to our knowledge. Whatever its basis, learning how to learn (sometimes called "the formation of a learning set" in contemporary jargon) is undoubtedly an important aspect of human learning. So far, we lack enough information to utilize this phenomenon for practical ends. It has only begun to be studied relatively recently, and so the variables that affect the process are hardly known at all.

Nonreinforcement and Learning Sets

Eventually, training on a number of two-choice discrimination problems leads to equal predictability regarding behavior subsequent to the *first* choice a subject makes on any two-choice problem. A clue to the learning set phenomenon may be contained in the fact that the solution of a two-choice problem seems more likely to occur during the earlier stages of the development of a learning set if a subject's first choice on a new problem is of the negative stimulus than if it is of the positive stimulus. This might have ramifications for reinforcement scheduling effects; that it might relate to the roles of reinforcement and nonreinforcement in simpler discrimination situations is also a quite provocative hypothesis.

All in all, however, each of the three phenomena just considered makes the same point—we do not understand how to relate the particulars of a given transfer situation to the general model devised by Bruce (42), Osgood (202), and others.

Warm-Up

Unlike many psychological terms, this means almost exactly what it does in the vernacular. To "warm up" means to go through any activities that subsequently facilitate the performance of some specific task.

Warming up is an almost perfect example of positive transfer of training: it involves performing components of the R's of task 2 in the presence of S's almost identical with those of task 2. The practice throws on the mound with which any baseball pitcher begins an inning illustrate this phenomenon.

Another example of this phenomenon should be familiar to every reader. Each of us, when he sets out to study, goes through a certain ritual of arranging his books and paraphernalia, getting into a certain location and bodily position, donning particular clothes, and so on. All such actions are part of what may be called warm-up. These, if they are not too inflexible and not too complicated, may be helpful (as will be seen more clearly in Chapter 12); when these practices are helpful they are considered to be kinds of "effective study methods." Warm-up, thus, is a special instance of the learning-how-to-learn phenomenon. In what is generally its most effective form, warm-up reflects what is seemingly a most important aspect of a good learning set: effective warm-up maximizes the stimuli that have previously been associated with good performance, *and minimizes irrelevant stimuli*. As will be seen in the next chapter, monkey learning sets seem to be distinctly a matter of learning what not to respond to. Even if this is not a correct appraisal, the relationship of warm-up to learning sets seems quite clear: the former is a generic term for those techniques that facilitate either the acquisition or the performance of habits.

Methodological Implications of Learning-Set Phenomena

The warm-up and learning-how-to-learn processes *may* occur in almost any transfer study. They must, therefore, be controlled in experiments designed to show the amount and kind of transfer due to S and R similarities of the tasks involved. It is possible, for instance, that positive transfer in predifferentiation, reversal, or transposition experiments may largely be due to warm-up or learning-set effects.

The generality of warm-up and learning-set effects, and the necessity of special controls for them in transfer studies, may possibly be another reflection of our fundamental ignorance about transfer phenomena. While these two phenomena *are* steps in the direction of a more analytic approach to the role of prior experience, they do not surmount the basic hurdle in the field of transfer of training. The problem of predicting the extent or direction of warm-up or learning-set effects is exactly the same as the problem of predicting any transfer effects.

Transfer of Training and Individual Differences

Basically, there are two ways in which transfer of training is presumed, by many psychologists, to form a bridge between the principles of simple habit formation and the facts of complex (human) learning. One of these ways, as we have seen, is most simply described by the statement that early learning facilitates, very generally, later learning via the formation of learning sets.

But transfer of training effects need not necessarily lead to greater homogeneity in the behavior of individuals. On the contrary, transfer may be the agent for *increasing* individual differences.

We must remember that, in nature, the environment that confronts an organism is usually complex. Even if we assume that two organisms come into a given complex environment with exactly the same prior training, it is possible that they would subsequently be more different in behavior than before. This is because in a complex, uncontrolled environment it is possible for different subjects to learn R's in relation to different aspects of the same total S situation.

When it is recognized that subjects rarely do come into a given environment with precisely the same experiential backgrounds, it should be easy to see how the interaction of successively formed habits would lead to very diverse personalities. This is not to say that learning phenomena account for all individual differences. Nevertheless, learning phenomena can certainly be considered as a major way of magnifying these differences.

The Laboratory vs. Nature

The laboratory study of learning is devoted to the minimization of individual differences. This is the main reason for laboratory experiments: to reduce the possible number of causes of variation during the investigation of any given environment-behavior relationship.

As a result, the student of learning often gets the impression that transfer of training is a phenomenon only a little less rare *outside* the lab than simple habit formation. Nothing could be more in error. As the preceding paragraphs have sought to show, transfer of training is one of the most pervasive influences on the course and outcome of specific learning situations for any given organism.

In short, it is with transfer of training that the study of learning begins to get down to those problems that seem (in the abstract, at least) to have some bearing on everyday learning situations. Because the seeming relevance of transfer is so extensive, yet so far exceeds psychologists' abilities to apply a workable set of principles to these phenomena, the lack of useful information in this area is particularly frustrating.

SUMMARY

Transfer of training is the second major class of simple habit interactions, so called because transfer refers to any case in which the acquisition of one habit subsequently influences the acquisition and/or performance of another habit.

Transfer effects may vary in their *extent*, and also in their *direction*. These two dimensions of variation correspond, respectively, to the S and R components of the model. Unfortunately, a general schema for describing and scaling either S similarity or R compatibility is lacking.

There are several phenomena that are typically given distinctive names, but that seem, in the final analysis, to be variations of the basic transfer design. These are Stimulus Predifferentiation, Discrimination Reversal, Transposition, Warm-Up, and Learning How to Learn. The first three of these are generally believed to contain potentially important clues about the mechanisms that determine stimulus similarity. The last two, in addition to any theoretical significance, are sources of positive transfer in a wide variety of specific transfer situations; as such, their effects must be controlled in any experiment seeking to investigate the role of more specific variables in transfer-of-training effects.

Transfer effects are presumably responsible in large part for the complex, rapid, and highly adaptive changes in, and formation of, habits that are the outstanding characteristics of the learning behavior of higher organisms. It is also assumed by many psychologists that there is a fairly straight path connecting simple habit *formation* with simple habit *interaction;* once this connection is found, the rationale goes on, we shall have most of the tools necessary for making penetrating analyses of, and predictions about, complex learning.

These statements are, at best, hypotheses that have not yet received sufficient test to be evaluated. At worst, they are mere articles of faith. The missing link *seems to be* the lack of useful methods of scaling the similarity (compatibility) of complex stimuli and responses.

CHAPTER 8

*

*

* SIMPLE HABIT INTERAC-
TIONS: III. "ELIMINATING"
(CHANGING) SIMPLE HABITS

When people turn to the techniques of learning (wittingly or not) as a means of controlling the behavior of others it is often for the purpose of "teaching him (them, it, her, etc.) not to do that," or "to stop their doing that." While one of the themes of this chapter will be that it is a futile approach to learning and behavior that puts a premium on what the organism is *not* doing, it cannot be denied that there are techniques designed for this purpose, and that these have been quite extensively studied by psychologists.

What does it mean to say that someone "got rid of" a habit? Using our root definition of a habit as some systematic relationship between an S and an R, it follows that one has rid himself of a habit when there is no longer any predictable relationship between the stimuli and responses concerned. It is also reasonable to expect that, since habits are formed and maintained by reinforcement, a habit could be broken by making some event other than reinforcement now become the consequence of performing R_L. As we have already seen, there are two classes of consequences that do not have the effect of reinforcing responses: (1) *nonreinforcement,* which is a shorthand expression for the elimination of whatever X event was formerly used to support a habit (in other words, R_L now is followed by *no* immediate, systematic event), and (2) *noxious stimulation,* which is any kind of event that an organism is known to prefer to stay away from if given a choice. As with reinforcers themselves, whether a specific event can be placed in either of these classes depends upon a great many conditions; with few exceptions, however, it is not difficult for independent observers to agree upon the classification of specific events as nonreinforcing or noxious.

The continuous nonreinforcement of a habit is called *extinction,* following Pavlov's terminology. In speaking of the habit elimination procedure that involves noxious stimulation, psychologists use the same term as do laymen: they called it *punishment.* Extinction and punishment have many characteristics in common: the ultimate aim of both techniques is the same, and the progress of each method is described in terms of the tendency for some response to *fail to occur.* Since the essential element in each technique—the type of consequence that is made to follow R_L—appears to be so different from that used in the opposite case, it is quite easy to overlook the many important similarities these methods have. Actually, the problems concerning the application of the two are much the same, and so also are the variables that seem to be most important in determining their effectiveness as methods of behavioral control. For this reason I present the discussion of the two under the common title of methods of changing habits.

We have already considered the use of both nonreinforcement and noxious stimulation in the formation of simple habits. Nonreinforcement plays a paramount role in all forms of discrimination learning; noxious stimulation is an essential feature of escape and avoidance learning. Extinction and punishment differ from these other learning situations in that the former emphasize the deterioration of an S-R relationship rather than the establishment of such a relationship.

This distinguishing characteristic of extinction and punishment situations seems to have been a source of conceptual confusion to students of these problems. A traditional way of viewing the behavioral processes involved in extinction and punishment has been to consider them as the opposites of the simple habit formation process. After all, if a basic feature of all learning situations is the reduction in variability of an S-R relationship, and if extinction and punishment cause such relationships to become more variable, it is logical to assume that the processes involved in decreasing and increasing variability are mirror images of one another.

Evidence from many sources suggests, however, that once habits are formed they can not be "unformed," but only replaced. It appears that once an organism has learned one habit,

$$S_1\text{-}R_1,$$

then only when another habit,

$$S_1\text{-}R_2,$$

has been made even stronger, will R_1 cease to be predictably related to S_1.

By way of explaining this, consider the following statements: "The moon is not made of green cheese" and "Roger is not biting his nails any more." Logically, these statements both say nothing. Our knowledge of what the moon *is* made of is advanced very little by rejection of the cheese hypothesis, and similarly we have no idea what Roger *is doing* any more. Just as we can be sure that the moon is actually made of *something*, a living organism *must* be responding in some way at all times; the one thing he is not likely to do is to do nothing. In this sense, an organism does not literally learn "not to respond," because this term has no behavioral counterpart. It is, without question, simpler to describe the *general nature* of the outcomes of extinction and punishment in terms of what the subjects do not do. A certain lawfulness can be discerned in the mass of research with such tools. Nevertheless, these techniques can not be effectively applied to the individual case (which is always the ultimate goal of psychology) without realizing that habits are only lost by being supplanted.

The elimination of a habit is most efficiently achieved by the substitution of another response for the one that is being extinguished or punished. In fact, it even seems legitimate to posit that all instances of habit elimination, to the extent that they are effective, actually do involve some crude kind of habit substitution. When there is no systematic attempt to develop substitute habits, these will, of course, be rather unpredictable in their acquisition. Insofar as this is true, furthermore, it makes the comparison of various extinction or punishment experiments difficult. Subjects in different experiments can, due to differences in apparatus and procedure, acquire different substitute habits (and acquire them with different degrees of ease). It is not surprising to find that a given independent variable can occasionally be shown (in different experiments) to have quite contradictory effects upon behavior.

The general point that I wish to make at this moment is that the simplified description of extinction and punishment procedures as being the inverse of the learning process itself is convenient but inaccurate. A response disappears from an organism's repertoire only when it is replaced by another response. While simple habit formation does not provide us with the proper framework for analyzing the present subject matter, another part of the preceding material does. Extinction and punishment, I believe, can best be discussed as special cases of transfer of training.

EXTINCTION

Extinction was first observed systematically by Pavlov; in his learning situation, extinction was the procedure of withholding the UCS while continuing to present the CS. The ultimate result was the failure of the CR to follow the CS. Exactly the same effect is obtained with operant habits if S_L is presented, but without reinforcement of any R_L occurrences.

When the effects of extinction are studied in detail, the following seem to be characteristic of nearly all types of extinction situations:

(1) The relationship of S and R becomes increasingly unpredictable, or erratic—just the reverse of what occurs during habit formation.

(2) There is always some finite number of nonreinforced occurrences of S and R that will result in the failure of R to follow further presentations of S.

(3) The deterioration in an S-R relationship is, at least in a gross way, gradual and progressive.

(4) If, between blocks of extinction trials, there is any period during which the organism is not exposed to S, or similar stimuli, the S-R relationship will be observably better at the beginning of any extinction series than it was at the end of the previous block. This, as we noted in Chapter 2, is called *spontaneous recovery*.

(5) Spontaneous recovery is itself weakened by continued non-reinforcement. In general, it becomes easier to produce an unstable S-R relationship with each block of extinction trials.

The exact course of these general extinction effects will be determined by a large number of variables. Before going into the examination of these, however, we must pause to consider one methodological problem that is relevant to all of the research to be discussed.

When Is a Habit "Eliminated"?

Frequently psychologists report that they continued extinction trials until the subject "ceased responding." We know, in accord with the discussion above, that this is an oversimplification of the actual events that occurred. We can never be sure that a subject would never again perform some R_L that has been repeatedly non-reinforced. What is meant by the assertion that R_L ceased to occur is that, *given a certain number of opportunities of the sort that were formerly sufficient for the occurrence of R_L, that response did not occur*. This is quite reasonable and legitimate, of course, but it adds to the difficulties of formulating general principles that describe the course of extinction under various conditions.

When extinction is being studied in a free operant situation, "opportunities for R_L's occurrence" are measured in units of time in the presence of S_L. Sometimes S_L may be withdrawn and then re-presented one or more times (as by putting a rat in a Skinner box for 30 mins. daily for a week), but the basic criterion for asserting that extinction has accomplished its purpose is the failure of R_L to occur within a specific period of time while S_L is present. Controlled operant extinction, on the other hand, is fundamentally a matter of the number of specific S_L presentations in a row that are not accompanied by R_L; even in these cases it must still be decided how long the subject is to be permitted to remain in the presence of S_L before "No Response" is recorded for a given trial. For example, extinction trials in a straight runway may be continued until a rat has three successive trials on which it does not enter the endbox within two minutes after being placed at the starting point; on such trials the animal is considered not to have responded. Since most controlled operant situations (excluding simultaneous discrimination problems) were modeled directly upon Pavlov's experimental set-up, essentially the same criteria of "No Response" are employed in the latter case, too.

All criteria of extinction (i.e., the bases for asserting that an R_L has ceased to occur) are necessarily arbitrary. Although often determined by considerations that are irrelevant to the purpose of the research (such as convenience in scheduling experimental sessions), they are usually reasonable. That is not the problem; the difficulty arises when we try to compare the results of different experiments in order to derive some general principles about the factors affecting extinction. Although this is an impediment to the resolution of some issues in this area, there are also a great many factors that affect behavior in many extinction sessions in essentially the same way.

Many times, of course, habit deterioration is so great that it can be agreed that the habit in question has, for practical purposes, been eliminated. In still other cases, the *relative* amount of deterioration is of more importance than is an absolute evaluation; this will only be true when there are the controls necessary to permit useful relative evaluations to be made.

All in all, however, there is a need for standardized criteria for deciding whether a habit is functionally effective. This applies as well to the *establishment* of habits as to their *extinction*. Criteria are needed because without them many pseudo-issues can be created and/or perpetuated by basically ambiguous experimental findings.

Resistance to Extinction

It is misleading but quite convenient to have a general name for the over-all changes that take place during an extinction session. The term that has come to be used by psychologists for this purpose is *resistance to extinction*. This refers to the rate at which a subject's habit deterioration approaches some criterion of no response. Anything that facilitates the effects of extinction causes a *decrease* in resistance to extinction. Any condition that *increases* resistance to extinction, on the other hand, is a condition that counteracts the effects of extinction. It must be kept in mind that any experimental conclusion about factors affecting resistance to extinction may not necessarily apply to other situations in which a different criterion of no response is used. It may or it may not be generalizable; only further research can tell. But then, this is always to some extent true in fields of knowledge that stress their empirical base.

Now that we know some of the reservations about the soundness of the conclusions that can be drawn from research in this field, we are ready to consider in detail the variables whose effects on resistance to extinction (and allied phenomena) can now be summarized.

Reinforcement Factors as Determinants of Resistance to Extinction

The reinforcement conditions that were used prior to the extinction sessions are the most important determinants of extinction effects. For the most part, the effects on extinction behavior can be deduced from an undersanding of the effects of the various reinforcement procedures on habit acquisition itself, but there are a few surprises.

Schedules of Reinforcement

The stability of a habit is directly related to its resistance to extinction. Since we know what the relationship between reinforcement scheduling and habit stability is, it should be simple enough to figure out the effect of different schedules of X upon resistance to extinction: the more often and the more irregularly X has followed R_L during the habit maintenance period, the greater will be the resistance to extinction of the habit. This is the one most important determinant of extinction effects. Almost every other factor that can influence resistance to extinction does so only within the restrictions imposed by the particular reinforcement schedule that is being used; this point will be discussed more in the next section.

In addition to the relationship between irregularity of reinforcement and resistance to extinction, the three basic types of intermittent schedules (fixed-ratio, fixed-interval, and variable) each produces its own distinctive pattern of responding during free operant extinction. These patterns are essentially those that have been previously established during habit maintenance. For example, responding during extinction after prolonged training with a fixed-ratio schedule shows the bursts of responding that were developed by the schedule. Once an organism begins responding at any time during extinction, he tends to make about the number of responses that he formerly had to make before being reinforced; as extinction continues, these bursts occur more and more infrequently, but once responding begins it usually persists until the formerly reinforced number of R's has been made.

Space limitations prevent a more detailed description of the effects of various schedules on subsequent extinction behavior. The results of extensive work on this topic in free operant situations have been summarized in Skinner (247), and Ferster and Skinner (75). One of the unfortunate gaps in our current knowledge of behavioral principles arises from a lack of a comparable amount of data about the effects of schedules and extinction effects in controlled operant situations. The main reason for this may be the apparently prohibitive amount of time required to collect the equivalent information in controlled operant situations. Perhaps this is true, but even some tentative attempts toward filling in this area might be very revealing. Lacking such data, our discussion of other reinforcement effects on extinction behavior must be tempered by the realization that most of the principles to be described have only been shown to hold when initial habit maintenance was by continuous reinforcement. There are some exceptions to this limitation, of course, and in general such studies happily suggest that our present knowledge of the interactions between scheduling and other reinforcement effects may be fairly accurate.

Frequency of Reinforcement

Traditionally, the number of reinforcements given to a certain habit was presumed to be the pre-eminent determinant of such behavioral measures as resistance to extinction. It is now clear that only vast differences in frequency of reinforcement actually result in differences in performance.

Consider any controlled operant situation in which the occurrence of R_L and the occurrence of X are both under the experimenter's control to some extent. With such conditions it typically can be shown that a habit formed or maintained by almost any intermittent schedule of reinforcement will show greater resistance to extinction than a habit nurtured on continuous reinforcement, *despite the fact that the continuously reinforced habit has been reinforced up to twice as often as the intermittently reinforced habit.*

Of course, if the type of schedule is held constant, then resistance to extinction is again a direct function of frequency of reinforcement. This statement is limited by the fact noted earlier (Chapter 5) that increases in frequency of reinforcement, beyond some indefinite point, restrict the variability and, ultimately, even the intermittence of any schedule.

Quality of Reward and Resistance to Extinction

It is still not clear whether amount of reward is systematically related to resistance to extinction. *If* there is a relationship, it is the opposite of what you might first guess; there is some research that indicates that low reward (which is continuous) leads to greater resistance to extinction than high (32). Other experiments (e.g., 158) have failed to show any reliable relationship between amount of reward and extinction effects.

Logan and his students (171) have reported research on the interaction of X_{rew} amounts and reinforcement schedules in relation to extinction. In a controlled operant situation with less than 100 training trials it appears that shifts between high and low amounts of reward have the same effect as shifts back and forth between high reward and no reinforcement.

There has literally been no useful research on the effect of reward quality in extinction. This is not surprising; I have already pointed out the current transitional state of the quality and quantity dimensions of X_{rew}. Until this matter is resolved, we can not expect much parametric work in these areas.

Delay of Reward Effects

It is extremely difficult to set up a legitimate design for comparing the resistance to extinction of habits formed under different delay of reinforcement conditions. In general, all other factors constant, a small number of delayed reinforcements produces a markedly weaker habit than the same number of reinforcements presented immediately; in such cases, the results of running these habits through an extinction series would be trivial. Weak habits will certainly have less resistance to extinction than strong ones. On the other hand, if the learning situation is juggled so that a delayed-reward habit attains the same strength as a habit equally reinforced without delay, the delayed-reward habit will probably show the greater resistance to extinction. After all, a subject who has learned under such conditions has already learned to tolerate a delay between R_L and X_{rew} (this is true by definition, of course); this is most likely because there are mediating S^r's, as described in Chapter 5. Such additional reinforcers may persist during the extinction period, producing greater resistance to extinction. By way of summary, then, the effect of delayed reinforcement on resistance to extinction varies according to its original effect on habit strength; when a delayed X technique is perfected or employed for so long that it produces a habit equal in strength to one formed without delayed X, then the former habit will probably show the greater resistance to extinction.

"Frustration Effects" in Extinction after Rewarded Learning

When habits are established by the use of rewards, the early phases of extinction do not always show a steady weakening of habit strength, nor, indeed, *any* weakening. This is especially true if habit maintenance has taken place by continuous reinforcement. Instead, during the initial phases of extinction, the learned response may show one or both of these effects:

(1) The response may increase in vigor—i.e., may be performed more quickly or more frequently.

(2) There may be shifts between periods of stable, vigorous performance and periods of erratic, generally deteriorated responding. In other words, the habit weakening is not steady, although the ultimate result is the same as if it were.

The current views of extinction tend to view continuous non-reinforcement as a frustrating procedure, following the Dollard, *et al.* (66) definition of frustration as the interruption of a reward-oriented response sequence. The major contribution of the frustration hypothesis to the understanding of extinction effects is the suggestion that there are emotional consequences that interact with the habit-weakening results of this procedure.

It is hard to evaluate this position, for two interrelated reasons. First and most critical, there are no definitive studies of extinction that have involved habit formation by non-reward reinforcement; obviously, therefore, we cannot be sure that similar emotional effects might not occur during the extinction of habits that were established without the use of reward. The second reason is that the hypothesized effects of frustration are themselves so diversely defined by different psychologists that almost any behavioral change during extinction could be so labeled (163); when such confusion surrounds a concept, its usefulness diminishes.

Intermittent Reinforcement and "Frustration Effects"

If we recognize a frustration effect as one consequence of extinction, then one effect of intermittent reinforcement could be called that of increasing frustration tolerance. At any rate, it is certainly reasonable to argue that intermittent reinforcement, involving as it does the essential features of extinction, in some way prepares an organism for later, more prolonged periods of nonreinforcement. There is a great deal of diverse evidence supporting the fact that the more irregular a reinforcement schedule is, the more resistant to extinction is the habit so established (at least, when X was a reward).

We do not yet know the exact mechanism by which the variability in reinforcement occurrences affects performance under continuous nonreinforcement. One recurring suggestion is that even such a subject as the rat is somehow capable of integrating the after-effects of a series of X and NoX events into a sort of "super-S" to which R_L is associated. Continuous nonreinforcement, being only a partial change from intermittent reinforcement (since the latter involves some nonreinforcement), produces a cumulative S much like the "super-S" above; thus high positive transfer (positive because R is the same in each case) from habit maintenance to extinction sessions.

Weinstock (284), however, produced the standard differences in resistance to extinction following intermittent vs. continuous reinforcement when all training and extinction trials were spaced 24 hours apart. His subjects were rats, and his dependent variable was running speed in a straight runway. Although some of us may be able to accept (albeit not explain) that a rat can somehow assimilate the effects of several experiences that occur in close temporal contiguity, it is straining things somewhat to assert that this will occur even when the critical experiences occur at 24-hour intervals.

Weinstock's own suggestion was that intermittent NoX trials tended to reduce variability in R_L by eliminating irrelevant aspects of this series of responses. He later verified this by showing that after extended training on a one-trial-a-day routine, rats reinforced only intermittently stabilized at a faster running speed than that of continuously rewarded rats (284a). This finding, which duplicates the effect already known to hold for the simple, free operant R, only displaces the essential problem here: the basis of carrying differential effects of X and NoX events over a 24-hour period.

Weinstock's work points up one matter that I will soon emphasize at great length: resistance to extinction can almost always be predicted with great accuracy from an understanding of (1) the range of variability in the S's, R's and X-like events that occur during training, and (2) the extent that these ranges differ from those that occur during extinction. In Weinstock's studies, for instance, intermittently reinforced rats showed less variability in R_L during the latter stages of training and also through the earlier extinction trials.

S^r and Extinction

Every secondary reinforcer, by definition, attains and maintains its effectiveness as a reinforcer in the same way as does an operant habit. So everything we have reviewed concerning the factors that determine habit changes during extinction seems to apply as well to the changes that develop when an S^r is repeatedly presented without further pairing with some more permanent X. S^r's, in short, are subject to extinction. Because of this high similarity, there has been in recent years an increasing skepticism regarding the usefulness of the resistance-to-extinction method of verifying that a neutral stimulus has truly become a reinforcer. Using that technique, it is not necessarily true that habit changes due to shifting from some sort of S-R-S_n + X procedure to an S-R-S^r + NoX situation reflect the degree to which the given S_n has become an S^r independent of the changes to be expected in the habit itself. That is, when are we to say that the weakening in a habit after several occurrences of S-R-S^r-NoX is due to the extinction of the secondary reinforcer rather than to extinction of the habit itself? There are techniques imaginable whereby such a decision could be made objectively, but they are not commonly used now in secondary reinforcement research.[1]

We have already seen the great relativity of the effects of various reinforcement procedures; let us now consider some experiments by Bitterman and his students (27, 69) that suggest an analogous effect in the case of secondary reinforcement strength. The crucial group in the Bitterman studies was one in which rats were trained to make a runway approach response on a straight runway under

[1] These techniques are sometimes used in studies of extinction where it is deemed necessary to *eliminate* S^r effects on the nonreinforced trials.

1:2 fixed-ratio reinforcement. On rewarded (food) trials, a white endbox was in place; on nonreinforced trials, there was a black box present. The apparatus was constructed so that a subject could not see which endbox was in place until the R_L was completed. (There were several other controls—and control groups—that we need not examine in detail; let it suffice to say that the controls were adequate.) The important comparison was between the performances of subjects given extinction trials with the white—S^r—box present and those undergoing extinction with the black—NoX—box in place.

The results were hardly those to be expected from a simple interpretation of behavior as a function of the occurrence of reinforcers, including experimentally established ones. Rats who consistently found the black box on extinction trials showed *greater* resistance to extinction than did rats who found the now-empty white box. In other words, stimuli previously associated with X_{rew} did not produce as much resistance to extinction as did stimuli that had been associated with NoX.

In terms of the model, these animals' training period consisted of two sorts of trials:

$$\text{S-}R_L\text{-}S_w + X_{rew}, \text{ and}$$

$$\text{S-}R_L\text{-}S_B + \text{NoX},$$

where S_w and S_B represent the white and the black endboxes, respectively.

For one group, the extinction sessions involved

$$\text{S-}R_L\text{-}S_W + \text{NoX},$$

while the other subjects found this combination on extinction trials:

$$\text{S-}R_L\text{-}S_B + \text{NoX}.$$

According to our means of schematizing learning situations, there is more similarity between the extinction trials and the training trials with the second-named extinction procedure than there is with the first. Apparently, this is an important difference.

Bitterman's results need not be interpreted as questioning the validity of the S^r concept. Saltzman (227), for instance, used a training procedure (described on pp. 84–85) essentially the same as Bitterman's and subsequently demonstrated the superior reinforcing effectiveness of the stimuli originally paired with X_{rew}. It seems more likely, instead, that Bitterman's work provides an important demonstration of the fact that a continuous nonreinforcement procedure is *not* merely the inverse of some habit formation situation.

Other Factors Traditionally Considered Important in Extinction

Effort as a Factor in Extinction

One of the latter-day developments from Pavlov's explanation of extinction was an attempt to relate the concept of inhibition to that of work, or physical effort. Mowrer and Jones (198) reported an experiment that appeared to verify the hypothesis that resistance to extinction is inversely related to the amount of work required to perform the R undergoing extinction; this fact, in turn, was used to elaborate the hypothetical inhibitory factor that was assumed to be the determinant of extinction results—this theoretical position was described in Chapter 2.

Other psychologists doubted that the relationship of work to habit formation or to extinction was a fundamental one. Perhaps this skepticism was due to the fact that in order to vary the effortfulness of a response, it was necessary to permit R_L itself to vary. In short, R's of different degrees of effortfulness are usually discriminably different R's. As the response differentiation experiment described on p. 189 brought out, not only psychologists but even rats can distinguish between R's that may accomplish the same result (in this example, lever depression), while differing in the effort expended in doing so.

Different implications easily follow from differences in the definition of basic terms. Specifically, in the case of the work variable, when R's differing in effortfulness came to be regarded as actually being different R's, new experiments and new ways of analyzing old experiments became apparent. These innovations produced evidence that *any* change in effort (i.e., in R_L itself) that was inaugurated along with the start of an extinction session would produce less resistance to extinction than *no* change.

Although there had been earlier critics of the Mowrer-Jones work, a report by Maatsch, Adelman, and Denny (175) was the first to reflect a real skepticism about the necessity of a work-produced-inhibition concept as an explanation of the usual relationship between effort and resistance to extinction. Maatsch *et al.* first trained all their rats to press a lever with a 40-gm. counterweight; then the subjects were assigned to groups for which the counterweight was either 10, 40, or 80 gm. After extensive training under one of these work conditions, subjects were given extinction sessions under the same work condition as that on which they had most recently been trained. Four different measures of resistance to extinction failed to show any differences in the average extinction performance of the three groups. This is contradictory to a work-produced-inhibition account of extinction, but is consistent with the assumption that S_L-R_{10}, S_L-R_{40}, and S_L-R_{80} are *different* habits (because they involve different responses). In the Maatsch experiment the training conditions were designed to keep these habits' strengths as equal as possible; doing this, it turned out, sufficed to eliminate the effort factor as an important source of variation during extinction.

Lawson and Brownstein (160) approached this topic in much the same way as had Maatsch, Adelman and Denny, except that we used an R_L requiring a lot of effort (jumping a series of hurdles in a straight alley) without providing much training on the low-work R that half of their rats performed during extinction. The animals that were required to continue jumping hurdles during extinction showed reliably greater resistance to extinction than did those shifted to an easier R—no hurdles—when extinction began.

In other words, reducing the effortfulness of a response can reduce that response's resistance to extinction. At least that would be the conventional and possibly paradox-provoking way of describing the Lawson-Brownstein findings. There is, however, a less puzzling way of viewing those data. Let us schematize the training conditions in the usual manner:

$$S_L\text{-}R_L\text{-}X$$

The extinction condition for the High-Work group would be depicted as:

$$S_L\text{-}R_L\text{-}NoX$$

On the other hand, the extinction session involved changes in all facets of the model for the Low-Work subjects:

$$S'_L\text{-}R'_L\text{-}NoX$$

S_L is changed due to removal of hurdles; the same change affects R_L as well—it can no longer be performed as it was formerly.

It should be clear how Brownstein and I found less resistance to extinction in the group required to expend less effort per response. The procedures by which we reduced the effortfulness of R changed the situation to such an extent that there was less positive transfer from the training conditions to the extinction session for the low-work group than there was for the high-work group.

There is, then, no simple relationship between effortfulness of R and habit performance. Differences in effort amount to differences in R's, so that all studies of the effort variable are actually studies either of (1) transfer of training, or of (2) the functional equivalence of R's reinforced in the same way under the same (S) conditions. Studies of the first type are those in which a subject has to perform R's requiring different amounts of effort at different times. In studies of R equivalence the comparisons are between the performances of subjects required to do different amounts of work for identical reinforcement in the same (or nearly the same) environment.

If one concluded that the above analysis suggests that most research on the "work variable" is of little value, he would be wrong. The conceptualizations of the problem being studied may have been inadequate, but many of the studies themselves were very ingenious (see 10, 198, 252 for critiques of much of this work). As means of attacking the problem of scaling R compatibility (discussed in Chapter 7), many of the techniques used to study effort effects look as if they might be very helpful.

Distribution of Extinction Trials

Extinction is the procedure of withholding reinforcement when a learned R occurs in the presence of the previously appropriate S's. Resistance to extinction is most directly reflected by the number of times in succession that R has occurred without additional reinforcement. We have already seen that the speed with which S-R-X, S-R-NoX, and so on follow each other can influence the ease of learning. The effects of *distribution of practice*, as this variable is called, can be noted in extinction, just as in learning. In general, massed extinction trials lead to more rapid habit-weakening than do spaced extinction trials. There *are* exceptions to this generalization, however, perhaps the most noted of which has been, in recent times, provided by the results of Virginia Sheffield's research (239).

Sheffield's design was as follows. Half of her rats received their daily blocks of training trials in a straight alley under massed conditions (15 secs. between the end of one trial and the start of the next one); the other subjects' trials were spaced 15 mins. apart. All subjects were then given a fixed number of extinction trials; for half of the subjects the intertrial interval remained the same as it had been during training. Half of the subjects in each training group, however, had their intertrial interval switched when the extinction sessions began. This design is summarized in Table VI.

TABLE VI
Times between Training and Extinction Trials Used by Sheffield (239)

Group	Time Between Training Trials	Time Between Extinction Trials
Massed-Massed	15 seconds	15 seconds
Massed-Spaced	15 seconds	15 minutes
Spaced-Spaced	15 minutes	15 minutes
Spaced-Massed	15 minutes	15 seconds

The standard prediction in this experimental situation would be that the animals given a 15-minute rest between extinction trials would show greater resistance to extinction than would those subjects having only a 15-second separation. Sheffield found just the opposite relationship—massed extinction trials, according to her interpretation, were associated with greater resistance to extinction than were spaced extinction trials.

The Effect of Measures of Resistance to Extinction on the Conclusions Drawn from Studies of Extinction

The rather unusual discovery of Sheffield's was eventually reconciled with more standard lines of thought by W. C. Stanley, another graduate student in the Yale laboratory (where Sheffield did her work). Sheffield had actually used a quite indirect measure of resistance to extinction. All her subjects received thirty consecutive nonreinforced trials, and the *speed* of response on each one was recorded; there were very few failures to respond on these trials, so that her measure of performance was most directly related to response speed. Now, changes in response speed under continuous reinforcement should certainly be correlated with (or be another way of *defining*) resistance to extinction. But traditional measures of resistance to extinction used an all-or-none definition of R; resistance was measured by the *number of trials* on which R occurred. Extinction trials were continued until the experimenter was satisfied that R, as he defined it, had ceased to occur. It was *this* measure of resistance to extinction that had been used in the studies antedating Sheffield from which the generalization about distribution of trials and resistance had evolved.

Stanley's contribution (260) to this problem was via a situation in which he varied distribution of extinction trials while using both Sheffield's measure and the traditional way of evaluating resistance to extinction. This was accomplished by using a number of extinction trials that was the same for all subjects (making Sheffield's measure appropriate), but that was great enough so that failures to respond eventually became prevalent in all subjects' records (thus permitting a trials-to-no-response score). This dual measurement technique revealed that everybody was right.

Specifically, Stanley found that when resistance to extinction was measured by trials to failure-to-respond, resistance was less with massed extinction trials than with spaced. On the other hand, average response speed during extinction was faster for subjects given massed trials. In brief, subjects undergoing massed extinction respond more vigorously when they respond at all, but they do not respond as frequently.

Spontaneous Recovery

We know that when an extinction procedure first produces sufficient habit weakening to result in no R in the presence of S_L, this is no guarantee that the given S-R relationship has permanently reverted to a random one. Pavlov had noted that the effects of extinction could be partially reversed by temporarily removing the subject from the experimental situation. Spontaneous recovery, as Pavlov called it, is as apparent in operant learning as in Pavlovian conditioning, and follows exactly the same empirical laws in both cases.

This behavioral event demonstrates that habits are not necessarily eliminated when they cease to occur, since they recur later. This raises some problems with respect to a general, abstract theory of learning. Spontaneous recovery has been regarded as such a pivotal problem that nearly all learning theorists have taken up the matter of spontaneous recovery during the early development of their systems of learning. It has typically been assumed that whatever principle is the basis of spontaneous recovery is also the basis of many other effects on habits of variations in the spacing of S-R occurrences. One of the most famous of such extensions was that made by Clark L. Hull (124), who showed how Pavlov's concepts of inhibition and conditioned inhibition could be used to predict most of the other effects on habits that are due to spacing factors. This is because one of the most important determinants of spontaneous recovery is the amount of time that elapses between successive extinction trials and/or extinction sessions, as we saw when discussing the Sheffield-Stanley research.

Extinction as a Type of Habit Interaction

In Chapter 6 the concept of a habit was broadened from that used in the first five chapters. The revised definition of habit made it a term for any systematic change in a stimulus-response relationship due to the repeated occurrence of some S-R-X situation. An S-R-NoX procedure was considered to qualify as a habit formation situation; nonreinforced responses were found to show predictable and important changes during the course of discrimination learning. This system of analyzing learning situations pointed up the continuity between simple habit formation (and/or maintenance) and discrimination learning; it seems that a similar mode of analysis could be applied to extinction phenomena, and it should be beginning to be apparent how such an application would look. In terms of the standard symbols, the basic extinction procedure involves two steps:

(1) S-R-X

(2) S-R-NoX

Actually, of course, step 2 alone describes the extinction situation per se. Step 1 is of great importance, however, in the understanding of extinction phenomena; almost all of the important determinants of resistance to extinction that we can now identify result from procedures employed in step 1, and/or from the similarity of step 1 and step 2 procedures.

There now seems to be sufficient evidence for us to formulate a general statement about this particular type of habit interaction: *Resistance to extinction is directly related to the similarity between the training (or maintenance) situation and the extinction situation.* In fact, it does not seem unreasonable to regard this as the basic *Law of Extinction.*

As with all scientific laws, or capsule descriptions of a number of specific variables, a lot of elaboration is necessary. And some of this elaboration poses quite important problems that are as yet unsolved.

For instance, it should be clear by now that when a psychologist talks about similarity he is usually expressing little more than a hunch. The difficulties with the notion of similarity that plagued us in the analysis of discrimination and transfer crop up here again, and limit our ability to test the Law crucially.

Dimensions of Variation in Training-Extinction Situations

Granting that there are ambiguities in the meaning of similarity in contemporary psychology, we can still see the *sources* of possible variation in similarity as an organism shifts from a situation that is conducive to habit formation (or maintenance) to one that reverses this S-R stability.

1. Variations in X

Obviously the extinction of an S-R relationship must involve at least a change from continuous X to continuous NoX. Other degrees of transition from maintenance to extinction schedules of reinforcement are possible, of course; for example, going from variable-ratio X to continuous NoX would seem to be less of a change than a shift from 100 per cent to 0 per cent reinforcement. We have already seen that irregular, intermittent reinforcement does, indeed, produce the greatest resistance to extinction of all reinforcement conditions.

As evidence of this we can look at the results of an experiment by Lewis and Duncan (169). I cite this one out of the innumerable experiments available for reasons that are well put by the experimenters themselves:

The purpose of this study was to determine the effect of different percentages of reward upon extinction of a lever-pulling response. The study differs from most others in the area of partial reinforcement in three principal ways. First, a larger number of different percentages of reinforcement is used than have previously been employed. Second, the reward used [money] was highly meaningful to the human [subjects]. And third, the task used—playing a slot machine—was one that had considerable intrinsic interest for the [subjects]. (169, p. 23)

There was first a series of trials on which the subjects were paid off according to one of a number of variable-ratio schedules each of which resulted in a different percentage of X's per eight R's (the percentages used are shown on the abscissa of Figure 19). Reinforcement (5 cents) occurred without regard to the combination of symbols that appeared on any play. The results are shown in Figure 19.

FIGURE 19

Resistance of a "Gambling Habit" Following Various X/R Percentages

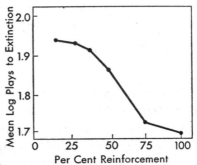

Per Cent Reinforcement

Adapted from Lewis and Duncan (169), in the *Journal of Experimental Psychology*, vol. 54, p. 116. Used by permission of the American Psychological Association.

Even in a situation in which the subject has nothing to lose by continued responding (since he could play as often as he wished without losing any previous winnings), the tendency to keep on playing under continuous NoX shows a steady inverse relationship to the irregularity of reinforcement that preceded the extinction period.

1a. Variations in S's associated with X and/or NoX.

The most important features of this source of training-extinction variation were noted a few pages earlier in connection with Bitterman's experiments (pp. 258–59). Actually, by way of control conditions, Bitterman's studies provided comparisons between more groups than were described in the earlier account of his work. The total number of training-extinction relationships provided by the researches in question are shown in Table VII; in that table the extinction conditions are shown in the right column, from highest down to least, according to the degree of resistance to extinction associated with each.

TABLE VII

Resistance to Extinction as a Function of
Relationship between S_n's and X and/or NoX
on Training and Extinction Trials

TRAINING CONDITIONS	EXTINCTION CONDITIONS
$S_w + X_{rew}$ and $S_w + NoX$	$S_w + NoX$
$S_w + X_{rew}$ and $S_b + NoX$	$S_b + NoX$ $S_w + NoX$ $S_g + NoX$

S_w, S_b, and S_g represent, respectively, a white, a black, and a gray endbox that were at the end of a straight runway under the indicated conditions. The groups shown in the second column are in order from most to least resistance to extinction, as summarized from the results of two experiments by Bitterman *et al.* (27, 69).

2. Variations in S

In view of the lengthy discussions of this topic that have already been presented in Chapters 6 and 7, further elaboration hardly seems necessary here. Suffice it to say that whenever similarity in S's *can* be quantified, resistance to extinction is less the greater the difference between the S of the training and that of the extinction trials.

It was pointed out in Chapter 2 that the trial-to-trial variability in S is an important determinant of (1) the smoothness of acquisition curves for individual subjects (280), and (2) the resistance to extinction of habits (177).

In general, intertrial variability in S seems to be an important determinant of at least some sorts of mediated stimulus generalization. As such, it is an influence on discrimination learning, transfer of training, and—consequently—on extinction.

3. Variations in R

As was pointed out in relation to the variable of effort (pp. 260–63), resistance to extinction will be affected by any shift in the R that is required (and/or permitted) as a shift is made from maintenance to extinction conditions. It is difficult to assess the relative importance of this factor alone, however, because it is hard to create situations in which a predictable shift from R_L (in training) to R'_L (during extinction) can be accomplished without also changing S_L.

4. Summary of Possible Variations between Training and Extinction Conditions

When there are the foregoing number of possible variations in S, in R, and in X that can be manipulated rather independently, the variations that could be created by the joint alteration of extinction determinants in more than one dimension are rather staggering. I emphasize this because many psychologists have treated extinction as an extremely simple procedure for which the *sole* defining characteristic is continuous NoX. The point I am developing here is that extinction need not be that simple, and, in actual practice as a research tool, is rarely that simple.

NoX as a Cue

The "learning how to learn" experiments described in Chapter 7 indicate that nonreinforcement *can* serve as an important cue in discrimination learning. Harlow and Hicks (108) have shown that for rhesus monkeys a single nonreinforcement of the choice of an object that then becomes the negative member of a simultaneous discrimination problem facilitates the solution of the problem more than does a single reinforcement of the choice of the to-be-correct stimulus. This is shown in Figure 20. These data show, in brief, that a single trial on which the monkey is shown what is wrong is of more assistance to him in solving the discrimination than is a single trial on which he is shown what is right.

An even more sophisticated reaction to NoX is revealed in the discrimination reversal experiment. Discrimination reversal refers, as we have seen, to the situation in which a subject is trained on a

FIGURE 20

Performance on First Simultaneous Discrimination Trials as a Function of Whether NoX or X Was Given as Pretraining

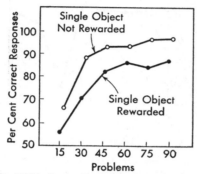

From Harlow and Hicks (108), in the *Psychological Review*, vol. 64, p. 106. Used by permission of the American Psychological Association.

simultaneous problem until he is always making the correct response, i.e., either S-R or S'-R'. Then the problem is reversed; now the relationships S-R' and S'-R are reinforced. Initially, this produces negative transfer, but if rhesus monkeys are given a large number of such reversal problems they begin to "catch on," as we might say. In fact, merely being well trained on two-choice discrimination problems in general seems to be sufficient; again, this phenomenon seems to be limited to the primates. The data in Figure 21 show the average performances of four rhesus monkeys on 96 discrimination reversal problems; prior to these problems, they had no reversal experience at all, but they had received a total of 611 two-choice discrimination problems without reversal. When you consider that Figure 21 thus includes the monkeys' performances on the very first reversal problem they ever had, it is clear that the effect suggested by the data in Figure 20 (above) is quite general.

In other words, the monkeys learn a general reaction of not repeating an S-R relationship that has just been nonreinforced, even though it may have been reinforced earlier.

FIGURE 21

Average Performance by Four Rhesus Monkeys
on 96 Discrimination-Reversal Problems

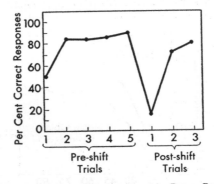

These data are from the control group of an experiment by Braun, Barnes and Patton (33). From the *Journal of Comparative and Physiological Psychology*, vol. 50, p. 642. Used by permission of the American Psychological Association.

In the foregoing cases NoX was a cue for the alteration of the monkey's behavior so that it could again obtain X_{rew} a high proportion of the time. NoX can, however, become an S for various R's even when no further X_{rew} is forthcoming—i.e., even when extinction continues.

Adelman and Maatsch (3) have shown that resistance to extinction can be determined by the R that is associated with NoX. Using rats that had first been trained to run a straight alley under 100 per cent X_{rew}, they ran each of their subjects under one of the following three conditions:

Compatible R

These rats were removed from the apparatus only after they had jumped up on a ledge that went around the top of the endbox. Jumping to this ledge first required that the animal enter the endbox.

Therefore, if we regard the jumping response as the R in a habit, the S part of which is NoX$_{rew}$ (and the X, removal from the apparatus), this habit does not tend to interfere with the previously established habit of running from the starting box to the endbox.

Incompatible R

Unlike those in the other two groups, these rats were permitted to leave the endbox again after they had entered it. In fact, they were required to do so: if they entered the endbox these rats were not removed from the apparatus until after they had partially retraced their steps and re-entered the alley proper.

Standard

These rats entered the endbox, and after 20 secs. were removed from it without regard for what they were doing at that time. This is the typical procedure used in the extinction of a controlled operant R.

In all cases, an animal was removed from the apparatus (wherever he was) if he had not entered the endbox within two minutes after being put into the starting box. The experimenters reasoned that the subjects who jumped out of the endbox—*Compatible* R—were learning a habit that did not interfere with the earlier approach habit, whereas teaching the rats to *go out of* the endbox—*Incompatible* R—was directly contradictory to the earlier habit. The average resistance to extinction of the *Standard* group was expected to fall between that of the other two groups. Different standard subjects, removed without regard for their behavior in the presence of NoX, should learn different habits—some of which would be interfering with, some complementing, the earlier approach habit—thus *on the average* their resistances to extinction should be intermediate to that in the other two groups.

How well this prediction was confirmed is revealed in Figure 22. I am, of course, particularly impressed by this experiment because of its very straightforward support of the habit-interaction interpretation of extinction.

A final bit of evidence that suggests that NoX—in a situation where X_{rew} has previously been forthcoming—can serve as a cue is that offered by Levy (167). Levy first trained his rats on a simple "discriminative stimulus" type of problem; the sound of a buzzer or no buzzer (i.e., no systematic sounds) were the S's. For half of

FIGURE 22

Resistance to Extinction as a Function of the R Associated with NoX

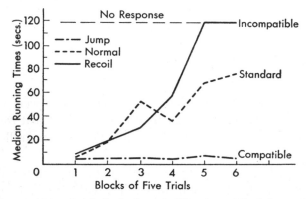

From Adelman and Maatsch (3), in the *Journal of Experimental Psychology*, vol. 50, p. 64. Used by permission of the American Psychological Association.

the subjects a simple approach R was reinforced when it occurred in the presence of the sound of the buzzer, but not when there was no buzzer; for the other rats, X_{rew} followed R_L on silent trials, but not when the buzzer was sounded. Subsequently, all these rats were given a delayed reaction problem to learn. This is a problem in which the subject is first shown the one of three boxes that contains food, but he is not permitted to approach the correct box immediately. During and after the delay period, the critical cues are absent. Levy embellished this technique by adding delay of reward *after* either R_L or R'_L as well as between S_L and R.

Levy's most important experimental manipulation was the presentation of the same sound conditions *after* R_L and R'_L that had previously preceded (or occurred simultaneously with) reinforced and nonreinforced R's, respectively, during the earlier phase of the experiment. In other words, if the buzzer had earlier been associated with reinforced pairings of S_L, it then was associated with correct (rewarded) responses in the delayed reaction situation. On the other hand, if the buzzer had previously sounded on nonreinforced trials, it also signified the same event (NoX) in the delayed reaction problem; the buzzer, that is, sounded only when the rat made a wrong choice.

Levy found that the delayed problem was solved more quickly by those rats for whom the buzzer again stood for NoX than by those for whom the buzzer, owing to its previous pairing with X_{rew}, was an S^r. The fact that an S that is associated with NoX_{rew} in one situation could serve as a rapid inhibitor of R'_L's in another situation was, quite reasonably, considered by Levy to be a demonstration of conditioned inhibition in operant learning. This interpretation is not, however, incompatible with the viewpoint being put forth here: When NoX is the only, or the most important, difference between two learning situations, some organisms may learn to use this difference as a cue for changes in behavior.

Generally, discrimination and extinction data fit together quite well in their emphasis on the importance of NoX as a determinant of response changes in habit interaction cases. Equally important, however, is the fact that, as a result of changes in the NoX conditions, new habits have been formed only in situations where another systematic relationship between an R and X supplants a previous R_L-X association. Fundamentally therefore, reinforcement remains of the greatest importance in the control of learning situations. The point that has been brought out by the preceding discussion is that nonreinforcement is not necessarily equivalent with nothing happening. In situations in which X has previously followed behavior in some predictable fashion, the occurrence of NoX may be quite a significant event.

THE ROLE OF PUNISHMENT IN HABIT ALTERATION

In accordance with the general definition of punishment (p. 247), our concern here is with the results that are obtained when some R_L is followed by S_{nox}. The evidence is fairly consistent that the immediate effect of pairing almost any R and an S_{nox} is the suppression of that R, suppression being defined by the same criteria as are used, in extinction studies, to define "no response." The classic demonstration of this was carried out by Estes (71). Estes' fairly exhaustive study of the role of S_{nox} in free operant behavior further revealed, however, that this suppressing effect is not permanent. There are a number of experimental manipulations (all involving the elimination of more S_{nox}, of course) that could be used to revive a response following a period in which it was punished.

Estes' results seem to be in conflict with common sense. Almost everyone can cite occasions (1) on which he has manipulated others' behavior, and (2) on which his own behavior has been controlled by the use of punishment. It seems that the effects of punishment may or may not be permanent. Such apparent ambiguity in the observable facts usually means that there are other variables that also need to be evaluated in order to predict the effects of the use of punishment.

Punishment and Escape Learning

Following the schematic representation used for extinction, a punishment situation can also be depicted as involving two steps:

(1) $S_L\text{-}R_L\text{-}X/NoX,$[2] then

(2) $S_L\text{-}R_L\text{-}S_{nox}$

Now, *escape learning* (pp. 87–89) is a situation in which a subject develops a stable response to an S_{nox} itself. This occurs if the

---

[2] The symbol "X/NoX" is a shorthand denotation than an S-R relationship has been followed by both reinforcement and nonreinforcement according to some intermittent schedule.

organism can develop a response that consistently terminates S_{nox}. It certainly is possible that some punishment situations might develop in this sequence:

$$S_{L_1}\text{-}R_{L_1}\text{-}S_{nox}\text{-}R_{L_2}\text{-}X,$$

where X is now the *termination* of S_{nox}. This is the basis for our first type of habit interaction that involves punishment: the type in which the earlier-established habit is described by the symbols $S_{L_1}\text{-}R_{L_1}$, and the second habit is $S_{nox}\text{-}R_{L_2}\text{-}X$.

This type of habit interaction will occur whenever the punishment—S_{nox}—*can* consistently be terminated by a given response. When this is so we have a situation in which there will be a high *degree* of transfer of training (because S_L is a part of both the original and the punishment situations). The *direction* of transfer, of course, will be determined by the "compatibility" of R_{L_1} and R_{L_2}. What the direction is will determine how effective the use of punishment is to be.

If there is *negative* transfer, punishment will be effective (i.e., R_{L_1} will be eliminated), for three interrelated reasons. First of all, R_{L_1} is being subjected to extinction, since it is no longer followed by any reinforcement. Secondly, the sequence $R_{L_1}\text{-}S_{nox}$ will momentarily reduce the organism's tendency to repeat R_{L_1}. Finally, R_{L_2} *is* being reinforced, concomitantly with the suppression of R_{L_1}, because R_{L_2} accompanies the elimination S_{nox}.

If, on the other hand, R_{L_2} is compatible with R_{L_1} (*positive* transfer), then the strengthening of Habit₂ should tend to counteract the effects of weakening Habit₁. In such a case, punishment will only eliminate Habit₁ slowly, if at all. Admittedly, it may be rare, either in nature or in the lab, for R_{L_1} and R_{L_2} to be highly compatible, though there is at least one example of such a situation in everyday life; some parents occasionally resort to physical punishment as a means of trying to get a child to stop crying. This may be satisfactory as a means of giving vent to one's exasperation, but as an effective training device it obviously leaves much to be desired.

Counter-conditioning Revisited

In many, if not most, punishment situations, S_{nox} is terminated without regard for the behavior of the organism being punished. In such cases there is no possibility for any type of *operant* $Habit_2$ establishment. But some S_{nox}'s have many of the characteristics of UCS's. This facet of punishing stimuli would be most important when their onsets and terminations are both independent of the actions of the organism, since this latter relationship is typical of the way in which many UCS's are actually employed in Pavlovian situations. Let us explore the implications of S_{nox} as a UCS.

When S_{nox} is cast in the role of a UCS, punishment situations take the following form:

$$S_{L_1}\text{-}R_{L_1}\text{-}UCS_2\text{-}UCR_2$$

Such a description is highly reminiscent of a technique of response elimination that was discussed several chapters ago, the process of *counter-conditioning* (p. 61), wherein a learned R is eliminated by presenting the S's for a strongly competing UCR.

There is little direct evidence of the ease with which predictions can be made about interactions between operant and Pavlovian habits. Logically, however, such an amalgamation does not suggest any unique complications. The counter-conditioning case of punishment should follow the principles already cited in the analysis of the escape learning type of punishment situation: the compatibility of CR_2 and R_{L_1} will determine the effectiveness of $S_{nox}-UCS_2-$as a means of eliminating R_{L_1}.

Punishment and Avoidance Learning

It should be clear now that the most effective use of punishment would be purposely designed to result in R_{L_2} (some response to S_{nox}) *replacing* R_{L_1} (the undesirable response) as the response associated with the original S_L. The most direct method of achieving this should be familiar by now: it is *avoidance learning*.

The earlier discussion of avoidance learning (pp. 89–96), however, brought out that the development of an avoidance habit was not dependent upon the prior acquisition of an escape response to S_{nox} itself. It seems sufficient to associate S_{nox} with some other consistent feature of the environment in which it occurs; the latter S feature then becomes fear-producing (or noxious) in its own right. An organism may try to avoid such an S, but never learn to escape S_{nox} itself. So avoidance learning provides us with a paradox. On the one hand, it can be the most effective way of eliminating responses via punishment; it can also be the most ineffective, for either of two reasons:

(1) The simplest sorts of avoidance R's are fear (flight) reactions. Such reactions are often not socially acceptable. In many human learning situations, we hope to minimize the occurrence of certain kinds of behavior without substituting fright reactions to the stimuli involved. For example, in our culture people need to learn to appreciate the dangers of electricity without developing a morbid terror of anything using that source of energy; similarly with fire.

(2) Often, in everyday situations, there are stimuli that precede the occurrence of S_{nox} and are distinct from either S_{nox} itself *or* S_{L_1}. Such a situation would be diagrammed as:

$$S_{L_1}\text{-}R_{L_1}\text{-}S_2\text{-}S_{nox}\text{-}R_2 \ldots$$

Furthermore, S_2 may occur before R_{L_1}, thus:

$$\left.\begin{array}{c} S_{L_1} \\ + \\ S_2 \end{array}\right\} \text{-}R_{L_1}\text{-}S_{nox} \ldots$$

In such a case the possibility is quite good that the organism might form a discrimination between the foregoing instance and this case:

$$S_{L_1}\text{-}R_{L_1}\text{-}NoS_{nox}.$$

Discrimination could occur whenever some S_2 was the inevitable precursor of S_{nox}. Thus, the *combination* of S_{L_1} *and* S_2 might inhibit R_{L_1} while S_{L_1} *alone* would continue to be associated with the occurrence of R_{L_1}.

To illustrate this second problem with punishment-derived avoidance, consider the problem of teaching a two-year-old child to stay from some highly attractive stimulus object such as a Christmas tree (for fear that he might injure himself by pulling it over, or by causing an electrical malfunction). A typical approach is for the parents to punish the child whenever he touches the tree *in their presence.* Does this guarantee that the child will stay away from the tree when his parents are not in the room? Probably not. What the child is most apt to do is to discriminate between the S complex, tree-plus-parents —i.e., S_1 *and* S_2—and the tree-alone condition—S_1—because the consequences of responding are different under the two S conditions.

Introducing S_{nox} without Stopping X_{rew}

Another potential difficulty that might be seen in the foregoing example could stem from the fact that the undesirable response (touching the Christmas tree) might be intrinsically rewarding. One certainly ventures into rough waters whenever one invokes concepts such as "intrinsically rewarding," but at least certain types of behavior might justify the use of that term; erotic behavior (e.g., thumb-sucking, playing with one's genitals) and curiosity are cases in point.

Whenever we punish a response, the mere occurrence of which is rewarding, we are asking for trouble. If R_1 is followed *first* by X_{rew} and *then* by S_{nox}, the best we can hope for is the development of conflict behavior. The determinants of conflict resolution, however, concern an entirely different set of variables than those involved in punishment situations. In other words, this effect of S_{nox} is to create more problems than it solves.

The Effect of Delayed Punishment

Discussion of the case in which R_1 is intrinsically rewarding, so that X_{rew} inevitably must precede S_{nox} by some small amount of time, leads directly to that in which S_{nox} is quite perceptibly separated from the R that is supposed to be eliminated. The results of such a procedure can easily be summarized: it doesn't work at all. The little bit of research on this problem that can be found is in agreement. S_{nox}, apparently, can only influence those R's that are temporally contiguous to its occurrence. Delayed punishment, therefore, seems even more likely to alter behavior in unexpected ways than delayed reward sometimes does.

Just as with delayed reward, delayed punishment *may* occasionally work with human beings if the response and the punishment can be linked together symbolically, or via some other mediating stimulus. All societies, for example, require their members to be their own policemen in respect to certain taboos; people are expected to inhibit certain actions even when it is perfectly obvious that there could be no immediate punishment if they were performed. The mediating stimuli for such situations are what we call anxiety, guilt, or conscience. At present, psychologists generally hold that these effects are produced by procedures analogous to those of avoidance learning.

By and large, however, punishment must be immediate if it is to be effective at all. This accounts for the failure of our law enforcement and penal systems to act as highly effective *deterrents* to crime. The delay between the occurrence of a criminal act and the time when the criminal is caught (not to mention his even later imprisonment) is usually sufficiently great (even if it is only a matter of hours) that it is not particularly surprising to find criminals who associate being arrested not with the crime, but with some subsequent behavior on their part. Thus, responses such as, "If I'd only had another hour you guys would never have got me," do not reflect simply a callous, antisocial attitude; in terms of learning principles per se, such a viewpoint is "reasonable."

In addition to the fact that delayed punishment may affect the wrong behavior, delay is also ineffective because it increases the possibility for the undesirable response to be reinforced in some way. We can see this fact, too, in the criminal's case. If capture is not immediate, then there is indeed a good chance that the act of breaking a law will be immediately reinforced. No matter what the long-range consequences turn out to be, from the criminal's point of view the fact may still remain that sticking a gun in someone's face *was* followed by the acquisition of money; ergo, armed robbery "obvi-ously" works, the problem being not to get caught *later*.

Punishment and Discrimination Learning

The Azrin-Lindsley demonstration (Chapter 3), by which the essentials of operant learning were introduced, served also to illus-trate how fairly complex, human behavior could be controlled and predicted by an extrapolation from principles largely worked out in unnatural (i.e., well-controlled) situations using infra-human sub-jects. A study that I now wish to describe in some detail is intended to serve the same dual purpose: it illustrates the most effective use of punishment as a way of altering behavior, and also shows another successful excursion of basic behavior theory into the more complex field of social psychology.

The rationale and procedure of the experiment in question have been quite clearly described by the experimenter himself, Dr. J. B. Sidowski: [3]

The study of conditioning in the laboratory, and the development of conditioning theory, are justified in part by the hope that the principles derived will ultimately enhance the understanding of human behavior in complex situations including social ones. In the present study an attempt is made to re-evaluate the essential features of a social situation viewed entirely within the framework of conditioning theory, and to investigate the simplest situation that could be considered truly social within this framework. . . .

In this analysis it will be assumed that the main factors controlling social behavior are reward and punishment. Within this framework, the essential features of a social situation are: (*a*) Two or more subjects [4] have at their disposal responses which result in rewarding or punishing effects on other subjects. (*b*) The principal sources of reward and punish-ment for any subject depend on responses made by other subjects. (*c*) The responses controlling reward and punishment are subject to learning . . . [and] at least the above features are present in any social situation.

[3] From the *Journal of Experimental Psychology*, vol. 54, pp. 318–19. Used by permission of the American Psychological Association.

[4] As already noted in Chapter 2 (p. 49), quotations from the journals are modified (without notation) on certain minor stylistic differences.

It is of interest to determine what learning would be predicted on the basis of these conditions alone, assuming only that the principles of conditioning theory are operating. This was the purpose of the present experiment.

Two subjects isolated from each other were provided with push buttons by means of which each could give the other reward or punishment. In this situation, if a subject makes a response, he does not "suffer the consequences" directly. A subject can change the rewards and punishments he receives only to the extent that this action may change the behavior of the other subject. Thus, if A makes a response which results in a reward for B, B may be expected to continue with, or to repeat, his immediately preceding behavior; if A makes a response which results in a punishment for B, B may be expected to discontinue his immediately preceding activity. Such changes in B's behavior would have a direct effect on the reward and punishment being received by A. In this way, A would receive some consequences from his own responses, but in an indirect way.

It is not intended that this situation be directly comparable to familiar everyday encounters. People generally enter social situations already equipped with a massive amount of prior learning relating to the effects of their behavior on others. This makes rigorous control of a given social experiment next to impossible. However, much of social control of other people's behavior is through stylized ways indicating approval and disapproval that are in effect methods of rewarding and punishing others. With adults, most of the rewarding and punishing techniques are conventional, but in many situations the responses learned are no longer appropriate. New responses must be learned. The process through which this learning and relearning takes place will be central to any extension of conditioning theory into the realm of social behavior. One may ask, Is face-to-face contact and "understanding" of the relationship between subjects necessary for "social" learning? . . .

. . . The subjects [in this experiment] were divided into two major groups, an Informed and an Uninformed group. All subjects in the Informed group were told that another subject was serving in the experiment. In the Uninformed group . . . subjects were not told [nor did they guess] that they were in a social situation . . . The two major groups were subdivided into three Reward-Punishment subgroups in which (a) Subjects could give each other Shock only, (b) Subjects could give each other Score [reward] only, and (c) Subjects could give each other both Shocks and Scores. (242, pp. 318–19)

The results of this experiment are shown in Figure 23. Two points are clear from these data. Learning occurred when punishment was combined with reward, but learning would occur just about as well when no punishment was involved, only reward. Second, with the possible exception of the case of Reward Only, knowledge that the situation was a social one did not alter the operation of the reward and punishment conditions. This second result is important, of course, but in the context of our present discussion the first conclusion is the one that I wish to emphasize most: punishment is effective in altering behavior only to the extent that some alternative behavior is strengthened. Sidowski's situation, then, illustrates another method by which this may be accomplished: the independent reinforcement of one response (some R_2 in the terms of our schematization) concomitant with the punishment of the undesirable R_1. In other words, the reinforcement need not be related to the occurrence of S_{nox} at all, except coincidentally.

SUMMARY: HABIT "ELIMINATION" AS HABIT CHANGE

Several principles of behavior manipulation have been introduced and/or brought into focus in the present chapter. The most important principles presented, or reviewed, here were the following:

(1) Basically, in order to eliminate a habit, all reinforcement of that habit must cease. This is called a continuous NoX schedule of reinforcement.

(2) Once an organism has learned a habit, he can not literally unlearn it. A habit is not destroyed, it is only *replaced* by a stronger, incompatible habit.

(3) Resistance to extinction, then, depends upon two factors:

(3a) First, there is the criterion of extinction employed. This, in effect, is the definition of "no response" that one has decided upon. Clearly, it will be easier to get a subject to reach some criteria of "not responding" than it will to attain others.

(3b) Second, there is the similarity between the habit-formation and/or habit-maintenance conditions (for the response now being eliminated) and the extinction conditions. There must invariably be differences in the X dimension, and the degree of difference (i.e., the

FIGURE 23

The Role of Reward and Punishment in a "Minimal Social Situation"

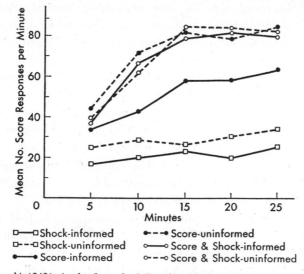

From Sidowski (242), in the *Journal of Experimental Psychology*, vol. 54, p. 320. Used by permission of the American Psychological Association.

The measure here is frequency of responses that produce reward for the *other* subject in the situation. Curves with dashed lines are for subjects who do not know another person is involved, solid lines are for the subjects who do know that another person's behavior determines their score. Open circles are for groups controlling both the rewards and punishments of their partner, closed circles are subjects who could reward each other, but not punish each other (they received no shocks), and X's are for groups that could punish each other, but not reward each other (they received no rewards). All subjects were instructed to try to get as many scores (signified by a flash of light) as possible.

relative occurrence of NoX during training and maintenance compared to the continuous NoX schedule that holds during extinction) is a fundamental determinant of resistance to extinction. But extinction situations can also involve deviations from the S or R features of the original behavioral conditions; such deviations also hasten the extinction procedure.

(4) In short, extinction is a new learning situation. To the extent that we actively attempt to supplant one response with another dur-

ing extinction, the more effective and permanent will be the use of extinction as a method of habit alteration.

(4a) In this connection, the laws concerning discrimination situations and transfer of training situations are applicable. A knowledge of these should enable one to design the most efficient and most effective extinction procedures.

(4b) It is important to recognize that nonreinforcement can, under some circumstances at least, be just as critical in the determination of an organism's future behavior as can reward. When a subject is not reinforced, it is not true that this is always equivalent to having nothing happen. NoX may evoke learned or unlearned R's that can themselves be reinforced. The compatibility (or lack of it) of these R's and the response(s) being subjected to extinction will be an important determinant of resistance to extinction.

(5) Changing habits by punishing some response is, basically, the use of extinction *plus* an active, momentarily effective suppressor of the R that immediately precedes punishment.

(6) As with extinction (NoX), punishment—S_{nox}—will evoke new responses. Just as in extinction, therefore, the results of using punishment will be determined by what sorts of such responses are reinforced. Again the principles of transfer of training and discrimination learning have an important bearing on the outcome to be expected in any given situation. Quite typically punishment situations involve the establishment of a new, competing habit via the processes of escape learning, avoidance learning, or counter-conditioning.

(7) Whether extinction or punishment is used, habits will be eliminated better the more control that we exercise over the habit that comes to replace the old one. This control is exactly the same as that used in any habit formation situation.

SUPPLEMENTARY NOTES

"Operant Level" as a General Criterion of Extinction

One of the more promising attempts to solve the problem of the arbitrariness of most extinction criteria was developed within the modified Skinnerian approach that characterized learning research at Columbia University in the decade following World War II. The method involved the concept of the *free operant level*. This level is the performance of any given R_L when the following conditions hold:

(1) The means for performing R_L are readily available under essentially the same conditions as those to be employed when learning is reasonably expected to occur, except that

(2) There is not, and has not previously been, any reinforcement of R_L during the period of operant level measurement.

As originally used, the operant level applied to free operant situations only; as such, it was restricted to measures of rate of responding. There is no logical reason why the operant level should apply to that measure and those conditions alone. Conceivably, the performance of R_L prior to any training could be a useful baseline for evaluating the effects of reinforcement and subsequent extinction no matter what measure of performance is used in a given situation. In other words, extinction would be considered to have been completed (within a given session) when behavior returns to the same degree of variability that had shown during pretraining determinations of the subjects' operant level behavior in the same situation. Admittedly, this suggestion is not characteristic of current practices. Even free operant situations rarely employ such a criterion of extinction, and the concept of the operant level, to my knowledge, has never been extended to measures of response strength other than rate by anyone but myself (159).

*
*
* # FACTORS PRESUMED
* # TO COMPLICATE THE
* # SIMPLE LEARNING
   # MODEL

INTRODUCTION TO SECTION III

In the preceding eight chapters I have attempted to relate a large variety of behavior-environment relationships to each other via the S-R-X model. Although I feel that this model can adequately deal with all the phenomena that fall within the topic of Learning, it would be quite misleading to create the impression that all psychologists are unanimous in their agreement on this matter. In the following section we shall consider experimental work that is related to two major exceptions to the belief in the adequacy of the model used so far.

One exception is the assertion that the model is definitely inaccurate. Some psychologists doubt that reinforcement is as essential to learning as has been presented here. Other psychologists question whether overt responding is always necessary in order for a habit to be formed. Experiments that provide an empirical basis for these reservations are taken up in Chapter 9.

The other exception to the model I have used is that it is incomplete since it does not emphasize the importance of a basic factor, or factors, called "drive" and/or "motivation." In Chapter 10 we review the thinking and the experimental evidence that characterize the various "motivational approaches" to learning. Some attempt will also be made to relate the motivational viewpoint to the learning model as it now stands.

CHAPTER 9

*
*
* LEARNING SITUATIONS
THAT DO NOT SEEM TO
FIT THE MODEL

The group of learning situations now to be considered are those in which it can be shown that learning has occurred, even though the situations themselves do not appear to fit the S-R-X model of learning situations.

Now, we have noted lack of correspondences between the model and some instances of Pavlovian conditioning and operant learning, but these were attributed to overconcentration by experimenters on only one phase of these types of situations. This may not be the most satisfactory way of conducting research, but it is understandable. After all, in any psychological experiment there are an over-whelming number of events that could be observed and described in detail, so a happy medium must be developed; there must be a compromise between a stark condensation of the independent and dependent variables in experimental reports, and a compulsive description of everything—including, for instance, barometric pressure at the time of each training trial. Just what might constitute a satisfactory compromise between copious detail and hardly any detail in experimental reports must always be worked out by trial and error. It is an inefficient process, but a necessary one.

This trial-and-error process usually must begin all over again whenever a new phenomenon is reported. Thus it is with many of the learning situations we are about to consider: the final decision has not yet been reached concerning the degree of detail that is necessary in order to determine whether a phenomenon can be rendered comprehensible in terms of current perspectives in learning.

The deviations from the model to be noted in the following pages were *not,* for the most part, accidental discoveries. The experimenters who discovered or subsequently studied these instances of learning were usually working with the conviction that a process such as implied by the model did not exhaust the possible ways in which learning could be effected.

One discrepancy between our model and some of the situations below is in the intentions of the model vs. those of the theories underlying these experiments. The model describes the conditions that are both sufficient *and* efficient ways of getting learning to occur. All these conditions, however, may not be absolutely *necessary* for some kinds of habit formation to take place. The minimal conditions under which learning can occur are of great theoretical interest, however, and the primary instigation for much of the research to be described in this chapter was the desire to compare one theory of learning with another.

Many of these phenomena are puzzling (in terms of the model) because they have not been given the systematic study that other learning situations have received. Unfortunately, when the resolution of a point of dispute between any two theories becomes the paramount concern of scientists, there is a tendency to be content with the simple demonstration of behavioral changes that are perplexing to the opposing theory. Apparently, the implicit assumption is being made that if an advocate of Theory A can produce an experiment that is perplexing to Theory B, then this somehow is a point *in favor of* Theory A. There is, in fact, no logical justification for this assumption.

Other discrepant situations are ones that involve the interaction of many habits acquired by the subjects before the experiments began (a kind of complex transfer of training). Insofar as this is the case, then such situations—although entirely legitimate instances of learning and performance—are not strictly comparable to the ones we discussed initially. In other words, some of these situations do not reveal basic learning principles, but rather show some of the complex learning types discussed in Sections II and IV of this text.

Still and all, a few of the situations to be described may reveal truly unique means of forming habits.

It is most important to understand, however, that regardless of the fact that these situations deviate from the model and regardless of the reasons why they do so, the following phenomena *are* instances of behavioral change of the sort that we identify as learning and as such are worthy of attention. They are also deserving of far more experimental investigation and analysis than many of them have so far received.

INCIDENTAL LEARNING

"Incidental learning" is just about ready to forego its place among the learning phenomena that have been demonstrated but not analyzed. Some aspects of this phenomenon have been studied rather extensively. Incidental learning can be classed as one of the "mysteries of learning" only because, for all of its recent examination, psychologists still do not understand incidental learning. With sufficient training, any intelligent person can be taught to become a successful "operant trainer," or "Pavlovian conditioner"; that is, we know enough about the variables and about the effects of manipulating them in these sorts of learning situations so that, given sufficient control over an organism's environment, we can attain a high degree of control over changes in the organism's behavior by what we call Pavlovian or operant methods. In most cases of incidental learning, a comparable degree of control can not yet be achieved, because psychologists are still uncertain about the environmental factors that are most pertinent for this kind of learning.

GENERAL CHARACTERISTICS OF
INCIDENTAL LEARNING

The foregoing is not as sad a commentary on the skill of modern psychologists as it may seem, not when you consider that incidental learning has the following characteristics:

1. The Subject Is Not Motivated

At least the subject is not motivated in a way that would presumably favor the acquisition of the habits that can later be shown to have been learned during what we will call the *exposure period* (because all that appears to be happening at this time is that the subject is exposed to or brought into the presence of certain stimuli).

2. There Is No Apparent Reinforcement of Any R's Made in the Presence of the Experimental Stimuli

The experimental stimuli are those that the subject is eventually going to be asked to recall or to respond to. The subject may be "doing something" in the presence of the experimental stimuli during the exposure period, but this "something" is not systematically reinforced; usually, precautions are taken to insure against any obvious sort of reinforcement for such R's.[1]

3. There May Be No Observable R's Made in the Presence of the Experimental S's during the Exposure Period

This is not a universal characteristic of incidental learning situations; sometimes, especially when the subjects are animals, the

[1] There is one body of research that is frequently described as a type of incidental learning, but in which there are definite, manipulated consequences of the subjects' responses. This research area might be called the study of awareness of reinforcement (for an extensive bibliography and review see 154). The basic question that seems to concern those who work in this area actually seems to be whether it makes any difference if the subject can or can not describe verbally the R_L-X relationships that the experimenter decides to set up. Now, to the best of our knowledge, infra-humans could never "describe what had happened to them" in a learning situation. This obviously does not prevent such subjects from learning new habits. In view of this, it is hard to see that the awareness-of-reinforcement research has any great significance for the development of laws of learning.

R's made in the presence of the crucial stimuli may be very close to those to be evoked during the test period. With both humans and animals, incidental learning is somewhat better if this has been the case. But the standard definitions of this phenomenon do not make the overt, observable occurrence of R_L's a necessary requirement of incidental learning.

Incidental learning is defined by negations—it appears to occur *in the absence of* many of the events that I said were necessary for learning. Negative definitions, of course, are extremely slippery and very hard for scientists to use. Any scientist who makes the statement, "I definitely saw Q occur *in the complete absence of* P," is straining the credulity of his colleagues. To assert that he failed to observe P may only show that he is not so perceptive, not so skilled an observer as he might be. The way out of this quandary, of course, is for this scientist to devote himself to isolating the conditions that can now only be called "not P" under which the phenomenon, Q, *does occur*. Recent developments in research on incidental learning suggest that positive statements of this sort may soon be possible in this field.

Vague as the critical events in the production of incidental learning appear to be, we can identify several types of experimental situations having the above characteristics. These fall into three major categories, all of which may be further subdivided. When human subjects are used in such studies, either the term *"incidental learning"* or the term *"learning without awareness"* is used. With animal subjects, we ordinarily identify two major types: *latent learning* and *sensory preconditioning*.[2]

---

[2] The nomenclature practices in this field (i.e., in the titling of original research papers) have been quite inconsistent. The use of several terms sometimes as synonyms and at other times to refer to different procedures or phenomena is quite unsatisfactory for pedagogical purposes. For simplicity in exposition, therefore, I am suggesting in this chapter a somewhat arbitrary basis for a consistent application of the terms prevalent in this area of learning. I have tried, when possible, to associate a given label with the situations by which they have most frequently been defined in the literature. As far as I can tell, no important theoretical issues have been prejudged by my particular system of classification.

Learning without Awareness [3]

How many times have you discovered that you can remember the automobile license number on the car of a friend, or the name of a restaurant that you only passed while driving through a strange town, or the face of a person whom you only saw somewhere without meeting or having any contact with him? We all have had such experiences, but in any specific case it might be possible—if all of the facts were known—to show that there was some reinforcement involved. As usual, if clear-cut evidence of learning without awareness can be found we must be able to specify controlled situations that can be arranged in the laboratory to find it. There are two conventional experimental situations with human learners:

1. The Irrelevant Set Design

A common form of this study is the one in which subjects work in pairs—as in a beginning experimental psychology lab class. One student is told that he is the "experimenter" and that his task is simply to administer the materials to his partner—the "subject"— according to a prescribed plan. The subject is told to learn the material shown to him by the experimenter. After the subject has done so, both he and the experimenter are tested to see how much of the material they remember. Since the subject is an intentional learner, he should—and usually does—remember a great deal. The experimenter was never aware that he needed to learn anything about the particular materials used; nevertheless, he typically can be shown to have learned something about the material. He is called an incidental learner.

2. The Irrelevant Learning Design

In this kind of situation, the subject *is* reinforced for learning certain habits; unknown to him, however, these are not the ones on which he will subsequently be tested. Whenever he makes the response(s) correct for the training problem as explained to him,

---

[3] The terms "aware," "awareness," and "set" are used only as shorthand means of describing that the subject is not told to remember the material.

he also exposes himself to certain other stimuli that were not described as relevant to his particular task. In the test situation, however, he is asked to indicate in some way whether he did develop any systematic responses to these "irrelevant" stimuli at the same time he was acquiring the other habits.

Essentially, this design seems to be asking the question of the extent to which verbal instructions restrict the sorts of S-R relationships that can be learned by a human subject. That is, there are several possible systematic relationships between stimuli and responses, and a subject has been informed that only certain of such relationships will, if performed, be reinforced. Does such a condition prevent the subject from learning other systematic relationships (or potential relationships) not mentioned in the instructions? As one might expect, no one general answer will fit all cases of this problem.

Stevenson (262) has shown an instance in which irrelevant learning is obtained. Three groups of children were presented with a problem that, aside from some controls we will not describe, consisted of searching inside a yellow box until they found a key. This key opened the lock on a blue box, and inside the blue box was a reward (in this case, as in many experiments with children, the reward was simply an inexpensive object that they were allowed to keep). They were told at the start that the key was somewhere in the yellow box, so their trial-and-error behavior was restricted solely to activities inside of this box. For one group the key was on top of all the other objects (a random collection of medium- and small-sized paraphernalia); for another, the key was placed just below either a purse or a matchbox; in the third group, the key was placed *inside of* either the purse or the matchbox. All children had experience with both the purse and the matchbox. The test for incidental learning was to show a child either a purse or a matchbox identical to those in the yellow box, and ask, "Do you know where to find a purse (or matchbox) just like this one?" The proportion of children locating the object was sufficiently high, especially when the key had been inside it, to infer that many of the children had indeed learned the location of the objects to which their attention had not been directed specifically at any previous time during the experiment.

On the other hand, as Postman and Senders (212) have shown, it is possible by the instructions so to control subjects' behavior that different subjects exposed to the same material (but told to respond in different ways) learn entirely different habits with little overlap in their learning. A group of college students were all shown the the same block of reading material, but half were asked to count the number of "e's" in it, while the others were told that they would be tested on its content. All students looked at the same material, but there was a clear-cut difference in the performance of the two groups when they were *all* asked to answer questions about the content of material.

Neither the Stevenson nor the Postman-Senders effect is particularly mysterious (from the standpoint of conventional learning principles such as we have already examined), especially when their experimental procedures are considered in detail. Such phenomena seem to be over-glamorized by labeling them with such phrases as "learning without awareness," "latent learning," and so on. It may be amusing to demonstrate learning in situations in which the experimenter does not control (i.e., understand) the variables that are most pertinent to the observed behavior changes, but it is hardly profitable.

Most everyday examples of learning without awareness (symbolized as LWOA) are really examples of faulty observation. Real life and laboratory life are quite different milieux; if this were not so, there would be no need for laboratories. The purpose of experimentation is *not* to recapitulate natural events in all their complexity. On the contrary, the primary aim of laboratory research is *to isolate classes of homogeneous events* (these classes are "variables") and *to determine the functional relationships between such events.* This is true for the laboratory study of learning, just as it is true for the laboratory study of atomic phenomena. Real life learning situations, on the other hand, are rarely simple situations. Nor are they easily described in terms of discrete variables. If there are, for example, fifteen different conditions that can each facilitate

learning, should we expect to find that these variables typically operate in isolation from each other? Our own experience provides the
answer. Quite the opposite, most natural learning situations involve
an unsystematic, myriad jumble of variables. It is frequently impossible for a skilled observer, sophisticated in the identification of
the means of producing habit acquisition, to state unequivocally the
reasons why, e.g., Johnny usually does learn to read (at least, a
little bit). Add to this confusion an untrained observer, and it is
not hard to see why many people might find it easier to regard
LWOA, rather than operant learning, as the normal mode of habit
acquisition.

Although LWOA is *defined* in terms of variables that are *not*
operating, thus making the phenomenon difficult to study, some
progress has been made toward the understanding of this kind of
habit formation. Progress in science means only one thing—the development of functional relationships between variables. Therefore,
our understanding of LWOA is to be measured in terms of the
number and importance of the relationships that can be identified
in this kind of learning.

Variables that Affect the Degree of Learning without Awareness

(1) Human subjects who are skilled at forming associations to
verbal material (i.e., who are "reminded of" more things by specific
words and phrases) are good incidental learners (210). Possibly related to this is the fact that when there is little opportunity for re-
hearsal in intentional learning, there is little difference in the degree
of learning obtained by the intentional and incidental methods. Specifically, Saltzman and his students (200, 228, 230) have shown that
when verbal material is presented at rapid rates there is little difference in the two methods, but at slower speeds intentional learning
is appreciably better. It is possible that at fast presentation rates intentional learners have no more opportunity to rehearse and associate the material voluntarily than incidental learners may do "un-
consciously."

(2) The means used to expose a subject to the experimental stimuli also influence the amount of LWOA. If the subject can be

"tricked into" rehearsing (i.e., saying out loud, thinking to himself, writing down, or otherwise specifically attending to) the crucial stimuli, he will remember them better, even when he is not specifically motivated to learn them (229). The techniques for accomplishing this are numerous, of course, but their effects are all similar—the subject makes the desired R's (the R_L's, that is) in the presence of the appropriate stimuli.

(3) Since learning is not, fundamentally, a "thing," but rather an inference from certain observations, it follows that the amount of learning that can be inferred from any set of observations depends, in large part, on the kinds of observations themselves. Postman and Tuma (213) have provided evidence that LWOA—measured by retention—is a function of the method used to measure retention (e.g., recognition vs. recall tests). We shall develop this point in greater detail in Chapter 12; the important consideration at the moment is that this relationship between method of testing retention and observed degree of retention holds just as well for material used in an LWOA situation as for material learned under conventional (motivated, reinforced) conditions.

Summary: Characteristics of "Learning without Awareness" Situations [4]

The amount of learning without awarness that occurs in any situation is usually compared with the retention of the same material by subjects exposed to it under more conventional conditions of motivation, orientation, and reinforcement. For any given S-R relationships there is some optimal set of conditions, a set of circumstances in which learning shows the most rapid progress, and/or results in the most permanent improvement. It should follow, then, that performance due to learning without awareness will resemble that developed as a result of motivated, reinforced learning to the extent that, for the incidental learners, all conditions that do not violate the definition of "incidental" are made as nearly optimal as possible. In particular, temporal and stimulus factors can be ad-

---

[4] Dr. J. K. Adams (2) published a good review of the literature in this field prior to 1956. Although his analysis is somewhat different than the one here offered (and seems equally reasonable), our conclusions are essentially alike.

justed toward maximum efficiency in an LWOA situation without going against current definitions of incidental learning. As the research findings accumulate, learning without awareness becomes less and less a curiosity among learning phenomena. Eventually, it would be interesting to see the result of some careful study of the terminal events in a LWOA "trial." There *must* be *some* kinds of terminal events, but in most accounts of LWOA studies these are not clear.

The most succinct summarization of learning without awareness, as it is understood today, would be to say that it appears to follow all the laws of learning except those that we have suggested as the fundamental ones: the reinforcement of an explicit R in the presence of a stimulus. LWOA research has not, it must be stressed, *proved* that the latter do not operate in these cases. All that has been shown is that some learning *can* occur without the specific manipulation of certain R and X factors.

Latent Learning [5]

Latent learning is another name for incidental learning. The distinctive characteristics of learning without awareness are shared by latent learning: Neither the subject's responses, nor the reinforcement schedule—if, indeed a reinforcing event can even be designated—are controlled in the ways that are the most certain means of obtaining learning. Latent learning differs from learning without awareness only in the kinds of subject employed; latent learning research has traditionally, though not invariably, involved infra-human subjects with limited experiential backgrounds. We shall apply the term "latent learning" *only* to experiments on incidental learning having that qualification. There are three major types of latent learning situations:

1. The "Blodgett Effect": One Reinforced Trial Follows Several Unreinforced Ones

Blodgett's procedure (29) consisted of (1) giving hungry rats repeated, unrewarded exploration trials in a complex maze (i.e., a

---

[5] A review of this field was written at the time of its peak importance in learning theory by Thistlethwaite (266). This now classic paper is "must" reading for any serious student of learning.

maze having several choice-points) and then (2) placing food at the opposite end of the maze from the point at which the rats started a trial. On the first trial after the rewarded one, rats thus treated show a marked decrease in errors (entries into blind alleys). The decrease appeared to be more than would ordinarily follow a single reinforced run through the maze. In fact, this post-reinforcement level of performance was not reliably different from that of subjects who had had an equal number of maze experiences, but all of them rewarded. There is serious doubt, however, that Blodgett's rats actually did their learning "latently." Attempted replications of this experiment have led to the conclusion that the rats have some mild aversion to blind alleys. There *is* some incipient reduction of errors during the presumably exploratory period. Thus, this learning is not so latent as Blodgett may have thought.

This form of the latent learning experiment is of historical interest primarily; but its historical effect was great—it provided the impetus for a host of latent learning studies. Some of these latter turned out to be quite challenging to an S-R-X view of learning.

2. The "Seward Effect": Maze Experience Followed by a Change in the "Significance" of one Part of the Maze, Where Such Change Is Separate from Maze Experience

We refer again to Seward (237), but to a different experiment this time for a representative example of this brand of latent learning situation. All things considered, this is probably the most convincing demonstration of "true" latent learning that is to be found.

Hungry rats explored a simple T-maze (one choice-point) that had differentiable endboxes (e.g., black vs. white) at each end of the cross-bar. After such exploration, each rat was placed directly into one of the endboxes and fed (this actually occurred directly behind the starting box of the apparatus; whether this is crucial or not is unknown). When returned to the maze immediately after eating in the endbox, a significant majority of the subjects ran to the position of the endbox in which they had just been rewarded. Eating-in-endbox and getting-to-endbox-from-starting-point are both R's, but prior to the test trial Seward had never permitted the pairing of these two R's. It appears that the rats had, in effect, some-how learned the locations of the two endboxes during unreinforced exploration of the maze. When the "value" or "significance" of one endbox was changed radically by associating it with food (but without having the rats go through the maze to get to it), most rats showed a correlated shift in their preference for one side of the maze as against the other.

There are two variations of this design. Both consist of starting the rats on a regular S-R-X set-up during original training. Then, analogously to Seward's procedure, the significance of a formerly rewarding endbox is altered, and the ensuing behavior noted.

Tolman and Gleitman (270) gave rats nondifferential training in a T-maze that had differentiable endboxes. That is, the subjects were rewarded equally often in both endboxes, so that they had little or no preference for either a right or a left turn at the choice-point. Then they were placed directly into one of the endboxes and given a severe shock. When later replaced in the maze, most rats made a turn at the choice-point that took them *away from* the location of the endbox in which they had just previously been shocked.

Similarly, Deese (59) taught rats to run consistently into a spe-cific, differentiable endbox at one of the ends of a T-maze. Then each rat was put directly into this endbox, but it now contained no food. When next given a series of non-rewarded (extinction) trials, rats with this pre-exposure to the empty goalbox required *fewer* trials to cease turning toward it than did rats without prior experi-ence of this sort. This is sometimes called "pre-extinction." [6]

Actually, the Tolman-Gleitman and the Deese studies are not as puzzling as Seward's. In the former cases S, R, and X are all speci-fiable. The only unusual characteristic of these situations is the demonstration of the fact that the extinction or punishment of the final R's of a series will affect the later performance of earlier R's of the series. Such an effect is not unusual in serial learning situ-ations, as we shall see. Seward's study is more perplexing, however,

---

[6] Moltz (192) has presented a response-reinforcement interpretation of this phenomenon. Since it depends quite heavily upon hypothetical response processes, instead of observable R's, it is not easily summarized in the terms of this text.

since there are *no* strong habits involved at all. Perhaps it is for this reason that latent learning of this type is not always easy to obtain experimentally.

3. Irrelevant Incentive Learning

Here the subject is allowed to observe the location of substances that are not now, but would be under other conditions, acceptable as rewards. Afterwards, the subject is motivated for such rewards. The question is, Will the subject go to the position where this reward was previously located?

With rats, the typical reward is food or water. The pretraining may be done with the animal neither hungry nor thirsty, or with one of these active, the other absent. In the latter case, food is present in one arm of a simple maze, water in the opposite position; the rat is motivated to consume only one of these substances at the time of training. Afterwards, the motivation is reversed, and if latent learning has occurred, the rat will go to the location of the previously "unacceptable" reward.

An experiment by Kendler and Levine (145) provided a clear demonstration of this kind of latent learning; the complete experimental design is shown in Figure 24. For the essentials of the study, we can turn to these experimenters' own report:

Three groups of white rats were trained in a T maze when satiated for food and water. Both endboxes were empty for Group O, while food was in one endbox and water in the other for Groups C and R. During the test series, the [subjects] received daily trials under conditions of food or water deprivation. The location of the food and water was the same for all groups, being in the positions that prevailed for Group C during training, while being reversed for the [rats] in Group R, i.e., if food had been in the left endbox during training, it was placed in the right endbox during the test series.

It was found that Group C achieved the criterion of learning [four successive correct responses] most rapidly. The performance of Group O, although significantly poorer than Group C, was significantly superior to Group R. The results of the performance of the three groups provided marked evidence of irrelevant-incentive learning under conditions of satiation. (145, p. 273)

This experiment utilizes the simple principles of *transfer of*

training as means of verifying that the rats learned something
during the exposure period. Group C subjects were shown the
food and water in the same locations during the exposure period
as they appeared when the subjects were motivated for one of these
rewards. Therefore, if these rats had actually learned where the food
and water were during the exposure period, they should have

FIGURE 24

Schematic Outline of the Kendler-Levine Study
of Irrelevant Incentive Learning (20)

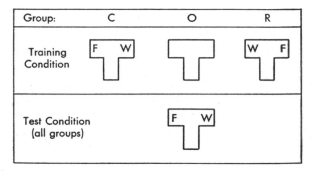

readily learned to perform the proper turn when they were later
motivated for one of these rewards. For Group R rats, anything
learned about the locations of the food and water during the exposure period would impede their performance when motivated,
because the locations had been switched. Group O subjects, not
having a chance to learn either the correct or incorrect locations of
the incentives would be expected to solve the test period problem
at a rate intermediate to the subjects' in Groups C and R.

Since T-maze learning proceeded at just the relative rates predicted by the above reasoning (C faster than O, O faster than R),
we can justifiably infer that the premise upon which the reasoning
was based may be true. The premise was, of course, that when rats
discover food and water (but do *not* consume them), this is sufficient
to predispose the rats to return to the locations that are appropriate
when they are later on deprived of one of these incentives.

The Theoretical Significance of Latent Learning

Clearly, interest in latent learning could stem merely from a simple, legitimate curiosity about the conditions under which such phenomena as we have just reviewed could be produced. Obviously, even infra-human animals are capable of fairly intricate learning of a sort that resembles the end product of understanding, reasoning, and so forth in humans. It is certainly of great interest to figure out how reasonable behavior can be produced in a nonverbal animal. This has not, however, been the main motivation for latent learning research.

The study of incidental operant learning in infra-humans (to give latent learning its full title) has been predominantly inspired by certain theoretical issues of questionable testability. Demonstrations of any latent learning phenomena have been, and are still, regarded by some psychologists as proof of such propositions as: (1) reinforcement is not necessary for learning, or (2) learning does not always involve the association of an S and an R.

Latent learning research played an important role in helping us to realize that early behavioristic definitions of S, R, and X terms were not entirely adequate. To this extent, this body of experimentation has contributed to our knowledge. More positive or constructive products from this area were noticeably absent until recently. Happily, this trend is now showing a reversal, with the result that latent learning—as well as most other forms of incidental learning—are beginning to reveal more features also common to the better understood learning phenomena.

Certainly latent learning can not occur under just any circumstances. It is also reasonable that some of the favorable conditions for its occurrence are more favorable than others. Desiderato (64) has recently described some factors influencing performance on the test trials in latent learning demonstrations of the second (Seward) type. Rats forced to keep active (running on a treadmill) before the test trial did not perform as well as rats kept in activity-restricting environments; presumably the latter were more generally motivated to run. Upon removal from the endbox following the feeding experience (i.e., just before the test trial), if the rat was rotated 360°, this apparently disrupted its ability to locate the correct endbox on the test trials.

Christie (51) has shown that performance in the irrelevant incentive situation is facilitated by prior experience either with being deprived of food or water, or with exploration trials in any maze; both types of prior experience combined (exploration while deprived) produced the most irrelevant incentive learning. Furthermore, the consensus of irrelevant incentive learning studies strongly suggests that the phenomenon occurs more readily (or is easier to demonstrate, at least) when there is no strong motivation operating during the preliminary exposure sessions.

Finally, it seems characteristic of the habits acquired by most of these incidental learning procedures that they differ most from habits established by more controlled operant techniques in their resistance to interferences. Both the interferences from new learning or those from more transient environmental influences can affect incidental habits more seriously than they can affect habits with a known and explicit S-R-X history (e.g., 139). Nor have the most striking and perplexing latent learning procedures (the Seward effect, for instance) been shown to increase in their influence on behavior by continued, repeated application. It is probably no accident that no one has ever reported a latent learning study in which the training conditions were given daily for as long as, say, three months. It is hard to imagine that some of the effects described above could still be produced. (Obviously the same is not true for the reinforcement of overt responses.) Well, then, does a procedure whose effect on behavior can be eradicated by further use of that same procedure qualify as a learning situation? Perhaps so, if the theoretical problems in learning are merely problems in establishing the preeminence of a certain set of definitions.

Sensory Preconditioning

The essential steps in this procedure are the following:

(1) The subjects are repeatedly exposed to two neutral stimuli presented together. These stimuli are always clearly identifiable

changes in physical energy. The neutrality of such stimuli is presumably the same as the neutrality of most S_n's in Pavlovian conditioning experiments—i.e., they do not elicit the R_L that is involved in the next step.

The paired presentation of such stimuli is done a great number of times (at least, when animals are used), but without regard to any response patterns of the subject. The subject is not motivated in any special way, either. In other words, this pairing is made as irrelevant as possible.

(2) If the previous step is symbolized as:

$$S_{n_1}\text{-}S_{n_2}$$

then this next step can be written:

$$S_{n_1}\text{-UCS}_1 \text{ or } S_{n_2}\text{-UCS}_1$$

In other words, one of the two S_n's is paired with a UCS. This is Pavlovian conditioning, of course. Sometimes Pavlovian conditioning's next of kin—operant avoidance learning—is used at this stage. The important point is that one of the previous S_n's now becomes the S of a learned S-R relationship. The other S_n is never presented during this phase of training.

(3) After a response has been associated with one of the neutral stimuli, the other neutral stimulus of step 1 is presented in the same general setting (e.g., in the presence of the same apparatus). If sensory preconditioning has taken place, then this second S_n will now elicit essentially the same CR or avoidance R. This, despite the fact that S_{n_2} has never been paired with the learned response itself; the only connection S_{n_2} has had to the later experiences of the subject is that it had been repeatedly paired with S_{n_1} *before any response had been systematically associated with S_{n_1}.*

A more clear-cut demonstration of sensory preconditioning is often achieved by comparing the rate of learning the R of step 2 to S_{n_2} for subjects having previously had $S_{n_1}\text{-}S_{n_2}$ pairings with subjects who have not. Both groups, of course, would have $S_{n_1}\text{-UCS}_1$ training.

A desirable control in any sensory preconditioning experiment would be a group that has both (1) S_{n_1}-UCS_1 training, and (2) as frequent exposure to S_{n_1} and to S_{n_2} as the experimental subjects get, but with the latter stimuli spaced in occurrence (e.g., on alternate days) so that little association between them is likely.

Variables Affecting Sensory Preconditioning Effects

Sensory preconditioning research began to focus on what variables aided the production of the phenomenon more quickly than did most incidental learning work. Possibly this was because most of the work on the topic is fairly recent. Sensory preconditioning was discovered by Brogden (35) in an experiment using dogs. It has since been obtained with rats (15, 244) and humans (37, 140).

Here again the data seem to indicate that sensory preconditioning effects are influenced by many well-known learning variables. Bitterman, Reed, and Kubala (28) showed that an S_{n_1}-S_{n_2} pairing (step 1) involving a short delay between the onsets of the two stimuli was a more efficient procedure than the older method of simultaneous presentation of the two. This bears a similarity to the relative effectiveness of different stimulus time relationships in Pavlovian conditioning that is too striking to miss. The similarity between sensory preconditioning's first phase and the usual Pavlovian procedure was noted by Silver and Meyer (244). These men worked from the notion that a truly "neutral" stimulus probably does not exist. In their own words:

. . . The presentation of paired reconditioning stimuli is likened [by us] to classical [Pavlovian] conditioning. Each stimulus is considered to be a UCS for a response that is not directly observed, and potentially a CS for a second response similar to the one elicited by the other stimulus. Prior to preconditioning, both responses occur only if both stimuli are present. After preconditioning, a response which resembles the entire complex follows presentation of either stimulus. . . . Since a CR is most readily established if the CS precedes the UCS, asynchronous [i.e., delayed] forward presentation of the preconditioning stimuli should facilitate acquisition of the mediating CR. The amount of transfer should be correspondingly greater than that obtained after simultaneous or backward presentation. (244, p. 57)

Various representative pairings of S_{n_1} and S_{n_2} in the ways described led to the results predicted.

The notion that step 1 of the sensory preconditioning procedure provides more chances for systematic S-R associations to develop than would seem possible at first glance is not dwelt upon by most investigators. This view, however, received a shot in the arm from work by Bahrick (14) in which the level of irrelevant motivation was varied during preconditioning (step 1).

Sixty-nine albino rats were exposed to 400 [simultaneous] paired presentations of a sound and a light while they experienced varying degrees of hunger and thirst deprivation. The animals were all satiated at the end of this experience and were then taught an avoidance response to the sound by pairing that stimulus with electric shock. Later they were taught the same avoidance response to the light by pairing the light with electric shock.

It was found that those animals which had gone through the paired presentation of buzzer and light under higher degrees of deprivation learned the final avoidance response significantly faster than other animals who had experienced the early training under low degrees of deprivation. These differences were shown to be at least partially independent of performance differences during the acquisition of the first avoidance response, and partially independent, also, of differences in the amount of time elapsing during the experiment. It was also shown that the variable of feeding subsequent to the paired presentations of buzzer and light was probably not an important determinant of the results. (14, p. 197)

Bahrick's findings support the Silver-Meyer hypothesis that many stimuli are UCS's for hard-to-detect R's, and that preconditioning consists of the association of such UCR's with either S_n's, thus making the S_n's involved functionally similar. Bahrick's data could be considered compatible with this view, since one effect of increasing motivation is to increase the frequency with which S-R connections (either learned or not) can be evoked. Therefore, highly motivated subjects would make UCR's to both S_n's, during preconditioning, more often and with greater strength than would less motivated subjects. This, in turn, makes it more favorable for the establishment of a response-mediated similarity between the two S_n's with highly motivated subjects than with poorly motivated ones. The final outcome should be a greater indication of preconditioning in the highly motivated subjects, and this is what Bahrick found.

The Theoretical and Practical Significance of Preconditioning

At present, then, there is at least indirect support for an S-R analysis of preconditioning. This is contrary to the implication contained in this phenomenon's full name, *sensory* preconditioning. Current opinions about the preconditioning process, however, are subject to radical revision by future results. It is only fair to tell the student that there are no masterpieces of experimental design in the preconditioning literature. The most common error in such studies is the failure to counterbalance the use of S_{n_1} and S_{n_2} in steps 2 and 3. We are not simply splitting hairs by mentioning this; Bahrick (15) has done a preconditioning experiment in which a definite difference existed in the ease with which an avoidance R could be established to a light and to a buzzer. Since this source of bias does not obscure the general preconditioning phenomenon, psychologists have not seen fit to control it. So it goes whenever scientists seek to test theories prematurely (i.e., before having sufficient basic, empirical knowledge about the phenomena involved in such tests).

As far as explaining the role of reinforcement in preconditioning is concerned, how can we determine whether or how X occurs in step 1 if we are uncertain as to what is being associated during preconditioning? If, as the Silver-Meyer hypothesis states, preconditioning is a special case of Pavlovian conditioning, then the problem of discovering X in this case is not unique, although it is not solved, either. If, on the other hand, preconditioning is, as some psychologists believe, a kind of learning that involves only the association of stimuli (rather than of stimuli with responses), then the possible reinforcing agents become even less apparent than they are in Pavlovian conditioning.

Historically, "cognitive" or "S-S" views of learning have rejected the notion that reinforcement is necessary for learning, just as they have opposed the definition of learning as an S-R relationship. These two dogmas have become so firmly linked that evidence for one of these principles is occasionally treated as support for both (thus compounding the fallacy of attempting to prove axioms by experiment). There is certainly no *logical* necessity for rejecting both the

S-R definition of learning *and* the concept of reinforcement together or not rejecting either one. So a cognitive approach to preconditioning does not help us, either conceptually or factually, to identify the factors that facilitate the association of whatever is associated in preconditioning. This is no surprise, since we have seen that hypotheses about the variables that do *not* influence learning (1) are hard to test, and (2) aid scientific progress, at best, in only a negative way (i.e., by turning attention away from unprofitable approaches).

Preconditioning clearly has little practical significance. This is another small point of similarity between this phenomenon and Pavlovian conditioning—everyday learning situations rarely provide the controls necessary to achieve either one. Insofar as learning can occur with relatively passive exposure to specific stimulus patterns, however, preconditioning *may* be related to the next phenomenon to be considered.

Can We Learn While We Are Asleep?

It has been claimed, by various sources, that the repetition of verbal material to a sleeping person can improve his ability to recite this material later on. This idea in its most extreme form was described by Aldous Huxley (126) in his *Brave New World;* he imagined infants who were instilled with social and personal attitudes while they slept. College students, for obvious practical reasons, are especially intrigued by the possibility that a person can learn while asleep. Even after discounting the observations of disillusioned professors that this *must* be an effective way of learning, because so many of their students use it, it is still true that evidence for learning during sleep has been claimed by some researchers. A belief in this phenomenon has been the basis for some commercial ventures, too.

Simon and Emmons (245) carefully studied the available evidence, and concluded that an important question was the degree to which the subjects in the experiments reporting positive results were actually asleep. "Actually asleep," of course, is a matter of definition, but most of us could probably agree that being asleep usually refers to a condition in which stimuli of normal to low intensity elicit no noticeable reaction by the sleeper. Now, it has been discovered that the "brain waves" of many people reflect the depth of their sleep, or lack of consciousness (by the above definition of these terms). Different brain wave patterns characterize different levels of wakefulness.

Simon and Emmons (246) exploited this relation between bioelectric brain action and wakefulness in an experiment that is a model of careful, definitive research. To describe all their procedural exactness would require too much time and space, but they concluded that no learning occurred when phonograph records of verbal materials (statements of historical facts, definitions, and so on) were played to a person who was "truly" asleep (by both behavioral and brain-wave definitions). Some retention occurred when subjects listened while they were in what we would call a "drowsy state."

Of course, even learning while drowsy might offer advantages over the practices now advocated as good study habits, if it were sufficiently effective. Research is needed before such a comparison can be made satisfactorily, but I interpret the findings of Simon and Emmons as indicating that learning during drowsiness improves performance no more than does incidental learning. Since incidental learning is an inferior type of learning, the grim prospect is that if we want to learn anything we are still going to have to work at it.

Place Learning

Place learning is another phenomenon like sensory preconditioning that allegedly demonstrates that learning does not consist of the association of responses with stimuli. There are two basic types of experimental situations in which place learning has been studied: (1) The subject is taught one response (or a series) to a set of cues, then the cues are rearranged so that the old response(s) is no longer appropriate; if the subject responds in accord with the new positions of the stimuli, he is considered to be a place learner. (2) The subject is exposed to a series of stimuli leading to an X_{rew}, but presumably he is not actually making the response of "going along the path to goal" himself. If he subsequently shows a preference for this path over alternative ones, he is considered to have learned the place for getting the reward without having practiced the responses necessary to get there.

Place learning studies of the first type have received a lot of attention in the past fifteen years, and it is now possible to make a fairly definitive evaluation of their implications for learning in general. Such an evaluation has been done by Restle (219), whose description and analysis is so well presented that a couple of quotations from his paper will suffice to wrap up the discussion of the first form of place learning research:

The place-vs-response question has been approached largely through the use of the T maze, rotated in its visual surround. A typical arrangement showing runs reinforced in "place" and "response" learning is shown in Fig. [25], along with the fixed-maze problem in which both place and response may be learned. In both place learning and response learning, the maze is rotated on alternate trials at random. The place learner is [defined as one who is] always to go to the same place in the room, responding consistently to extra-maze cues but making different turns on different trials. The response learner [by definition] makes the same turn on all trials, going to different places. One supposed test of whether place or response learning is more dominant is to compare rates of learning on these two problems. Another test is to train animals with the maze in a fixed position (place + response learning), and then rotate the maze for a test trial. The animal can now either make the same turn he has learned or go to the same place he has been going to, but not both. In this direct opposition experiment, the relative number of animals taking each choice is a test of the relative dominance of place and response.

In 1946, Tolman, Ritchie, and Kalish [271] proposed that in such a situation place learning is more natural and primitive for the rat than response learning, and place will dominate response in all tests. Their experiment supported the hypothesis, but some later repetitions have found response dominating place, or have found no difference. . . .

. . . There is nothing in the nature of a rat which makes it a "place" learner, or a "response" learner. A rat in a maze will use all relevant cues, and the importance of any class of cues depends on the amount of relevant stimulation provided as well as the sensory capacities of the animal. In place-response experiments, the importance of place cues depends on the amount of differential extra-maze stimulation. (219, pp. 217, 226) [9]

In a sense, the procedure for demonstrating the second type of place learning is exactly the opposite of that used to demonstrate latent learning of the Seward type. McNamara, Long, and Wike

FIGURE 25

Presumed Differences between Place and Response Learning

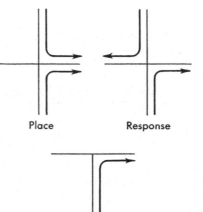

Place   Response

Place + Response

After training on a T-maze in the position shown in the top figure, the maze's position in the experimental room is rotated 180°. The two lower figures show how "place" and "response" learning are defined by workers in this area. Place learners still run to that part of the room in which the reward formerly was presented, response learners continue to make the formerly reinforced turn in the maze itself (i.e., they still go to the right-hand side of the maze).

(184), for example, repeatedly carried a rat along a T-maze in a basket, sometimes taking him to the end of the cross-piece where there was food. There the animal was released and allowed to eat. When later released in the starting box and allowed to locomote for themselves, rats trained in this way went to the rewarded side of the T-maze as often as did animals given equal, but more conven-

[9] From the *Psychological Review*, vol. 64, pp. 217, 226. Used by permission of the American Psychological Association.

tional (trial-and-error) training in the maze. This sort of learning is called place learning because, it is asserted, the rat has had no opportunity to perform the critical response (turning right or turning left) during the training period—so this response per se can not have been learned; yet, when given the chance the animal *does* make the appropriate response.

As McNamara *et al.* (184) and also Gleitman (86) have shown, place learning can not be shown under all conditions. If there are few differential cues associated with the correct and incorrect paths of a maze, for instance, animals given this passive exposure do not learn the location of the food, although animals trained by more conventional methods can still do so.

The two experiments referred to in the preceding paragraph constitute the clearest examples of place learning. They also point out the following limitations of such learning: (1) It is not clearly differentiable from transfer of training—after all, even laboratory rats have had much previous experience at going toward stimuli associated with reward; and (2) it is fairly unstable, compared to response learning. The fact that it can be demonstrated, however, gives us some assurance that the albino rat is not the feeble-minded, untalented vertebrate that the critics of his use in experimental psychology sometimes assert.

Place learning is not a crucial challenge to an S-R model of learning, although it is sometimes so regarded. The fact remains that in order to prove that a rat "knows where the food is," the rat must eventually go there under his own power. In other words, the rat must have already learned how to translate cognitive maps into action; must have learned this so well, in fact, that it is a highly generalizable ability. As long as differential responding remains the only way of demonstrating that learning has occurred, then a description of learning in S-R terms surely can not be illegitimate.

Imprinting

Imprinting is a type of learning that has, so far, been noted only in the neonates of many species of birds and fowl. Specifically, it has been observed that very young birds will tend to follow practically any moving object that they see during early infancy. If they do this frequently enough with the same object (or highly similar ones) the "following response" becomes strongly entrenched. Since the moving object that it is most likely for them to see is an older member of their own species (particularly the mother), the adaptive value of this process is quite high.

This sort of behavior was first studied in detail by the famous European naturalist, Konrad Lorenz (172), who described its unique characteristics as a type of learning: (1) It can only occur during a critical period of infancy—i.e., if not exposed to moving objects until a few days old, birds do not develop this tendency to follow such objects, and (2) once established, the "following response" is not subject to forgetting, interference, or extinction. It was this latter characteristic in particular that gave this phenomenon the name "imprinting."

Experimental work in England (see 215) has questioned whether either of these characteristics can be unfailingly noted in the following response. Especially is the idea of a critical period being challenged, although the argument is partly a semantic controversy. In some species it has been noted that after a few days the young bird develops a fear, or flight, reaction to unfamiliar moving objects which supersedes the tendency to follow them. Thus, it is argued, the critical period is not a stage of peculiar "neural readiness" for certain kinds of learning, but rather it is a period during which a moving object is a UCS for the "following response," permitting the practice of this kind of response. When, later on, moving objects become UCS's for other kinds of responses, imprinting obviously can not take place. The only objection to this interpretation might be that the UCS's followed during the neonatal stage never become UCS's for flight reactions later on; clearly, learning has taken place, and it is a kind of learning that can not occur (in just the same way) at any other developmenal stage—therefore, it should be permissible to speak of this period when imprinting is possible as a "critical period."

In America little experimental work on imprinting has been done.

Jaynes (128) has verified the general phenomenon and shown that once it is established in the young chick it may be generalized to other, similar objects later on. Jaynes (129) has also shown that imprinting is easier to obtain the younger the subject, but that it is stronger (more permanent, so to speak) the later in the critical period at which such training takes place; beyond the critical period (54 hours old in Jaynes' chicks), of course, no imprinting occurs. Imprinting is greater, the greater the opportunity for practice of the "following response" during the neonatal period (130). Furthermore, the later generalization of the "following R" is inversely related to the strength of the imprinted R itself; the stronger the tendency of the adolescent bird to follow the object exposed in infancy, the less the tendency to follow other objects (131).

This phenomenon has no known practical significance for human learning, of course, but that should not diminish the value of understanding the phenomenon. Although limited to a fairly specific R in a small segment of the animal kingdom, imprinting may provide us with important information regarding the role of neural development (i.e., maturation) in learning. Another possible outcome of the interest in this phenomenon could be the development of more interchange of information between the ethologist and the experimental psychologist, whose fields of study clearly seem to supplement each other.

SUMMARY

In Table VIII the phenomena discussed in this chapter are listed along with a capsule review of how they fail to fit our S-R-X model. Clearly, it is the reinforcing agent that comes out most poorly. Evidence, if measured by frequency or weight, against the necessity of reinforcement in learning is most impressive. We have repeatedly mentioned our reservations about such evidence, however, and need only repeat here that the learning allegedly found in the absence of something has never yet been shown to aid in the prediction of an individual's behavior. Since statistical, or aggregate, effects (e.g.,

TABLE VIII

A Summary of the Learning Phenomena that Do Not Fit the
S-R-X Model, and How They Do Not Fit

PHENOMENON	PART OF THE MODEL THAT IS NOT APPARENT	
	R	X
Learning without Awareness		
"Irrelevant Set" Type	Sometimes Not Clear	Not Apparent
"Irrelevant Learning" Type	Not Apparent	
Learning During Sleep	DOES NOT OCCUR	
Latent Learning		
Blodgett Effect		Sometimes Not Clear
Seward Effect		Not Apparent
Irrelevant Incentive Learning	Not Clear	Not Apparent
Sensory Preconditioning	Not Apparent	Not Apparent
Place Learning	Sometimes Not Clear	
Imprinting		Not Apparent

The evaluations above take the reported research on each phenomenon at face value.
There are three degrees by which any of these learning situations may be judged to depart
from any part of the model: *Not Apparent* means that no direct observation has been reported of events fitting the indicated portion of the model. *Not Clear* means that there are
experimental conditions that could be the indicated aspect of the model, but it is not
certain that they actually are so. *Sometimes Not Clear* means that the indicated part of
the model has been observed in some experiments, but not in all.

18, 240) can occur for reasons quite independent of the experimental
conditions, demonstrations relying on such effects are not necessarily
destined to contribute much to a science of individual behavior.

CHAPTER 10

*

*

* MOTIVATION

As a concept in behavior science, motivation has exactly the same characteristics as does the concept of learning. These characteristics were discussed in detail in the first chapter. Learning is not a specific phenomenon that can be described in terms of a single set of events. Delayed Pavlovian conditioning can be described by empirical references alone, and so can fixed-ratio, free-operant learning; these are specific instances of the general class called learning. This general class concept (learning), then, applies to a variety of specific functional relationships between environmental conditions and behavioral changes. All such relationships must share some common characteristic if the concept of learning is to be a useful one; the S-R-X model to which we have continually referred is one example of the sort of basis upon which a learning concept may be founded. In the final analysis, however, the decisions as to which environment-behavior relationships to include and which to exclude from the topic of learning are decisions to be made by the individual behavior theorist. To repeat, we do not study learning, we define it—what we study are the consistent relationships between environmental events (past or present) and behavior (present or future) that fall within the definition agreed on.

Now, motivation is just like learning as a psychological concept. There are a variety of environment-behavior relationships that may reasonably be included under this rubric. Just which relationships will and will not be included is, again, up to the psychologist who seeks to systematize the information available in behavior science at any given time.

The methodological similarity between these two concepts of learning and motivation results in an empirical overlap as well. The broadest definitions of motivation used by contemporary psychologists include many of the same environment-behavior relationships that are included in the most encompassing definitions of learning. While a more sophisticated science would hardly notice a temporary inconsistency of this sort in its terminology, the motivation/learning overlap has been treated by many psychologists as a theoretical controversy about which they *must* hold an opinion. Much energy has been spent in attempts to support with empirical evidence the various possible standpoints on this matter.

PROBLEMS INVOLVED IN INCORPORATING MOTIVES INTO THE STIMULUS-RESPONSE FRAMEWORK

From a behavioristic standpoint, the basic problem of psychology is this: Given an organism, A, and an environment, Z, are there any methods and principles that will enable us to become capable of predicting at least some of the things that will happen when organism A is confronted with environment Z on a given occasion? It would not be misleading to describe this entire textbook as an attempt to answer the above question. Up to now, my answers have utilized the implicit assumption that a given environment can be divided conceptually into two kinds of stimuli (each of which rarely occur in equal proportions, of course)—unconditioned and "conditionable." By "unconditioned" I mean just what Pavlov did—UCS's that will almost always elicit some specifiable R in most members of a given species. By conditionable S's I mean the broad class of stimuli for which there are only negligible unlearned R's that are very easily modified by the process that we call learning.

Can the outcome of placing organism A in environment Z on a given occasion actually be predicted solely from an understanding of the stimulus factors of which Z is composed and of A's probable reactions (due to learning, mainly) to such stimuli? Most psychologists say no. The very complexity of the S's in any ordinary environment, it is said, precludes accurate prediction on the basis of knowledge about the subject's S-R experiences alone. We at least need some basis for making an educated guess, this argument goes on, as to the S's most likely to attract the organism's attention. Many psychologists are of the opinion that the best, and perhaps the only, basis for predicting behavior in a normally complex environment is an understanding of the motivation of the organism under observation.

In other words, modern psychology in general tends to emphasize motivation as a *causal* factor in behavior, sometimes to the exclusion of any consideration of the causes of different motivating conditions themselves. The reasons for this tendency are too manifold to delineate here, but its outcome is simple to describe: It has developed another general orientation to behavior science that is not quite an alternative to, not exactly a supplement to, nor yet something isomorphic with an analysis of the sort we have been developing in the preceding chapters.

Not all psychologists who identify themselves in one way or another with a motivational viewpoint would agree that they had thereby dissociated themselves from the S-R approach to behavior. The attitude of some of these psychologists is that there are other operations besides the manipulation of stimulus and reinforcement conditions that play an important role in the determination of observed behavior. The basic "motivation vs. learning" problem that is seen by those of this persuasion is the description of these environment-behavior relationships that are not typically contained in the scope of learning research. That is, are there any important ways of controlling and manipulating behavior that are not explicitly recognized and systematically incorporated in standard treatments of the control of behavior via learning?

I have more or less parenthetically implied several times that hungry animals are more easily taught than those who are not hungry. The interpretation of the significance of a fact such as this is one example of a motivational problem in learning.

Motivational behaviorists, if that term is not too oppressive, feel that there is at least one set of empirical relationships in addition to those covered by the S-R-X model that must be understood. These relationships are called "drives."

A drive concept itself and its relationship to the concept of learning raise (more explicitly, perhaps, than do some other motivational approaches) certain practical, methodological problems. All dependent variables in psychology are measures of behavior, i.e., of responses to (or in the presence of) certain stimuli. Very few demonstrations of drive effects can be made without requiring the subjects to acquire or perform some habit.[1] Are we, therefore, confronted with a "chicken vs. egg" controversy if we attempt to differentiate learning and nonlearning relationships in the study of behavior? Certainly the psychologists who feel this way are in the minority. Accordingly, we must examine the kinds of data that are considered important by those behaviorists who have sought to blend these two areas.

"BIOLOGICAL" DRIVES

What, then, are the general features of these conditions called drives? The basis of the drive school of thought seems to lie in the discovery that the manipulation of variables that have known (or suspected) effects upon the physiological mechanisms of an organism also have a diversity of effects upon this organism's behavior. The following characteristics seem to have been generally agreed upon by psychologists who are interested in defining drives:

(1) The arousal of drives is not entirely dependent upon the immediate, external conditions of the environment. Earlier, antecedent conditions may have produced physiological changes that now serve as the determinants of behavior. Whether one wishes to associate such effects with the concept of S as I have used it so far

---

[1] The complexity of this problem is in no way reduced by the current belief (e.g., 23, 278) that an absolute differentiation between "learned" and "unlearned" behavior is logically and empirically impossible.

in this text depends on the strictness of one's adherence to, and one's interpretation of, the statement that independent observers can agree that something has happened in the organism's environment. Whether what has happened must have been the result of immediately preceding events was not, as far as I know, a prerequisite for identifying a source of stimulation. Furthermore, one can invoke all the internal stimuli that can be identified with specific operations of the experimenter; whether to class them as such or not can only be decided on the basis of what schematic system is the most productive for further research.

(2) Presumably more convincing evidence of the necessity of a drive concept comes from the fact that the strength of certain environment-behavior relationships can be made independent of the S-R relationships that prevail at a given time. In other words, with the immediate S conditions constant, as well as the prior training of the organism in the presence of S, behavioral differences can still be produced that vary with variations in conditions other than those of the momentary environment.

(2a) Directly related to the foregoing is the fact, worth mentioning on its own, that the intensity and/or persistence with which both learned and unlearned S-R relationships are performed will fluctuate directly with the strength of drives.

The General Techniques of Drive Arousal

There are three major classes of antecedent conditions that seem to be especially pertinent to the discussion of behavior-environment relationships which we might choose to label as "drives." These are: (1) deprivation, (2) presentation of certain UCS's, and (3) a combination of the first two techniques.

Deprivation

Deprivation refers to situations in which certain R's are prevented from occurring by withholding for a time the necessary S's, following which these S-R relationships show greater strength than they show when occurring ad libitum. The basic class of events in this category are those conditions that, if allowed to persist, and/or if carried to the extreme, would result in the death of the organism so treated. These include the conditions called hunger, thirst, pain, sleeplessness, being too hot or too cold, and lack of oxygen. For this reason, these conditions are labeled "biological." All of these have specifiable determinants as well as specifiable remedies. Such remedies are almost always considered to be rewards. The sexual drive is also an important influence on organismic activity. Even though it is not fundamental to individual survival its manifestation is a direct function of deprivation.

Recently, there has been a great deal of interest in behavior that is regarded by many psychologists as reflecting a drive to explore the environment. This curiosity drive (sometimes called an "exploratory drive," or a "manipulatory drive,") is, as with sexual desires, not crucial for individual survival, but such a drive would certainly *aid* survival because it leads to increased contact with the environment. All increments in contact with the environment, of course, will afford increased opportunities for learning.

From the standpoint of human learning, the curiosity and manipulatory drives may actually be the most important of the primary drives. In a prosperous society such as our own, in which the physical needs of most infants are taken care of rather readily, the amount of learning that is directly related to the maintenance of life and physical comfort seems to be only a small portion of the habits that are formed even in the earliest years. Parents and educators, to speak of them in a rather stereotyped way, probably do not utilize children's curiosity to the fullest advantage in the education process.

External Stimulation

Another obstacle to the amalgamation of learning and motivation concepts is the differentiation between motivational stimuli—denoted by S_{mot}—and the observable, external stimuli of the environment—indicated by S_{ext}. Such a differentiation tends to impose unrealistic restrictions on the motivation concept itself. With people especially, much of what we consider to be the means of arousing motivation is done by the presentation of external stimuli. Words, for example, are probably our primary means of arousing those around us to some sort of action. The evidence of external control of many presumed motivational effects is also beginning to accumulate at the infrahuman level. So we find less than a sharp distinction between environmental stimuli and motivating conditions. But control of organismic activity by variations in S_{ext} seems to fall under the category of learned behavior. Again we are confronted with an inability in many cases to distinguish between motivated behavior and learned behavior, except by using very arbitrary criteria for identifying these two phenomena.

Our treatment of avoidance learning has already introduced the notion that *some UCS's can be thought of as ways to arouse drives.* The most apparent class of such UCS's are those that we have labeled "noxious stimuli." Pain, excessive heat or cold, a prolonged excess of carbon dioxide in the lungs, and abnormally intense stimulation of any receptor modality are the most typical kinds of S_{nox}'s.

Many species show nonsexual reproductive activity and maternal behavior that does not seem to be a result of learning only. If, as some students of behavior choose to think, such response patterns indicate rather specific drive conditions, then such drives would also be classed with those manipulated primarily by unconditioned stimuli.

This assumes that we can classify the manipulation of hormonal and allied physiological factors as unconditioned stimuli.

The treatment of UCS's as means of arousing drives seems to reflect, to the fullest extent, the view of drive as a generic term for almost any unlearned environment-behavior relationship. Consider, for instance, the data reported by such an outstanding student of learning as Prof. K. W. Spence (256). His dependent variable in these studies was the frequency of conditioned eyeblinks,[2] and intensity of the air puff used as the UCS was the independent variable. A positive relationship was found between UCS intensity and occurrence of CR's—both during initial training and at a later time. The assumption of such a relationship was fundamental to our

---

[2] The method of conditioning the eyelid reflex was described in conjunction with the discussion of Voeks' experiment (p. 49).

hypothesis that the study by Bahrick (described on p. 311) was also relevant to the Silver-Meyer account of sensory preconditioning (outlined on p. 310), i.e., drive intensity should increase the strengths of UCR's and thus aid in the conditioning of CR's related to these UCR's.

The only question here is the persistent one: since CS intensity (within the ordinary limits) also is known to affect CR strength positively, without any hypothesis about drive being mentioned in such a case (e.g., 207), why should a similar relationship between UCS and UCR need to be referred to drive phenomena? As usual, the answer to this question lies not in any facts, but in one's way of interpreting these facts. Spence's interpretation of his data, therefore, is justifiable, though (as he himself points out) not the only possible interpretation.

UCS's Plus Deprivation

Some drives appear to require *both deprivation and the presentation of UCS's*. The drives for which both of these manipulations most clearly seem important are the sexual drive in many male animals and the exploratory drives. In most of the female members of the animal kingdom, sexual motivation is highly correlated with hormonal balance; in such cases we would class the drive as one manipulated by UCS's alone. These variations in the sexual drive of the female are accompanied by changes in secondary characteristics such as color, odor, or behavior which, in turn, act as UCS's for the sexual drive of the male. While these UCS's are essential to sexual arousal in the male, the *degree* of arousal, in many vertebrate males at least, relates to the *amount of deprivation*.[3]

Curiosity appears to be a joint function of both of these kinds of antecedents. The introduction of novel (unfamiliar) stimuli into an organism's environment seems to act as a UCS for exploratory behavior (61). Obviously, the more times an organism is exposed

---

[3] To be sure, this is an extremely oversimplified account of a very complex determinant of much organismic activity. For a glimpse at how complex this problem is, read some of the reports by Prof. F. A. Beach of his excellent research in this field (e.g., 22, 24).

to a given stimulus, the less novel this stimulus becomes, and the repeated exposure to a stimulus is called "satiation," which is the procedural opposite of deprivation. Just as an organism is more likely to pay attention to food stimuli if such stimuli have been absent from his environment for a long time (deprivation), so the organism is more likely to attend to stimuli of other types if they have been absent from his environment. Evidence for a satiation effect in exploration drive has been reported by Welker (286); Bahwell and Premack (16) have also presented data that appear to confirm in a more direct way the role of deprivation in the manipulatory drive's strength. A complicating factor in the assay of deprivation and satiation factors in the field of curiosity drives, however, is that the satisfaction of such drives should be rewarding. Therefore, the activities leading to such satisfaction should be strengthened; this strengthening would, however, retard or eliminate the expected decline in manipulation or exploration. This interaction of reward and satiation—with the dominance of the former—is shown in data described by Harlow, Blazek, and McClearn (106); their young monkeys showed progressive improvement, not deterioration on manipulatory tasks for which the only possible reinforcement was successful (in a purely objective sense) manipulation—e.g., undoing a hook such as is commonly found on screen doors.

Experimental work on curiosity is a rather recent development in psychology, and as yet we have not determined the specific quantitative relationships between the strength of this drive and its antecedent conditions. One puzzle that must be dealt with in the process of determining the antecedents of a curiosity drive is that some kinds of unfamiliar stimuli arouse fear instead of curiosity, particularly in children and animals. Hebb (109) has described experimental anecdotes suggesting this, and Montgomery (193) made observations that he regarded as confirming the interplay of these two drives in novel situations. At present, the factors that produce one effect instead of the other are not understood; there is a possibility that the fear of the unusual may be largely due to learning, at least in some of the species that are most frequently studied.

Frustration

A fourth method of producing drive that has frequently been suggested is the procedure called "frustration." Frustration involves the prevention of an organism from completing goal-directed responses by means other than the withholding of the relevant stimuli (which latter technique, of course, fits our deprivation definition). The signal evidence for this assertion is considered to be the often-observed fact that organisms tend to try harder (i.e., show greater response strength) after frustration than before (e.g., 183). Since frustration involves nonreinforcement *by definition*, it has been supposed by some psychologists (38) that increased vigor following non-reward is most readily explained by assuming that frustration momentarily increases an organism's total drive level. I. E. Farber (73), a psychologist who has kept his head in the general controversy over the role of drive in behavior theory despite his unabashed predilections toward a strong drive position, has skillfully pointed out the noncrucial nature of most research cited in favor of a frustration drive.

The essence of the objections to regarding frustration as a drive-producing technique might well be leveled against many procedures that are generally considered as specific examples of the first three classes of methods discussed. The logical necessity of a drive notion, it was noted earlier, stems from apparent temporal gaps between antecedents and consequents, such as between the removal of food from a rat's cage and the rat's behavior many hours later. In the cases of frustration, curiosity, and even sexual activity (viewed from one standpoint), no such problem exists, since there are immediate external conditions that can be related to observed behavior.

While temporal parameters of deprivation can be brought to the rescue of sex and curiosity as drives, a similar defense can not be invoked for the aftereffects of frustration. The case for a frustration-produced drive rests on inductive reasoning almost entirely. The importance of this issue, as the student should see, does not evolve from a concern about the observable effects of frustration. No one seriously questions these. The "frustration-produced drive" controversy, however, raises some fundamental issues about the status of the drive concept in general. For this reason, the various interpretations of frustration experiments are currently being subjected to intense scrutiny (e.g., 163).

DRIVE AS A PSYCHOLOGICAL CONCEPT

Drive as an "Intervening Variable"

Drive is the same kind of psychological phenomenon as is learning; we observe neither directly, we only see their effects. In 1936, Tolman (269) described the essential procedure for evaluating the role of drive in behavior, and some fifteen years later H. G. Yamaguchi (294) actually performed an experiment carrying out Tolman's suggestions. The essential feature of this experiment is that different groups of rats were given identical training and extinction treatments in identical external environmental conditions. The subjects in all groups learned the same S-R relationship; the same reinforcement—food—was administered in the same way and for the same response with all subjects, and the external stimulus conditions —a straight runway—were the same for all. The only way in which the groups differed was in the length of time that had elapsed since the subjects in each group had last had a chance to eat.

It is clear from Figure 26 that the groups did differ in the persistence of responding after they were no longer rewarded for running to the former goal area. This persistence is systematically related to the degree of hunger. Since all other factors known to influence behavior in this sort of situation (and in the observed manner in which the behavior was affected) were affecting all groups equally, we may assume that the differences observed between the groups directly reflect the differences in their average strength of drive at the time of the test trials. In effect, we can consider the values on the ordinate of Figure 26 as indicators of relative drive strength, rather than a specific behavioral measure. Thus it was possible for Yamaguchi to conclude that he had determined the relationship between drive and hours of food deprivation, even though he had not directly observed any event that could be called drive. Furthermore, if we grant the possibility of an underlying drive factor, then these data are equally interpretable as a description of the relationship between drive and response strength.

Why do we consider it necessary to talk about drive in reference to the empirical relationship of hours of deprivation and response strength? The reason is the same as that discussed when we talked

FIGURE 26

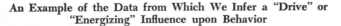

An Example of the Data from Which We Infer a "Drive" or "Energizing" Influence upon Behavior

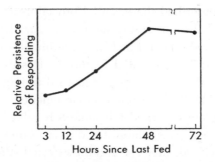

The points on this curve represent the relative resistance to extinction of rats trained under identical conditions and given extinction trials under conditions also identical except for the time since the animals had last eaten. No exact values are given for the ordinate scale, since the *relative* persistence is most important for the illustration. The decline between 48 and 72 hours is attributed to the weakening effect of prolonged semi-starvation. (From Yamaguchi (294), in the *Journal of Experimental Psychology*, vol. 42, p. 112. Used by permission of the American Psychological Association.)

about avoidance learning (Chapter 3): in and of itself, the absence of something can not constitute part of a causal chain. The absence or nonoccurrence of something must imply the presence or occurrence of something else just as observable, or at least potentially just as observable.

One of the persistent difficulties confronting scientific conceptualizations is that most of the world's languages permit—indeed, encourage—us to speak of the null class (the absence of something) as if it were truly the opposite of some positive, observable event.

Thus, in the popular jargon it is considered to be a fact or a discrete event that an organism has not eaten for a certain period of time. In science, however, we can not grant "time since last meal" the status that a term such as "having four legs" has, although the rules for making both measurements are equally clear. Instead, it is assumed by scientists that events that developed during the "time since last meal" and were in effect at the time of the experimental tests could be the only determinants of test behavior. Now, the deprivation of food or water is known to produce changes in the physiology of living organisms, the most extreme of which is death. These changes, and others not yet known or understood completely, are presumably related to what we call drive. In the final analysis, at this stage of biological advancement, drive is simply an inference, an expression of scientific faith, so to speak, that physiological changes and behavioral changes will eventually be more highly correlated than they now are. For this reason, drive is most properly called a *hypothetical construct* or an *intervening variable*.[4] It stands for whatever the actual empirical determinants might be of the differences in S-R strengths such as Yamaguchi produced by food deprivation (Figure 26).

Nonspecific Effects of Drive

Hull's theory of behavior (124) incorporated one of the most explicit hypotheses about the nonspecific effects of drive. Drive, he said, increased the subject's random activity. No matter what the specific S's were in any situation, nor what R's might be associated with them, drive had the same fundamental effect: all such S-R connections were more likely to be evoked, and if evoked, the behavior would be quite vigorous.

---

[4] MacCorquodale and Meehl (176) have discussed the pros and cons of using these terms as synonyms vs. using them to express subtle, but presumably important, differences in the empirical status of scientific concepts of the type represented by "drive." They defend the latter alternative. Marx (179) has defended the synonym position in a paper that also attempted to expand the possible referents such concepts could have. No budding devotee of the philosophy of science as applied to psychology can afford to overlook these two important papers.

The potential survival value of such an effect clearly is great. If an organism grows increasingly hungry and, concomitantly, grows more active, his chances of discovering and consuming whatever food may actually be available are enhanced. If increases in drive, by way of illustrative contrast, tended to *immobilize* organisms, there would probably not, at this late stage in the earth's history, be many organisms left to note this fact. However well this hypothesized effect of drive may fit our Darwinian predilections, such a fit does not make an hypothesis a fact. There are empirical as well as dogmatic bases for the hypothesis that the major role of drives is to increase the strength of whatever S-R relationships are to be expected in a given situation anyway:

(1) Yamaguchi's experiment (see Figure 26) demonstrates one of the main types of evidence used by most psychologists who argue for the use of some "drive" or "motivational" factors in accounting for behavioral variability, especially when learning factors alone would not lead one to expect such differences. This study exemplifies the situation that is often supposed to occur in which drive energizes an S-R relationship that is already predominant for other reasons (e.g., training and habit acquisition factors). In other words, divergences in the performance of habits—either by a group of individuals, or in the same individual from time to time—may not be due to differences in the habit itself, but in the drive conditions.

We speak of the effect of drive as being nonspecific in cases such as this because the drive energizes whatever R's are aroused by S_{ext}'s. The drive condition does not directly determine which R's will be aroused, and it would have affected hurdle-jumping, barpressing, or any other S-R relationship in the same way as it does whatever R is under observation.

(2) Another easily observed, nonspecific effect of drive is upon the variability in the performance of learned R's. As drive strength increases, most subjects' R's show less variability from observation to observation. Under low drive there is typically a great deal of intra-subject variability—sometimes the organism will make a given R quickly, only to make it sluggishly the very next time; as we in-

crease drive, however, we decrease such inconsistencies. Similarly, the variability between subjects on a given learning trial (when they have all learned the same habit to the same degree) rises and falls with decreases and increases, respectively, in drive.

Presumably, this effect on variability is a subsidiary outcome of the energizing characteristic of drive. Clearly, there is a physical maximum for response strength. There *is* a limit, for example, to how fast even John Landy can run the mile; even the legends about Paul Bunyan recognize some kind of limit to ability. Now, increasing motivation to its maximal energizing effect must push response strength up to its maximum also. So the limits of one's ability impose a fairly strict upper limit, while the strength of the drive affecting one imposes a lower limit of performance. As these two limits come closer to one another (by raising the latter, usually, since it is the easier to manipulate), there must be less variability in performance. It seems to be for reasons similar to these that psychometrists try to administer intelligence and achievement tests under optimally motivating conditions, so as to get an estimate of the upper limits of the subject's abilities.

Learning and the Effects of Drive

We will now examine the ways in which some fairly fragmentary work on drives has influenced and/or aided the understanding of learning phenomena. The following discussion treats the distinction between drive and learning as legitimate. The student should bear in mind, while studying the following, the many reservations about such an assumption that have been discussed from time to time in the text. But the assumption of a difference between drive and learning is here to be regarded only as a convenience in communication, *not* as a pivotal notion in behavior theory, nor as the issue of paramount importance in the following discussions.

The Stimulus Characteristics of Drives

The simplest sort of control over drives is to be able to manipulate conditions so that a given drive is either present or not. But such control would be of little value if we could not also predict the behavioral consequences of producing or eliminating a drive. Insofar as drives are UCS's we can control the occurrence of the related UCR's by controlling the presence or absence of a specific drive. We actually can do much more than this, however, because it can be shown that drives have much in common with more conventional stimuli; organisms can learn to make different responses in the presence of different drive conditions.

The experimental evidence for this stimulus function of drives was first obtained by Hull (123) and by Leeper (165). They worked separately, but their experiments were very similar. Both used mazes that looked like the one shown in Figure 27. There were no differ-

FIGURE 27

The General Shape of the Maze Used in the Hull and the Leeper Experiments on Drive Discrimination

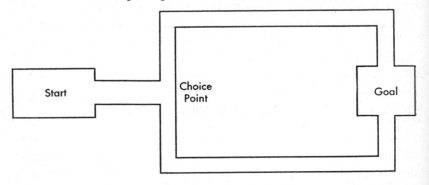

ential cues on either side of the maze, neither inside it nor outside. The problem situation was basically this: when a rat had been deprived of water, a turn to the left at the choice-point, say, would be rewarded by the availability of water in the goal area; if the rat turned right, however, no water was available. On other days, though, the same rat was no longer thirsty, but *was* hungry. Now a turn to the left culminated in an entry into an empty goalbox, but a right turn was rewarded by the opportunity to eat food. In other words, the solution was "when thirsty, go left; when hungry, go right." There was no possibility of "place learning," nor of irrelevant incentive learning in these experiments—the subject always ended up in the same general area no matter what its choice had been, and there were no irrelevant incentives offered.

It takes a rat a great while to learn such a problem, but rats *can* learn to solve it. This indicates unequivocally that there are distinct stimulus-like aspects to different drive conditions. In the absence of any external cues, knowledge of the organism's current drive (hunger or thirst) was the only cue to the correct path on any given day. Since rats presumably can not obtain knowledge through verbalization, their ability to use this cue suggests that drives can function in and of themselves as stimuli. We now are using the term "stimulus" in a purely functional sense, of course; what we mean specifically is that different R's can be associated with only one class of events—S's; therefore, drives have S components. To many students this may only be an elaboration of the obvious; apparently the notion of drives and motives as S's is among the earliest conceptualizations that are formed about motivation.

Kendler (144) and Bailey (17) elaborated on the Hull-Leeper technique. They made hunger and thirst *irrelevant* (i.e., these drives were not related to the reinforcing agent). The fundamental problem facing their subjects (albino rats) was to learn to turn off a bright light. This could be done by pushing on one of two panels; sometimes pushing on the white panel was followed by a reduction in illumination, sometimes the black panel was correct. The cue as to which panel should be pushed to turn the light off was whether the subject was hungry or thirsty (i.e., had most recently been deprived of food or water); for example, if a rat was hungry the correct panel was the black one, if thirsty, the white. Although this might seem to be an impossible problem for an albino rat, this animal (or the members of one strain, at least) can solve it if given enough time (about 450 trials).

To put the foregoing briefly, the *absence* of certain substances (deprivation) can provide cues that are capable of being attached to R's by the usual methods of habit formation. Organisms *can* learn specific habits involving not the presentation of external S's, but the "arousal of needs." But it takes a long time.

Drives as Responses

It turns out that not only can specific, observable R's be associated with drives, but—to further complicate things—drives can be associated with specific, external S's. At least, the drive we call "fear" can; the evidence for the learning of other drives is still ambiguous.

The notion that drives can be manipulated in essentially the same ways that we can manipulate responses seems to have become fundamental to much of the theorizing that goes on in the fields of psychology such as personality, abnormal behavior, and psychotherapy, to name but a few. Clearly, such an idea underlies all assumptions that behavior can be controlled by controlling the subject's motivation—an assertion that pervades the "applied" areas of psychology today.

We have already (Chapter 3) described the classic demonstration by Neal Miller (189) of the conditioning of a drive. His apparatus was a long, thin box divided into two compartments. The walls of one compartment were painted white, the walls of the other were black. The floor was an electric grid which could be turned on in the white compartment while remaining off in the black one. Between the black and white compartments was a door; this door was always open during the initial stages of training.

Since the compartments were differentiable, the white box might be expected to become a signal for the impending shock. Indeed, it did so; the rat learned to flee from the white box as soon as he was placed into it, without waiting for the shock. This, as we have seen, is called avoidance learning. Psychologists generally consider this phenomenon to be best explained by assuming that the white chamber comes to elicit a fear response, so that this cue's own termination is rewarding. Proof of this is that rats can learn an entirely new response, never associated with shock or shock reduction, the reinforcement for which is the elimination of (escape from) the acquired fear-producing S. To show this, Miller closed the door between the two compartments, and inserted a lever alongside the door. When the lever was pressed the door opened, permitting escape from the white box. Rats did learn the lever-pressing response, although the only reinforcement was escape from the white box; shock was never associated in any direct way with lever-pressing.

Whatever doubts might exist that the rats did actually learn to fear a shock compartment were removed by a study by Goodson and Brownstein (87) that is a model of well-designed experimentation. In this study, the rats were trained just as in the first stage of Miller's study—to run from a shock box to a different, safe compartment—but they were originally equidistant between the compartment where they had formerly been shocked and a neutral box (one they had never seen during shock trials). Goodson and Brownstein found that the rats had a strong preference for the neutral box in this choice situation, and that they did not delay long in making their choices. It would appear that they were afraid of the former shock chamber.[5]

In both of the above experiments the rats learned a discrete R to the shock chamber itself—viz., to get out of it in a hurry. In contrast to this, Amsel and Cole (6, see text p. 93) performed an experiment in which no specific overt R was systematically reinforced during the fear-conditioning stage. Rats were simply confined in a small box and repeatedly shocked after a light had flashed for a brief interval. The light foreshadowed the shock, as in the studies just described, but here the rats could do nothing to escape or to avoid the shock. Next, the animals were made thirsty and allowed to drink all that they could during twice-daily half-hour sessions in a special box, one quite different from the shock box. After the rats developed a stable rate of water consumption during such sessions, they were required to drink while the flashing light from the shock situation—but no shock—was presented intermittently. Their water consumption dropped sharply when the light was flashing. Presumably the light elicited an acquired drive—fear—for which water was an irrelevant incentive and for which drinking was not an appropriate response.

The most important aspect of this experiment was that apparently

[5] The similarity of this experiment to that by Gleitman (p. 317), which was discussed (by Gleitman) in quite different terms, should be noted.

no specific instrumental response was being learned during the light-shock pairings. If this was actually the case, then the light's effect upon the previously unrelated drinking response was not due to the arousal of other, interfering R's by the light itself. Instead, the light's effect upon behavior could be attributed to the fact that the presence of the light altered the subjects' drives.

Actually, it is not too unreasonable to assume that many members of a genetically homogeneous group of laboratory-raised albino rats might make similar UCR's to the UCS of shock; from what we have seen in the case of Pavlovian conditioning, the sequence, S_n-UCS-UCR, contains all the elements necessary for learning to occur. Perhaps, therefore, many of Amsel and Cole's subjects did indeed associate some overt R with the blinking light CS. Furthermore, if a CR were to be established by this procedure, it would probably not be compatible with a water-drinking R. During the test sessions, therefore, we could predict that the light would interfere with water consumption—which was the observed outcome—without ever using a drive notion.

The fact that some experiments, such as that by Amsel and Cole, do not clearly differentiate between the learning of overt responses and the acquisition of drives is an indication of the difficulties that are confronted when we try to study motivation experimentally. These difficulties are slowly being overcome, however, and there has been a gradual accumulation of evidence that, taken altogether, seems to verify the hypothesis that at least some drives can be modified by learning.

At present, the weight of the experimental evidence appears to be on Mowrer's side as far as the fear drive is concerned (cf. the discussion on p. 91 above). For the other biological drives (sometimes called "primary drives"), however, it is not at all certain that they can be associated with S_{ext}'s by the usual learning procedures. Anderson (8) once reported data that he interpreted as an instance of "hunger-drive conditioning," but his work has been traditionally cited—and justifiably so, I think—as one of the early demonstrations of secondary reinforcement establishment. With secondary reinforcement and irrelevant incentive possibilities eliminated, Danziger (58) was unable to find any evidence of hunger-drive conditioning. Calvin, Bicknell and Sperling (46) reported a more adequate test of the drive-conditioning hypothesis with hunger, but they failed to control for exploratory motivation; a subsequent study for Siegel and MacDonnell (243) did not confirm their results even though they repeated it in its essentials (as Calvin himself admitted).

Logically, the skepticism about the likelihood of conditioning hunger and thirst drives centers about the question of their developments. If such drives (and thus their presumed neural concomitants) develop gradually, then they would be highly unsatisfactory UCS's. On the other hand, we spoke several pages back of one effect of hunger being the UCS for crying and sucking R's in the infant, and Hebb (110) has noted that one 24-hour period of food deprivation is not sufficient to obtain a high level of activity in laboratory animals (although such an interval can become the sufficient antecedent of a high activity level, granted enough repetitions). Organisms seem to require time to learn when they are to be fed, rather than simply to be deprived in order to develop a high level of activity. All in all, it seems that we have not yet worked out the methods crucial to a test of the general drive-conditioning hypothesis. Whether behavioristic approaches (as opposed, e.g., to physiological techniques) to this question will ever prove satisfactory still remains to be seen.

Hidden in this question of whether drives with relatively slow onsets can be associated with S_{ext}'s according to the more well-known learning procedures is an issue of paramount importance to the problem of resolving motivational and learning approaches to behavior. This is the matter of whether anything but responses can be associated with stimuli, and, further, whether the identification of a learned response in the context of a drive-conditioning study frees the learning-oriented psychologist from the problem of discussing drive conditioning. Put more simply, the question is, are the most important consequences of the conditions that produce drives UCS's or UCR's, and does the answer to this question affect the answer to the subsequent question, Can drives be conditioned? We are in no position to take a stand on this issue; nor, for that matter, is any psychologist, since it is a problem in theoretical dogma. Our aim has been to clarify somewhat the issues involved.

How Drives Affect Learning

Can drives literally affect learning? Can we talk about the effects of drives upon learning in the same way that we can discuss the effects of enzymes upon ingested food, or the effects of exploding gasoline and oxygen upon an automobile piston? No, we can not, for psychologists do not refer to entirely differentiable events when they talk about drives and about learning.

We have already discussed (Chapter 1) the fact that learning is not a "thing," but a term referring to a series of events. It is a description of some of the ways in which an observable event in the present is to be related to events in the past. Drive is the same sort of concept; it is a shorthand way of stating the relationships between events that occur at different moments in time.

In psychology the event observed in the immediate present is always some behavior change; this is true no matter what the hypothesis, theory, or practical problem that may have stimulated any particular research. Now, behavior can be measured on only a finite (and, as yet, actually small) number of dimensions, but concepts such as "drive" and "learning" do not squabble over the possibilities available—they are both defined in terms of almost all classes of behavioral changes now used in laboratory research. Drives and learning differ, thus, not so much in terms of their behavioral symptoms, but in the events leading up to these effects; in other words, they refer to different sets of antecedent conditions and their relationships to behavioral changes. Much of the difficulty involved in differentiating between the concepts of drive and habit stems from the vagueness with which their respective antecedents are discussed and described.

Drives and learning, then, are both merely terms, and the question as to how drives affect learning can not have any literal, scientific meaning.

The best understood and the most widely applicable types of

learning situations are those in which specified responses are reinforced in the presence of certain stimuli. Therefore, the question of
how drives influence learning is to be answered by considering the
ways in which drives could affect the exact nature of particular
S-R-X sequences. Since we have already considered the effects of
variations of motivation upon the S-R-X model, in a general way,
we have actually answered the question now before us. A brief
review, however, may be beneficial.

(1) Increasing a subject's drive level increases his responsiveness
to the environment. This should often have the effect of increasing
the chance that he will make an R in the presence of some S under
conditions where this sequence might be reinforced. This role of
drive is most often utilized in operant learning situations. It is only
one of several means used simultaneously to speed up the rate at
which repetitions of the S-R-X sequence can occur.

A fact that perhaps is not emphasized enough is that the use
of drives as general activators will, by itself, rarely bring about
efficient learning. (It is equally or even more important, for instance, to arrange the external features of the environment in which
learning is expected to occur in such a way that the subject will not
make a lot of irrelevant responses.) A strong drive is not essential
for efficient learning; a variety of other procedures—such as those
used in Pavlovian conditioning and some of the incidental learning
experiments—can also increase the chance that the appropriate R's
will occur at the proper times.

Joel Greenspoon (91) was the first of several experimenters to
employ a method of modifying human verbal behavior that does not
require experimental manipulation of a subject's motivation. The
initial instructions to the subject were similar to those used in "irrelevant set" incidental-learning studies; the subject was asked
simply to recite aloud all the common nouns that occurred to him
during the experimental session (this period varied from 20 to 60
mins. in different studies of this phenomenon). Whenever the subject happened to mention a plural noun, the experimenter made
some verbal remark of a generally reinforcing (or rewarding) kind—
e.g., Greenspoon simply said, "uh huh." Three different studies of

this phenomenon, at least, have shown that the relative frequency with which a general class of R's—such as plural nouns—increases over a period of time is just the same as that with which a *specific* R increases during more typical operant learning sessions.

Among many interesting features of this experiment, it illustrates that effective learning situations do not necessarily require the control of the subject's motives—except in a loose way. Subjects rarely discerned that they were in a learning experiment; an appreciable minority did notice, or suspect, that there was a consistent relationship between their behavior and the experimenter's reactions (such as "uh huh" responses), but even when this insight included a knowledge of what part of their own behavior elicited an R by the experimenter, there were few subjects who felt any obligation to learn. Greenspoon's study—which has been confirmed several times since—is a perfect case of incidental learning that does not depart from the S-R-X model.

That learning can be obtained in the absence of relevant motivation is of great importance for behavior theory; from a practical standpoint the fact is interesting, but less fundamental. When a person wishes to teach an organism to do something, it will usually be wise to consider first the possibility that the subject can be, as we say, "motivated to learn" the desired habits.

(2) Drive can also enter into the S-R-X scheme at the X stage. That is, some reinforcers vary directly in effectiveness with changes in drive conditions. The general relationship has already been discussed earlier in this chapter. At present, we know only a limited number of relationships between drive changes and changes in reinforcement effectiveness that would be pertinent here.

The most striking example of this phenomenon is to be found in an experiment by Reynolds, Marx and Henderson (224). Rats were trained to operate a lever in a Skinner-type box, with the reward for half of them being a large food pellet and for the remainder, a small pellet. Half of the high-reward rats were trained under high drive (48-hour food deprivation), half under low (24-hour deprivation); similarly for the low-reward rats. So there were four groups, essentially:

High-Reward—High-Drive   High-Reward—Low-Drive
Low-Reward—High-Drive   Low-Reward—Low-Drive

All subjects were given extinction sessions during which the same drive conditions as during training prevailed.

A significant interaction was obtained between drive condition and reward amount. Under high drive, subjects that had got low reward had greater resistance to extinction than did subjects who had been receiving high-reward amounts under high drive. For the rats trained and tested under low drive the results were more in line with common sense. Here, rats previously receiving high reward had greater resistance to extinction than rats getting low-reward amounts.

Historically, the relationships observed between some drives and some reinforcers led many psychologists to support the notion that the fundamental class of reinforcers consisted of those events that were "need reducing"—the general name for all conditions important for individual and species survival. The effectiveness of all reinforcers, as this still popular theory goes, can be traced back to some relationship—direct or acquired—with need reduction. Currently, such a theory of reinforcement is not regarded by most psychologists as consistent with all the facts; nevertheless, it can not be considered a bankrupt idea, nor has it been an unproductive hypothesis.

(3) We know that drives have stimulus characteristics. This fact leads to the possibility that drives themselves can become involved in habits. If so, the arousal of a drive already associated with some R could affect the speed of learning in a new situation, for it is known that a number of S's presented simultaneously may serve as an S complex to which a specific R may be associated. This can be true even if all of the S's do not fall on the same physical dimension. Among the elements of such a compound may be stimuli arising from some drive condition. Now, if an R is associated with this compound, and the drive-produced S's constitute a large portion of the total S elements in the compound, what will be the effect upon the habit of varying the relevant drive condition—either qualitatively or quantitatively? Assuming, as most psychologists do,

that the number or intensity of stimuli varies directly with the intensity of the drive, we would expect the habit also to vary at least with the *intensity* of the drive conditions.

This process—called transfer of training—is described in detail in Chapter 7; for the present, it is sufficient to say that the evocation of an older S-R relationship during a new learning situation is not inevitably a help, nor yet is it a hindrance. Its influence upon the new learning situation depends upon the compatibility of the old and new R's, and the similarity of the two relevant S's. This, in capsule form, is the prosaic fashion in which behaviorists describe some of those often awe-inspiring examples of human conduct that seem superficially unrelated to the conditions that prevail at a given moment.

The Basic Designs of "Drive-Learning Interaction" Studies

In the earlier portions of this chapter we reviewed many of the ways in which the drive-producing operations could affect behavior. Experimenters working on the role of drive in learning have not concerned themselves with most of the ways in which these two sets of operations could interact, instead restricting themselves almost exclusively to the method of deprivation—either of food or water—on the drive side. Some psychologists (e.g., 47) have studied different intensities of electric shock in this context, using, however, the same approach as that used with hunger and thirst. The basic experimental designs for all such research are shown in Table IX. Almost all such research has also involved the albino rat as the subject.

The only effects of drives that have been identified and explicitly controlled are their stimulus characteristics. If high- and low-drive levels are accompanied, as seems reasonable, by stimuli of different intensities, then the performance under a given drive level of a habit learned under a different drive level might be expected to show some deterioration. This follows from the principle of *stimulus generalization,* discussed on pp. 52–54 and 100–105.

Furthermore, a shift from a high-drive level to a lower one, and a shift from a low level to a higher degree would not have equal generalization effects. This is because it is assumed (justifiably)

TABLE IX

The Designs Used to Study the Role of Drive in Learning

NAME OF DESIGN	DRIVE LEVEL DURING TRAINING	DRIVE LEVEL DURING TESTING
Reversal	Group 1: High Group 2: Low	Group 1: Low Group 2: High
Counterbalanced	Group 1: High Group 2: Low	Group 1a: High 1b: Low Group 2a: High 2b: Low
Randomized	All subjects given High and Low drive conditions randomly	Group 1: High Group 2: Low

Many of the actual experiments in this field used more than two levels of drive at one or both of these stages. This elaboration, however, has not yet resulted in designs that are more than permutations of those described in this table.

that the variations in stimulation that accompany variations in drive level are primarily variations in the intensity of stimulation. When variations of stimuli are along the intensity dimensions, the typical stimulus generalization effects are modified somewhat.

Recall that R strength varies with the intensity of the S presented (this is true whether the S-R relationship in a given example is learned or not). As a result, reducing S intensity from that originally used during the establishment of the habit should produce a decrement in the performance of the R involved, even if no generalization factor has to be considered; increasing the intensity of S, on the other hand, should lead to a stronger R. But the generalization effect can not actually be ignored. Any change from the original S in a learned S-R relationship will produce a decrement in the performance of the given R.

The interaction of stimulus generalization and stimulus intensity effects was named *stimulus intensity dynamism* by Hull (125). This joint effect is especially important in predicting the effects of shifts of drive following the acquisition of a habit. The first design described ("Reversal") in Table IX does not take these into account. The other two designs do, but in different ways.

Current Understanding of the Role of Drive in Learning

Of the three general designs, only the Counterbalanced has received extensive study. Deese and Carpenter (60) used the Reversal design and failed to find what would be expected from a stimulus-intensity-dynamism hypothesis. Specifically, the rats that shifted from high to low drive in their study did not show the depression of performance that would be expected by stimulus intensity generalization. Those which shifted from low to high did show the overgeneralization that would be predicted in such a case.

Using the Randomized design and a very sophisticated method of analyzing his data, Cotton (55) was hesitant to reach any final conclusions about the general nature of the drive-learning interaction. The randomized design, however, brings in a new factor—it involves shifting from variable training conditions to standard testing conditions—and this general problem has yet to be examined, so we can not tell whether Cotton's results are most pertinent to drive theory or to the effects of simulus variability during learning.

The greater amount of attention given to the counterbalanced design has not resulted in a clarification of the general problem. The majority of studies with this design have revealed no statistically reliable effects of training drive level on performance of the habit under test drive levels (e.g., 60, 112), but there are some disturbing exceptions to this generalization (e.g., 68). If we assume that these studies were equally adequate in execution, then the disparity in their results must be due to some factor such as suggested by Campbell and Kraeling (48): viz., that the evaluation of the influence of drive on learning will itself be affected by the measure of performance, or habit strength, that is employed during the testing period.

The Campbell-Kraeling hypothesis is probably correct without being sufficiently explicit. To be more concrete, we would point out that there are *several* ways in which drive could affect learning *indirectly*. (The effects can only be indirect since neither drives nor habits are things.) Drives affect behavior. Learning, or much of it that is of practical importance, depends upon behavior; simple habits (i.e., those not involving generalization or transfer effects) require reinforced occurrences of R in the presence of S's.

Drives can often determine the effectiveness of a given reinforcing agent, and drives can also influence the chances of a given R occurring in the presence of S. Ergo, drives can affect learning, but we have little data on the exact processes.

They must be processes, instead of a single type of interaction, since drive has no single relation to behavior. There can be no fewer relationships between drive and learning than there are between (1) drive and behavior, and (2) behavior and learning.

If the foregoing hypothesis is a valid—albeit highly abstract—description of the logical possibilities in this area, then the needs for future research are rather apparent: (1) For one thing, we can not continue to restrict such research to the rat. (2) Even with the rat, however, we need to clarify the differences in behavior and/or R-X relationships that are associated with variations in drive level during original training on any given habit. (3) Finally, it must be realized that no conclusions about the *general* effects of drives can be based upon the study of just a few of the conditions that are typically considered to be "drive-producing."

Beyond Biology: A Brief Critique of "Drive"

The ancestral impetus for the research and thinking that lie behind the study of biological drives is to be found in the writings of Charles Darwin. The theory of evolution, of course, has been a primary influence on every branch of biological science (of which experimental psychology is one). No one was more aware than Darwin himself, however, that the struggle for survival was a concept more appropriate to the aggregate than to the individual. Only under extreme conditions is it true that the individuals of a complex species (i.e., one capable of great individual variation in reactions to many environmental conditions) will be solely, or even mainly, concerned with self- and/or species-perpetuation. For example, *The Origin of Species* was not the result of an individual organism's struggle to stay alive. In other words, evidence is accumulating that the behavior of the more complex organisms (which is generally considered to be the fundamental concern of psychologists) is not primarily determined by primary needs or drives, except under extreme environmental conditions.

It should not be surprising, therefore, to discover that the foregoing review of the actions of primary drives does not provide a smooth entrance to the complexities of the other kinds of allegedly motivated behavior. Most vertebrates, at least, can be aroused to action by a number of procedures, none of which is directly related to survival. There is a discontinuity in our understanding of nonlearning variables that influence behavior and the usual formulations of the drive and motivation concepts. Neither concept fits the known data, and, in view of this, they do not fit each other. When we proceed, as we now shall, to the topic of motivation, you will probably find it quite a change in frame of reference.

MOTIVATION AND THE S-R-X MODEL

Let us now consider the effects upon behavior that may sometimes be attributed to motivational factors. This review of the commonly hypothesized effects of motivation will be done in the context of our model of behavior.

Any extensive discussion of the ways in which motivation affects behavior would surely mention, at least, the following points: (1) Motivation is regarded as the factor that instigates a person's behavior; it is said to *select* and *direct* the actions of the person. (2) It is also frequently referred to as the means of keeping the organism in action; not merely maintaining action, but actually determining the strength or persistence of this action. This usage of the motivational concept is that most frequently given the distinguishing label of "drive." (3) Motivation may also be considered in relation to the consequences of responding; abrupt changes in motivation may be rewarding or punishing, and motivating conditions may determine whether other events will be reinforcing.

Motivation as an Activator of Behavior

$$\begin{array}{c} \text{Mot} \\ + \text{-R-X} \\ \text{S} \end{array}$$

In terms of the model, the concept of motivation as an elicitor of R's means that a motivating condition forms part of the total stimulus complex with which the R in question has been associated. Evidence suggests that this particular function (an S function, it is often called) of motivation can operate in perhaps as many as three somewhat different ways:

(1) All parents are familiar with the role of *motivation as a UCS.* Both the crying response and the spontaneous sucking response of the small infant are originally UCR's for which hunger (or some other form of discomfort)—in any case, a motivating condition—*appears* to be the sufficient stimulus. As with all UCR's, these actions are modifiable, but initially they seem to be elicited directly by motives alone.

(2) *Motivation may be the primary S for a series of learned responses.* If you feel hungry, you will probably go through a series of responses that terminate in eating. Such a series may be of considerable complexity—the college student living in a dormitory may have to put on warmer clothes, operate an automobile, and talk to a restaurant employee—and the specific characteristics of the sequence will be determined by many other stimuli besides the hunger itself. Nevertheless, it seems reasonable to say that the entire sequence was initially evoked by the motivating condition.

In his analysis of verbal behavior, in fact, Skinner (251) regarded deprivation (and some other motivating conditions) as the basic antecedent for one of the fundamental forms of such behavior. He called this class of behavior the "mand," and it includes such verbal acts as requests, pleas, and commands (e.g., "Give me a glass of water.") Skinner's opinion is that although the occurrence of these R's may be modified by being brought under external stimulus control, they are primarily governed by motivational fluctuations. In the present terminology, this position would be compatible with the statement that motivation can play the same role that we have assigned to S in our model.

(3) *Motivation may be the determining S* in a situation where several habits are equally likely. Most of the time we are in environments where there are S's for a variety of R's; sometimes this produces dilemmas, but not often. Usually we respond to one S complex instead of another without hesitation. One basis for the easy resolution of most of these potential conflicts is the motivating condition prevalent at any moment.

From a learning standpoint, we account for this effect of motivation in the following manner: Assume that the environment at a given moment consists of two major stimulus-complexes—S_1 and S_2—to which responses R_1 and R_2, respectively, have been associated. We also assume that the subject is motivated in a specific way—symbolized by S_{mot_1}. S_{mot_1} is not a stimulus in the external environment, but rather "in the subject," so to speak. Therefore, as the subject's attention to the external environment shifts, he is, in effect, confronted by series of compound S complexes—for example, $S_{mot_1} + S_2$.

Now, if it has been the case that the sequence, $S_{mot_1} + S_1\text{-}R_1$, has often been followed by reinforcement, but the other sequence, $S_{mot_1} + S_2\text{-}R_2$, has not been reinforced, then we can readily predict which response will occur when the subject is under the motivating conditions symbolized by S_{mot_1}.

This is, of course, a complicated way of describing how it happens that a music-lover will go to a restaurant instead of a record store when he is hungry. This complexity, however, permits the consistent use of the S-R-X model.

In some ways there is only an arbitrary distinction between the stimulus functions of motivation that are described by cases 2 and 3. I use the distinction to point out two facets of what may well be, for some purposes, considered as a single process: the association of R's with motives in the same way that R's become associated with external S's. These cases do differ, however, in that case 2 describes a purely "S_L-like" role of motivation, whereas the selective action is pointed up in case 3 as well. In fact, case 3 describes the situation that is often referred to by many psychologists as the "selective perception of stimuli due to motivational factors."

Motivation as an Energizer of Behavior

$$\begin{array}{c} \text{Mot} \\ \text{S- } + \text{ -X} \\ \text{R} \end{array}$$

Another major way in which motivation is hypothesized to affect behavior is not as an elicitor of R's—i.e., not as an S—but as an *energizer*. In this case the R is elicited primarily by external stimuli, and the role of motivation is that of governing the intensity, frequency, or persistence of the response. As we have said, when this effect of motivation is referred to, the term "drive" is frequently used. In fact, some psychologists would prefer to treat this function of motivation as the basic effect of the condition, and they have attempted to derive all other effects attributable to motivation from this drive factor.

The Effects of Motivation on Reinforcers

$$\begin{array}{c} \text{Mot} \\ \text{S-R-}+ \\ \text{X} \end{array}$$

There are two ways in which motivation can affect reinforcement conditions:

(1) *Changes in motivation may themselves be reinforcing.* Motivational changes subsequent to the occurrence of some R, if they are abrupt enough, easily fit our definition of a change in the S conditions (i.e., our basic definition of a reinforcer)—since we have seen that motivation can often be considered part of the S complex. When deprivation is reduced, or S_{nox} is removed, we usually speak of "drive reduction," and this is considered by many psychologists to be the fundamental type of reinforcement. But increasing an organism's motivation should logically be an effective reinforcer, too, since it is also a change in the total stimulus situation. As we

have seen (p. 276) this is not the usual effect of raising (or arousing) a subject's drive level. Increases in motivation frequently act as punishers (i.e., as noxious stimuli), and we have already noted that punishment is an exception to our general definition of a reinforcing event. Not all increases in drive are noxious, however; at least we need not accept this premise as universally true as long as the validity of the Sheffield, Wulff and Backer experiment (Chapter 4) remains unchallenged. If uncompleted sexual activity is more likely to stimulate than to sooth, this experiment represents an instance in which drive arousal has been shown to be an effective reinforcer.

(2) *Motivation may influence the effectiveness of reinforcers.* As one simple illustration of this effect, consider the fact that praise does not always work equally well as the reinforcer for a given person's behavior in all situations. This shifting in the effectiveness of a reinforcing agent we are quite prone to attribute to changes in the subject's motivation instead, since the external (environmental) conditions—such as the expression of verbal approval, as in this example—appear to remain the same from situation to situation in which this X is employed. Such an "explanation" of the fluctuations in reinforcement effectiveness with human subjects actually comes, via analogy, from observations made with rats for the most part. With laboratory animals it is relatively easy to show variations in the reward and/or reinforcement value of given substances that are highly correlated with variations in the nature and intensity of the subjects' motivating conditions. To put this more simply, food is not so likely to reinforce a response that is made by a well-fed rat as it is to reinforce an R made by a hungry rat.

WHAT IS MOTIVATION?

Our extensive survey of drive was necessary because nearly all concepts of motivation that have points of contact with experimental psychology make some reference to drives. The more conventional ways of relating motivation, drive, and learning usually stress either or both of the following ideas:

1. Motivation as "Drive Plus Learning"

According to this view, drives are universal, biological factors that influence the behavior of organisms in fairly standard ways. Despite this universality of the occurrence and of the essential effects of drives, organisms develop a wide variety of means and ends in relation to drives. These differences, especially those in the goals sought by biologically similar organisms, are considered to be motives, as opposed to drives. In other words, this definition of motivation emphasizes how learning provides the variety that is to be observed in the manifestations of drives by many species, especially man. Most beginning psychology texts develop this idea very well. The chief drawback to this definition is that it makes motivation merely a higher-order description of the outcomes of learning, which is hardly the status accorded the concept by many psychologists—especially those, of course, who regard motivation as a term that applies to the relationships and processes basic to the comprehension of behavior.

2. Motivation as Drive Conditioning

This viewpoint relates learning and biological needs in a way that attempts to derive the occurrence of nonbiological drives from already known principles of learning and drive. The mechanism invoked for this purpose is Pavlovian conditioning, by which technique it is assumed that drives can be brought under the control of external stimuli. Then it is further posited that the behavioral component of a conditioned habit may, as often happens during conditioning, differ from its unconditioned predecessor. If such transformations were to occur repeatedly—via higher-order conditioning, for instance—the later-conditioned changes in the organism might not resemble the original, unconditioned drive state at all. Probably the most convincing advocate of this concept of motivation has been O. H. Mowrer.

Unfortunately for this position, the two crucial links in the hypothesized chain of events are not supported by much available data. Drive conditioning, for one thing, has not been demonstrated in enough different situations to guarantee that it might occur frequently in natural conditions. This same criticism is even more applicable to the phenomenon of higher-order conditioning. United States psychologists have rarely reported a clear case of higher-order conditioning.[6]

These points of view, no matter what their specific shortcomings, represent the two major approaches to blending motivation and learning concepts in a single behavior theory. On the one hand, the concepts may refer to essentially the same phenomena—alterations in behavior due to practice and reinforcement. Against this is the position that while learning may affect specific motives—just as it can be considered to alter drives in specific instances—motivation is a unique concept, referring to influences on behavior that are, at least, a special class of habits.

More extreme views of motivation tend toward an emphasis on the difference between man and other animals. We must resist these remnants of the pre-Galilean view of man as the center of the universe and the epitome of nature's creativity. Nearly all behaviorists are committed to the general evolutionary theory that pervades most aspects of biology. Therefore, they are skeptical of assertions that there are uniquely human behavioral phenomena, except in the sense that species with different sensory and motor equipment do differ in the specific forms of much behavior. The principles governing behavior are presumed to be essentially the same for man and at least his closer biological kin. This assumption has been the basis of some very sophisticated, and some very silly, controversies, a most interesting and detailed account of which may be found in Wendt's In Search of Adam (287).

A most common complaint registered against behavioristic treatments of human behavior is that these do not consider, nor provide any means for considering, the roles and origins of the long-range goals or motives of individuals. This has been a special source of irritation to psychologists such as Gordon Allport (1), who express an aversion to both behaviorism and psychoanalytic theory (probably the two most important general influences upon con-

---

[6] An exception to this statement might be the work of Eccher and Culler (67) who used an "escape" type of learning situation.

temporary American psychology, aside from functionalism). The complaint is certainly legitimate to some extent, but the complainants frequently go so far in the breadth of their objections and in the severity of the suggested cures (e.g., dispensing with the behavioristic approach entirely) that the problem has become clouded by many irrational arguments. Although behaviorism was born and raised within a similarly revolutionary *milieu* in which the discarding of the "ancients" (e.g., Titchener and the whole structuralist framework in American psychology) was wholesale, behaviorists have become more conservative now (as do all successful old revolutionaries). Some behavioristic writers have revealed a deep interest in the more encompassing features of life and living. It is no longer literally true (if, indeed, it ever was) that a panoramic or long-range view of the determinants of human behavior is incompatible with a behavioristic approach. Behaviorism, in short, has become more of a methodology than a philosophy; its residual philosophic characteristics are, for the most part, concerned with the philosophy of science—*not* the "philosophy of life."

On the other hand, it is indeed possible to question the assertion that long-range goals are persistent influences upon a person's development and adjustment—influences, that is, of the sort with which scientists can deal. These allegedly pervasive determinants of action might, for example, simply be retrospective simplifications of the inherently complex past history that can be described for any organism whose age can be measured in years. Even those who most aggressively champion the study of life-long goals and needs have never offered much evidence in support of its usefulness, nor even a workable program for the collection of such material, except in reference to the psychotherapeutic situation—a situation not exactly as conducive to as careful research as would seem to be necessary in order to test hypotheses about uniquely human motivation. Actually, the variety of processes encompassed by the field of learning—especially the almost omnipresent factor of transfer of training—seems to provide just as promising a basis for the comprehension of the enduring or repeatedly important goals and habits that can be noted in any individual.

"Incentive Suggestion" as a Motivational Technique

There is at least one way, however, in which human motivation does seem to be unique—human beings appear to be easily put into action by the information that certain goals or rewards are potentially available in their environment. The presentation of such information we shall call *incentive suggestion,* and this concept points out—but does not as yet explain—the most important means of motivating humans. Incentive suggestion is obviously a large class of specific procedures that is just as extensive as is the class of things that the individual will react to as rewards. There are few readily apparent experimental analogues of incentive suggestion that will influence the behavior of infra-human laboratory subjects.

Even in the prehistoric period of man's existence it was probably common knowledge to the merchants of those times that they could dispose of more of their goods if the people needing such goods knew who had them to sell or barter. It has always paid to advertise, in other words. But imagine the excitement of the first ancient trader to discover that by telling people in advance what he had to offer he actually *increased* the demand for his goods. (Probably our hypothetical retailer's second, almost simultaneous, insight was that, come to think of it, he hadn't known how much *he* wanted to own a sack of dog's teeth until his customer showed them to him.) More simply, and without the historical fantasy, the point is: the act of telling a person that some reward or goal is potentially available in a given situation has effects on behavior that are similar to those produced by the other motivating techniques we have discussed.

Only two types of animal experiments appear to contain the analogous steps. One of these is represented by the prefeeding experiments of Bruce (42) and Morgan and Fields (194). These studies showed that rats trained to run to food or water (when deprived of one of these rewards, of course) would start out such runs significantly faster if first given just a taste of the reward awaiting them at the end of their runs. Seward's latent learning study (described on p. 303) could also be considered to have used a type of incentive suggestion procedure. As a final example, Finch (76) has reported behavior by chimpanzees that could be classed with these others; when teased with a piece of banana (highly desired by the chimp), most subjects made R's that in the past had been followed—*not* preceded, as during the "teasing" period—by this delicacy. The procedures just reviewed might be considered to be similar to the incentive suggestion technique, but differ from it in that the rewards were *actually* presented prior to R, instead of being represented only *symbolically*, as is usually true with human beings. Only more research can tell us whether this distinction that we have drawn is too fine to be theoretically or practically useful.

Incentive suggestion appears to play a versatile role in human behavior largely because of humans' ability to respond differentially to stimuli that are symbols of past, present, and future events. It is generally, though not universally, agreed by psychologists that animals may respond to symbols; we know, for instance, that animals can respond to stimuli owing to their association with events that are no longer present—e.g., the cues enabling avoidance learning to occur. It does seem that a concept of the future need for pain reduction need not be assumed as part of an animal's knowledge in order to account for avoidance reactions in animals (see the discussion on pp. 89–91 for more consideration of this point); some psychologists do not regard this assumption (of a concept of the future in nonverbal subjects) as important in an account of human symbolic behavior, either, but this position can only be defended by some fairly subtle reasoning.

The rarity of observations of the motivating effect of incentive suggestion on animal behavior is in itself a cause neither for rejoicing nor for despair by psychologists or philosophers. Perhaps there are extenuating conditions that make such a procedure difficult to demonstrate with rats, monkeys, and the like. Since incentive suggestion amounts to dangling a reward in front of a person, common sense would suggest that the object or event so used as a means of motivating someone must have two general characteristics: (1) It should be one that a subject would be expected to respond to readily if it were actually available, and not just symbolically presented, and (2) it should be able to retain its reward value long beyond the time its possible attainment is first suggested. The general method would seem to be closely related to the methods of establishing secondary (acquired) rewards that were considered in Chapters 4–5. Any further discussion of how incentive suggestion might come to be a motivator would be entirely speculative. There is no more directly relevant data to be cited, deplorable as this ignorance may be.

Since they rest not upon facts, but upon the interpretations of facts, arguments about the nature and the extent of differences between human and infra-human behavior are fruitless pastimes for scientists whose main interests lie in other endeavors and accomplishments. Psychologists do learn a great deal about the principles that apply to human behavior by watching animals under the proper conditions; ultimately, however, hypotheses about human behavior must be tested by observing human behavior. The study of incentive suggestion seems to be a case in which this last statement, trite though it may sound, appears to be especially relevant.

Acquired Drives as General Personality Characteristics

Acquired drives are frequently thought of, especially by clinical psychologists, as being fairly stable personality characteristics, or traits. One of the most extensive research projects that has developed from such an assumption is that instigated by the work of Prof. Janet A. Taylor (263).

Taylor tested the assumption that people who could be said to have "high anxiety," defined by clinical criteria, would have a higher general drive level than people diagnosed as being low in anxiety. She first constructed, by selecting items from the MMPI, a paper-and-pencil test that would differentiate at least between people manifesting very many and very few overt symptoms of anxiety. This Manifest Anxiety Scale (MAS) was administered to a large number of college students. Later, the people whose scores were among the highest 20 per cent of all the scores made on the MAS, and those from the lowest 20 per cent, were recruited for an experiment in eyelid conditioning. These groups were considered to be subjects with high and low anxiety, respectively.

All subjects were actually treated alike in the conditioning sessions. They were all given a standard eyelid conditioning procedure; no reference was ever made to the paper-and-pencil test, and the subjects did not know that they had been specially selected for this study. The independent variable of the experiment was in reality the subjects' relative standing on the MAS, of course. Taylor reasoned that if subjects with superficial symptoms of high anxiety did have a higher general drive level than people with few such symptoms, there should be a difference in the strength or frequency of avoidance CR's made by subjects from these two groups. This prediction was strikingly confirmed: after the initial stages of training, "high anxiety" subjects as a group reached and maintained a higher frequency of conditioned eyelid responding than did low anxiety subjects.

Although Taylor's research led to the most exhaustive comparison of paper-and-pencil test performance with performance in controlled laboratory situations (see 264 for a review), this line of research has not yet shed much light upon the problem of acquired drives. Work such as this can only lead to the formulation of *R-R laws*, as Spence (255) has called them—which are laws stating the relationships between classes of responses. Such laws may be useful for a variety of purposes, but they do not *directly* contribute to the fundamental goal of behavior science, which is to establish relationships between antecedent (environmental, genetic, etc.) factors and behavioral events. Spence called these latter relationships *S-R laws*. Failure to keep the distinction between S-R and R-R laws clear has often resulted in confused and unnecessary arguments between applied and scientific psychologists.

SUMMARY

(1) Although the complete details are not yet available, there does seem to be an empirical basis for identifying both drive and learning factors in behavior.

(2) Drive is defined as the relationship between procedures—

such as deprivation—to behavior changes—such as increased response strength—under conditions where learning could not be invoked as the direct or indirect determinant of such changes. These conditions are often hard to specify with certainty, of course, and therein lies the chief problem in this area.

(3) Drives can function as S's, and thus become integrally related to habits.

(4) At least the drive condition produced by noxious stimulation can be brought under the partial control of external stimuli, apparently by Pavlovian conditioning techniques.

(5) There is a great deal of overlap between the typical meanings of the concept of motivation and the concept of learning in contemporary psychology. It is doubtful that they can be completely differentiated. For example, the presentation of an X_{rew}, or its symbolic representative, is generally regarded as a motivating condition, but this is clearly not entirely independent of nor entirely dependent upon prior habit formation.

(6) The relationship of the concepts "drive" and "motivation" is likewise unclear. Presumably, the only way in which this relationship will be clarified is by first determining the relationship of each of these concepts to that of habit.

(7) Most of the problems mentioned in the foregoing item seem to be problems of organization and classification, rather than empirical problems.

SECTION IV

*

*

* *"COMPLEX"*

* *LEARNING*

* *CASES*

INTRODUCTION TO SECTION IV

In the first eight chapters of this book I presented what I honestly believe to be samples of the most fruitful research done in the field of learning. Other learning psychologists will undoubtedly take exception to specific points I made, but most will probably agree that something such as I have described forms the foundation of this area of psychological knowledge. The more important question for our present purposes is whether the type of knowledge and thinking outlined in the preceding chapters has relevance for any other fields, or problems, of psychology.

I know of no polls taken on this matter, but I suspect that a majority of laymen (and of psychologists as well) would reject the proposition that any important, useful information has (or could) come from the kinds of situations that were predominant in the preceding descriptions. There are two common objections to the usefulness of the research on which the field of learning is based.

First, there is the charge that the learning psychologists' reliance on animals as subjects seriously limits the applicability of their findings to human behavior, because of the manifest differences between animals and humans. Second, there is a general skepticism about the artificiality of many learning situations as studied in the laboratory. One common way of putting this is that such situations are unrepresentative because of their simplicity. Simple situations, it is charged, can only generate simple laws the operation of which in other (more complex) situations is to be questioned.

The pragmatic reasons for using animals were discussed in Chapter 1, and I hope that sufficient evidence has subsequently been presented to show that many of the principles discovered through animal research do indeed apply to human behavior. Differences among species may, of course, produce differences in the details of the operation of various principles, but so far the similarities discovered have seemed to outweigh the obvious differences. So the mere fact that the rat, for instance, is incapable of verbal behavior does not mean that the study of the rat can not give us any insight into organisms that are capable of verbal behavior. It is always true, however, that animal research can only *suggest* principles that may apply to human behavior. Ultimately, we must test this application directly, and indeed this has been done in the majority of cases, but only sparingly.

Similarly, the charge of artificiality is not an *ipso facto* argument against laboratory research. The purpose of the laboratory is not to recreate the superficial chaos of nature, but to set up situations in which specific relationships can be unequivocally traced. As with the specific case of animal research, it is always true that the applicability of laboratory-derived principles to non-laboratory situations must be checked by direct testing. So far the history of science gives us little reason to believe that the laboratory is not an excellent place to start in the search for the solutions to even highly practical problems.

As to the related criticism of simplicity, what does simplicity mean? It is not entirely facetious to assert that simple phenomena are those that we understand, and complex phenomena are those that we do not. The immediate question before us is whether our attempts at the simplification of learning lead in the direction of creating an artificial world, or in that of aiding our understanding of behavior as it occurs in nature.

As in most cases concerning the application of scientific knowledge to matters in which non-scientists are also greatly interested, both sides must give a little. The scientist must be willing to accept practical results as a reasonable objective toward which to apply his methods. The layman, in turn, must be prepared to alter markedly his ways of thinking about whatever phenomena may be involved in the problems that he has asked the scientist to help him solve.

We will be confronted with all the foregoing problems in some degree during these final two chapters, which are concerned with what is most often called human or complex learning. My mode of presentation in them is intended to display the potential applicability of the data and rationale already explained in the preceding pages.

I must admit that much of what we have so far covered does not apply too well to the kinds of *research* we are about to go into. It is my prejudice that much of the lack of fit between simple habit research and studies of complex learning is due more to the inadequacies of the latter than of the former. These inadequacies are of two general types:

(1) The failure to *try* to apply the principles of learning so far examined. The controlled application of efficient reinforcement practices is especially deficient.

(2) There is also the tendency to pursue lines of research that are intriguing from a methodological viewpoint, but seem to be rather sterile in terms of developing our understanding of the role of learning in human behavior. I shall not dwell on this point in the next two chapters, because it obviously is a matter of opinion. In terms of developing a learning text of reasonable length, however, some things must be touched upon lightly, if at all. I have chosen to do much of my abbreviating in the area generally called "human learning." This is not because human learning is unimportant—far from it! It is, instead, because much of what is now recognized as research in human learning does not, in my opinion (and I want to stress "opinion"), aid our understanding of many learning situations of any sort.

CHAPTER II

✳
✳
✳

THE ACQUISITION
OF HABITS
IN COMPLEX SITUATIONS

The final group of learning situations that we have to consider are those in which a relatively large number of responses are associated with a variety of stimuli at the same time. Everyday examples of complex habit formation are such things as learning to read and write, learning to drive a car, and memorizing a speech. In terms of the underlying principles, the distinction between complex habits and the earlier topic of simple habit interactions is highly arbitrary —much more so than that between the interactions and simple habit formation. The situations in which complex habit formation has been studied do have some at least superficially distinguishing features.

Conditions Generally Unique to Complex Learning Situations

(1) A large number of S-R associations are formed, or are combined into a new sequence.

(2) Usually the S's, and also the R's, are quite similar.

(3) Furthermore, S's and R's may even be similar to each other; the consequences of the occurrence of one response, in fact, may be the major stimuli to which a subsequent response is associated.

(4) Relative to the number of S-R connections that are involved, reinforcements of the kinds that we have most often discussed in the preceding pages are exceedingly rare.

CLASSIFYING COMPLEX HABITS

Despite the fact that the history of science repeatedly reveals that an adequate taxonomy greatly facilitates effective research, complex learning is an area in which cataloguing has been minimal. Classification is, at best, a risky way to earn a living; it involves emphasizing some specific differences while overlooking others in the phenomena being catalogued. In the case of complex learning, psychologists seem to have erred almost entirely in the latter direction. Only a few simple dichotomies are typically used to differentiate subtypes in this field. The result has been a tendency to generalize specific research findings to too large a group of types of learning situations, simply because the given behavioral types have traditionally been lumped together. This does not aid the most efficient delineation of meaningful environment-behavior relationships.

The standard differences emphasized in complex learning situations have been of three kinds:

"Verbal" vs. "Motor" Learning

Anatomically, at least, this is a perplexing basis for differentiation. Certainly the behavior studied in "verbal learning" research has obvious motor (i.e., muscular) involvement. While it may be helpful to have terms for differentiating habits that require the subject to use words from those that do not, there is not now any clear rationale for the assumption (or, at least, the implication) that these kinds of behaviors necessarily follow different laws.[1] As has

[1] Skinner's conceptualization of verbal behavior (251), already mentioned in Chapter 10, gets at the essence of this behavior. Verbal behavior is that which is reinforced only by a change in the behavior of another organism. This definition, reasonable as it indeed appears, has not been even the implicit basis of the research that most often appears in the psychological literature under the title of "studying verbal behavior." Not even Skinner's definition, however, offers any suggestion as to an adequate definition of the alternative term, "motor learning." Skinner's definition, of course, was not presented in the context of the verbal-motor dichotomy; I only mention it to show that even a satisfactory definition of one of these terms does not imply the adequacy of the dichotomy itself.

been implicit throughout the development of this book, the latter criterion seems to me to be the most meaningful basis for any scientific classificatory scheme. Accordingly, we shall use the verbal vs. motor distinction only when it is helpful for descriptive purposes to make a crude, functional segregation of complex habits.

"Serial" vs. "Rote" Learning

The serial vs. rote subdivision refers, basically, to the logic of presentation of the various habits in a given complex learning situation. "Serial," in this usage, implies only that the subject is exposed to first one habit, then another, and so on, in a systematic, functionally related order; "rote" then implies the opposite—the habits involved have no necessary relationship to each other. This distinction brings out an important dimension of various complex learning situations. There are five focal points on this continuum:

(1) First, there are complex learning situations in which the presentation of the stimuli for the second habit in a given sequence can occur only upon the performance of the response appropriate to the first habit in the chain. In learning to play an instrument such as the harmonica, accordion, or trumpet, one must first learn how to make noise before one can even begin to learn to make music. The habits appropriate to squeezing, blowing, and/or puckering must be accomplished to some degree before any other learning can proceed. Of course, as in the examples given, $Habit_1$ does not have to be perfected before practice on $Habit_2$ begins, but some degree of $Habit_1$ proficiency is essential.

(2) A second type of complex learning involves a series of habits, each of which can be learned independently of any other, but which must be ordered in a specific sequence before the terminal reinforcement will be presented. A simple example would be the learning of the combination to a safe; you can have the third series of dial movements down pat, but a lot of good it will do you if you are still uncertain about, say, the second or fourth of such series. Failure to receive terminal reinforcement, in addition, may not (as in the above example) provide any clue as to the source of the erroneous performance.

(3) Somewhat different from the preceding would be those cases in which there is more than one sequence of habits that will attain the same goal, but each sequence is different from any other. For any given sequence, the conditions are as in No. 2 above—only one combination of separable habits will work. In cases 2 and 3 the reinforcement problems are the same; the difference is in the sources of possible confusion between S's and R's.

(4) A minor variation on the foregoing would involve those situations in which a number of sequences might accomplish the same end result, but with the additional restriction that "some ways are better than others"—e.g., in terms of speed, efficiency, expenditure of energy, and so on. Here the problem of *differential* reinforcement for various modes of responding is added to those already noted.

(5) Finally, there is "rote," or random, complex habit formation. In this case the various habits to be learned are independent of each other. The only aim of the learner is to acquire as many of them in as little time as possible. In other words, there are numerous combinations that will attain the same end result, and these combinations are not mutually exclusive. It should be especially noted, however, that "functional independence" does not mean there are no similarities in the habits being acquired by rote.

This type of scaling of complex learning situations probably comes as close to being meaningful in terms of the preceding chapters as any classification could. The important thing to recognize is that different simple learning procedures may apply to different specific instances of complex learning situations.

"Recombination" vs. "New Learning"

Another dimension along which most complex learning situations might be scaled is that having as its extremes (1) situations involving only the rearrangement (recombination) of habits already well entrenched in the subject's behavior (e.g., learning a new telephone number), as against (2) situations requiring the establishment of brand-new habits as a prerequisite to any serialization process (e.g., learning a foreign language that has a different kind of alphabet from one's native tongue). Clearly, there would be a number of gradations to a dimension such as this.

Dimension R and Complex Learning

In Chapter 3 it was noted that distinctions among types of operant responses could be discerned, but they were quite arbitrary. We return to exactly the same problem when we try to slice up the field of complex learning. Is this a coincidence or does it suggest that some common characteristics are shared by simple operant and complex learning situations? There is a growing opinion that the latter alternative is closer to the truth.

Specifically, there is reason to believe that the effects of irregular and complex reinforcement schedules are to produce behavior not unlike that which we have traditionally called complex, except that only one R_L is involved throughout the complicated operant cases. The patterns of R_L that are produced, in short, resemble the crude beginnings of complex learning.

The findings of Ferster and Skinner (75), indeed, argue convincingly for the use of the "repeated R" operant technique (see Chapter 3, p. 79) as a simple way of determining some of the basic features of complex learning. They have found that the pigeon can gear its pecking response to remarkably complex sequences of rapid shifts in reinforcement schedules, with or without associated changes in external S conditions. Denny, Wells, and Maatsch (63) have shown that frequency of food-trough investigations decreases the longer a rat has been bar-pressing on a fixed 5:1 ratio; this effect begins to appear quite early in the application of such a schedule.

Observations like those just noted serve to emphasize the point already made (Chapter 3) that distinctions along Dimension R of operant learning are quite arbitrary. One of the themes of the present chapter, however, is that it is not necessarily the distinctions between categories of Dimension R that are arbitrary; it could be the distinction between simple and complex learning situations that puts an unrealistic emphasis on the manifest differences in these situations while overlooking similarities in the underlying principles of their control. Both of these attitudes probably oversimplify the problems that are raised by attempts to relate simple and complex learning situations. Such statements do, however, put stress on the search for similarities (or, at least, less trivial differences than are usually noted) in these situations; for this reason alone they are worth dwelling upon.

Classifications of Complex Learning Summarized

The main point I have sought to make in this section is that there is no one set of principles that can dictate how the learner and/or the teacher should proceed in *all* complex learning cases. To the questions that have traditionally been raised in this field of research ("Is massed practice better than spaced?" "Should the whole or the part method be used?" "When is it best to give knowledge of results?" "When is the best time for rest periods?" and so forth) there must, unfortunately, be only one answer: "It all depends."

It all depends, that is, on the exact nature of the learning situation that is being referred to in such questions. One of the points that I hope has come through in this book is that there can be no discussion of learning that is completely detached from any reference to concrete events. Learning is the association of responses with stimuli, usually (if not always) by reinforcement; it is a procedure, and the specifics of this procedure vary with the details of the given situation in which we seek to employ it as a means of controlling behavior. This becomes especially pertinent in reference to complex learning. Since complex learning can have so many forms, it is fantastic to expect that a few simple formulas will describe how all complex learning can be most effectively accomplished.

All is not lost, however; there does seem to be order in this area. As an important step toward the detection of this order, let us examine a procedure that directly relates simple habit formation to complex learning—the technique called *shaping*.

SHAPING: FROM SIMPLE TO COMPLEX
LEARNING SITUATIONS

As a very dramatic, but also very accurate, illustration of the general nature of shaping, let us consider the following, a quite unusual clinical case report [2]:

The subject [was] a white, single male who [had been] admitted to the Anna State Hospital [19 years earlier]. He is classified as Schizophrenic Reaction, Catatonic Type, and has remained mute since [soon after admission] . . . For the past 12 years he seems to have crystallized into a chronic catatonic who is mute, withdrawn, and exhibits little psychomotor activity.

He was placed in a group therapy situation with other chronic schizophrenics [who were verbal], but he did not communicate. Cigarettes were furnished the group by the therapist, but the patient would accept none. At one session, when the therapist removed the cigarettes from his pocket, a package of chewing gum came out with them. The patient's eyes moved toward the gum, but he refused a stick when offered one.

Arrangements were then made for the therapist to see the patient 3 times a week in a small testing room. . . . The following sequence of procedures was then introduced. . . .

Weeks 1, 2. Gum was produced and held before [the patient]. When he looked at the gum, it was given to him. At the end of the second week, he looked at the gum when it was held before him.

Week 3. The gum was held before him as he looked at it. When movement was noticed in his lips, it was given to him. By the end of the week, he moved his lips when the gum was held before him.

Week 4. The gum was now held before him until he made a sound; this was occasioned by the gum by the end of the week.

Week 5. [The therapist] now said: "Say *gum. Gum,*" holding up the gum. The gum was given [to the patient] any time he made a sound approximating the word.

Week 6. This procedure continued, during which time [the patient] said: "Gum, please," following such a statement by [the therapist] as

[2] The material quoted here is from a paper distributed at the 1958 meetings of the Midwestern Psychological Association, "Reinstatement of verbal behavior in a catatonic, mute for 20 years prior to conditioning," by Wayne Isaacs, Anna State Hospital. I am grateful to Prof. Israel Goldiamond, Southern Illinois University, for making this material available to me. A version of this research has been published in the *Journal of Speech and Hearing Disorders* (126a).

he held up the stick of gum. At the end of this week [the patient] began answering questions regarding his age and name.

Three months have since gone by (to April 11). During the last two therapy sessions of last month he spoke first to the therapist when the therapist entered the group therapy room. Until then, he did not make conversation, but did respond to questions in the group sessions. During the past month, he has been talking to [the therapist] outside the sessions.

On April 11, generalization procedures were introduced. A nurse was present during the private sessions. [The patient] smiled at her. He also read, at [the therapist's] request, from signs in the room, and did so fluently.

This remarkable demonstration illustrates all the important features of shaping. There are five learning principles employed in this technique; all of them should be familiar to you from earlier discussions throughout this text:

(1) An organism can not learn a given S-R relationship if he can not perform the R in question. All learning situations, therefore, begin by utilizing responses that the subject is already known to be able to make. This is a difficult concept for most people to grasp because the vernacular is filled with terms such as learning a new response, and the like. So let us examine this idea in some detail; it is very important for the understanding of the intricacies of complex learning cases.

Learning psychologists sometimes amuse themselves by teaching pigeons to play a rudimentary form of ping-pong.[3] Clearly, we should all agree that "pecking a ping-pong ball over a net" is not a response that a pigeon will usually make. So, if we can teach a pigeon to make this response, are we not teaching him a new response?

This is where the accomplishment definition of responses shows an inherent weakness. By that way of describing R's, "pecking a ball over a net" is certainly novel behavior for a pigeon. But how do we get a pigeon to do this? Well, we start by reinforcing an R that the pigeon *can* make, we strengthen this R, we tie it to certain S's, then we demand finer and finer differentiations and discrimina-

---

[3] I thank Prof. Harold Babb, Hobart College, for suggesting how this particular example could be used to exemplify the point now being made.

tions. In the end, we have the organism "doing something quite different" than it ever did before. At no time, however, did we attempt to reinforce an S-R relationship that involved an R that the organism was quite unlikely to perform; it is simply impossible to get learning to occur in that way.

(2) By the technique of response differentiation (Chapter 6), R_L can be made as precise as the organism's anatomy will permit. The concept of "precise response," of course, is defined in terms of the degree of variability in the R_L that will be permitted (i.e., reinforced) from occasion to occasion. As suggested above, we are always, at least by implication, using an anatomical definition of R_L—as when we reinforce certain combinations of vocal sounds but not other, similar ones.

(3) The successive discrimination technique (Chapter 6) reveals that, as with response precision, the specificity of the S that can be made appropriate for a given R is only limited by the accuracy of the organism's receptors.

(4) All the learning described in the preceding three statements is most easily established by starting with the reinforcement of R's that only generally resemble the one that you ultimately seek to establish, then gradually increasing the strictness of your definition of a correct R (i.e., the one that will be reinforced); on the stimulus side a similar procedure is followed, generally lagging somewhat behind the response differentiation program. Ultimately, only a very precise R is being reinforced, and only when it occurs in the presence of a very specific stimulus pattern.

(5) Even a continuously reinforced habit has *some* resistance to extinction, so that once it has been established, reinforcement can be withheld without immediately disastrous results. Thus, during the random activity that follows when reinforcement does not occur at its usual time (after the successful performance of the first habit), something akin to the R that you wish to make part of the second habit may occur (how likely this is can only be determined by observation of similar subjects under similar conditions). Now the process begins all over. At first, only a random, crude representative of the next response is reinforced; after a while, only a precise

response is reinforced, and only if it immediately follows acceptable performance of the preceding habit in the chain. This first habit may have to be directly reinforced occasionally in order to maintain it at full strength during the establishment of the second habit. Eventually, by following this procedure, you can establish as complex a habit as you wish.

An important principle that is supported by the shaping technique is that, as pointed out in Chapter 1, S and R are arbitrarily defined in any given learning situation. Sometimes they are defined more specifically than at other times. It does not matter. As long as both S and R are as distinguishable to the subject as they are to the teacher, he can learn to associate them if these S-R contingencies are reinforced in the proper manner. If reinforcement does not systematically follow the correct S-R relationships, the *ease* with which such relationships are formed will certainly follow the laws of simple transfer noted in Chapter 7. There is a good chance, too, that the same laws will apply if reinforcement is administered in a meticulously correct fashion. In general, however, the operation of the principles of reinforcement is paramount over principles such as those of transfer of training.

The most efficient progress in complex learning situations is made by utilizing the principles of shaping. Just as with simple habits, complex learning proceeds best when just the right R's are unambiguously reinforced only when they occur in the presence of just the proper S's.

The traditional approaches that most experimental psychologists have followed in the study of complex learning, however, have not emphasized the relation of shaping to this class of learning situations. They have, instead, chosen to emphasize the complexity of the variables that can affect learning when the training conditions deviate markedly from those that are most effective. In particular, the reinforcement conditions in many studies of complex learning have been especially unclear; it is perhaps for this reason that incidental learning situations such as studied by Postman (e.g., 211) and Saltzman (e.g., 229) have been found to compare favorably with the results of ordinary rote learning procedures (see Chapter

9). It is not that incidental learning is such an effective method, but rather that standard rote learning is such a poor one.

It is a trivial accusation, however, to note that the methods developed by Ebbinghaus in the late nineteenth century for the study of complex learning have only been elaborated and refined (but not radically revised) in the ensuing sixty-odd years of research in this area. While such rigidity in technique does not indicate an appreciation of modern advances in our comprehension of the fundamentals of learning, it does reflect a continuing attempt to understand complex learning in terms of the normal (poor) circumstances in which it is required to occur. This is quite legitimate; it is just as interesting to study the effects of a given variable under less than optimal conditions, as to discover the optimal conditions—especially when the latter rarely occur in the usual course of events. On the other hand, it *is* difficult to see why a more equitable distribution of labor has not yet been worked out between the study of *poor* complex learning conditions and the study of *effective* complex learning conditions.

If we consider, as indeed we must, *what has been* rather than *what might have been* in this area, then we find that the problems noted with respect to simple habit interactions return to haunt us. There are also a few new questions that seem equally recalcitrant to general solutions. Let us consider these problems in order according to the sequence of events in our basic model.

STIMULUS FACTORS IN COMPLEX LEARNING

To the extent that given complex learning situations simply constitute more elaborate versions of the simple habit interactions previously considered, the discussions of stimulus variables in Chapters 6 and 7 apply here. That is, when the S's in some or all of the habits concerned are similar, there is a tendency for stimulus generalization to influence the rate of successful completion of complex learning.

More often than not, similarity of S's impedes the rate of learning complex habits, especially if the habits are verbal. This is in keeping with the general rule that negative transfer is most easily produced when there is: (1) high similarity among S's and (2) minimal clarity to the subject regarding what R goes with what S—i.e., little immediate reinforcement.

Of course, making the subject clear as to what he is to do also depends upon a complicated prior history of learning. Especially concerned is learning that leads to the integration of verbal and nonverbal modes of behavior, with the primary aim of bringing the latter under the control of the former. Nevertheless, the almost exclusive use of adult subjects in human engineering experiments means that not much in the way of truly *new* learning is usually being tried. Pressing a subject to the limits of his abilities to discriminate S's and differentiate R's may be a new experience for the subject, but it has not yet been shown to produce unique problems for the application of learning principles.

RESPONSE FACTORS IN COMPLEX LEARNING

One way to make complex learning difficult is to keep the subject uncertain as to whether a given response is appropriate or not; this is most easily accomplished when the teacher is also uncertain as to what exactly the subject is supposed to be doing. A subject is "uncertain" about the "appropriateness" of his responses whenever a specific S_L-R_L relationship is not reinforced to the exclusion of all others. Similarly, we infer that a teacher is "uncertain . . . about what the subject is supposed to be doing" whenever the teacher does not arrange a situation in which specific S_L-R_L relationships will be reinforced to the exclusion of all other combinations. This may seem to be a trivial or facetious statement, but I believe it actually points to the basis of much of the complexity in complex learning situations. Unfortunately, the situation—absurd as it is—portrayed in the first sentence of this paragraph is a reasonably accurate description of a good part of our formal education system (see 249 for a discussion of this).

Much natural learning, regrettably, takes place (or is expected to take place) in an abyss of confusion like that just described. Psychologists, therefore, can not be condemned, *ipso facto*, for recreating such chaos in their laboratories. Nevertheless, one wonders how long it will be before it is recognized that it is impossible to generalize from one ambiguous learning situation to another; that this is like trying to prove the null hypothesis.

It is becoming increasingly clear that the traditional view of laboratory studies of simple learning situations has not fully appreciated the significance of such research. The traditional view has been that these situations provide only a rudimentary introduction to, rather than a true understanding of, human learning situations. We now recognize that the learned behavior that can be produced in the laboratory is by no means simple, although the techniques used to produce it may be. Who would have asserted, in advance of reading Chapter 3, that the establishment of even one instance of co-operative behavior in young children could be accomplished with the ease described by Azrin and Lindsley (p. 69)?

In short, the ideas and knowledge about learning gleaned from the study of such phenomena as are produced by shaping and reinforcement schedules are not simply ways of *introducing* learning to the student; properly developed, such phenomena *are* the field of learning—if the objectives of this field are viewed as those of achieving better control and prediction of behavior. In our culture, people are concerned with learning what the variables influencing a phenomenon are for one main purpose—in order to control the manifestations of this phenomenon. The traditional approaches to complex learning have shown a preference for the older approach to scientific understanding—the simple demonstration of antecedent-consequent relationships. Although there is basically no difference between understanding and control, the appearance of such a difference can be created by lowering one's standards of what constitutes learning. Thus, much complex learning research has not sought to evaluate the effects of things as spacing of trials, similarity of S's and R's, and so forth within the context of procedures that we know to be *effective*, but rather in the context of procedures that are definitely known to be *inefficient*.

A number of variables can be shown to affect learning to some slight degree if inefficient procedures are used. But the effort that it would involve to develop techniques for maximizing (or minimizing, in some cases) the effects so demonstrated would probably not be as easy to put into effect as it would to be to institute the procedures of the so-called simple learning situations. In the latter case, at least, there would be more chance of dramatic success.

INHIBITION AND COMPLEX LEARNING

Among the many interesting developments that arose during Prof. Hull's period of greatest influence on thinking in the field of learning was an extension of the roles assigned to the concepts of inhibition and conditioned inhibition. We have already seen (Chapter 2) how Pavlov used these concepts (or hypotheses) in dealing with extinction phenomena; Hull extended this same line of reasoning to the extinction of operant habits. In addition, Hull found many applications for these concepts in complex learning situations.

It was Kimble (148) who made a major synthesis in the field of complex learning starting from the Pavlov-Hull notions about inhibition. Specifically, Kimble filled in the details relating motor learning phenomena to the concepts originally designed to apply to extinction situations. Among the empirical relationships that were handled by Kimble's theory were: (1) the superiority of spaced practice trials over massed, and (2) the phenomenon of reminiscence.

Reminiscence

It has often, though not invariably, been found in complex learning situations that if a given period of relativity massed practice is ceased and the subject allowed to rest, his performance when practice is resumed may be superior to any previous level of performance. This effect, shown in Figure 28, seems to be a case of *improve-*

ment in the absence of practice. Although this description may capture our fancy, it is scientifically untenable, because there can be no change in a dependent variable that is not a consequence of some kind of change in some independent variable. This is not to say that reminiscence is not related to any independent variables.

FIGURE 28

Reminiscence as a Function of Length of Interpolated Rest

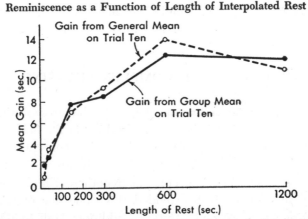

From Kimble and Horenstein (150), in the *Journal of Experimental Psychology,* vol. 38, p. 242. Used by permission of the American Psychological Association.

After ten 50 sec. trials, spaced 10 secs. apart, on a complex motor task (the pursuit rotor), subjects were permitted to rest for 10, 30, 150, 300, 600, or 1200 secs. then given two final 50 sec. test trials. The relative amounts of improvement in performance after different rest periods are shown in the curves, each of which uses a different method of estimating pre-rest performance. In general, the curves both show that when subjects are permitted to rest for a period longer than the standard intertrial interval, they perform better than if they had no rest. This improvement due to rest is called reminiscence.

There are, in fact, two major determinants of the amount of reminiscence. One is the amount of time (i.e., rest) between the practice and test periods; the longer this time, up to a limit which varies with specific tasks, the greater the reminiscence (e.g., 127). The other is the time between successive practice periods or practice items; the longer this time, the less the later reminiscence (119).

Kimble combined Hull's suggestion that *any* occurrence of a response tended to build up inhibition with Pavlov's earlier hypothesis that inhibition dissipated with rest (nonoccurrence of the given response). From the first of those ideas it should follow that as massed trials are piled upon each other, the competition between inhibition and the positive effects of practice begin to cancel each other out. If a rest period is interjected, though, the inhibitory factor diminishes, but the effects of practice will not. Therefore, performance after a rest period may exceed any prerest level of performance.

The concept of inhibition achieved great popularity among students of complex learning. Its major weakness was that it attempted to ignore the specific differences in a tremendous variety of learning procedures. Extensions of the inhibition concept tended to emphasize brain processes more, the possibility of specific R interference less. With this shift in emphasis it became increasingly difficult to predict specific experimental results from the highly general effects that this term came to stand for.

The alternative to the assumption of a general inhibitory process is the notion of interference between overt (or potentially overt) R's. We have already seen how this idea can be applied to extinction situations. Insofar as the interference theory eliminates the initial empirical necessity for a hypothetical inhibitory state, the extension of inhibition to other learning situations becomes a dubious enterprise. The continued attempts to manipulate "inhibition" in complex learning at last began to reveal that the more flexible "interference" hypothesis seemed better equipped to deal with the variegated results obtained (1, 3, 261).

STIMULUS-RESPONSE INTERACTIONS IN COMPLEX LEARNING

Whenever possible, humans in complex learning situations quickly discover the *general* nature, at least, of the S's and R's with which they must deal in said situations, usually by the relation of verbal behavior to nonverbal. Thus, most of the confusion that can be observed in complex learning situations is pretty well restricted to confusion as to what goes with what, rather than confusion as to whether a given R or S is at all relevant.

The major outcome of the process called "learning how to learn" is that the organism can more quickly isolate those features of a situation that are relevant to the final attainment of a complex sequence of habits. Granting this ability, and granting that much complex learning proceeds under cover of ambiguity, it is not surprising to find that psychologists view stimulus and response generalization as the basic impediments to complex learning. That confusion in complex learning situations is especially prevalant in a sequence of the rote type (see p. 370), in which an arbitrarily paired series of S's and R's must be performed, is not surprising, either. Thus, Murdock (199a) finds that R's appropriate to a later stage of a series are made when S's of an earlier stage are presented; so, too, with early R's and late S's. In either direction the erroneous associations apparently can be just as strong.

But the concept of directionality is misleading here. What is happening is that R's and S's are generally confused. That R_{10} should occur occasionally when S_1 is presented is no more perplexing than that S_{10} should sometimes be followed by R_1. There are various names for these phenomena: "backward and forward associations" and "anticipatory and preservative errors" are two of the popular labels. By any name, however, there is not now any good evidence that such effects can be predicted for the individual learner.

Studies of generalization effects in complex learning situations have relied almost entirely upon the statistical approach. There is nothing inherently wrong with that approach to a research problem, of course, as long as the findings of such research are not intended to be applied to the individual case. Very little work in the field of complex learning today, however, is explicitly oriented toward the prediction of average trends in large groups of college students (who form the samples in many experiments in this area).[4] It is not

---

[4] The major exception to this statement is the research performed with young military personnel as subjects. Here it may literally be true that all that is sought is a generalization that applies to other young military personnel "on the average." Similarly, perhaps, with most large groups of students, no matter what age.

that remote associations do not occur, but that our present ability to control their occurrence (either an increase or a decrease) is poor in the individual case.

Plateaus

There is an interesting phenomenon that sometimes occurs when a complex learning situation involves both the formation of relatively novel S-R habits (simple), and the organization of these

FIGURE 29

Schematic Representation of a Learning Plateau

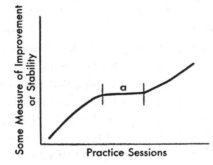

The plateau is indicated by the portion of this curve marked "a."

into a variety of equally strong, alternative habit combinations. It is called a *plateau*. As shown in Figure 29, a plateau is a period of no discernible improvement as a function of continued practice; it is somewhat the opposite of reminiscence, which we considered earlier. The frustrating feature of this effect is that it follows an initial period of rather steady improvement with practice.

Although there is a lot of anecdotal evidence for the plateau phenomenon, its experimental reproducibility has begun to be questioned (143). Plateaus have most often been identified in non-verbal learning situations—e.g., learning to play a musical instrument. This is probably because the standard laboratory studies of verbal learning are not sufficiently comprehensive to encompass this phenomenon.

Very few verbal learning problems in the laboratory meet all the conditions that are presumed to occur in situations where plateaus appear. These conditions are:

(1) The S's and R's are fairly novel to the subject, as well as the specific S-R relationships themselves. Thus the first stage in such learning situations involves at least two of the three basic types of discrimination learning: (a) discriminating S's, (b) differentiating R's, and (c) associating specific pairs of such S's and R's.

(2) The next stage involves the learning of patterns of R's to be made to patterns of frequently recurring S's. Many real-life, complex-learning situations include a number of subsidiary S-R combinations that repeatedly must be performed; for example, skilled typists learn to respond to complex stimuli such as the written words, "the," "and," and so on, with the equivalent combination of R's. As practice proceeds, these complex S-R patterns may become as well organized as are simpler habits; in fact, they may become functionally indistinguishable from simple habits.

(3) Finally, both the simple and the subtypes of complex habits must undergo the process described as formation of a learning set (Chapter 7). That is, these individual habits have to become sufficiently free from irrelevant or undependable kinds of S's so that they can easily be recombined into a variety of specific sequences. We have seen (Chapter 8) that learning what to ignore seems to be an important part of learning sets.

Plateaus are most likely to occur when stages 2 and 3 above are imposed on the subject nearly simultaneously. In other words, periods of no improvement during continued practice are typically periods when there is a mixture of new learning (stage 2) and "unlearning" (which is characteristic of much of stage 3, as described here). These effects will be magnified when the reinforcement conditions are inadequately associated with the relevant S-R pairs—as they frequently are, of course.

REINFORCEMENT FACTORS

The persistent theme of this chapter has been that if effective, manipulable reinforcers are applied in a systematic way to S-R relationships, then complex learning is not essentially different from simple learning. It is not customary, however, for the formation or recombination of multiple habits to proceed by the rules of simpler discrimination and differentiation methods. Since a certain degree of learning does, nevertheless, occur, there must be some factors that serve the same function as direct reinforcement would.

Speculation about possible reinforcers (or substitutes for X) in complex learning faces the same difficulties as did a similar attempt with respect to Pavlovian conditioning (see Supplementary Notes, Chapter 4). Since most experimenters have not actively sought to manipulate reinforcement at every step in complex learning studies, their experimental reports (quite unintentionally) often do not contain sufficient details about procedural matters that might be important to the discovery of the actual reinforcement factors (if any). Another obstacle is that the vast majority of complex learning studies have used S or R differences as their independent variables, and, therefore, provided essentially the same possible reinforcement conditions for all groups concerned; obviously none of *those* studies could provide evidence crucial to any hypothesis about the reinforcement effectiveness of this or that procedure.

With the foregoing reservations in mind, let us consider the features of complex learning situations that *could* strengthen the habits involved. Some of these conjectures can be supported by evidence, while others can not.

The Effects of the Terminal Goal

In all complex learning situations there is some final consequence of the successful performance of all the S-R relationships involved. With nonverbal subjects this consequence must be a distinct, extrinsic reinforcement like those employed in simple learning cases. Such terminal reinforcers may also be used in teaching complex habits to sophisticated, verbal subjects, but do not seem to be absolutely necessary. Instead, a more complicated terminal goal, *the removal of the necessity for further practice,* may suffice with experienced learners.

Two questions about terminal goals immediately suggest themselves. A basic problem is the ways in which (and the degree to which) terminal reinforcers can by themselves provide the basis for all other, more specific reinforcements in complex situations. The second question concerns the differences in the relationship between terminal and subgoal reinforcers that stem from differences in the nature of the terminal reinforcer itself.

Closely related to a distinction in types of ultimate goals is the difference between complex situations depending upon aversive (avoidance) motivation, and those utilizing approach motives. Here again, the question is whether the subgoals differ in kind or in effectiveness according to the affective nature of the end goal. All the questions in this and the previous paragraph merit our close investigation.

The General Effects of Terminal X's

Terminal reinforcement can provide the basis for specific reinforcements throughout the course of a complex learning sequence via a process that has already been revealed in simple learning situations—specifically, learning with delayed reward. As you should recall, simple habits can be formed even when X_{rew} does not immediately follow R_L *if* some systematic pattern of stimuli fills the lapse of time between the occurrences of R_L and X_{rew}. Many complex learning situations satisfy this requirement. Thus, the specific S-R relationships that comprise a complex habit may become stabilized because they are followed by *secondary reinforcers* that have been established because of their sequential relationship to each other and, ultimately, to the terminal reinforcement.

In other words, most of the S-R formations in many complex learning situations can be considered as a special case of delayed reward learning. As in all such cases, a habit will be stabilized to the extent that it eventually comes to be followed immediately by S^r's. S^r establishment is quite a likely possibility in many instances of complex learning because of the relatively systematic series of S's and R's that may arise. In this way, a terminal X_{rew} may be the sufficient basis for all the reinforcers in a complex problem.

If the terminal X is the sole determinant of all X's, however, learning will proceed slowly. Any delayed reward situation involves two stages—the establishment of an S^r, *then* the fixation of the S-R combination that immediately precedes a given S^r. When numerous S^r's and numerous S-R associations must be established, you can see that the time required for the successful stabilization of all components of a complex habit could be very great.

The Interaction between X Delay and S-R Generalization Effects

If complex learning proceeded strictly and solely by the principles of delayed reward learning, there should be a direct relationship between the time elapsing between a given S-R occurrence, the presentation of the terminal reinforcer, and the ease of establishing that habit. Habits practiced earliest should be hardest to learn, assuming that all the habits in a complex are practiced equally, and one right after the other. This rarely happens, however. When complex learning situations require the acquisition of many different (but similar) R's to similar S's, and reinforcement is primarily via S^r's related to the final goal, the *earliest* habits are learned most rapidly (excepting, perhaps, the habits that occur just prior to terminal reinforcement). The habits that follow these tend to *increase* in difficulty until near the end of the entire series. This phenomenon is sometimes called the *serial-position effect*.

The gradient of intra-serial difficulty seems to be due primarily to S and R similarities and spacing of practice, rather than to differential reinforcement. Lack of familiarity with the S's and R's also contributes to this gradient. As previously pointed out, confusion among the various habits in a complex situation occurs most often when reinforcement is used ineffectively. Trying to establish a group of habits while simultaneously building up the effectiveness of the reinforcing stimuli that are necessary for habit establishment is clearly not going to minimize a subject's confusion.

The Role of Terminal X's with Verbal Subjects

With subjects who can talk, it is an easy matter to indicate to them the nature of the terminal consequences of acquiring a complex habit series even before they have practiced any of it. It is also possible to tell the subject what will constitute a subgoal reinforcer; often, however, sophisticated learners can generalize from their past experiences to determine when they are making progress toward the ultimate goal.

Under the proper circumstances, prior information about either the ultimate and/or the immediate reinforcers in a complex learning situation can eliminate the problems that are associated with delayed reinforcement.

Prior information about the terminal reward can also (as noted in Chapter 10) serve as a powerful motivator to get the subject to practice, assuming that the terminal reward is one that is valued by the subject. The subject will even repeat a complex sequence several times without actually receiving the terminal reward, as long as there are indications that its attainment is becoming more likely.

Sophisticated, verbal learners can, in short, reach a stage where they can learn a great many complex habits with only very little X_{rew}; in fact, with little reinforcement of any kind. But people have come to rely too much on this talent, rather than on the skillful arrangement of complex learning conditions. In many natural situations the conditions for learning will, of course, be poor, and it is fortunate that organisms can learn despite the deviations from perfection. It does not follow, however, that when we *can* control and manipulate the conditions of learning (as in most phases of formal education, job training, many forms of psychotherapy and rehabilitation, and so on) that we need to settle for less than the best.

Telling the subject what he is supposed to do, and what he will get for doing it, is an imperfect substitute for a good learning situation. There are few languages that are not steeped in ambiguity—and English is certainly not one of them. How many words in even a condensed dictionary have only one meaning given? How many of such words refer to behavioral events or features of the environment that are not rather exotic?

Attempts to improve the clarity of linguistic communication are limited in their possibilities by the lack of control over the varieties of behavior that may, for any individual, become associated with any given abstract symbol. Either the behavior, the goals, or both may be misunderstood when instructions are substituted for the effective employment of reinforcement. There are two basic ways of using reinforcement effectively: (1) by providing for the immediate reinforcement of every correct S-R relationship involved in a given complex learning situation, or (2) as reinforcement is used in shaping.

Terminal X Events in Serial and Rote Learning

A major difference between these complex learning cases, as defined here, seem to be in the most plausible possibilities of reinforcement. In serial learning, the occurrence of S_2 can come to serve as the reinforcer for R_1, and so on; in rote learning, S_2 will occur whether or not R_1 has been performed correctly, so some other means of differentially reinforcing the correct behavior must be found.

In both cases, of course, there is usually a change in stimulation following a subject's response to any S in complex situations. In true serial learning only the correct response can be followed by even the most innocuous change in S, but in rote learning some types of reinforcement are just as apt to occur following a "wrong" R as they are to strengthen a proper one.

Some Special Reinforcement Phenomena

We now turn to some effects of reinforcement that appear to be unique to complex learning situations. This apparent uniqueness may be only because they have always been studied in complex learning cases. In line with the argument of this chapter that the differences between simple and complex learning are minor when compared to their similarities, I must at least mention the possibility of some of these effects of reinforcement occurring under other circumstances.

Spread of Effect

Many years after he formulated the Law of Effect (Chapter 4), E. L. Thorndike added another stipulation to his concept of the effect of reinforcement. Not only did reinforcers strengthen the S-R relationships that they immediately followed, but, according to Thorndike, other S-R relationships that happened to occur relatively close (in time) to the occurrence of a given reinforcing event would also be strengthened somewhat (even though not directly reinforced themselves). The amount of strengthening was directly related to the temporal proximity of an S-R sequence to the occurrence of reinforcement. Most important, this *spread of effect* (i.e., of reinforcement) was bidirectional—a given reinforcing event could just as well strengthen an S-R pairing that had not yet occurred as it could influence some habit that had occurred an appreciable time before the X event.

In the standard spread-of-effect experiment, the subject is given a series of meaningless stimuli (e.g., nonsense syllables); the series usually has about 10 items. The subject's task is to discover, by guessing, which one of a finite group of R's is supposed to go with each of the stimuli. Most often, the digits from 0 to 9 comprise the R group. Unknown to the subject, it has been predetermined that only one of his guesses on the first run-through of the stimuli will be reinforced (by the experimenter saying, "right," or via some other, equivalent sort of S^r). So that intra-list confusion will be constant for all subjects, *any* R that a subject makes to a specific stimulus in the list in reinforced, but no R's to any of the other S's are.

Thus, different subjects will have different R's (of the prescribed class) reinforced, but all of these R's are reinforced following their occurrence in the presence of one specific S in the list. Most important, this S occurs in the same numerical position in the list for all subjects. In order that it will be equally possible to trace the occurrence of both fore- and after-gradients of repetition of "errors," [5] an R to a stimulus in the middle of the series is nearly always the one to be reinforced.

The critical events are the guesses that occur on the second presentation of the series of stimuli. If a subject could recall with perfect accuracy each of the guesses made on the first trial, he would, of course, repeat only one of the S-R pairs that occurred on that trial. Because of the paucity of reinforcement on trial 1, and because the entire situation is conducive to great intra-series confusion, there will be some recurrences on trial 2 of S-R pairs that were made (but not reinforced) on trial 1. The spread-of-effect hypothesis stems from the observable fact that "errors" in some places in the list are more frequently repeated than they are in others.

The reinforced S-R pair, of course, is repeated by a majority of subjects. Using the serial position of this habit as a reference point, the frequency of error repetitions increases as this point is approached, reaches its maximum in the "first 'after' position" (shorthand for the first serial position after the position of the reinforced pair), and decreases less rapidly than it developed.

The history of the discussion about and investigation of the spread-of-effect hypothesis (180) is both discomfiting and illuminating with respect to the way in which words can get in the way of the understanding of empirical relationships. If we take Thorndike literally (as he apparently meant himself to be taken), he proposed an extremely radical revision of the concept of the role of reinforcement. Traditionally, X has been treated an as event that can only influence behavioral events that have *preceded* it. Thorndike not only proposed that behavior that *succeeded* an X could be affected by that X, but the results of many spread-of-effect experiments seemed to indicate that this latter phenomenon was the more easily produced sort of "spread." Oddly enough, it was not this implication that first focused attention upon this problem.

[5] In spread-of-effect studies, "errors" are all nonreinforced S-R occurrences. Remember that the subject believes it is possible for him to discover "right" responses for each stimulus in the list.

The critical examination of spread of effect mushroomed only after the publication of an uncritical reiteration of Thorndike's views with respect to the crucial nature of the spread phenomenon for all reinforcement approaches to learning data (111). This stimulated a relatively intense study of the phenomenon that largely supported the essentials of Thorndike's early research, but also caused a reformulation of his interpretation of his findings.

First of all, both statistical and experimental control procedures showed that the phenomenon might be accounted for entirely by the principles of S and R generalization. Furthermore, the after-gradient has been easier to reproduce than the fore-gradient; this makes it improbable that any conventional sort of remote effect of reinforcement could be playing an important role in this phenomenon.

The alternative to Thorndike's hypothesis starts with the realization that people do not guess numbers at random. In a culture such as ours, a young adult has had extensive training in the use of numbers. This experience produces two interrelated biases (deviations from randomness) in a person's guessing behavior: (1) Over a long series of guesses, some numbers will occur much more frequently than some others; in other words, the probabilities of the occurrences of all R's in a class (such as one-digit numbers) are *not* equal even when a subject is trying to "guess at random." (2) Responses such as numbers are repeatedly combined into sequences that a person learns—telephone numbers, historical dates, addresses, many of the labels by which a complex society keeps track of its members. We all learn different sets of such sequences, and some sequences we learn better than others. The net result is that once a given number is "guessed" this tends to limit the alternatives from which the second R will be chosen; up to a point, this restriction in randomness increases as more numbers are given in a sequence. This second guessing bias is especially pertinent to the spread-of-effect data.

In brief, if there is any factor that predisposes a subject to make a particular number response, then the immediately ensuing number-R's will also be less than random. Is there any factor in the spread-of-effect situation that predisposes the subject to make any given response less than randomly? The single reinforcement on trial 1 obviously fits this description. This produces a strong tendency for one repetition on trial 2 of an R made (for whatever reason) on trial 1. If this R is a member of some previously learned number sequence (as it almost certainly is), then the R's that are likely to follow the occurence of this one are predictable with more than a chance probability of accuracy. Furthermore, the first R after the reinforced one can be predicted best, the second one less accurately, and so on. Thus, insuring (by reinforcement) that *one* R is going to be made in the presence of the same S on trials 1 and 2 actually tends also to improve the chances that R's following the reinforced one will also be repeated. So "spread of effect" does occur, in one sense; a single reinforcement of an S-R pair does affect the persistence of other (not directly reinforced) responses to similar stimuli.

One investigator has continued to reject the "response bias" explanation of the spread of effect as being entirely sufficient. M. H. Marx has reported a series of ingeniously designed and analyzed experiments in which a after-gradient spread can still be detected, even when guessing habits, etc., are controlled (181, 182).

Knowledge of Results

Any time a learner is given information about his performance he can be considered to be receiving "knowledge of results." There are two basic ways in which knowledge of results has been manipulated as an experimental variable:

(1) The accomplishment of every relevant R is communicated to the subject at the time he makes it. This may or may not differ from the procedure that I have heretofore called reinforcement. Suppose that one is shooting at a target, with the ultimate goal of becoming so skilled that he will hit the bull's-eye every time he shoots. If one is told immediately after every shot whether he had or had not hit the bull's-eye, then he would be learning by the most direct application of the simple reinforcement method: he would be reinforced whenever he hit the target, not reinforced when he

did not. But one might be informed in some way, instead, by how much and in what direction all failures to hit the bull's-eye had erred. In the latter case, there would be a basis for describing the method of altering one's behavior as involving more than simple reinforcement. One type of knowledge of results, thus, is only a complex form of response differentiation that ultilizes previous verbal learning by the subject. The basic requirements for the use of this method are these:

(1a) The subject must be able to conceptualize the ultimate, desired effect of his behavior. To put this much more simply, it must be possible to reward the subject by telling him that he is on target. This is why I assert that knowledge of results utilizes previous verbal learning. This "awareness" of the ultimate goal may, however, serve as a motivating condition without directly affecting the pattern of behavior variation that precedes learning. In the knowledge-of-results case, the subject's ensuing behavior in a learning situation will depend upon his "perception" of the degree of congruence between the immediate results of his R's and the desired results.

(1b) In other words, the subject's "ability to discriminate" between the obtained and the desired results will determine his subsequent behavior.

But how do we know whether an organism can discriminate between the two events? By noting that he behaves differently following their separate occurrences; i.e., when these events consistently evoke different UCR's, or different learned R's.

So different effects following differences in the organism's knowledge of results are due primarily to prior learning? Yes; few stimuli that are used to convey knowledge of results evoke strong UCR's with a great resistance to modification (the stimuli used most, of course, are words). Any consistent, differential R's that follow such cues as, "You're just a little under it" or "That was right on it," are due to previous learning.

(1c) In the final analysis, knowledge of results is a complicated case of shaping. The organism makes an R, certain environmental changes then occur, and the organism again responds. The "certain environmental changes" that occur may be new S's primarily—i.e., they produce R's different from those that have just occurred; they may be X's—fixating the preceding R's. In a case in which the announcement of results follows a series of somewhat independent R's, it may, of course, have both S and X effects concurrently. That is, it may reinforce one R, and also lead to the occurrence of a subsequent one.

Once again, then, the subtlety of the differences between simple and complex learning situations is revealed. Shaping stems directly from procedures that are used to establish simple habits and simple habit interactions, yet the result of shaping can be a behavior pattern that qualifies as "complex." Similarly, the knowledge-of-results method is an obvious elaboration of the way in which NoX is used to get a subject to refine or add to the R's he has already begun to associate with S's in a simple learning situation.

Like conventional reinforcers in simple learning, the effectiveness of the knowledge-of-results technique depends upon the immediacy of its application (92). Like X_{rew}'s, however, delay is not fatal; if there is some basis for mediating the association between a reinforcer and the relevant R, some temporal lag can occur. By definition knowledge of results provides such a mediating basis in many cases. As with any "backward" mediation of a delay in X, there is always the risk that the subject will associate the wrong response with the reinforcer.

Is knowledge of results superior to response differentiation with only X and NoX (with subjects for whom they would both be effective)? There have been no systematic studies of this question, but it is hard to imagine that there could be an absolute answer. If both methods were used in the maximally effective ways, the best guess would be that learning would progress equally well under either method. Possibly, however, if both were employed inefficiently, knowledge of results would have a slight edge in most situations. Reinforcement must be immediate and accurately correlated with R_L's if it is not supplemented by verbal information; conceivably this would not be *as* important with the knowledge-of-results technique, although delay does influence it (92).

(2) The second type of situation that is generally considered to

involve knowledge of results is that in which the subject makes a great many R's and only after this behavior is he given some information about his performance. The most common example of this type of aftereffect of complex performance is the exam grade—a student makes many verbal R's and is eventually told "how many points he got" on the test. This technique does appear to produce learning occasionally, but systematic work relating it to reinforcement or any other standard class of learning variables has not been done. As a result, we can only speculate about the dynamics of this procedure and the circumstances that determine its effectiveness.

SUMMARY

Many standard discussions of complex learning imply that it is a drastically different set of phenomena from those that come under the heading of "simple habit formation." Considering the confusing conditions under which learning—especially human learning—is often required to take place, it is not hard to see how the belief in the distinction between simple and complex learning could arise. This seems, however, to be a classic instance of the cart before the horse.

As long as inefficiency is not a part of the definition of "complex," then the boundary between simple and complex learning situations becomes indistinct. First of all, a positive definition of complex learning brings out two characteristics, neither of which is unknown to simple learning situations. One characteristic is that several S-R sequences are involved, and another is that the S's and R's involved are often highly similar. Many intermittent reinforcement, free operant situations meet these criteria, too. Secondly, when the knowledge derived from the studies of simple habit interactions is added to that from simple learning research, there seems to be little that is perplexing in complex learning situations. If we ask how complex learning can proceed *most effectively*, the answers seem to be contained in our understanding of simpler learning situations.

In short, the major discrepancy between simple and complex learning conditions arises from the fact that the former have been studied with the intention of gaining *control* over them, while the latter have been taken at face value as they occur in nature. Under such circumstances, the inability of learning psychologists to relate one set of complex learning conditions to others is understandable, though not particularly praiseworthy.

CHAPTER 12

*

*

* RETENTION

Retention is the generic name for that part of the field of learning that deals with the phenomena that are more popularly called "memory," "remembering," or "forgetting." "Retention" and "memory" are practically synonymous, both referring to the measurement of the amount of remembering that an organism demonstrates. The following "equation" describes the relationship between remembering and forgetting:

amount remembered + amount forgotten = amount originally learned

Forgetting, in short, is the opposite of remembering; anything that helps the one hinders the other.

THE BASIC CHARACTERISTICS OF RETENTION STUDIES

All studies of retention share at least the following features:

(1) There is an initial period of practice on the habit(s) the retention of which is to be studied. Ideally, we would want to observe the entire span of the acquisition of this habit, or set of habits; for this reason this period is called the *Original Learning Period* (which often will be abbreviated to OL Period).

(2) There is a period during which the subject no longer practices these habits. This will be called the *Interpolated Rest* [1] *Period* (IR

---

[1] "Rest" refers only to respite from practice on the material under consideration; the subject actually may be quite active during the IR Period.

Period). The minimum requirement for an IR Period is that the S's and R's under consideration at least do not occur in the same combinations as during the OL Period.

(3) Finally, the subject is confronted with a situation in which the occurrence of the habits formed during the OL Period could reasonably be expected. The comparison of the level of performance of these habits during this final stage with their performance during the last portion of the OL Period provides us with a measure of the amount remembered (or forgotten). Accordingly, this final stage is called the *Retention Test Period* (RT Period).

Thus, three discrete stages must occur before it is reasonable to talk about what a subject does or does not remember. Factors operating at each of these stages can, at least theoretically, be influential in determining the amount retained. The consideration of such factors is the next major topic. Before going on to that, however, it may be helpful to mention a couple of technical matters.

Methodological Considerations in Retention Studies

In order to make an accurate, objective assessment of an organism's retention, it must be possible to describe quantitatively his performance at the end of the OL Period and also during the RT Period. The kinds of learning situations in which this is easiest to accomplish are those described in Chapter 11 as being near the true rote learning end of the continuum of complex learning cases. Whenever a learning situation consists of a series of relatively independent simple habits, then an obvious measure of retention would be to compare the total number of such habits correctly performed at the end of the OL Period with the number correctly performed in the RT Period. Such a measure is quite comparable over a variety of specific experimental conditions. Because of the simple and extensive applicability of this measure, most laboratory studies of retention have utilized situations in which this counting of correct S-R relationships is a sufficiently accurate measure of performance.

When we are interested in retention in serial learning situations, other measures are necessary. In a case in which each habit must be performed correctly before the next one can be performed at all, the measure described above would clearly be inappropriate. If the subject had forgotten Habit$_1$, for instance, this would prevent him from showing whether he remembered Habit$_2$, Habit$_3$, and so on.

A reasonable solution to this problem is to provide some means for "reminding" the organism of any given habit (during the RT Period) to see if this will enable him to reproduce the next habit in the sequence. Of course, any habits that can not be performed without a "reminder" would be counted as errors, just as in the rote learning cases.

With nonverbal learners, it is not very easy to remind a subject about the correct R for a given S if the presentation of S itself is not sufficient to produce the R. Usually we must resort in such a case to permitting the subject to go through a trial-and-error period similar to that during which the habit was originally learned. When this is done the measure of retention becomes more complex, since it must now involve some statement about the time required to arrive at the correct R, the number of irrelevant R's made first, and so forth. These considerations also apply to cases in which our primary interest is in the retention of a single, simple habit.

I have taken the space for this digression in order to rectify a quite common popular misconception about retention. Implicit in many of the layman's discussions of retention is the attitude that it is an all-or-none phenomenon. The preceding consideration of the problems of measuring retention should have made it clear that this is not necessarily true at all.

A final technical matter that needs to be mentioned for the sake of clarifying many of the matters soon to be discussed concerns the basis of distinguishing between the Original Learning and Interpolated Rest Periods. If we take our definition of the IR Period most literally, any break in practice during initial acquisition could be considered an Interpolated Rest Period. But this is too cumbersome and too subtle for the discussion of most retention phenomena. For the sake of convenience, therefore, we shall arbitrarily define the OL Period to include all periods of practice, and any possible periods of rest—no matter how long—that occur before the subject and/or teacher are satisfied that the habits have reached sufficient strength. The facts to be considered in deciding when no further practice is necessary are, of course, many and varied.

As we shall soon see, the amount of retention *will* be influenced by the relationship between the spacing of practice sessions during the OL Period and the length of the IR Period. But this is not a sufficient basis for making a more complicated distinction between the two stages.

ORIGINAL LEARNING CONDITIONS AND RETENTION

We have already discussed all the principles important to this topic. The fundamental law concerning the OL Period with respect to retention is very simple: the better a habit has been learned, the less likely it is to be forgotten.

Most of the preceding material in this text has dealt with the ways in which habits can be most rapidly and most permanently established. It would be redundant, therefore, to re-examine these principles anew. Certain special OL conditions can be important in the light of the IR and RT conditions that are going to prevail in some specific situation, but these can better be taken up in the discussions of these stages themselves. Let us, therefore, proceed directly to these topics.

INTERPOLATED REST CONDITIONS AND RETENTION

Time and Forgetting

A law of forgetting that has been almost universally recognized since ancient times is that the longer the time since something was learned, the harder it will be to remember. In our terminology, this reduces to the statement that retention is an inverse function of the length of the Interpolated Period. Although there is a great deal of evidence that gives ostensible support to this principle, a more careful examination reveals other factors than the mere passage of time to be of greatest importance in determining retention. By way of introducing this alternative interpretation of the crucial characteristics in the IR Period, let us take up one more technical matter.

How Forgetting Differs from Extinction

Although the *results* of the procedures called "forgetting" and "extinction" are essentially the same, the *means* by which these procedures take place are quite different. Extinction, as we have seen, results when the S-R combinations that were originally learned occur repeatedly without reinforcement. Forgetting, on the other hand, appears to result from the *nonoccurrence* of the critical S-R relationships. Procedurally, at least, the two phenomena are quite distinct.

While it will be helpful for the beginning student to know the above difference, he should be forewarned that the ensuing discussion will go a long way toward reducing the clarity of the distinction. This is because conceptually extinction and forgetting have quite similar bases. It is this proposition that we now want to take up.

Retroactive Inhibition

The basic design for demonstrating retroactive inhibition in the laboratory is this:

	Step (1)	Step (2)	Step (3)
Retroaction Group	Learn A	Learn B	Test for Retention of A
Control Group	Learn A	"Rest"	Test for Retention of A

If, as is almost invariably the case, the first group shows less retention of the habits involved in A, the learning of the B habits is said to have had a retroactively inhibiting effect on the A habits. It was not long before psychologists interested in memory began to recognize that the retroaction design had relevance for the topic of retention in a variety of cases. This insight was buttressed by many lines of evidence, all of which boiled down to one generalization: the greater the similarity in the S's of the habits involved in A and B, and the greater the incompatibility of the R's involved, the less the retention of the habits in A.

The above principle has been shown to hold in numerous studies in which the material of task B and its acquisition are controlled and manipulated (see 121, 203, 292 for detailed reviews of the traditional findings). In addition, there is some information that suggests the operation of the same principle even when—as is most often the case with forgetting—the events of the Interpolated Period are not controlled, except negatively. Lidell (170), for example, found that sheep who were subjected to treatments that produced "neurotic" behavior did not show any forgetting even after as much as two years away from the laboratory. The IR Period for these sheep was spent in a typical farm environment where they had no contact with anything or anyone connected with their lab experiences. Therefore, although the R's of the IR and OL Periods were quite incompatible (roughly, contentment vs. neuroticism), the dissimilarity of the stimuli in the two situations was so great that the farm habits had little effect upon the lab habits. When the sheep were brought back to the lab, they behaved with about as much emotional disturbance as they had formerly shown. There had been, in other words, no forgetting of the OL experiences.

We saw in Chapter 9 that there is no evidence of learning while an organism is asleep. This perhaps regrettable discovery has its positive side, too, however, for it has also been shown (132) that a subject who sleeps through the IR Period forgets far less than one who does not. Thus, an IR situation that provides little opportunity for *any* learning also does not offer much chance for forgetting to occur.

The Interference Theory of Forgetting

As a result of evidence such as that just reviewed, many psychologists have become convinced of the generalization that most, if not all, forgetting is due to the formation (or additional strengthening) of habits during the IR Period that compete with those that have been built up during the OL stage.

Those who do not accept an interference theory as a complete explanation of retention phenomena point, quite reasonably, to the fact that no one has yet been able to devise an IR situation that will produce *no* forgetting. Even subjects who sleep through most of the IR Period, for instance, do forget some of their original learning. Theoretically, of course, if interference is the determinant of forgetting, it would seem to be possible to create an interpolated situation in which there was no interference—thus, no forgetting.

A theory can be refuted only by empirical results when all the conditions of the theory have been met in studies that do not obtain the results predicted by the theory. In order for this to happen, the theory in question must be extremely explicit in its description of the conditions necessary to test it. By this criterion, the interference theory is not a good (i.e., completely testable) theory. There are several reasons why not:

(1) First of all, there is the problem of the inexplicitness of the meanings of the terms "similar S's" and "compatible R's." This is the same problem that plagued us in discussing transfer of training, extinction, and so forth.

(2) The practical inability of the typical experimental procedures to prevent *any* occurrence of interfering habits being performed during the IR Period is another difficulty. Without using drugs (which have their own complications), it is almost impossible to have a subject go deeply to sleep immediately after an OL Period; inevitably there is going to be some activity, some dreaming, and the like.

(3) Finally there is the possibility that not all sources of interference are localized in the IR Period. This brings us to the phenomenon called Proactive Inhibition.

Proactive Inhibition

The basic design for studying this effect is:

	Step (1)	Step (2)	Step (3)	
Proaction Group	Learn A	Learn B	Rest	Retention Test on B
Control Group	Rest	Learn B	Rest	Retention Test on B

It has generally been found, with adult humans as subjects, that the retention of the B material is impeded by the prior learning of similar material. This effect, which shows up best when all the materials learned are relatively unfamiliar and/or arbitrarily combined, is called *proactive inhibition*. Here the emphasis is upon the effects on retention of *previous* learning rather than *interpolated* learning.

Relative to the sufficiency of the interference theory of forgetting, Underwood (276) has presented an effective argument for the view that proactive inhibition effects can account for most of the forgetting that retroactive inhibition does not. He has shown that numerous studies, when combined, reveal a positive, monotonic relationship between the amount forgotten and the number of similar learning tasks that have preceded the task that goes through the standard retention sequence. Underwood's summary is reproduced in Figure 30.

This phenomenon noted by Underwood seems to be in contradiction to the "learning set" effect. In the latter case, of course, previous learning *aids* future learning in a general, invariably positive manner. The cumulative proaction effect just noted, however, is a case in which increased experience with similar tasks has a negative influence on the retention of a task that is subsequently learned.

Just how the different effects of *apparently* similar quasi-transfer situations might be reconciled is not now clear. Retention and acquisition *are* different sorts of procedures; perhaps it is fallacious to assume that a complex process like learning how to learn should affect both in a similar fashion. Rather than raising any doubts about either the learning set or the proaction phenomena, this discrepancy might go far toward clarifying the differences between learning and remembering.

At any rate, Underwood considered his findings to be consistent with an interference theory of forgetting. The proaction effect, to him, simply pointed out another source of interfering habits. While the interference theory developed from a study of IR Period effects on retention, the theory need not necessarily be restricted to these effects alone.

Time as a Variable

At the bottom of the interest in such questions as the validity of the interference theory is an attempt to clarify the meaning of "the passage of time." Literally, time refers only to the number (or

FIGURE 30

Retention as a Function of Amount of Similar Prior Learning

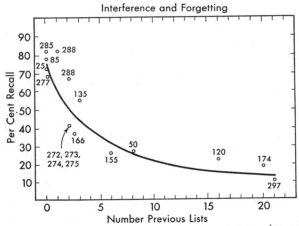

From Underwood (276), in the *Psychological Review*, vol. 64, p. 53. Used by permission of the American Psychological Association.

Each point on this graph summarizes the results of the studies denoted by the number(s) adjacent to them; the numbers, as usual, indicate items in the reference list. The smooth curve shown here was constructed by Underwood, who also reported a rank-order correlation of −.91 between the x and y values of the points shown.

fraction) of revolutions the earth has made on its axis, starting from some basal relationship in the positions of the earth and the sun. As we all know, many other natural relationships are conveniently described in terms of the relatively reliable changes in that physical relationship. It is a purely arbitrary basis for description, though, and as such does not *explain* the reliability of the phenomena described.

The relationship between forgetting and time since the OL Period is one of the most easily verified in the field of learning, but for the reasons just mentioned this does not tell us much about the variables that *are* operating to produce forgetting. Time, per se, is not a psychological variable; it can only be a convenient way of marking changes in factors that are directly relevant to behavioral changes. The interference theory is an attempt to explicate these factors in the case of forgetting; I have stressed it so much because

FIGURE 31

Retention as a Function of the Length of the IR Period

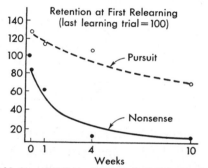

From Leavitt and Schlosberg (164), in the *Journal of Experimental Psychology*, vol. 34, p. 410. Used by permission of the American Psychological Association.

In this graph, retention of verbal (nonsense syllable list) and motor (pursuit rotor performance) habits are shown. Although the retention of the two types of habits is quite different, they both show the same trend in forgetting: Performance is best immediately after learning, and drops off at a decreasing rate as the IR period becomes longer. Note that reminiscence is obtained after one week (and to some extent after four weeks) on the pursuit rotor task.

it is, as of now, the most positive attempt to handle the facts of forgetting—especially the correlation between the length of the IR Period and the amount retained.

One of the widely accepted rules of forgetting is that it is a negatively accelerated function of the lapse of time between the OL and RT Periods. This is shown in Figure 31. What is it that happens during this time lapse? The interference concept holds that the things most likely to occur are other S-R combinations, and that these compete with those of the OL Period. This competition is presumed to follow the same principles of S and R confusion that can be noted in complex learning situations. Thus, the name interference theory.

OL- and IR-Period Response Factors in Retention

The preceding discussion leads smoothly into this topic, which should serve primarily as a further review of the interference position.

A rough scale of types of responses and their susceptibility to forgetting seems to be in the process of being identified. Generally, it runs from Pavlovian-conditioned habits, which are easily retained for long periods, to complex verbal habits, which are quite readily forgotten. This gamut makes sense in interference terms.

As we have previously noted, Pavlov's technique for producing learning is fairly "unnatural." Because of this it should be relatively easy to devise OL and IR Periods that are quite different—in other words, involving quite different S's and R's—when the OL Period follows Pavlov's procedure. If so, interference between the habits of the two periods should be at a minimum; thus, little forgetting. This is also true for motor learning as studied in the lab (5).

Complex verbal learning must of necessity involve behavior that can vary over only a limited range. There are, after all, a finite number of motor acts that are employed in any kind of verbal behavior. Similarly, there is a much larger, but still finite, class of S's that must nearly exhaust the possible S's that could be involved in verbal habits. For those reasons, truly distinct OL and IR Periods should be hard to contrive when the OL material is verbal. This should enhance the possibilities of forgetting.

Much more difficulty is met when we attempt to fill in the intermediate steps on this scale of "ease of retention." The difficulty stems, of course, from the general problem of stating any useful, universal definition of response compatibility. As I have repeatedly suggested, a really good scaling of R's as to their tendency to interfere with each other (or to facilitate each other's acquisition) would break up a lot of log-jams that now block the search for widely applicable principles of learning.

Retention and Distribution of Practice

I have already pointed out that when there is any rest between practice periods the distinction between the IR and OL stages of a retention study becomes an arbitrary one. This situation also raises the seeming paradox of spaced practice being, in general, an asset to learning, but a detriment to remembering. To be specific, spaced practice *usually* results in a more rapid rate of acquisition of complex habits, relative to the total amount of time spent in practice, than does massed practice; in fact, in many complex learning situations a high level of performance can *only* be obtained by permitting some interpolated rest periods (situations in which reminiscence occurs, for example). On the other hand, if the IR Period contains any possibilities of interference, then the longer that period the greater the forgetting that will occur (80).

This seems to be an inconsistency that stems directly from the basic difference between an OL Period and an RT Period—in the former, warm-up of a fairly specific nature may be permitted, and knowledge of results or some type of reinforcement will usually be available to the subject (127). A retention test, on the other hand, closely resembles an extinction session quite often—every attempt is made to keep the subject in the dark about the effectiveness of his performance.

Another factor influencing the relationship of spaced practice to the length of the IR Period could be something analogous to the hypothesis of Virginia Sheffield about spaced and massed trials and frustration (Chapter 8). Extrapolating from her reasoning, the following hypothesis might be tenable: The more similar the lengths of the periods that occur between successive practice sessions to the length of the interval after which retention is to be tested, the better will be the retention. This is based on the assumption that, on the average, essentially the same interpolated events will occur between practice sessions and between the final OL session and the RT session, if the lengths of these periods are always the same. Therefore, the subject will come to each of these sessions with rather similar degrees of adjustment to the learning situation (i.e., warm-up) necessary. This settling down may become part of the relevant S's in the learning situation; if a similar effect occurs at the time of the retention test, remembering should be facilitated because of the similarity of the conditions to those that prevailed during at least part of each learning session. This effect should be enhanced if practice is repeatedly and frequently interrupted; this brings up another condition of learning that is necessary to consider: the whole vs. part methods of practice.

The Whole vs. Part Methods

Directly related to the question of distribution of practice is the issue of what and how much of a complex learning task to try to handle at one practice session. This is ordinarily called the "whole vs. part" problem. The "whole" method (practicing all the components of a complex task within each practice session) is a kind of *massed* practice. The part method may or may not involve spaced practice, however; for one thing, it depends upon whether each part is practiced to perfection before another segment of the material is taken up. Even in the latter case, each part may be acquired by massed or spaced methods. Thus, to some extent, the efficacy of these two methods will be determined by the considerations already discussed with respect to the spacing of practice.

Another factor that will determine when the whole method would be more or less desirable is whether, and to what extent, the shaping technique is being utilized. Shaping, by definition, is a use of the part method. If, on the other hand, more conventional kinds of transfer of training are relied upon extensively during the OL Period, the whole method may be most efficient.

In the last analysis, then, the whole-part problem is simply a special instance of the general problem of efficient acquisition in complex learning situations. To the extent that quite unfamiliar S-R relationships are to be acquired, the part method seems preferable; when the learning consists mainly of recombination of well-practiced R's, the whole method is better. Of course, there is nothing to prevent one from using different methods at different stages in practice—going from the part to the whole method would probably be the usual progression; college students do this sometimes—studying the material as it is assigned (or as it becomes pertinent to the lectures), then reviewing all of it prior to an exam. Eventually, however, one wishes to bring his practice sessions (their spacing, the amount they cover, and so on) as nearly in accord with the conditions that will prevail as the IR Period transition to the RT Period occurs.

RETENTION TEST CONDITIONS AND AMOUNT REMEMBERED

Now we come to a principle that is, from the standpoint of applying laboratory findings to concrete memorization problems, of the greatest importance. The principle is this: The greater the similarity of the OL and the RT Periods, the better the retention.

The importance, in terms of application, of this principle is that it suggests some things the individual learner may do to improve his memory. From the standpoint of the general principles of learning also, this rule is important because it shows how still another facet of the field of learning is interrelated with all of the others. The following explication of the OL-RT interaction will show the basis for these two assertions.

Similarity in OL and RT Stimulus Conditions

All approaches to learning theory, as shown in Chapter 9, agree that stimulus factors are essential elements of any learning situation. Thus, there is hardly any dissension possible from the statement that remembering will be best when the crucial stimuli of the original learning period are reproduced almost exactly during the retention test session.

At our present level of understanding of S factors in general, it is hard to give a very specific definition of crucial stimuli that would apply well to most complex learning situations. Literally, of course, crucial stimuli are those in the presence of which the appropriate R's (and only those responses) are reinforced. But so many complex learning situations do not permit the clear-cut occurrence of this series of events that this definition is not as useful as it should be. The obvious possibility, of course, would be the S's in the habits concerned. Other crucial stimuli might be the general features of the OL Period environment, whether or not warm up typically occurred—in general, any environmental conditions that frequently or consistently occur during original learning (and not at other times) should be present during the retention test in order to obtain the maximum degree of remembering.

Laboratory studies of retention generally use constant environmental conditions for the OL and RT sessions as a standard control procedure. There has not, therefore, been a lot of evidence relevant to this point. As will be mentioned in a subsequent section, however, this seems particularly important for the application of retention principles to the individual case.

Learning sets also play a role in this relationship. One characteristic of a sophisticated learner is that he learns to ignore many features of situations in which he is aware that he is supposed to learn something. Insofar as this held for a given subject, it would reduce the importance of the similarity of extraneous S conditions in retention, of course, but to just what extent can not be specified in advance for a new situation at our present stage of development in this field.

Finally, there is the fact already mentioned (Chapter 2) that when learning occurs under widely varying S conditions the habits produced are more resistant to extinction (177). Since extinction is a variation of the transfer-of-training model, and so is the relationship between OL and RT conditions in retention, that fact may have some pertinence to the present relationship. In particular, there is good reason to believe that learning under varied conditions is the basic quality of those situations that are productive of learning sets that have highly adaptive values.

All three of the items just reviewed point out factors that mitigate the importance of S similarities between the OL and RT Periods, other than in the seemingly trivial case of the S's directly involved in the habits concerned. This trivial case, however, is often surprisingly important in practical situations, as we shall see in a little while.

Similarity in OL and RT R Conditions

When the specific R's learned during the OL Period are the same as the R's that have to be performed in the retention test, remembering will be at its best. Insofar as the required R's are different in the two stages, forgetting can be expected. In the context of all of the discussion that has preceded in this book it may seem ridiculous to mention this determinant of the amount of retention, but many of the traditional methods of measuring retention make it quite important.

An unusual aspect of most retention tests (especially with human subjects) is that they deviate more from at least an implicit recognition of the S-R approach to behavior than do any other standard laboratory or everyday learning situations. We often expect ourselves or others to remember things that have never been learned. An example of this is the reliance on the testimony of eyewitnesses to events that happened rapidly (which is often erroneously treated as an example of perceptual variability in psychology texts). Here a person must give a *verbal report* of a situation during the occurrence of which he may not have had a coherent thought, much less actually have *said* anything relevant.

The conventional way of describing the effect of R similarity between the OL and RT stages is by the statement that amount of retention is a function of the method used to measure retention. While this is generally true, it obscures some of the critical factors that produce this effect.

Measures of Retention

Terminology varies here, and there is some overlapping of concepts, but three major kinds of retention test situations are easily differentiable:

The Recognition Method

Here the subject is shown a number of stimuli. Some of these stimuli were previously presented in a similar form during the OL Period; symbolic representations of the R's originally learned may also be used. Others of the RT S's were *not* part of the OL situation. The subject's task is to pick out those S's that occurred during the OL Period. A classic example of this sort of retention test is the multiple-choice, so-called objective examination.

The recognition method will generally produce high retention scores even on the first retention trial. This follows from the definition of the method; it provides a situation that has some resemblance to many forms of original practice.

The Recall Method

This method requires a subject to reproduce a large number of previously learned R's in the face of S's that may be only roughly similar to those of the OL Period. An example known to most college students is the essay examination. This will generally produce the poorest retention scores, because it is the RT situation most likely to deviate markedly from the OL situation that preceded it.

The Relearning Method

This is most often employed in cases where the amount of forgetting is known (or expected) to be great. The method amounts to repeating the OL conditions almost completely and observing the amount of practice that a subject needs to reacquire a level of accuracy or proficiency comparable to that attained in the OL situation. All things equal, this method should produce the greatest degree of remembering, following the principle stated at the beginning of this section, because it most nearly replicates the OL conditions in their entirety. Especially important is the fact that this method most assures that exactly the same R's are appropriate to both the OL and the RT Periods.

As a practical method of measuring retention, however, the relearning method leaves something to be desired. First of all, it requires that the original learning take place under conditions that permit of objective and comparable quantitative measures of performance. This is rarely applicable to conventional learning situations such as schools. Even more important, though, is the fact that we often do not aim during the OL Period merely to establish a group of habits that can be more easily relearned later on. Many applied learning situations seek to establish habits to such a degree that further learning is not necessary. At least, that is often the manifest aim of formal training situations; it may, indeed, be an unrealistic goal in many cases. A contemporary example of the attempt to train subjects to a point where they will be easier to retrain, should the necessity arise later, is the peacetime draft.

Similarity in OL and RT Reinforcement Conditions

Since, by definition, no test of retention except the relearning method usually involves *any* reinforcement, this will not often be a variable determining OL-RT similarity. Certainly it has not been studied as such.

There is one case in which the absence of X's during the RT Period could significantly affect the similarity of the two stages. That would be whenever some of the reinforcers used to strengthen given S-R relationships also become part of the S complexes for other habits in the OL Period. This is not too unlikely in some types of serial learning. To the extent, then, that an attempt is made to exclude these X's during retention, some components of the S's involved will also be eliminated. It thus becomes a special case of stimulus similarity between the OL and RT Periods.

There has been no systematic study of the effects of different types or schedules of reinforcement using the relearning method.

SUMMARY AND DISCUSSION: THE
LEARNER AS HIS OWN TEACHER

Most of the layman's questions about applying the principles of learning for his own improvement are questions about how to aid retention. There are many books and pamphlets devoted exclusively to these questions, and they usually contain much useful information.

One principle that is often underemphasized, or not spelled out sufficiently, is the effect of the similarity of the OL and RT Periods. Usually this relationship will determine for the most part what constitutes good learning procedures during the OL Period. By far the most widely applicable rule of retention is that the OL Period should be made as much like the RT Period as possible. By the same token, the IR Period should be kept as free from the performance of habits that compete with those of the OL (and thus ideally the RT) Period.

Now, in most real-life analogs of the experimental study of retention, the learner has the most control over the events of the OL Period, next most over those of the IR Period, least of all over the RT conditions. The *absolute* degrees of control that a person may have in a specific case will, of course, vary with a great number of circumstances, but these *relative* degrees will hold most of the time.

Many people who have difficulty with the retention of material fail to recognize the significance of this differential control over the various stages of the retention sequence. The attitude is often expressed that, in effect, (1) there is one best method of learning (or memorizing) that invariably applies, and (2) since the nature of any retention test is in the lap of the gods, it can not have anything to do with one's method of learning. It should now be clear that these statements are false.

Knowledge of the nature of a retention test is usually an important clue to the method of study that will be most profitable. This is implicit in the question asked by many college students at the start of a course, "Will the exams be essay or multiple-choice?" Experienced students know that these alternatives usually require different sorts of preparation.

To the extent that a learner is unable to control certain relevant features of the IR Period that is to occur, it is necessary to contrive an OL method that maximizes the differences between it and the IR Period, as well as the similarities with the RT Period. This may be difficult, may require a great deal of ingenuity, but it can be done.

The most effective means of carrying out the general principles just reviewed will be via an analysis of a given learning situation in terms of S's and R's. Now, as we come to the end of this survey, I hope it has become apparent that an S-R approach to behavior does not necessarily commit one to a specific philosophy—except a belief that behavior is lawful. While there *are* epistemological arguments for this approach, these are debatable. I have chosen, instead, to stress the pragmatic value of the S-R approach. In short, this sort of analysis *works* as a guide to the control of behavior. Control is the key to understanding of natural phenomena. It remains to be seen whether our ultimate understanding of things psychological can adequately be expressed in S-R terminology. This need not influence our decision to use or to discard the behaviorist approach *now*. I have, admittedly, tried to present the case for the continued use of this frame of reference at present—preferably, of course, the intelligent, continually self-correcting use of it.

SUPPLEMENTARY NOTES

Physiology and Learning

The contemporary alternative to the interference theory of forgetting is some kind of neural theory. Naturally, the present state of our knowledge of brain functions and their relations to behavior being what it is, neural theories of memory are none too specific. In fact, it is hard to see in exactly what way the "brain approach" is in opposition to the interference theory, though it is often presented as such.

Fundamentally, no one can deny that there must be physical changes that accompany the behavioral changes from which we infer the occurrence of learning. It is axiomatic in all of science that there can be no effect without an immediate cause. Thus, the events of yesterday, last week, and so forth can not affect today's behavior unless there is some immediate "representative" of those past events. The most reasonable guess is that the past events effect some rather permanent, although subtle, changes in an organism's structure. And since the organismic system about which we know the least is the nervous system, and its connections with behavior are the most obvious, this is the most likely candidate for the locus of such changes.

The interference theory does not rule out neural events as being important in retention. Whatever controversy there is seems mainly to center around the degree to which it is deemed necessary to understand the neural basis of retention in order to be able to comprehend the behavioral phenomena of retention. The interference theory proponents hold to the traditional behaviorist viewpoint that a thorough knowledge of S-R events is necessary before the neural links can be discovered. Physiological psychologists see the understanding of the role of the organism's structure as essential to an explanation of the S-R relationships.

No one can foresee from what line of investigation the next important breakthrough in knowledge is liable to come. Also, good scientists will nearly always follow their own talents and interests rather than the prevailing dogma. In the light of these considerations, the "physiological vs. behaviorist" controversy seems a little futile.

The advanced student of learning may regard the preceding statements as a pretty belated gesture toward open-mindedness, considering my exclusion of physiological studies relating to learning. This exclusion admittedly *has* reflected my own leanings in this matter. It has also a more objective basis. As yet, while there are many provocative lines of physiological research related to learning, there is little of a sufficiently definite nature to merit the detailed comments on the methods and interpretations of such research that would be necessary.

Unfortunately, good physiologists rarely perform good behavioral experiments. At least this has been true so far. One may hope there will be more blending of talents in the future.

*

*

*

REFERENCES

1. Adams, J.A: A source of decrement in psychomotor performance. *J. exp. Psychol.*, 1955, **49**, 390–94.

2. Adams, J.K.: Laboratory studies of behavior without awareness. *Psychol. Bull.*, 1957, **54**, 383–405.

3. Adelman, H.M., & Maatsch, J.L.: Resistance to extinction as a function of the type of response elicited by frustration. *J. exp. Psychol.*, 1955, **50**, 61–65.

4. Allport, G.W.: Scientific models and human morals. *Psychol. Rev.*, 1947, **54**, 182–92.

5. Ammons, R.B.; Farr, R.G.; Bloch, Edith; Neumann, Eva; Dey, M.; Marion, R.; & Ammons, C.H.: Long-term retention of perceptual-motor skills. *J. exp. Psychol.*, 1958, **55**, 318–28.

6. Amsel, A., & Cole, F.K.: Generalization of fear-motivated interference with water intake. *J. exp. Psychol.*, 1953, **46**, 243–47.

7. Amsel, A., & Rousell, Jacqueline: Motivational properties of frustration: I. Effect on a running response of the addition of frustration to the motivational complex. *J. exp. Psychol.*, 1952, **43**, 363–68.

8. Anderson, E.: The externalization of drive: III. Maze learning by non-rewarded and satiated rats. *J. genet. Psychol.*, 1941, **59**, 397–426.

9. Antonitis, J.J.: Response variability in the white rat during conditioning, extinction, and reconditioning. *J. exp. Psychol.*, 1951, **42**, 273–81.

421

10. Applezweig, M.H.: Response potential as a function of effort. *J. comp. physiol. Psychol.*, 1951, **44**, 225–35.

11. Arnoult, M.D.: Stimulus predifferentiation: some generalizations and hypotheses. *Psychol. Bull.*, 1957, **54**, 339–50.

12. Atkinson, R.C.: An analysis of the effect of nonreinforced trials in terms of statistical learning theory. *J. exp. Psychol.*, 1956, **52**, 28–32.

13. Azrin, N.H., & Lindsley, O.R.: The reinforcement of cooperation between children. *J. abnorm. soc. Psychol.*, 1956, **52**, 100–02.

14. Bahrick, H.P.: Latent learning as a function of the strength of unrewarded need states. *J. comp. physiol. Psychol.*, 1952, **45**, 192–97.

15. Bahrick, H.P.: Sensory preconditioning under two degrees of deprivation. *J. comp. physiol. Psychol.*, 1953, **46**, 39–42.

16. Bahwell, R., & Premack, D.: Unpublished experiment on manipulation frequency as a function of time since last exposure to the manipulandum.

17. Bailey, C.J.: The effectiveness of drives as cues. *J. comp. physiol. Psychol.*, 1955, **48**, 183–87.

18. Bakan, D.: The general and the aggregate: A methodological distinction. *Percep. & Mot. Skills*, 1955, **5**, 211–12.

19. Barnes, G.W.: Conditioned stimulus intensity and temporal factors in spaced-trial classical conditioning. *J. exp. Psychol.*, 1956, **51**, 192–98.

20. Barnes, G.W., & Kish, G.B.: On some properties of visual reinforcement. *Amer. Psychologist*, 1958, **13**, 417 (Abstract).

21. Beach, F.A.: Sexual behavior in animals and men. *The Harvey Lectures, 1947–1948.* Springfield, Ill.: Thomas, 1950.

22. Beach, F.A.: The snark was a boojum. *Amer. Psychologist*, 1950, **5**, 115–24.

23. Beach, F.A.: The descent of instinct. *Psychol. Rev.*, 1955, **62**, 401–10.

24. Beach, F.A.: Characteristics of masculine "sex drive." In Jones, M.R. (Ed.): *Nebraska symposium on motivation*, Vol. IV, Lincoln: Univer. Nebraska Press, 1956.

25. Belmont, L., & Birch, H.G.: Reindividualizing the repression hypothesis. *J. abnorm. soc. Psychol.*, 1951, **46**, 226–35.

26. Birch, D.: Discrimination learning as a function of the ratio of nonreinforced to reinforced trials. *J. comp. physiol. Psychol.*, 1955, **48**, 371–74.

27. Bitterman, M.E.; Feddersen, W.E.; & Tyler, D.W.: Secondary reinforcement and the discrimination hypothesis. *Amer. J. Psychol.*, 1953, **66**, 456–64.

28. Bitterman, M.E.; Reed, P.C.; & Kubala, A.L.: The strength of sensory preconditioning. *J. exp. Psychol.*, 1953, **46**, 178–82.

29. Blodgett, H.C.: The effect of the introduction of reward upon maze performance of rats. *Univ. Calif. Publ. Psychol.*, 1929, **4**, 113–34.

30. Bourne, L.E., & Archer, E.J.: Time continuously on target as a function of distribution of practice. *J. exp. Psychol.*, 1956, **51**, 25–33.

31. Bragiel, R.M., & Perkins, C.C., Jr.: Conditioned stimulus intensity and response speed. *J. exp. Psychol.*, 1954, **47**, 437–41.

32. Branson, R.K., & Fuchs, A.H.: Resistance to extinction of a generalized response as a function of stimulus and amount-of-reward conditions during training. Paper read at Midwestern Psychological Assoc. Meetings, 1959.

33. Braun, H.W.; Barnes, H.W.; & Patton, R.A.: Effects of electroshock convulsions upon the learning performance of monkeys: IV. Discrimination-reversal learning. *J. comp. physiol. Psychol.*, 1957, **50**, 641–43.

34. Brody, A.L.: Statistical learning theory applied to an instrumental avoidance situation. *J. exp. Psychol.*, 1957, **54**, 240–45.

35. Brogden, W.J.: The effect of frequency of reinforcement upon the level of conditioning. *J. exp. Psychol.*, 1939, **24**, 419–31.

36. Brogden, W.J.: Sensory preconditioning. *J. exp. Psychol.*, 1939, **25**, 323–32.

37. Brogden, W.J.: Sensory preconditioning of human subjects. *J. exp. Psychol.*, 1947, **37**, 527–40.

38. Brown, J.S., & Farber, I.E.: Emotions conceptualized as interven-

ing variables—with suggestions toward a theory of frustration. *Psychol. Bull.*, 1951, **48**, 465–95.

39. Brown, W.L., & Gentry, G.: The effect of intra-maze delay. II. Various intervals of delay. *J. comp. physiol. Psychol.*, 1948, **41**, 403–07.

40. Brown, W.L.; Gentry, G.; & Kaplan, S.J.: The effect of intra-maze delay. I. Delay enforced by a revolving wheel. *J. comp. physiol. Psychol.*, 1948, **41**, 258–68.

41. Bruce, R.H.: The effect of lessening drive upon performance by white rats in the maze. *J. comp. Psychol.*, 1938, **25**, 225–48.

42. Bruce, R.W.: Conditions of transfer of training. *J. exp. Psychol.*, 1933, **16**, 343–61.

43. Bugelski, B.R., & Scharlock, D.P.: An experimental demonstration of unconscious mediated association. *J. exp. Psychol.*, 1952, **44**, 334–38.

44. Butler, R.A.: Discrimination learning by rhesus monkeys to visual-exploration motivation. *J. comp. physiol. Psychol.*, 1953, **46**, 95–98.

45. Butler, R.A.: Incentive conditions which influence visual exploration. *J. exp. Psychol.*, 1954, **48**, 19–23.

46. Calvin, J.S.; Bicknell, Elizabeth; & Sperling, D.S.: Establishment of a conditioned drive based on the hunger drive. *J. comp. physiol. Psychol.*, 1953, **46**, 173–75.

47. Campbell, B.A., & Kraeling, Doris: Response strength as a function of drive level and amount of drive reduction. *J. exp. Psychol.*, 1953, **45**, 97–101.

48. Campbell, B.A., & Kraeling, Doris: Response strength as a function of drive level during training and extinction. *J. comp. physiol. Psychol.*, 1954, **47**, 101–03.

49. Chambers, R.M.: Some physiological bases for reinforcing properties of reward injections. *J. comp. physiol. Psychol.*, 1956, **49**, 565–68.

50. Cheng, N.Y.: Retroactive effect and degree of similarity. *J. exp. Psychol.*, 1929, **12**, 444–58.

51. Christie, R.: The effect of some early experience in the latent learning of adult rats. *J. exp. Psychol.*, 1952, **43**, 281–88.

52. Collier, G., & Marx, M.H.: Frustration and performance. *Amer. Psychologist*, 1957, **12**, 458 (Abstract).

53. Coppock, H.W.: Stimuli preceding electric shock can acquire positive reinforcing properties. *J. comp. physiol. Psychol.*, 1954, **47**, 109–13.

54. Coppock, H.W., & Chambers, R.M.: Reinforcement of position-preference by automatic intravenous injections of glucose. *J. comp. physiol. Psychol.*, 1954, **47**, 355–57.

55. Cotton, J.W.: Running time as a function of amount of food deprivation. *J. exp. Psychol.*, 1953, **46**, 188–98.

56. Crespi, L.P.: Quantitative variation of incentive and performance in the white rat. *Amer. J. Psychol.*, 1942, **55**, 467–517.

57. D'Amato, M.R.: Secondary reinforcement and magnitude of primary reinforcement. *J. comp. physiol. Psychol.*, 1955, **48**, 378–80.

58. Danziger, K.: The operation of an acquired drive in satiated rats. *Quart. J. exp. Psychol.*, 1951, **3**, 119–32.

59. Deese, J.: The extinction of a discrimination without performance of the choice response, *J. comp. physiol. Psychol.*, 1951, **44**, 362–66.

60. Deese, J., & Carpenter, J.A.: Drive level and reinforcement. *J. exp. Psychol.*, 1951, **42**, 236–38.

61. Dember, W.N., & Earl, R.W.: Analysis of exploratory, manipulatory, and curiosity behaviors. *Psychol. Rev.*, 1957, **64**, 91–96.

62. Denny, M.R., & Dunham, M.D.: The effect of differential nonreinforcement of the incorrect response on the learning of the correct response in the simple T-maze. *J. exp. Psychol.*, 1951, **41**, 382–89.

63. Denny, M.R.; Wells, Ruth H.; & Maatsch, J.L.: Resistance to extinction as a function of the discrimination habit established during fixed-ratio reinforcement. *J. exp. Psychol.*, 1957, **54**, 451–56.

64. Desiderato, O.: The interaction of several variables in latent learning. *J. exp. Psychol.*, 1956, **52**, 244–51.

65. Dinsmoor, J.A.: A quantitative comparison of the discriminative and reinforcing properties of a stimulus. *J. exp. Psychol.*, 1950, **40**, 473–87.

66. Dollard, J.; Doob, L.W.; Miller, N.E.; Mowrer, O.H.; & Sears, R.R.: *Frustration and aggression.* New Haven: Yale Univer. Press, 1939.

67. Eccher, W., & Culler, E.: Reciprocal facilitation of the conditioned and conditioning mechanisms. *J. comp. physiol. Psychol.*, 1941, **31**, 223–31.

68. Eisman, E.; Asimow, Adele; & Maltzman, I.: Habit strength as a function of drive in a brightness discrimination problem. *J. exp. Psychol.*, 1956, **52**, 58–64.

69. Elam, C.B.; Bitterman, M.E.; & Tyler, D.W.: A further study of secondary reinforcement and the discrimination hypothesis. *J. comp. physiol. Psychol.*, 1954, **47**, 381–84.

70. Ellson, D.G.: Spontaneous recovery of the galvanic skin response as a function of the recovery interval. *J. exp. Psychol.*, 1939, **25**, 586–600.

71. Estes, W.K.: An experimental study of punishment. *Psychol. Monogr.*, 1944, **57**, No. 263.

72. Estes, W.K., & Burke, C.J.: A theory of stimulus variability in learning. *Psychol. Rev.*, 1953, **60**, 276–86.

73. Farber, I.E.: The role of motivation in verbal learning and performance. *Psychol. Bull.*, 1955, **52**, 311–27.

74. Ferster, C.B.: Sustained behavior under delayed reinforcement. *J. exp. Psychol.*, 1953, **45**, 218–24.

75. Ferster, C.B., & Skinner, B.F.: *Schedules of reinforcement.* New York: Appleton-Century-Crofts, 1957.

76. Finch, G.: Chimpanzee frustration responses. *Psychosom. Med.*, 1942, **4**, 233–51.

77. Finch, G., & Culler, E.: Higher order conditioning with constant motivation. *Amer. J. Psychol.*, 1934, **46**, 596–602.

78. Fitzwater, M.E.: The relative effect of reinforcement and nonreinforcement in establishing a form discrimination. *J. comp. physiol. Psychol.*, 1952, **45**, 476–81.

79. Fitzwater, M.E., & Thrush, R.S.: Acquisition of a conditioned response as a function of forward temporal contiguity. *J. exp. Psychol.*, 1956, **51**, 59–61.

80. Frankmann, Judith P.: Effect of amount of interpolated learning and time interval before test on retention in rats. *J. exp. Psychol.* 1957, **54**, 462–66.

81. Furchtgott, H.E., & Rubin, R.D.: The effect of magnitude of reward on maze learning in the white rat. *J. comp. physiol. Psychol.*, 1953, **46**, 9–12.

82. Gagne, R.M.: The retention of a conditioned operant response. *J. exp. Psychol.*, 1941, **29**, 296–305.

83. Gantt, W.H.: The nervous secretion of saliva: The relation of the conditioned reflex to the intensity of the unconditioned stimulus. *Proc. Amer. Physiol. Soc., Amer. J. Physiol.*, 1938, **123**, 74.

84. Geier, F.M., & Tolman, E.C.: Goal distance and restless activity. I. The goal gradient of restless activity. *J. comp. Psychol.*, 1943, **35**, 297–304.

85. Gibson, Eleanor J.: Intra-list generalization as a factor in verbal learning. *J. exp. Psychol.*, 1942, **30**, 185–200.

86. Gleitman, H.: Place learning without prior performance. *J. comp. physiol. Psychol.*, 1955, **48**, 77–79.

87. Goodson, F.E., & Brownstein, A.: Secondary reinforcing and motivation properties of stimuli contiguous with shock onset and termination. *J. comp. physiol. Psychol.*, 1955, **48**, 381–86.

88. Goodson, F.E.; Scarborough, B.B.; & Lewis, G.W.: Expectancy and the extinction of expectancy in the rat. *J. comp. physiol. Psychol.*, 1957, **50**, 563–66.

89. Goss, A.E., & Rabaioli, E.J.: Response strength in a modified Thorndikian multiple-choice situation as a function of varying proportions of reinforcement. *J. exp. Psychol.*, 1952, **43**, 106–14.

90. Graham, C.H., & Gagne, R.M.: The acquisition, extinction, and spontaneous recovery of a conditioned operant response. *J. exp. Psychol.*, 1940, **26**, 251–80.

91. Greenspoon, J.: The reinforcing effect of two spoken sounds on the frequency of two responses. *Amer. J. Psychol.*, 1955, **68**, 409–16.

92. Greenspoon, J., & Foreman, Sally: Effect of delay of knowledge of results on learning a motor task. *J. exp. Psychol.*, 1956, **51**, 226–28.

93. Grice, G.R.: The relation of secondary reinforcement to delayed reward in visual discrimination learning. *J. exp. Psychol.*, 1948, **38**, 1–16.

94. Grice, G.R., & Goldman, H.M.: Generalized extinction and secondary reinforcement in visual discrimination learning with delayed reward. *J. exp. Psychol.*, 1955, **50**, 197–200.

95. Grice, G.R., & Saltz, E.: The generalization of an instrumental response to stimuli varying in the size dimension. *J. exp. Psychol.*, 1950, **40**, 702–08.

96. Guthrie, E.R.: *The psychology of learning* (Rev. ed.). New York: Harper, 1952.

97. Guttman, N.: Operant conditioning, extinction, and periodic reinforcement in relation to concentration of sucrose used as a reinforcing agent. *J. exp. Psychol.*, 1953, **46**, 213–24.

98. Guttman, N.: The pigeon and the spectrum and other perplexities. *Psychol. Rep.*, 1956, **2**, 449–60.

99. Guttman, N., & Kalish, H.I.: Discriminability and stimulus generalization. *J. exp. Psychol.*, 1956, **51**, 79–88.

100. Hall, J.F.: Studies in secondary reinforcement: I. Secondary reinforcement as a function of the frequency of primary reinforcement. *J. comp. physiol. Psychol.*, 1951, **44**, 246–51.

101. Hamilton, W.F., & Coleman, T.B.: Trichromatic vision in the pigeon as illustrated by the spectral discrimination curve. *J. comp. Psychol.*, 1933, **15**, 183–91.

102. Harker, G.S.: Delay of reward and performance of an instrumental response. *J. exp. Psychol.*, 1956, **51**, 303–10.

103. Harlow, H.F.: The formation of learning sets. *Psychol. Rev.*, 1949, **56**, 51–65.

104. Harlow, H.F.: Learning and satiation of response in intrinsically motivated complex puzzle performance by monkeys. *J. comp. physiol. Psychol.*, 1950, **43**, 289–94.

105. Harlow, H.F.: Mice, monkeys, men, and motives. *Psychol. Rev.*, 1953, **60**, 23–32.

106. Harlow, H.F.; Blazek, Nancy C.; & McClearn, G.E.: Manipulatory motivation in the infant Rhesus monkey. *J. comp. physiol. Psychol.*, 1956, **49**, 444–48.

107. Harlow, H.F.; Harlow, Margaret K.; & Meyer, D.R.: Learning motivated by a manipulation drive. *J. exp. Psychol.*, 1950, 40, 228–34.

108. Harlow, H.F., & Hicks, L.H.: Discrimination learning theory: Uniprocess vs. duoprocess. *Psychol. Rev.*, 1957, 64, 104–09.

109. Hebb, D.O.: On the nature of fear. *Psychol. Rev.*, 1946, 53, 259–76.

110. Hebb, D.O.: *The organization of behavior*. New York: John Wiley & Sons, 1949.

111. Hilgard, E.R.: *Theories of learning* (1st Ed.). New York: Appleton-Century-Crofts, 1948.

112. Hillman, Beverly; Hunter, W.S.; & Kimble, G.A.: The effect of drive level on the maze performance of the white rat. *J. comp. physiol. Psychol.*, 1953, 46, 87–89.

113. Holder, W.B.; Marx, M.H.; Holder, Elaine E.; & Collier, G.: Response strength as a function of delay of reward in a runway. *J. exp. Psychol.*, 1957, 53, 316–23.

114. Holland, J.G.: Human vigilance. *Science*, 1958, 128, 61–67.

115. Homme, L.E.: Spontaneous recovery and statistical learning theory. *J. exp. Psychol.*, 1956, 51, 205–12.

116. Hopkins, C.O.: Effectiveness of secondary reinforcing stimuli as a function of the quantity and quality of food reinforcement. *J. exp. Psychol.*, 1955, 50, 339–42.

117. Hovland, C.I.: The generalization of conditioned responses: I. The sensory generalization of conditioned responses with varying frequencies of tone. *J. gen. Psychol.*, 1937, 17, 125–48.

118. Hovland, C.I.: The generalization of conditioned responses: III. Extinction, spontaneous recovery, and disinhibition of conditioned and generalized responses. *J. exp. Psychol.*, 1937, 21, 47–62.

119. Hovland, C.I.: Experimental studies in rote-learning theory: II. Reminiscence with varying speeds of syllable presentation. *J. exp. Psychol.*, 1938, 22, 338–53.

120. Hovland, C.I.: Experimental studies in rote-learning theory. VI. Comparison of retention following learning to same criterion by massed and distributed practice. *J. exp. Psychol.*, 1940, 26, 568–87.

121. Hovland, C.I.: Human learning and retention. In Stevens, S.S. (Ed.): *Handbook of experimental psychology*. New York: John Wiley & Sons, 1951.

122. Hubbard, W.R.: Secondary reinforcement of a simple discrimination in human beings. *J. exp. Psychol.*, 1951, **41**, 233–41.

123. Hull, C.L.: Differential habituation to internal stimuli in the albino rat. *J. comp. Psychol.*, 1933, **16**, 255–73.

124. Hull, C.L.: *Principles of behavior*. New York: Appleton-Century, 1943.

125. Hull, C.L.: Stimulus intensity dynamism (V) and stimulus generalization. *Psychol. Rev.*, 1949, **56**, 67–76.

126. Huxley, A.L.: *Brave new world*. Garden City, N.Y.: Doubleday, Doran, 1932.

126a. Isaacs, W.; Thomas, J.; & Goldiamond, I.: Application of operant conditioning to reinstate verbal behavior in psychotics. *J. Speech & Hearing Disord.* (In press, 1959.)

127. Jahnke, J.C.: Retention in motor learning as a function of amount of practice and rest. *J. exp. Psychol.*, 1958, **55**, 270–73.

128. Jaynes, J.: Imprinting: The interaction of learned and innate behavior: I. Development and generalization. *J. comp. physiol. Psychol.*, 1956, **49**, 201–06.

129. Jaynes, J.: Imprinting: The interaction of learned and innate behavior: II. The critical period. *J. comp. physiol. Psychol.*, 1957, **50**, 6–10.

130. Jaynes, J.: Imprinting: The interaction of learned and innate behavior: III. Practice effects on performance, retention, and fear. *J. comp. physiol. Psychol.*, 1958, **51**, 234–37.

131. Jaynes, J.: Imprinting: The interaction of learned and innate behavior: IV. Generalization and emergent discrimination. *J. comp. physiol. Psychol.*, 1958, **51**, 238–42.

132. Jenkins, J.G., & Dallenbach, K.M.: Oblivescence during sleep and waking. *Amer. J. Psychol.*, 1924, **35**, 605–12.

133. Jenkins, T.N.; Warner, L.H.; & Warden, C.J.: Standard apparatus for the study of animal motivation. *J. comp. Psychol.*, 1926, **6**, 361–82.

134. Johnsgard, K.W.: The role of contrast in stimulus intensity dynamism (V). *J. exp. Psychol.*, 1957, **53**, 173–79.

135. Johnson, L.M.: The relative effect of a time interval upon learning and retention. *J. exp. Psychol.*, 1939, **24**, 169–79.

136. Kalish, H.I.: Strength of fear as a function of the number of acquisition and extinction trials. *J. exp. Psychol.*, 1954, **47**, 1–9.

137. Kanfer, F.H.: The effect of partial reinforcement on acquisition and extinction of a class of verbal responses. *J. exp. Psychol.*, 1954, **48**, 424–32.

138. Kanfer, F.H.: Effect of a warning signal preceding a noxious stimulus on verbal rate and heart rate. *J. exp. Psychol.*, 1958, **55**, 73–80.

139. Kanner, J.H.: A test of whether the "nonrewarded" animals learned as much as the "rewarded" animals in the California latent learning study. *J. exp. Psychol.*, 1954, **48**, 175–83.

140. Karn, H.W.: Sensory preconditioning and incidental learning in human subjects. *J. exp. Pyschol.*, 1947, **37**, 540–45.

141. Kelleher, R.T.: Intermittent conditioned reinforcement in chimpanzees. *Science*, 1956, **124**, 679–80.

142. Kelleher, R.T.: Conditioned reinforcement in chimpanzees. *J. comp. physiol. Psychol.*, 1957, **50**, 571–75.

143. Keller, F. S.: The phantom plateau. *J. exp. anal. behav.*, 1958, **1**, 1–13.

144. Kendler, H.H.: The influence of simultaneous hunger and thirst drives upon the learning of two opposed spatial responses of the white rat. *J. exp. Psychol.*, 1946, **36**, 212–20.

145. Kendler, H.H., & Levine, S.: A more sensitive test of irrelevant-incentive learning under conditions of satiation. *J. comp. physiol. Psychol.*, 1953, **46**, 271–73.

146. Kessen, W.: Response strength and conditioned stimulus intensity. *J. exp. Psychol.*, 1953, **45**, 82–86.

147. Kimble, G.A.: Conditioning as a function of the time between conditioned and unconditioned stimuli. *J. exp. Psychol.*, 1947, **37**, 1–15.

148. Kimble, G.A.: Performance and reminiscence in motor learning as

a function of the degree of distribution of practice. *J. exp. Psychol.*, 1949, **39**, 500–10.

149. Kimble, G.A.: Shock intensity and avoidance learning. *J. comp. physiol. Psychol.*, 1955, **48**, 281–84.

150. Kimble, G.A., & Horenstein, Betty R.: Reminiscence in motor learning as a function of length of interpolated rest. *J. exp. Psychol.*, 1948, **38**, 239–44.

151. Kish, G.B.: Avoidance learning to the onset and cessation of conditioned stimulus energy. *J. exp. Psychol.*, 1955, **50**, 31–38.

152. Koch, Margaret B., & Meyer, D.R.: A relationship of mental age to learning set formation in the pre-school child. *J. comp. physiol. Psychol.*, 1959, **52**, 387–89.

153. Köhler, W.: *Gestalt psychology.* New York: Liveright, 1929.

154. Krasner, L.: Studies of the conditioning of verbal behavior. *Psychol. Bull.*, 1958, **55**, 148–70.

155. Krueger, W.C.F.: The effect of overlearning on retention. *J. exp. Psychol.*, 1929, **12**, 71–78.

156. Kuenne, Margaret R.: Experimental investigation of the relation of language to transposition behavior in young children. *J. exp. Psychol.*, 1946, **36**, 471–90.

157. La Berge, D.L., & Smith, Adrienne: Selective sampling in discrimination learning. *J. exp. Psychol.*, 1957, **54**, 423–30.

158. Lawson, R.: Amount of primary reward and strength of secondary reward. *J. exp. Psychol.*, 1953, **46**, 183–87.

159. Lawson, R.: Brightness discrimination performance and secondary reward strength as a function of primary reward amount. *J. comp. physiol. Psychol.*, 1957, **50**, 35–39.

160. Lawson, R., & Brownstein, A.J.: The effect of effort and training-test similarity on resistance to extinction. *Amer. J. Psychol.*, 1957, **70**, 123–25.

161. Lawson, R.; Cross, H.A.; & Tambe, J.T.: Effects of large and small rewards on maze learning after different prior experiences with reward amounts. Paper read at Midwestern Psychological Assoc. meetings, Chicago, 1959.

162. Lawson, R., & Dawson, D.R.: Seward's "Test of Guthrie's Theory"

refined. Paper read at Midwestern Psychol. Assoc. meetings, Detroit, 1958.

163. Lawson, R., & Marx, M.H.: Frustration: Theory and experiment. *Genet. Psychol. Monogr.*, 1958, **57**, 393–464.

164. Leavitt, H.J., & Schlosberg, H.: The retention of verbal and motor skills. *J. exp. Psychol.*, 1944, **34**, 404–17.

165. Leeper, R.: The role of motivation in learning: a study of the phenomenon of differential motivational control of the utilization of habits. *J. genet. Psychol.*, 1935, **46**, 3–40.

166. Lester, O.P.: Mental set in relation to retroactive inhibition. *J. exp. Psychol.*, 1932, **15**, 681–99.

167. Levy, N.: An experimental comparison of secondary inhibition and secondary reinforcement. *J. comp. physiol. Psychol.*, 1957, **50**, 29–34.

168. Lewin, K.: Environmental forces in child behavior and development. In C. Murchison (Ed.), *A handbook of child psychology.* Worcester: Clark Univ. Press, 1931.

169. Lewis, D.J., & Duncan, C.P.: Expectation and resistance to extinction of a lever-pulling response as functions of percentage of reinforcement and amount of reward. *J. exp. Psychol.*, 1957, **54**, 115–20.

170. Liddell, H.S.: Conditioned reflex method and experimental neurosis. In Hunt, J. McV. (Ed.), *Personality and the behavior disorders*, Vol. I. New York: Ronald Press, 1944.

171. Logan, F.A.; Beier, Eileen M.; & Kincaid, W.D.: Extinction following partial and varied reinforcement. *J. exp. Psychol.*, 1956, **52**, 65–70.

172. Lorenz, K.: Der Kumpen in Der Umwelt des Vogels. *J. Orn., Lpzg.*, 1933, **83**, 137–213.

173. Loucks, R.B.: The experimental delimitation of neural structures essential for learning: The attempt to condition striped muscle responses with faradization of the sigmoid gyri. *J. Psychol.*, 1935, **1**, 5–44.

174. Luh, C.W.: The conditions of retention. *Psychol. Monogr.*, 1922, **31**, No. 3 (Whole No. 142).

175. Maatsch, J.L.; Adelman, H.M.; & Denny, M.R.: Effort and resist-

ance to extinction of the bar-pressing response. *J. comp. physiol. Psychol.*, 1954, **47**, 47–50.

176. MacCorquodale, K., & Meehl, P.E.: On a distinction between hypothetical constructs and intervening variables. *Psychol. Rev.*, 1948, **55**, 95–107.

177. Mackintosh, Irene: The resistance to extinction of responses acquired under irregular conditions of learning. *J. comp. physiol. Psychol.*, 1955, **48**, 363–70.

178. Margolius, G.: Stimulus generalization of an instrumental response as a function of the number of reinforced trials. *J. exp. Psychol.*, 1955, **49**, 105–11.

179. Marx, M.H.: Intervening variable or hypothetical construct? *Psychol. Rev.*, 1951, **58**, 235–47.

180. Marx, M.H.: Spread of effect: A critical review. *Genet. Psychol. Monogr.*, 1956, **53**, 119–86.

181. Marx, M.H.: Gradients of error reinforcement in normal multiple-choice situations. *J. exp. Psychol.*, 1957, **54**, 225–28.

181a. Marx, M.H.: Some relations between frustration and drive. In Jones, M.E. (Ed.), *Nebraska symposium on motivation*, Vol. IV. Lincoln, Neb.: Nebraska Univ. Press, 1956.

182. Marx, M.H., & Goldbeck, R.A.: Error reinforcement in a modified serial perceptual-motor task. *J. exp. Psychol.*, 1957, **54**, 288–91.

183. Marzocco, F.M.: Frustration effect as a function of drive level, habit strength and distribution of trials during extinction. Unpublished doctor's dissertation, State Univ. Iowa, 1950.

184. McNamara, H.H.; Long, J.B.; & Wike, E.L.: Learning without response under two conditions of external cues. *J. comp. physiol. Psychol.*, 1956, **49**, 477–80.

185. Meyer, D.R.: The effects of differential rewards on discrimination reversal learning by monkeys. *J. exp. Psychol.*, 1951, **41**, 268–74.

186. Michels, K.M.: The effects of fixed-ratio random reinforcement on the response latency of monkeys. *J. comp. physiol. Psychol.*, 1955, **48**, 32–36.

187. Miles, R.C., & Meyer, D.R.: Learning sets in marmosets. *J. comp. physiol. Psychol.*, 1956, **49**, 219–22.

188. Miller, N.E.: Experimental studies of conflict. In Hunt, J. McV. (Ed.), *Personality and the behavior disorders*, Vol. I. New York: Ronald Press, 1944.

189. Miller, N.E.: Studies of fear as an acquirable drive: I. Fear as motivation and fear-reduction as reinforcement in the learning of new responses. *J. exp. Psychol.*, 1948, 38, 89–101.

190. Miller, N.E., & Kraeling, Doris: Displacement: Greater generalization of approach than avoidance in a generalized approach-avoidance conflict. *J. exp. Psychol.*, 1952, 43, 217–21.

191. Mitrano, A.J.: The principles of conditioning in human goal behavior. *Psychol. Monogr.*, 1939, 51, No. 4.

192. Moltz, H.: Latent extinction and the fractional anticipatory response mechanism. *Psychol. Rev.*, 1957, 64, 229–41.

193. Montgomery, K.C.; The relation between fear induced by novel stimulation and exploratory behavior. *J. comp. physiol. Psychol.*, 1955, 48, 254–60.

194. Morgan, C.T., & Fields, P.E.: The effect of variable preliminary feeding upon the rat's speed of locomotion. *J. comp. Psychol.*, 1938, 26, 331–48.

195. Mowrer, O.H.: Preparatory set (expectancy)—some methods of measurement. *Psychol. Monogr.*, 1940, 52, No. 2.

196. Mowrer, O.H.: On the dual nature of learning: A reinterpretation of "conditioning" and "problem-solving." *Harv. educ. Rev.*, 1947, 17, 102–48.

197. Mowrer, O.H.: Two-factor learning theory reconsidered, with special reference to secondary reinforcement and the concept of habit. *Psychol. Rev.* 1956, 63, 114–28.

198. Mowrer, O.H., & Jones, Helen M.: Extinction and behavior variability as functions of effortfulness of task. *J. exp. Psychol.*, 1943, 33, 369–86.

199. Murdock, B.B., Jr.: Transfer designs and formulas. *Psychol. Bull.*, 1957, 54, 313–26.

199a. Murdock, B.B., Jr.: "Backward" associations in transfer and learning. *J. exp. Psychol.*, 1958, 55, 111–14.

200. Neimark, Edith, & Saltzman, I.J.: Intentional and incidental learn-

ing with different rates of stimulus-presentation. *Amer. J. Psychol.*, 1953, **66**, 618–21.

201. Olds, J.F.: Physiological mechanisms of reward. In Jones, M.R. (Ed.), *Nebraska symposium on motivation: 1955*, Vol. III. Lincoln: Univ. Nebraska Press, 1955.

202. Osgood, C.E.: The similarity paradox in human learning: a resolution. *Psychol. Rev.*, 1949, **56**, 132–43.

203. Osgood, C.E.: *Method and theory in experimental psychology.* New York: Oxford Univ. Press, 1953.

204. Pavlov, I.P.: *Conditioned reflexes* (trans. by G.V. Anrep). London: Oxford Univ. Press, 1927.

205. Pavlov, I.P.: *Experimental psychology and other essays.* New York: Philosophical Library, 1957.

206. Perin, C.T.: A quantitative investigation of the delay-of-reinforcement gradient. *J. exp. Psychol.*, 1943, **32**, 37–51.

207. Perkins, C.C., Jr.: The relation between conditioned stimulus intensity and response strength. *J. exp. Psychol.*, 1953, **46**, 225–31.

208. Perkins, C.C., Jr.: Stimulus generalization. *Amer. Psychologist*, 1958, **13**, 391.

209. Perkins, M.J.; Banks, H.P.; & Calvin, A.D.: The effect of delay on simultaneous and successive discrimination in children. *J. exp. Psychol.*, 1954, **48**, 416–18.

210. Plenderleith, Mavis, & Postman, L.: Discriminative and verbal habits in incidental learning. *Amer. J. Psychol.*, 1956, **69**, 236–43.

211. Postman, L.; Adams, Pauline A.; and Phillips, Laura W.: Studies in incidental learning: II. The effects of association value and the method of testing. *J. exp. Psychol.*, 1955, **49**, 1–10.

212. Postman, L., & Senders, Virginia L.: Incidental learning and generality of set. *J. exp. Psychol.*, 1946, **36**, 153–65.

213. Postman, L., & Tuma, A.H.: Latent learning in human subjects. *Amer. J. Psychol.*, 1954, **67**, 119–23.

214. Powell, D.R., Jr., & Perkins, C.C., Jr.: Strength of secondary reinforcement as a determiner of effects of duration of goal responses on learning. *J. exp. Psychol.*, 1957, **53**, 106–12.

215. Proceedings of the Association for the study of animal behavior. *Brit. J. Animal Behaviour*, 1955, **1**, 35–38.

216. Razran, G.H.S.: Conditioned responses in animals other than dogs. *Psychol. Bull.*, 1933, **30**, 261–324.

217. Razran, G.: Backward conditioning. *Psychol. Bull.*, 1956, **53**, 55–69.

218. Reinhold, D.B., & Perkins, C.C., Jr.: Stimulus generalization following different methods of training. *J. exp. Psychol.*, 1955, **49**, 423–27.

219. Restle, F.: Discrimination of cues in mazes: A resolution of the "place-vs.-response" question. *Psychol. Rev.*, 1957, **64**, 217–28.

220. Reynolds, B.: The acquisition of a trace-conditioned response as a function of the magnitude of the stimulus trace. *J. exp. Psychol.*, 1945, **35**, 15–30.

221. Reynolds, B.: The acquisition of a black-white discrimination habit under two levels of reinforcement. *J. exp. Psychol.*, 1949, **39**, 760–69.

222. Reynolds, B.: Acquisition of a simple spatial discrimination as a function of the amount of reinforcement. *J. exp. Psychol.*, 1950, **40**, 152–60.

223. Reynolds, B.: Resistance to extinction as a function of the amount of reinforcement present during acquisition. *J. exp. Psychol.*, 1950, **40**, 46–52.

224. Reynolds, B.; Marx, M.H.; & Henderson, R.L.: Resistance to extinction as a function of drive-reward interaction. *J. comp. physiol. Psychol.*, 1952, **45**, 36–42.

225. Reynolds, R.W.: The relationship between stimulation voltage and rate of hypothalamic self-stimulation in the rat. *J. comp. physiol. Psychol.*, 1958, **51**, 193–98.

226. Reynolds, W.F.: Acquisition and extinction of the conditioned eyelid response following partial and continuous reinforcement. *J. exp. Psychol.*, 1958, **55**, 335–41.

227. Saltzman, I.J.: Maze learning in the absence of primary reinforcement: A study of secondary reinforcement. *J. comp. physiol. Psychol.*, 1949, **42**, 161–73.

228. Saltzman, I.J.: The orienting task in incidental and intentional learning. *Amer. J. Psychol.*, 1953, **66**, 593–97.

229. Saltzman, I.J.: Comparisons of incidental and intentional learning with different orienting tasks. *Amer. J. Psychol.*, 1956, **69**, 274–77.

230. Saltzman, I.J., & Atkinson, Rita L.: Comparisons of incidental and international learning after different rates of stimulus presentation. *Amer. J. Psychol.*, 1954, **67**, 521–23.

231. Sarason, I.G.; Sarason, Barbara R.; Miller, Marilyn; & Mahmoud, P.: The role of the intertrial interval in discrimination and reversal learning. *J. comp. physiol. Psychol.*, 1956, **49**, 77–79.

232. Schoenfeld, W.N.; Antonitis, J.J.; & Bersh, P.J.: A preliminary study of training conditions necessary for secondary reinforcement. *J. exp. Psychol.*, 1950, **40**, 40–48.

233. Schrier, A.M.: Amount of incentive and performance on a black-white discrimination problem. *J. comp. physiol. Psychol.*, 1956, **49**, 123–25.

234. Schrier, A.M., & Harlow, H.F.: Effect of amount of incentive on discrimination learning by monkeys. *J. comp. physiol. Psychol.*, 1956, **49**, 117–21.

235. Schwartz, M.: Conditioned-stimulus variables in avoidance learning. *J. exp. Psychol.*, 1958, **55**, 347–51.

236. Seward, J.P.: An experimental test of Guthrie's theory of reinforcement. *J. exp. Psychol.*, 1942, **30**, 247–56.

237. Seward, J.P.: An experimental analysis of latent learning. *J. exp. Psychol.*, 1949, **39**, 177–86.

238. Sheffield, F.D.; Wulff, J.J.; & Backer, R.: Reward value of copulation without sex drive reduction. *J. comp. physiol. Psychol.*, 1951, **44**, 3–8.

239. Sheffield, Virginia F.: Resistance to extinction as a function of the distribution of extinction trials. *J. exp. Psychol.*, 1950, **40**, 305–13.

240. Sidman, M.: A note on functional relations obtained from group data. *Psychol. Bull.*, 1952, **49**, 263–69.

241. Sidman, M., & Boren, J.J.: The use of shock-contingent variations

in response-shock intervals for the maintenance of avoidance behavior. *J. comp. physiol. Psychol.*, 1957, **50**, 558–62.

242. Sidowski, J.B.: Reward and punishment in a minimal social situation. *J. exp. Psychol.*, 1957, **54**, 318–26.

243. Siegel, P.S., & MacDonnel, M.F.: A repetition of the Calvin-Bicknell-Sperling study of conditioned drive. *J. comp. physiol. Psychol.*, 1954, **47**, 250–52.

244. Silver, C.A., & Meyer, D.R.: Temporal factors in sensory preconditioning. *J. comp. physiol. Psychol.*, 1954, **47**, 57–59.

245. Simon, C., & Emmons, W.H.: Learning during sleep? *Psychol. Bull.*, 1955, **52**, 328–42.

246. Simon, C., & Emmons, W.H.: Responses to material presented during various levels of sleep. *J. exp. Psychol.*, 1956, **51**, 89–97.

247. Skinner, B.F.: *The behavior of organisms*. New York: Appleton-Century, 1938.

248. Skinner, B.F.: "Superstition" in the pigeon. *J. exp. Psychol.*, 1948, **38**, 168–72.

249. Skinner, B.F.: The science of learning and the art of teaching. In *Current trends in psychology and the behavioral sciences*. Pittsburgh: Univ. Pittsburgh Press, 1954.

250. Skinner, B.F.: A case history in scientific method. *Amer. Psychologist*, 1956, **11**, 221–33.

251. Skinner, B.F.: *Verbal behavior*. New York: Appleton-Century-Crofts, 1957.

252. Solomon, R.L.: The influence of work on behavior. *Psychol. Bull.*, 1948, **45**, 1–40.

253. Spence, K.W.: The differential response in animals to stimuli varying within a single dimension. *Psychol. Rev.*, 1937, **44**, 430–44.

254. Spence, K.W.: The role of secondary reinforcement in delayed reward learning. *Psychol. Rev.*, 1947, **54**, 1–8.

255. Spence, K.W.: The postulates and methods of "behaviorism." *Psychol. Rev.*, 1948, **55**, 67–78.

256. Spence, K.W.: Learning and performance in eyelid conditioning as a function of intensity of the UCS. *J. exp. Psychol.*, 1953, **45**, 57–63.

257. Spence, K.W., & Norris, Eugenia B.: Eyelid conditioning as a function of the intertrial interval. *J. exp. Psychol.*, 1950, **40**, 716–20.

258. Spiker, C.C.: Effects of stimulus similarity on discrimination learning. *J. exp. Psychol.*, 1956, **51**, 393–95.

259. Spooner, A., & Kellogg, W.N.: The backward conditioning curve. *Amer. J. Psychol.*, 1947, **60**, 321–34.

260. Stanley, W.C.: Extinction as a function of the spacing of extinction trials. *J. exp. Psychol.*, 1952, **43**, 249–60.

261. Starkweather, J.A., and Duncan, C.P.: A test for conditioned inhibition in motor learning. *J. exp. Psychol.*, 1954, **47**, 351–56.

262. Stevenson, H.W.: Latent learning in children. *J. exp. Psychol.*, 1954, **47**, 17–21.

263. Taylor, Janet A.: The relationship of anxiety to the conditioned eyelid response. *J. exp. Psychol.*, 1951, **41**, 81–92.

264. Taylor, Janet A.: Drive theory and manifest anxiety. *Psychol. Bull.*, 1956, **53**, 303–20.

265. Terrell, G., Jr., & Kennedy, W.A.: Discrimination learning and tranposition in children as a function of the nature of the reward. *J. exp. Psychol.*, 1957, **53**, 257–60.

266. Thistlethwaite, D.: A critical review of latent learning and related experiments. *Psychol. Bull.*, 1951, **48**, 97–129.

267. Thorndike, E.L.: Animal intelligence: An experimental study of the associative processes in animals. *Psychol. Monogr.* 1898, **2**, No. 8.

268. Tinklepaugh, O.L.: Multiple delayed reaction with chimpanzees and monkeys. *J. comp. Psychol.*, 1932, **13**, 207–43.

269. Tolman, E.C.: Operational behaviorism and current trends in psychology. In *Proc. 25th Anniv. Celebr. Inaug. Grad. Stud.* Los Angeles: Univ. South. Calif. Press, 1936, 89–103.

270. Tolman, E.C., & Gleitman, H.: Studies in Learning & Motivation: I. Equal reinforcements in both end-boxes, followed by shock in one end-box. *J. exp. Psychol.*, 1949, **39**, 810–19.

271. Tolman, E.C.; Ritchie, B.F.; & Kalish, D.: Studies in spatial learning: II. Place learning versus response learning. *J. exp. Psychol.*, 1946, **36**, 221–29.

272. Underwood, B.J.: Studies of distributed practice: VII. Learning and retention of serial nonsense lists as a function of intralist similarity. *J. exp. Psychol.*, 1952, **44**, 80–87.

273. Underwood, B.J.: Studies of distributed practice: VIII. Learning and retention of paired nonsense syllables as a function of intralist similarity. *J. exp. Psychol.*, 1953, **45**, 133–42.

274. Underwood, B.J.: Studies of distributed practice: IX. Learning and retention of paired adjectives as a function of intralist similarity. *J. exp. Psychol.*, 1953, **45**, 143–49.

275. Underwood, B.J.: Studies of distributed practice: X. The influence of intralist similarity on learning and retention of serial adjective lists. *J. exp. Psychol.*, 1953, **45**, 253–59.

276. Underwood, B.J.: Interference and forgetting. *Psychol. Rev.*, 1957, **64**, 49–60.

277. Underwood, B.J., & Richardson, J.: The influence of meaningfulness, intralist similarity, and serial position on retention. *J. exp. Psychol.*, 1956, **52**, 119–26.

278. Verplanck, W.S.: Since learned behavior is innate, and vice versa, what now? *Psychol. Rev.*, 1955, **62**, 139–44.

279. Voeks, Virginia: What fixes the correct response? *Psychol. Rev.*, 1945, **52**, 49–51.

280. Voeks, Virginia W.: Acquisition of S-R connections: A test of Hull's and Guthrie's theories. *J. exp. Psychol.*, 1954, **47**, 137–47.

281. Warren, J.M., & Baron, A.: The formation of learning sets by cats. *J. comp. physiol. Psychol.*, 1956, **49**, 227–31.

282. Watson, J.B.: *Psychology from the standpoint of a behaviorist.* Philadelphia: Lippincott, 1919.

283. Webb, W.B., & Nolan, C.Y.: Cues for discrimination as secondary reinforcing agents: a confirmation. *J. comp. physiol. Psychol.*, 1953, **46**, 180–81.

284. Weinstock, S.: Resistance to extinction of a running response following partial reinforcement under widely spaced trials. *J. comp. physiol. Psychol.*, 1954, **47**, 318–22.

284a. Weinstock, S.: Acquisition and extinction of a partially reinforced running response at a 24-hour intertrial interval. *J. exp. Psychol.*, 1958, **56**, 151–58.

285. Weiss, W., & Margolius, G.: The effect of context stimuli on learning and retention. *J. exp. Psychol.*, 1954, **48**, 318–22.

286. Welker, W.I.: Some determinants of play and exploration in chimpanzees. *J. comp. physiol. Psychol.*, 1956, **49**, 84–89.

287. Wendt, H.: *In search of Adam* (trans. by J. Cleugh). Boston: Houghton Mifflin, 1956.

288. Williams, M.: The effects of experimentally induced needs upon retention. *J. exp. Psychol.*, 1950, **40**, 139–51.

289. Wolfe, J.B., & Kaplon, M.D.: Effect of amount of reward and consummative activity on learning in chickens. *J. comp. Psychol.*, 1941, **31**, 353–61.

290. Wolfle, Helen M.: Time factors in a conditioning finger-withdrawal. *J. gen. Psychol.*, 1930, **4**, 372–78.

291. Wolfle, Helen M.: Conditioning as a function of the interval between the conditioned and the original stimulus. *J. gen. Psychol.*, 1932, **7**, 80–103.

292. Woodworth, R.S., & Schlosberg, H.: *Experimental Psychology* (Rev. Ed.), New York: Henry Holt, 1954.

293. Wylie, H.H.: An experimental study of transfer of response in the white rat. *Behav. Monogr.*, 1919, **3**, No. 16.

294. Yamaguchi, H.G.: Drive (D) as a function of hours of hunger. *J. exp. Psychol.*, 1951, **42**, 108–17.

295. Young, P.T., & Greene, J.T.: Quantity of food ingested as a measure of relative acceptability. *J. comp. physiol. Psychol.*, 1953, **46**, 288–94.

296. Young, P.T., & Greene, J.T.: Relative acceptability of saccharine solution as revealed by different methods. *J. comp. physiol. Psychol.*, 1953, **46**, 295–98.

297. Youtz, Adella C.: An experimental evaluation of Jost's laws. *Psychol. Monogr.*, 1941, **53**, No. 1 (Whole No. 238).

298. Zeaman, D.: Response latency as a function of the amount of reinforcement. *J. exp. Psychol.*, 1949, **39**, 466–83.

299. Zeaman, D., & Radner, L.: A test of the mechanisms of learning proposed by Hull and Guthrie. *J. exp. Psychol.*, 1953, **45**, 239–44.

✳ INDEX